The Freedom of the Poet

JOHN BERRYMAN

The Freedom of the Poet

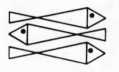

Farrar, Straus & Giroux

NEW YORK

PR
403
.B4
1976

Grateful acknowledgment to reprint is made to Houghton Mifflin, Little, Brown; New American Library, G. P. Putnam's Sons, Simon & Schuster, Trident Press, World Publishing Company, and to the editors of *American Review 22, The American Scholar, Commentary, The Hudson Review, The Kenyon Review, The New York Times, Partisan Review,* and *Sewanee Review.* Introduction to *The Monk* by Matthew G. Lewis is reprinted with the permission of the Grove Press, copyright © 1952 by Grove Press, Inc. "Stephen Crane's *The Red Badge of Courage*" is reprinted from *The American Novel from James Fenimore Cooper to William Faulkner,* edited by Wallace Stegner, © 1965 by Basic Books, Inc. and used with the permission of the publisher. The essays on *Macbeth,* Isaac Babel, Crane's *The Open Boat,* Hemingway, and T. S. Eliot are reprinted in revised form from *The Arts of Reading,* co-edited by Ralph Ross, Allen Tate, and John Berryman, by permission of the publishers, copyright © 1960 by Thomas Y. Crowell, Inc.

Library of Congress Cataloging in Publication Data
Berryman, John, 1914–1972.
The freedom of the poet.
1. English literature—History and criticism.
2. American literature—History and criticism.
I. Title.
PR403.B4   1976   820′.9   75–45162

CONTENTS

Contents

PREFACE

EIGHT MONTHS BEFORE HIS DEATH, JOHN BERRYMAN SIGNED a contract with Farrar, Straus and Giroux for a collection of essays and stories. It was dated May 13, 1971, but we had discussed the project at least as early as 1968, shortly after publication of *His Toy, His Dream, His Rest*, the concluding volume of *The Dream Songs*. First John sent me a tentative list of the items he was thinking of putting in the book. Later he drew up a formal table of contents, grouped in five sections, and on January 7, 1970, drafted a statement about his own practice of criticism that he intended to expand into a preface. In his letter he added, characteristically, "Hurrah for me: my prose collection is going to be a *beauty*."

His list of contents totaled thirty-seven pieces, eight of which were new, or at any rate unpublished. Those that had already appeared in print over three decades (see my bibliographical notes at the back) were readily obtainable, but none of the new ones reached me before John's death. With Kate Berryman's help, we found the essays on Marlowe, Cervantes, Walt Whitman, Joseph Conrad, and Anne Frank, and a two-parter entitled "Shakespeare's Last Word," the conclusion of which provided John with this book's title. But still missing were "Africa" (about which I had only John's penciled notation, "cf. 'Olive Schreiner Foaming at the Mouth'") and an essay on Job entitled "Man and the Lord." They were never discovered, and either were not written or were destroyed.

The contract for *The Freedom of the Poet* was drawn up and two copies were sent to John while his new book, *Love & Fame*, was going through the press in the early months of 1971. When the contracts did not come back, I began to wonder whether he had changed his mind about doing the book. Not at all. In early May, when I phoned Minneapolis, I found him in excellent spirits: he had mislaid "the damned contracts" but was keen to get the book out, because he had lots of ideas for other books. He told me Kate was expecting and wanted me to be the godfather, probably in the summer (I stood up for Sarah Rebecca in June), and he said he would mail the contracts as soon as he found them. They arrived on May 13, with a short letter that said a great deal—more than I realized at first. Written in his familiar mandarin hand, with his customary abbreviations, on a small University of Minnesota letterhead, it compressed much news about many matters into little space:

Tues. [May 11]

Dear Bob

Found the f. contracts and here they are. Can you suggest a *name* for this book? I am not intoxicated w. mine; on the other hand I agree w. you that *Sel. Essays* is no good. [There seemed in the end to be no better title than John's original.]

Very pleased w. our tel. talk. Kate glad abt god-fathering. Today is the Feast of St Isidore the Farmer [who converted] a consul & his household & a senator & *his* household of 68! There were Xtians in those days. Let me commend to you my fav. recent text: Luke, 13, 8.

Present plan:

1) vol. essays/stories—Spr. '72
2) *Delusions, Etc.*—Fall '72
3) *Recovery* (the novel)—'73?
4) *Shakespeare's Reality*—'74?
5) *The Blue Book of Poetry* (ed.)
6?) I am also doing a *Life of Christ*
for Martha [his daughter]:
illustrated—e.g. Titian's great
'Scourging' in the Pinakothek.

I enclose the syllabus of one of the present seminars that is driving me hard. [It listed readings from the New Testament, *The Tempest*, Whitman, Freud's *Civilization and Its Discontents*, *The Meaning of Death* edited by Herman Feifel, *The World of the Child* edited by Toby Talbot, and Tolstoy's *Master and Man*. At the end: "Test: Group-suicide, 3:00 p.m., last Tues. of Spr. quarter."]

Will you have Lady Pat [my editorial assistant, Pat Strachan] send me some of my own immortal works? [A list followed.] That should last me till kingdom come . . .

Aff'ly
John

There were two postscripts crammed into the margins, one apparently about his previous evening's reading: "*Rip Van Winkle* last nt.—his [Washington Irving's] failure to make any *use* of his excellent German material is pathetic. Poe was our first imagination after Edwards, then Emerson, *then* Walt." The other was about a former classmate of ours: "In a 2nd-hand bk I saw yest'y [he] praised my *HYMN to Mistress Br.*"

This short letter, so full of vitality, humor, and critical intelligence, cheered me enormously because I knew he was depressed over some of the reactions to *Love & Fame*. The list of works-in-progress was an encouraging sign. Even his "favorite recent text" has optimistic, as well as comic, implications—chapter 13 of Luke being the parable of the fig tree that was late in bearing fruit, and verse 8 containing the wise gardener's advice to his master: "Lord, let it [the fig tree] alone this year also, till I shall dig about it and dung it." At the same time there was something in the letter vaguely and inexplicably disturbing.

When I saw John, for what was to be the last time, a few weeks later at Sarah's christening, he seemed happier, more confident and serene than in all the years I had known him (we met in 1934, as fellow students of that great teacher, Mark Van Doren). He sounded convincing about having licked his drinking problem (he drank only non-alcoholic stuff during my stay in Minneapolis), and was enthusiastic about the progress of his novel, *Recovery*. "It will have the greatest number of technical details about alcoholism ever to appear in a book. I *know*, I'm an expert!" he said. One afternoon in his study he described with eloquence still another project, not listed in the May letter, entitled *Sacrifices*. When he showed me his sheaf of notes, I copied down this passage: "An entirely new kind of freedom manifested in several ways, in retirement, in death, but invariably in a special retirement or death that contains as one of its chief meanings a repudiation of the earlier 'freedom.' There is a *conversion*, in short, if we can employ the term without either religious or psychoanalytic overtones. Someone is changed, simply, into someone else." I still did not get the message, not until January 7, 1972, when I heard the incredible news of John's leap to his death from the high bridge over the Mississippi.

The Freedom of the Poet, as published, deviates from John's intention as I understood it in two instances, for which I accept the responsibility. I have added "Wash Far Away," one of his best stories, of whose existence no one was aware until Kate Berryman found it among his papers. I have also added "The Ritual of W. B. Yeats," the earliest piece of writing in this book. It dates from our senior year at college, when I published it in *The Columbia Review*, and belongs here for several reasons: it shows how early Berryman's individual prose style was formed and, in addition to its intrinsic interest as a close analysis of Yeats's dramatic work, it attests to his most important early influence, which he acknowledges on page 323: "I began work in verse-making as a burning, trivial disciple of the great Irish poet William Butler Yeats."

Berryman made several slight rearrangements in the order of the contents. For example, he originally led off with the stories, but finally —and properly, I think—put them last; and "Thursday Out," the account of his trip to India in 1957, ended up with the stories (though it had been with the essays), perhaps because it contains fictional elements. But he never really veered from his basic, pentadic pattern: the Elizabethans; other English and European writers; works of American fiction; poets and poetry; stories.

He should have the last word, in this book he planned for so long, with this statement about his work as a critic that he drafted two years, exactly, before his death:

> I think my critical practice has attached itself to no school, though it was influenced in its inception by T. S. Eliot, R. P. Blackmur, Ezra Pound, and William Empson. I have loved other critics, like Dr Johnson, Coleridge, my Columbia teacher Mark Van Doren, D. H. Lawrence, John Crowe Ransom. But I have also borne in mind throughout: remarks by Franz Kafka ('the story came out of me like a real birth, covered with slime and blood') and Joseph Conrad: 'A work of art is very seldom limited to one exclusive meaning and not necessarily tending to a definite conclusion. And this for the reason that the nearer it approaches art, the more it acquires a symbolic character . . . All the great creations of literature have been symbolic, and in that way have gained in complexity, in power, in depth and in beauty' (letter of 4 May 1918). My interest in critical *theory* has been slight.

ROBERT GIROUX

I

Marlowe's Damnations

SHAKESPEARE AND BEN JONSON APART, ONLY OF CHRISTO-
pher Marlowe among the playwrights of the first Elizabeth is enough
known personally to make feasible an exploration of those connexions,
now illuminating, now mysterious, between the artist's life and his
work, which interest an increasing number of readers in this century,
and the existence of which is denied only by very young persons or
writers whose work perhaps really does bear no relation to their lives,
tant pis pour eux. Marlowe was a professional secret agent, a notorious
unbeliever, a manifest homosexual, cruel, quarrelsome, and perhaps
murderous, his habitual associates scoundrels and traitors. He reminds
us, learned and drastic, rather of Villon or Rimbaud than of any English writer.

Let us take both the atheism and the homosexuality seriously,
because Marlowe did: he was missionary about both and he could
have been burned for either. As William Empson has remarked, he
was lucky to be murdered before he was burned. A French critic,
Michel Poirier, observes that Marlowe did not really write either for
money (plays brought too little) or for fame (plays hardly ranking as
literature). This last notion we had better qualify, for the playwright
seems to have revised *Tamburlaine* between its production and publication, in the light of his admiration for some things in the new
Faerie Queene, and he was dead too soon for us to decide whether he
would have gone on publishing his work. But though presumably
he liked applause, it is a fair impression that in an unusual degree he
wrote simply to gratify himself. His mind had no popular cast. He
works proverbs, for instance, less than any other serious Elizabethan
playwright, and Caroline Spurgeon (in *Shakespeare's Imagery*) has
shown how heavily Marlowe drew on classical learning for images,
how singularly little on contemporary life, sport, and so on. He
suited himself. He flaunted himself—perhaps to win converts. In
Edward II he fastens on what is shortly mentioned in the chroniclers,

3

the king's homosexual indulgence as a young man, and makes half his play with it. The king's extremely horrible murder, Empson once said, parodies his vice. In fact, Marlowe found this in Holinshed: putting "into his fundament an horne . . . through the same they thrust up into his bodie an hot spit" and so killed him—the point being to leave no sign of how he was killed. But how the poet's imagination has seized on this piece of history is clear from Lightborne's opening words "I must haue the king" and some even more ambiguous and startling lines later. But "Lightborne" (one of Marlowe's few real characters) is, as Harry Levin notices in his new book,* synonymous with "Lucifer." Marlowe has fused his two vices.

The fate of Faustus later can be understood in the light of this scene, with the help of an insight from a surprising source, the great textual authority Sir Walter Greg. The weakness of the middle acts of *Doctor Faustus* is to be accounted for partly by the probability that Marlowe did not write much of them. But Greg thinks he laid down the plan for his collaborator or collaborators, and the plan was this: Faustus, being damned from the moment of his bargain, naturally will disappoint the high expectations of the audience as to what he will do with his power—he deteriorates—and did not in the process interest Marlowe enough even to compose it. There are difficulties in the way of accepting this impressive theory. But it alone seems to reconcile the burden of the play as we have it (not so corrupt textually as criticism has been used to suppose) with the tragic profundity of Act I:

> FAUSTUS. Where are you damned?
> MEPHASTOPHILUS. In hell.
> FAUSTUS. How comes it then that thou art out of hell?
> MEPHASTOPHILUS. Why this is hell, nor am I out of it.

and the supreme terror of Act V:

> The stars move still, time runs, the clock will strike,
> The devil will come, and Faustus must be damned.
> Oh I'll leap up to my God! Who pulls me down?
> See see where Christ's blood streams in the firmament!

Now, under this conception, what does finally damn Faustus is his intercourse with Helen, a demon, the analogy to demoniality (Greg proves) being "bestiality." And therefore, again, Lucifer must have

---

* *The Overreacher: A Study of Christopher Marlowe*, 1952.

4

him. I pass by the masochism here, the sadistic images here and in *Hero and Leander,* the weird joke (iv. 7. 47.) about Faustus's committing incest with his father. The point is that twice at the summits of his art Marlowe has damned himself in a particular way for the same particular things. The impression is unavoidable that he *enjoyed* writing these scenes, *and* was excruciated. His sinister art ran exactly with his life.

Marlowe's life and the text of his work, which reaches us rather mutilated, have been examined at length by scholarship, but literary criticism has been oddly scanty. There was a history-of-ideas study by Paul H. Kocher, and then a pleasant, semi-psychological study by M. Poirier of the Sorbonne translated in England last year (1951). With Harry Levin's book, more ambitious and much better than these, the subject may be said to have become a going concern. His scholarship is careful, his range of reference wide, his quotations apt, his curiosity as to what the dramatist is up to genuine, his analysis of his heretical ambitiousness exemplary, and from the first page of his laboured preface to the last page of his ninth appendix, his book contains nothing unconsidered. Perhaps it may seem a little forbidding to most readers, a little fussy to some, and it has definite weaknesses. The beauty and the malice of this magnificent poet hardly appear. Instead, of one distich in a famous passage,

> Our soules, whose faculties can comprehend
> The wondrous Architecture of the world,

Levin admires "the enjambment that carries the first line so breathlessly into the second." But is there anything really unusual about that runover? On the other hand, a moment later, he is rescuing from the contempt of Victorian critics the splendid climax of this speech (*1 Tamburlaine* 11. 6.), which he rightly regards as blasphemous. So with his discussion of *Hero and Leander,* from which, except for some technical remarks and quotations, one would scarcely suppose the subject a work in verse, much less one of the finest sensuous poems in the language, rich with passages like this sly, exquisite creation of the church, which Eliot might envy as hard as Keats:

> So faire a church as this, had *Venus* none,
> The wals were of discoloured *Iasper* stone,
> Wherein was *Proteus* carued, and o'rehead;
> A liuelie vine of greene sea agget spread;
> Where by one hand, light headed *Bacchus* hoong . . .

On the other hand, Levin's analysis of Marlowe's special mythology in the poem (pp. 142–4) is immaculate. His third chapter, on the crosscurrents of faithlessness in *The Jew of Malta*, is intent, rapid, full, astute; and the pages on *Edward II* that follow are nearly as good, though some readers may feel he insufficiently emphasizes the superiority of its final scenes.

Of the imposing work that preceded these influential plays, *Tamburlaine*, and the intense fragment that evidently followed them, *Doctor Faustus*, his accounts are less satisfactory. Our taste seems bound to be uneasy with these simpler works. *Tamburlaine* is crude, humanly; most of *Faustus*'s middle is insipid; their actions are episodic, and their ends—sovereignties of power and knowledge—affect us as abstract or unreal; neither the bombast of *Tamburlaine* nor the plain and solemn style of *Faustus* is as attractive as the middle style of the other plays; there exist particular reasons why both works appear to us stupid. But Levin neglects an element, not indeed considerable in *Tamburlaine*, but striking. Bajazet, conquered and being bound, cries out,

> Ah villaines, dare ye touch my sacred armes?
> O *Mahomet*, Oh sleepie *Mahomet*.

When the Governor of Babylon is about to be hung up in chains and shot, he boasts,

> nor death nor *Tamburlaine*,
> Torture or paine can daunt my dreadlesse minde—

to which Tamburlaine:

> Vp with him then, his body shalbe scard.

In an art of grandiose overreaching and magniloquence these touches have an enlivening effect, and the critics by the way who have solemnly debated whether or not Marlowe possessed a sense of humour must have slept through this line.

But Marlowe had little enough humour, even of this grim sort. The two modes through which he speaks to us are the seductive, the languorous (displayed in *Dido*, the first half of *Edward*, and *Hero and Leander*), and the vast and atrocious (displayed nearly everywhere else in the extant intact work of high quality). These modes possess in common a certain self-indulgence and a concern with persuasion, but clearly in most respects they stand opposed. What I wish to claim is that his deepest dramatic effects are the result of an interpenetration of the modes which is not only mature but diabolical.

These effects are intimately associated with his life. It is true that once, briefly, in *Edward*, Marlowe was enlightened and drawn out of himself into emulation of the dexterous apportionment of interest among various characters *as well as* the concentration achieved by Shakespeare when he enlarged and rewrote the "Contention" plays (*2* and *3 Henry VI*); so that this play treats characters other than the single Marlovian hero-figure. But by the end of it he is back with his hero (Mortimer rather than Edward)—to whom in *Faustus* he then wholly returned.

Putting it once more: the union of the seductive and the atrocious has for its purpose an insolent defiance of salvation. We may disagree about Marlow's "atheism," depending on what we take the word to mean, but about his hostility to Christianity there can be little question except for churchmen reluctant to give him up. Not unnaturally, the service which his work shows him most sensitive toward, and most harshly satirical of, is the Commination Service. But I ought to add that it is just possible, if the unfinished *Hero and Leander* followed *Faustus* and was his final production, that Marlowe had begun to grow out of his hatred of God, or had become less insistent upon it. This poem is still obsessedly inverted (II, 181 ff., which Miss Tuve tries in vain to explain away), but its satire, such as that in the passage quoted earlier, nowhere deepens to blasphemy.

When Frizer's dagger entered his arrogant and corrupt brain, Marlowe was twenty-nine—an age at which Congreve had retired. Marlowe's dramatic accomplishment stands that comparison poorly. Some recent revivals cited by Levin tend to prove rather, as Poirier says, that his works have not survived on the stage than that they have. Kyd was a greater dramatist, as Eliot decided long ago. But Marlowe was a great poet, which Kyd was not, and his dramatic strokes were grander. He lives, however (the academic interest and his poetry's spell for a few readers, apart), and the same is true of his contemporaries, for a reason better still: that he helped in the initial formation of the most powerful artist the race has produced. Levin inclines to feel that Marlowe has received some injustice by being bracketed with Shakespeare. But in the first place he does certainly not *deserve* to be so bracketed, and in the second place what higher honour is conceivable? His role in Shakespeare's early development was not less vivid for having been exaggerated by most critics. He established a musical and strong verse on the stage; Tamburlaine and the rest eased the births of York and Richard III and the rest, Barabas of Shylock, Edward II of Richard II, his murderers of Shakespeare's,

7

his long poem inspired Shakespeare's early poems and echoes verbally sometimes through the plays all the way down to a song of Ariel's. It was even shown last year that one of Shakespeare's characteristic image clusters (Love-book-eyes-beauty) has its germ in *Tamburlaine*. Auden on the occasion of Yeats's death observed that one of a poet's real ambitions is to be useful in this technical way. A dramatic poet of civilization needs at hand developed materials for high achievement, and Marlowe out of his contumacy and agony produced them to his master.

1952

Thomas Nashe and

The Unfortunate Traveller

CONSIDERING HOW LITTLE WE KNOW OF HIS SHORT RESTLESS life, and how little we read his work, Thomas Nashe makes an oddly distinct impression. One sees a small man, passionate, racy, sharp ("young Juvenal, that biting Satirist, that lastly with me together writ a comedy"—so Robert Greene at the point of death*), Cambridge-trained, poor, writing like mad fantastic pamphlets, negligible plays, and parts of plays with Marlowe and perhaps others, one stunning lyric and a gay one and some bad and obscene ones, in trouble with the authorities; dying no one knows where or when, and pretty forgotten then for centuries. He wrote also a novel, this one, we hear, and it stands as practically the only work of his anyone reads, even scholars, though every scholar uses the index McKerrow made for his magnificent five-volume edition of Nashe fifty years ago.

But it is not a novel, nor should it be held even to be his best book—if it is proper to think of Nashe as writing books at all. Historically *The Unfortunate Traveller* may claim real interest, as a symbolic effort to wrench prose narrative out of euphuism and romance, and as perhaps the first historical "novel" in English (putting an imaginary hero among actual dead men and past events, to let him operate and listen). But it can hardly be seen as successful in itself or as in itself pointing to anything. Literary historians like to point, forward, backward. The view, well put by Walter Allen in his intelligent survey *The English Novel: a short critical history*, is surely the right one, that these Elizabethan narratives have nothing to do with the novel (*Robinson Crusoe, Emma, Ulysses*). They are just stories, and Nashe's is not a good story.

The usual potted account of it is misleading. Jack Wilton, we are

---

* It is not certain, though generally accepted and *very* probable, that Nashe is referred to. See *The Works of Thomas Nashe*, ed. R. B. McKerrow, 1904-10 (repr. 1958), V, 143-4; and Francis Meres in *Palladis Tamia* (1598) calls him "gallant young Juvenal."

told, servant, prince of rascals and good fellows, careers about the Continent hobnobbing with Luther and More and Erasmus, after sitting in on historic battles political and religious, is trapped with his master, Henry Howard, Earl of Surrey, by a Venetian courtesan, gets off with Aretino's help, adopts the Earl's name, and proceeds to Florence with a rich widowed beauty, is discovered by Surrey, and witnesses a great tourney, races to Rome, etc., etc. Here is a young Englishman projected from 1593 back into Henry's reign, and meeting: the supreme Reformer, the two greatest Northern Humanists, one of the most formative of all English poets, whores, scoundrels, murderers, Aretino. It all sounds good.

These things do indeed happen in the book. But the book is not like this. As a story, almost everything in it creaks. Little of what is encountered convinces (not that Nashe had visited these lands, by the way). Its major faults, free of synopsis, might be three. There is a hanging failure to *get on*—a banal anecdote will be strung out to its end. On the other hand, Nashe can be the most perfunctory and disconcerting of writers. Jack listens to Luther and Carlstadt in solemn disputations: they heap up words against the Mass and the Pope— they are vehement, Luther talks louder, Carlstadt pounds his fists more, "they uttered nothing to make a man laugh, therefore I will leave them." We do not hear them at all; that was that. Worse yet, the hero develops no personality or character. One never comes to care a straw what happens to him. Even Allen, who is very good-natured toward the book ("the most sheerly *enjoyable* of all Elizabethan prose fictions"), has nothing to say for Jack.

Well, how shall we set about accounting for the unmistakable attraction *The Unfortunate Traveller* still exerts? There have been half a dozen reprints in England and here during the last generation, a matter scarcely to be explained in terms of its academic interest. On what ought we to base the book's continuing claim?

Perhaps there is some deeper structure, non-picaresque? I wonder that no professor-critic desperate for a subject has waded in here, for clearly Nashe is a triadist, and the organization of his narrative, intended or not, is definite. There is the triple-war sequence: in France, at Marignano, at Münster. There is the triple-learning sequence: Erasmus and More (actual), the Wittenberg reception (farcical), Cornelius Agrippa's feats (magical, and superior)—after which we emerge into the real world. There are the ceremonies: at Wittenberg's reception, at Florence the tourney, at Bologna the execution. Leaving out all else, the fundamental triad plainly is that which justifies the epithet "Unfortunate" in the book's title: Jack's imprisonment for counterfeiting, for murder, and for cellar-door breaking. It is true that the last punishment is the worst (to become an anatomical specimen), so that a crescendo is observed; still, I see difficulties with this scheme. There are only two courtesans, only two epidemics; and there are four Italian cities. Venice-Florence-Rome will do; Bologna is extra. But Bologna is where the story's climax grinds. The professor triumphant has an answer: *Thrice* the story appears to start, and fails. When Jack goes back to England (there was no pretense of a story during all the pages before that point); when he meets Surrey and sets out—but nothing happens; when in Venice they are had. That it never gets going will never baffle an article. I like better the triple sense of a recent critic that Nashe's *Traveller* "begins as a jest book, continues as a mock chronicle, and concludes as an experiment in Italianate melodrama."*

The jest-book origin is certain. How far and where Nashe first intended to go with it, though, is not clear. Did he, as some critics say Cervantes did (to compare small things with vast), begin with little and see that he had opened a sort of mine? (Those critics are practically right, but wrong.) Or had he it all in mind at first? Where—we are postponing now the question of value—did this work, which has lasted so much better than the jest books, come from?

Prose fiction had not got very far in England. There had been John Lyly's *Euphues* (1578), Greene's romances through the following decade, Sidney's *Arcadia* (1590); Nashe reacts against all these. "*Euphues* I read when I was a little ape in Cambridge, and then I thought it was *Ipse ille*: it may be excellent good still, for ought i know, for I lookt not on it this ten yeare: but to imitate it I abhorre" (*Four Letters Confuted*, 1592). From the Continent had come a literature of roguery, the Italian *novelle*, and the anonymous *La Vida de Lazarillo de Tormes*, picaresque, "realistic," which had been translated and was no doubt read by Nashe but which is as different as possible from *The Unfortunate Traveller* and exerted no influence on it that anyone has been able to demonstrate. Classical narrative does not seem to be in question. Nashe was a great looter in details (McKerrow's notes are full of his borrowings or thefts and it has been shown since that he used a compendium, Textor's *Officina*, for the parade of learning in his apprentice work *An Anatomy of Absurdity*),† like many Elizabethans, but unless something turns up, McKerrow's judgment will have to stand: that the book is "in the main an original attempt in a hitherto untried direction" (iv, 252)—a judgment the more impressive for his careful arguments against Nashe's

---

* L. G. Salinger, in *The Age of Shakespeare*, ed. Boris Ford, 1956.
† D. C. Allen in *Studies in Philology* (xxxii), 1935.

familiarity with the works of either Aretino or Rabelais (v, 128–31). Some translated Aretino he may have read.

So he had no model, unless he intended a parody of the medieval knightly legends for which he had already explained his detestation, and not only is there no evidence for this but the jest-book outset is against it. He drew, of course, on this and that, the chronicles of Lanquet and Sleidan, conversation (certainly) with people who had visited Italy* (as Shakespeare pumped them also, or remembered), and a report, in Puttenham's *Art of English Poesy* (1589, but written much earlier), that Surrey had gone there, together with Surrey's "Geraldine" sonnet—not one of that poet's best sonnets, though it imitates, like his best, Dante's history of La Pia (end of Canto V, *Purgatorio*).

But the work has no respectable ancestry, then, leads to nothing (except Defoe and so forward), is rather a tale than a story, and is not internally organized as artworks are supposed to be and, from the *Iliad* to *The Bear*, mostly are.

Nashe's strength here, and elsewhere, is continually said to lie in his style. That is why, historians and critics and editors say, we read him.

It is a reason. The notion "style" points in two contrary directions: toward individuality, the characteristic, and toward inconspicuous expression of its material. The latter is the more recent direction (George Orwell a superb practitioner); we may range it with T. S. Eliot's intolerable and perverse theory of the impersonality of the artist; it may have something wrong with it. Nashe is an extreme instance, perhaps the extreme instance, of the feasibility of the first theory. (We are not saying anything, as yet, about the correctness of the critical sense that his style generated his power.) He is unmistakable, even among the wild men, brilliant Dekker, and their imitators.

Suppose we begin with an example. To Surrey's long discourse of his love for Geraldine, Jack responds mentally in the narrative as follows:

> Not a little was I delighted with this unexpected love storie, especially from a mouth out of which was nought wont to march but sterne precepts of gravetie & modestie. I sweare unto you I thought his companie the better by a thousand crownes, because he had discarded those nice tearmes of chastitie and continencie. Now I beseech God

* "I have not travaild farre, though conferred with farthest travailers" (*Lenten Stuff*, 1599).

love me so well as I love a plaine dealing man; earth is earth, flesh is flesh, earth will to earth, and flesh unto flesh, fraile earth, fraile flesh, who can keepe you from the worke of your creation?

I have taken, on consideration, a passage which no one would be likely to overpraise or to hold commonplace, a suggestive but median passage, though exalted in the close.

A spectrum of points, not exhaustive:

The word order of the first sentence is unremarkable, yet reminds me that Nashe is (I hope I do not exaggerate) one of the masters of English prose. Inversion or rearrangement for rhythm, emphasis, and simulation of the (improved) colloquial; examples are so common in the novel that tauter illustration seems unnecessary. Rapid, offhand, natural, the order is still highly periodic.

Note then how physical it is ("from a mouth") and how active ("march"): major notes of the style. It is a self-conscious style, but *alert*, not laboured. "Extemporal" was indeed the word Nashe most often used for his programmatic and instinctive sense of what he felt he ought to be up to ("give me the man whose extemporall veine in any humour will excell our greatest Art-maisters deliberate thought" —Preface to Greene's *Menaphon*, 1589). Anti-pedantic, spontaneous (apparently), but showmanlike; "Now I beseech God . . ." is between Madison Avenue and truth.

Nashe is a stylist queerly schizophrenic, even below the level of intention: More than half a thousand images, from this novel, lately collected by a student,* show more than half divided between, say, the Marlowe side [Learning] and the Shakespeare side [Daily Life]— the first static (example: "prince of purses"), the second dynamic ("march"). These come, in Croston's reckoning, to half his whole number (147 and 133), most of the rest (200) being from Animals and Body, and "Imaginative" (personifications mostly), a dim remainder (83) being credited to Nature, Domestic, and the Arts. There is no suggestion, in Nashe, of the image clusters explored in Shakespeare by E. A. Armstrong.

Now there is a complicated simultaneous double movement, both democratic (this non-Elizabethan trait in Nashe has been often remarked), and servantlike. Amusing as it may be, Jack's "swearing" to the pages (to whom the book is addressed) that he likes his master's (an Earl's) "companie" better now that they are matey, man to man— the word "companie" is dramatic—passes to a flick of greedy hope, in the "thousand crownes," that this new comradeliness may bring a

* A. K. Croston, *The Review of English Studies* (xxiv), 1948.

tangible reward; a suggestion reinforced by the implication (notwithstanding his earlier praise of Surrey, for Nashe is regularly inconsistent) that he has only tolerated the Earl's "companie," till now, for gain. At the same time, the Elizabethan hierarchy is at work in the passage: the pages ("you"), Jack ("I," a super-page, mobile), the Earl, and God—but then we return to Jack, and pass outward (not upward) to a sturdy common denominator, the plain-dealing man.

Follows a peroration at once highly rhetorical and rather casual, pathetic and joyous; and "realistic," you notice, after Surrey's tearful protestations. The vivid ambiguity of the whole passage comes to a head in the final phrase, where not only is frailty set against and with "worke" but "your creation" is perfectly double: both divine and sexual; that which we were created to do, and what which we do to create.

Next, two passages about Greene, from the *Four Letters Confuted*, addressed to his august antagonist, Dr. Gabriel Harvey of Cambridge. "A good fellowe he was, and would have drunke with thee from more *angels* than the Lord thou libeldst on *gave thee in Christs Colledge;* and in one year he pist as much against the walls, as thou and thy two brothers spent in three." Here an insolent *and* a spiritual alliance is effected between the poverty-stricken, generous London tosspot and God's rescuers, as against the arrogant, miserly (an angel was a coin, worth rather more than a dollar) Cambridge Fellow, which is really Pauline, and deadly. The word order in the opening is more important than in the other passage we were looking at. "He was a good fellow" would be entirely different, as failing to convey the thrust that *he* was good, though he seemed not, as *you* are not, though you seem so in your respectability and eminence. It is hard to measure what has been lost in our prose by the uniform adoption of a straight-on, mechanical word order (reflecting our *thoughtless* speech). Perhaps Nashe's prime instruction to modern writers might be located here. But the clause, though inverted, is anti-pontifical, and this might be a second lesson. Impromptu and searching, Nashe's prose often seems, not a *first* anything, but a *last* high achievement of the impromptu and searching vigor exemplified in Tyndale's Bible (1525): "And the Lorde was with Joseph, and he was a luckie felowe" (A.V.: "prosperous man," and the heart sinks; *Gen.* 29.2). For our generation, this inspired rendering associates itself with Tawney's *Religion and the Rise of Capitalism*, where it is used as an epigraph for the chapter on the Puritans, whom Nashe of course hated, and one wonders whether our prose has not become puritanical: straightforward, pompous. Finally, I remark the savage contrast between Harvey's impious hypocrisy ("libeldst") and Greene's unpretending physical ale-frankness ("pist"). Very few people write like this.

The second passage is deservedly celebrated and must be one of the most remarkable sentences that has come down to us from that time, Shakespeare always excepted. We might contrast it, for emotional and moral tone, with Essex's great cry at his trial, against Ralegh: "What boots it swear the Fox?" It comes just before the sentence we have been studying and is very simple: "Debt and deadly sinne, who is not subject to? with any notorious crime I never knew him tainted." The *weight* of the terrible likelihood for man of evil comes first in both clauses (likelihood?: *certainty*), followed first by resignation, second by a kind of freeing. A whole moral drama lives in the little thing, hopeless, rebuking.

Undeniably, then, Nashe writes well, better than well, at his best. But he is slovenly, uneven, and I would not care to fix in his style alone whatever claim he may be held to make on our attention. Before saying more about this, some discussion is in order of his chief lifetime reputation and his chief present controversial interest.

He was known in his age as a satirist, primarily. He flattered popular taste in various ways (cozening, pageantry, Italian crime, the wicked Jew, travellers' lies and wonders), but in nothing so much as in his mockery and abuse: of ridiculous captains, of university pedantry and entertainment, of the Pope's mistress poisoned. I am holding to *The Unfortunate Traveller;* actually his fame was a product of his invective against Harvey—so scandalous the flyting became that in 1599 all the books of both were ordered seized and no new ones allowed printed (whatever that means). But can this matter to us? I would think not, unless historically. The targets of a generation become indifferent. We pretend that genius transcends, even here, and perhaps it does, for *A Modest Proposal*, but who reads what Swift calls his masterpiece, *A Tale of a Tub* (of which an admirable modern edition exists)? As in all things human, scale obtains; trouble, attention, will be taken, paid, for and to a small work; not a large. *The Unfortunate Traveller* is in between; but I hardly see anyone reading it now for its satire. For Nashe's general powers, squandered on a war with a (rather attractive) pedant: there may certainly come a time when his pamphlets will be more attractive than they are now, but it is not yet. These are two obstacles, apart from our entire lack of interest in the matters at stake, if there were any, between Harvey and Nashe. We jib at cutting and humiliation, even of someone else; Housman's ferocity as a scholar toward his colleagues makes us more nervous than it entertains us—our exhausted and vague humanitarian-ism, sentimental, feels that this ought not to happen. But the second obstacle, emerging from the history of culture, puts Nashe further off still: a fight between two film stars is a topic—between two scholars, not. It is easy, even from here, to analogize the Nashe-Harvey controversy, imagining a war between Walter Winchell (gifted suddenly by God with a style) and Walter Lippmann (made a little dull, academized). But who, five years later, one season later, would care? Another problem here—the sincerity of the slashers—I postpone a little.

Currently there is some question as to whether *The Unfortunate Traveller* is picaresque or not. A *picaro* is a knave, and by showing Jack Wilton as heartless, financial, a servant, mischievous, Professor Bowers, whose style is rather mechanical,* has made an important contribution to nothing by emphasizing the possibility that Nashe conformed more to the picaresque (Spanish) model than we thought. It does remain a possibility.

It has also been claimed that Nashe is a master of psychology, leaving loose the wonder that he troubles to make Diamante innocent, as an accused wife, and then calls her courtesan.

A prose work will not live for its style alone, other factors ordinary. This is my difficulty, trying to account for the book's survival over three and a half destructive centuries. A poor story, brilliant. But do we truly only read for stories? Let's jump and re-trieve the term "Imagination"; one can write marvellously without it. For example, C. D. Broad, the British philosopher, in his obituary for McTaggart before the British Academy, has a cunning sentence: "Whatever else may be thought about McTaggart's work on Hegel, it cannot at any rate be denied that he has succeeded in producing from the Hegelian hat a large and fascinating rabbit, whilst others have produced only consumptive and gibbering chimeras, a feat the more remarkable in that the rabbit may never have been inside the hat at all, while the chimeras certainly were." It is brilliant, fanciful, has nothing to do with fiction at all. But style? wow. Now we put against it: "A pretie rounde faced wench was it, with blacke eie browes, a high forehead, a little mouth, and a sharp nose, as fat and plum everie part of her as a plover, a skin as slike and soft as the backe of a swan, it doth me good when I remember her. Like a bird she tript on the grounde, and bare out her belly as majesticall as an Estrich." Now this has little more to do with *fiction* than Broad's

* "Jack is not too exclusively a victim"; F. T. Bowers in *Humanistic Studies in honor of John Calvin Metcalf*, 1941.

sentence (though *something* more), but clearly it has a vast deal more to do with the possession and employment of Imagination. The operation of Fancy in Broad's splendid sentence—I am returning to Coleridge—"has no counters to play with, but fixities and definites," whereas the description of Diamante is surely a plain instance of the operation of Coleridge's "secondary Imagination": "co-existing with the conscious will, yet still as identical with the primary [Imagination as purely creative] in the *kind* of its agency, and differing only in *degree*, and in the *mode* of its operation. It dissolves, diffuses, dissipates, in order to re-create . . ."

Nashe is nothing even resembling a great writer then, but he is a really good one. It must be admitted that he is very spotty—but perhaps we are much too keen in the present period of criticism to require works even of the second order to be even wholes, which few of them are. It must be admitted also that he puts forward no settled view of life. This objection has been expressed most strongly, of late, by C. S. Lewis:* "In his exhilarating whirlwind of words we find not thought nor passion but simply images: images of ludicrous and sometimes frightful incoherence boiling up from a dark void" and Lewis goes on to compare Nashe with Bosch, the later Picasso, and James Thurber. Ignoring, if we may, the last comparison, I think this attractive view is somewhat exaggerated. Of course we are dealing always with the work of a young man, imperfect and forming. The steadiness and depth of Swift are out of the question. But when Lewis wonders whether Nashe's rage is real ("Even his angers seem to be part of his technique rather than real passions"), perhaps the critic, expert though he is in the literature of the Renaissance, may be felt as proceeding in his judgment rather from a modern than from a Renaissance or a classical sense of Sincerity. A shaky passage earlier in Lewis's fascinating book (p. 44) seems to make this certain, when he refers to the truth that "denunciations of vice became part of the stock-in-trade of fashionable and even frivolous writers. Perhaps nothing in our period is so surprising to a modern as the readiness with which a Lyly, a Nashe, or even a Greene, will at any moment launch out into moral diatribe of the most uncompromising ferocity. All our lifetime the current has been setting toward license. In Elizabeth's reign it was the opposite. Nothing seems to have been more salable, more *comme il faut*, than the censorious. We are overwhelmed by floods of morality from very young, very ignorant, and not very moral men. The glib harshness is to us a little repulsive . . ."

I doubt if this will do, though part of what it says is true enough.

* In *English Literature in the Sixteenth Century, excluding Drama*, 1954.

The larger truth might be we are uneasy *equally* with the enthusiastic and the censorious—with the enthusiastic, for instance, in Cummings's Harvard lectures and Jack Kerouac's *On the Road*—while an Elizabethan was at home with both. I think, therefore, that it would be as foolish to question the sincerity of Nashe's wonderful praise of poets as of his detestation of Anabaptists and Puritans. But our fundamental difficulty lies probably further on, and is not touched by Lewis's account at all, except in his phrase "at any moment." The real trouble is that, among the ghastly orthodoxies of the twentieth century, communist, fascist, democratic, we are suspicious of anything that is not *wholly* pro or con: in a rambling-free Elizabethan structure we are unready for either violent praise or blame. Perhaps in literature we stand in some need, decidedly, of more of the anti-categorical, and *ad hoc*, the flexible, the experimental, which Sir Isaiah Berlin, in an unusual article in *Foreign Affairs* several years ago, called desirable in Western statesmanship. Why does not, for example, some serious writer go to work against *Time* and *Life* as Nashe went to work against Harvey?

Our categorizing will be hard, so long as it continues, on Nashe. The split between journalist and imaginative writer, between "non-fiction" and fiction, does not apply to him any better than it applies to Swift. He is a minor case; not so small as a prose man; but the increasing irritability with storytelling observable in writers like Joyce and Saul Bellow might profit by a study of him. In Bellow, it is true, there is the parade of a view of life, as there is not in Joyce or Nashe. Nashe's concern—but his imaginative concern, I would say—is rather with the medium, with prose itself. He may suffer from the absence of Joyce's overall formal concern; but then Joyce's work suffers from its existence. It is pedantic, after *Dubliners*, magnificent and pedantic. Nashe hated, evenly, both the pedantic (inkhornism) and the monosyllabic (which he called "single money," or small change), and opposes himself thus as an artist both against Joyce and against Hemingway—paths that do indeed seem to have run into the ground.

To revive another analysis of Coleridge's, this time as of the visual arts, we appear to find Nashe unqualifiedly in the second part: "the beautiful in the object," Coleridge says, "may be referred to two elements—lines and colors; the first belonging to the shapely (*forma, formalis, formosus*), and in this, to the law, and the reason; and the second, to the lively, the free, the spontaneous, and the self-justifying."* I would not place him so simply. As our interest in narrative

* *Biographia Literaria*, ed. Shawcross.

18

declines—I would assert that it is, and has been for some time, declining, without in any way *approving* of the decline—our interest in the dynamics and art of particular passages is bound to increase, and Nashe's sense of rhythm in English prose that I would call the passages we have cited "shapely," like hundreds of his others. As a novelist, that is, he cannot much attract us; but his claim as a *writer* is permanent, and much of it will always attach to *The Unfortunate Traveller*, which therefore deserves to be read.

2

Of Nashe's hard-pressed, harum-scarum life (though he on one occasion defensively claimed that "it is as civill as a civill orenge") the best account is naturally, though oddly, to be collected from the austere pages of McKerrow's edition, volume V, which begin, however, with several open assertions so nearly eloquent that I know of nothing else like them in all McKerrow's works.* "Save Shakespeare alone," he observes, "there is perhaps no writer of the Elizabethan time whose work has been better known to students of the period, or who has been more constantly drawn upon for illustration of language and manners. Not that he was, or has ever been considered, one of the greatest of the Elizabethans—though he surely deserves to be counted among the most brilliant—but because of a certain actuality in his writings, a vividness of presentation which makes them more surely and entirely of their own time and country, more representative of the England of Elizabeth, than almost any others. In invective he stands perhaps without a rival: as a satirist of manners he had talent rather than genius, wit rather than wisdom; in eloquence and in profundity of thought he was surpassed by many a man long ago forgotten; he was indeed often faulty in language and crude in ideas, often careless, often ignorant, but what he saw he could describe, and what he thought he said in most effective words." As encomium this estimate hardly ranks with Housman's overwhelming survey of the mind and achievement of Arthur Palmer (most easily come by in Gow's *A. E. Housman*), but as the final view taken by one of the foremost modern scholars of English literature, of his major subject, it is very attractive.

* Few men more conservative can ever have lived. Sir Walter Greg, a lifelong friend, tells one extraordinary story in the memoir of McKerrow he did for the British Academy. McKerrow was interested in science and was heard, years after the Michelson-Morley experiment, when it was mentioned in his presence, to murmur regretfully to himself, "Yes, I suppose it is true."

Nashe was born in the autumn of 1567 (christened in November, no day given) of the second marriage of a Suffolk minister, at Lowestoft, and except for a two-year-older brother, Israel, he was the only survivor into adulthood of seven children, though a half-sister, Mary, from one of his father's earlier marriages also survived. When he was six his parents moved to West Harling (Norfolk) and in either 1581 or 1582 he went up to St. John's College, Cambridge, where he was doing we don't know what until his father's death in January 1587, and even for a year after that, when he left without taking his master's degree—although he probably was *not* sent down. He matriculated as a sizar of St. John's in October 1592 and was later a scholar of the Lady Margaret Foundation. Presumably he ran out of money at some point after his father's maintenance ended (the master's degree, now very cheap, was then expensive), or he was offered some sort of preferment in London, or a love affair (leading to "pensiveness," as he says) drew him away, or he went down to make a career in literature, taking a manuscript with him (*An Anatomy of Absurdity*, entered on the Stationers' Register, 19 September 1588, but not printed until much later)—or some combination of these and other motives. Of his six or seven years at the university we *know* only that he attended (or said he would attend) lectures on philosophy by a Mr. Rowly in 1588 (probably early on) and had some hand in a show called *Terminus & non terminus* (a title that Samuel Beckett might find useful if he ever runs out of his own anti-wonders). From an enemy we hear that his name had become proverbial for disorder in Cambridge—there would be nothing surprising in this, though nothing confirms it and various inferences are against it; from Nashe we hear that he could have had a fellowship at John's if he had desired it. He spoke always with affection of the university and his college afterward; but he never returned there, so far as we know, though in February 1592 he was some sixty miles out of London in the country, in a landscape like the fens out of which Cambridge and Ely protrude. None of these possibilities excludes the others, in life, as they do in scholars' notebooks. He went down. Maybe the active Puritan party in John's drove him crazy (McKerrow, v. 10²); who knows?

Now begin mysterious years.

He becomes one of the University Wits—Marlowe, Greene, Peele, Lodge, Lyly, to mingle the generations a little—whose education, usually at Cambridge, does not seem to have done so much for them as Shakespeare's self-education somewhere did for him; and was in London for some years apparently without break; and had published at once his preface to Greene's *Menaphon* (1589), a most enigmatic document even for the Elizabethan period, which testifies, however, in its existence to reputation beginning, Greene being very well known. Perhaps he got into the famous Marprelate controversy (see below); he certainly quarrelled with the old and boring poet Thomas Churchyard and evidently had to apologize; he was putting together (if the term is not too strong) the shapeless *Pierce Penniless;* he wrote a preface in 1591 to Sidney's *Astrophel and Stella.* But how did he live? *An Anatomy of Absurdity* had indeed appeared, in 1589 —an attack, larded with Latin, on women, on Puritans, and on luxury, interspersed with chaotic recommendations of poetry, learning, and study, and some pages on diet are intermingled—and, just possibly, some anti-Martinist tracts; but none of these things could let a man live. Even after *Pierce Penniless* (1592) had got him famous, and the war with Harvey had got him notorious, his writings did not support him. We are here in the very beginning of the possibility of living by writing, as no doubt Greene did (Shakespeare was of course an actor, and a poet with Southampton as patron, as well as a dramatist). Nashe's work, moreover, during these years apparently went largely unprinted ("I have written in all sorts of humors *privately,* I am perswaded, more than any yoong man of my age in England," 1592—my italics); nothing of his substantial work is thought lost by McKerrow, and the known stuff justifies no such statement. He was in debtors' prison at some point. Had he patrons?: Lord Strange, to whom perhaps he dedicated an obscene poem (*The Choice of Valentines,* printed by J. S. Farmer from several manuscripts in 1899) too badly written to quote; Sir Charles Blount, to whom *The Anatomy* was offered, but who was now mostly abroad and of whom we never hear again from Nashe; one of these, or another, to whom he acted as secretary? It is in 1592 and 1593 that Nashe emerges into sight.

A word, however, about the preface to *Menaphon,* in regard to which I am obliged to agree with Professor Lewis ("He clearly has something to tell us about English prose style but I have failed to understand him")—that even McKerrow's notes have not here made much plain. The spectacular lucidity of Shakespeare and Marlowe and Jonson has perhaps had too little attention, among the libraries of print devoted to them; Spenser, and nearly all contemporary witness to Shakespeare, is more in line with Nashe's mysterious Epistle "To the Gentlemen Students of both Universities." He seems to attack: Latin-taggers, tragic playwrights (*not* Marlowe, McKerrow argues), plagiarists, and—a passage that has tormented a century of scholars: "It is a common practise now a dayes amongst a sort of shifting companions, that runne through every Art and thrive by none, to leave the trade of *Noverint* [scrivener] whereto they were borne, and busie themselves with the indevors of Art that could scarcely Latinize their neck verse if they should have neede; yet English *Seneca* read by Candle-light yeelds many good sentences, as *Blood is a begger,* and so forth; and if you intreate him faire in a frostie morning, hee will affoord you whole Hamlets, I should say handfuls of Tragicall speeches." Later—the pun is atrocious but the passage sufficiently energetic, just quoted—he declines into a blast at some who "imitate the Kid in *Æsop,* who, enamoured with the Foxes newfangles, forsooke all hopes of life to leape into a newe occupation . . . Sufficeth them to bodge up a blanke verse with ifs and ands . . ." Both Greg and McKerrow resist the tendency to make this an attack on Thomas Kyd (son of a scrivener, author of *The Spanish Tragedy*) as author of a pre-Shakespearean *Hamlet.* Whether they are right I do not think our scholarship is yet in a position to say. We know very little about the drama of these years; more will come, in particular about Shakespeare; it is more and more likely that he wrote a *Hamlet* in the mid-1590's and then finally in 1600–1; why not first much earlier? *If* he is here being attacked by Nashe, either as of a *Hamlet* or for changing professions (actor to playwright—the substance of Greene's venomous remarks three years later), it would not be—but I cannot now go into this—the only early assault on the gaining dramatist of the age. The general literary problem involved is whether Nashe was deliberately obscure in the preface; and I do not think a solution is possible. He was slashing about, partly for Greene no doubt, and to cause comment, but until we shall know at whom, I see no way of measuring the degree of his dissimulation. If Shakespeare was here the target, it must be said that that author's reply (see below) was characteristically—though not comprehensibly—mild, or even friendly.

In 1592, as I said, Nashe becomes visible. He goes into the country in the late winter, *Pierce Penniless* is entered on the Stationers' Register on 8 August, about which time Greene's fatal banquet (according to Harvey) of herring and Rhenish wine, with Nashe and Will Moxon, takes place. Then Nashe is staying at Croydon, probably, and writing a very bad play for Archbishop Whitgift, *Summer's Last Will and Testament,* performed there privately in October (perhaps), in which Henry VIII's jester, Will Summers, alone comes to life,* and one great lyric by this poet who delivered so little, a plague song. What is he now, twenty-four?

> Beauty is but a flowre,
> Which wrinckles will devoure,
> Brightnesse falls from the ayre,
> Queenes have died yong and faire,
> Dust hath closde *Helens* eye.
> I am sick, I must dye:
>> Lord, have mercy on us.

Even in Elizabethan lyric the hovering and plunging grief of this stanza exceptionally sings. It is strange that we have so little verse of Nashe's. He now has definite patrons: besides the Archbishop, an "Amyntas" in *Pierce Penniless* probably to be identified with the "Lord" he speaks of here of having been in the country with for fear of the plague raging this year through London, and Sir George Carey, captain-general of the Isle of Wight, with whom Nashe was at Carisbrooke Castle in the coming winter. But his patrons seem always to have come and gone.

With *Pierce Penniless* he both became really known and developed fully his particular gift for taking the English language by the throat, at the same time clubbing it on the head, with passionate love. "Argument" there is none, except that the writer is determined to present a supplication to the Devil, finds a messenger, and gives it to him to read; he himself desires the support he deserves, and that all the gold locked up in rich men's coffers should be liberated. Many sins are then attacked: avarice, pride, envy, murder, wrath, gluttony, drunkenness, sloth, and lechery; and some classes: antiquaries, and enemies of poetry, and one person, Richard Harvey; then the "state" of hell is discussed, and the devil's nature, and "Amyntas" is praised. The work may seem to belong rather to what we should now call "popular culture" than to literature, but the distinction, fruitful now, had not then in fact arisen.†

The same thing is true of his famous quarrel with the Harveys, which here begins. I have said nothing, by the way, of the great

* Cf. M. C. Bradbrook, *The Growth and Structure of Elizabethan Comedy*, 1955.

† A study of the subject might begin with a page (312) in L. C. Knight's *Drama & Society in the Age of Jonson* (1937), and some of the papers, especially Clement Greenberg's and Dwight Macdonald's, assembled in the uneven collection *Mass Culture: The Popular Arts in America*, eds. Bernard Rosenberg and David Manning White, 1957.

Marprelate controversy, because it is far from certain now that Nashe had much or anything to do in this. Tradition long asserted for him a major share in it, on the bishops' side, of course, against "Martin Marprelate" and his Puritan associates. But McKerrow, as his edition progressed, grew increasingly doubtful, and in the end only thought it possible that Nashe may have written *An Almond for a Parrot* (1590)—for which the case has lately been somewhat strengthened* but remains too uncertain for confidence. Naturally there is no question as to Nashe's sympathy with the anti-Martinists. In any event, the *Almond* is a negligible production, to my sense as to Dover Wilson's, while some of Nashe's most spirited pages were called forth by Gabriel Harvey.

Nashe loved an enemy. "*Redeo ad vos, mei Auditores,* have I not an indifferent prittye veyne in Spur-galling an Asse? if you knew how extemporall it were at this instant, and with what haste it is writ, you would say so."† Here joined in one sentence bristle his major claims, to powers of invective and the offhand; to later critics he properly left the claims to mastery of rhythm, imagination, and the detailed administration of diction. You notice the three hid points in the sentence, administrative. "Indifferent" is a handsome quibble, meaning *first* "fairly hot" and *then* "unprejudiced"—and the second is double, i.e., both "you can trust me" and "I couldn't care less." There is thus a three-step descent, or ascent, into insolence. "Spur-galling" is a two-step-up operation: a spur you strike in—to gall is to wound. These first two stages of insult, though, have their (original) destination in the word "Asse"—by no means, now, just a rudeness, but that which you *ride,* steering, hurting, yourself not only careless but "right" (the truth is with you), and able; so that the whole triple process has now, in the mind of the alert reader, reversed itself to conclusion, and we feel with exactness—hard to come by in prose—how Nashe regards Richard Harvey. Moreover, owing to the complex of rhetoric and logic in the sentence, the terms of the writer's intellectual and even practical superiority to his victim look fixed; who could make his way back, for vindication, much less a new battle, through such a mine field? Other points, in this staggering crescendo from "indifferent" [me] to "Asse" [you], will easily be distinguished by the interested reader, but the culmination of the whole (backward) suggests—which might be missed—that nothing

* Donald J. McGinn in *PMLA* (v. 59), 1944.

† *Pierce Penniless.* Generally, I am quoting McKerrow's text, but with minor adjustments (three, here) for modern clarity.

forward (or more) is to be said; *and* the overall implication that the enemy is to be *ridden* to a goal not only amusingly contradicts that notion but tosses us into the center of Nashe's mind. With a first-class enemy, given our powers, we're in. Nashe loved an enemy.

The sentence just studied, I would diffidently suggest, is hard, if our study is true, on many accounts of the differences between poetry and prose, although we said nothing of its rhythm. The dynamics of the imagination I hope are clear. Pascal, on his own unit side, Lancelot Andrewes on the large-formal side, exemplify imaginative dimensions that seem never to have come up for Nashe; in prose. (In verse half a dozen of his lyrics in the play *Summer's Last Will* brought forward by Q in *The Oxford Book of English Verse*—a very good collection, after all, irresponsible textually and unreliable except in lyric—of 1900 give him a small but solid place.)

The intemperance, and length, of the Nashe-Harvey quarrel is not easy now to understand, nor is its origin exactly known. Probably religious motives were involved, as well as literary and personal. It began in 1590 with an attack by Richard Harvey (physician, pastor, and astrologer, who had made himself widely ridiculous in 1583 with a predictive work) on Nashe's preface to Greene's *Menaphon*. To this Greene replied, in the summer of 1592, with an attack on Richard and his brothers, Gabriel and John. The passage was at once cancelled, but now Nashe replied to Richard in *Pierce Penniless*. Gabriel published *Four Letters*, insulting over Greene, who had just died in poverty and ignominy, and attacking *Pierce Penniless*. Gabriel Harvey, best remembered now as Spenser's friend and Nashe's butt, was one of Cambridge's best-known scholars. This treatment of Greene is the worst thing we know of Harvey, apart from his style, but there seems to be little doubt that he was an arrogant man, withdrawn but quarrelsome. Nashe knew him very little, though he had praised Harvey's Latin verse; and even in *Four Letters* Harvey praises Nashe's poetry. Nashe hung back a bit, for which he was rebuked in Chettle's *Kind Heart's Dream*, before replying; then he threw the book at Harvey, with *Strange News, of the Intercepting Certain Letters* (entered on the Stationers' Register, 12 January 1593). "Hee that wraps himselfe in earth, like the Foxe, to catch birds, may haps have a heavy cart go over him before he be aware, and breake his backe." Harvey had picked the wrong man. Harvey is "a filthy vaine foole," a barefoot poet, impudent and calumnious, and moreover has no pride: he was in fact the son of a prosperous rope-maker and was very much ashamed of the fact, whereas "Had I a

Ropemaker to my father, & somebody had cast it in my teeth, I would foorthwith have writ in praise of Ropemakers, & prov'd it by sound sillogistry to be one of the 7 liberal sciences."

Harvey defended himself in *Pierce's Supererogation* (1593). The best sentence perhaps that he ever wrote occurs herein, begging the reader to give up Nashe and Greene and read serious works (of exploration, navigation, war): "Phy upon fooleries: there be honourable woorkes to doe; and notable workes to read." Nashe's style and works are satirized, his way of living deplored, even his originality denied. But at some point here there were offers of peace, through intermediaries or letter, and Nashe indeed has a handsome passage of retraction and praise, prefatory to his uninteresting *Christ's Tears over Jerusalem* (also 1593), which was long thought to be contemptuously repudiated by Harvey in his *New Letter*. McKerrow is of the opinion that Harvey had not seen the work but only *heard* that Nashe was repenting; and doubted it, for his *New Letter* is a blast. McKerrow also thinks that *Pierce's Supererogation*, though written long before, had not yet been published when the motions of peace occurred and culminated in the epistle to *Christ's Tears;* so that Nashe had not any knowledge of the two new attacks when he apologized, and Harvey had not the apology before him when he wrote them. One gets an impression of churlishness, however, from Harvey, as well as almost invincible ignorance of the figure he was cutting.*

Nashe, furious, set on his enemy again in a new epistle for *Christ's Tears* (1594: a passage about misappropriation of charity funds and bribery had caused trouble in London, so part of the work was reprinted and bound up with old sheets). He seems to have delayed, again, over his real reply, but it was well under way when, late in 1595, he met Harvey by chance in Cambridge (or rather *not* met, refused to meet, but lodged in the room next to his at the Dolphin and rejected his overtures—as, Nashe tells us, insincere already once before). *Have with You to Saffron Walden* (1596) is Nashe's masterpiece, I think, but I am not going to try to describe it; even McKerrow confessed that it "defies analysis"; copies or reprints of it may be found in respectable libraries. With it the controversy closes, for McKerrow is clear that *The Trimming of Thomas Nashe*, a scurrilous production of 1597, is not by Harvey and only once mentions him. A word in Harvey's favor, here at the end. He is one of the most unreadable of authors, and did not like *The Faerie Queene*, but his judgment in diction was nothing like so bad as

* McKerrow, quite unwarrantedly, I think, attaches no importance (v, 104) to Nashe's open assumption that Harvey was responsible for the publications.

26

Thomas Nashe thought—if we may trust the practice of posterity. Nashe drew up a list, in *Strange News,* of Harvey's "inkhornism," which begins with "Conscious mind" and continues—with some daisies admittedly—through "Ingenuitie" and "Rascallitie" and "artificiallitie," "addicted to Theory," to "Notorietie" and "negotiation"; all fair terms these days.

We have got ahead of our story, but indeed there is little left to tell. Nashe was very likely satirized on the stage at least twice—by Shakespeare, as Moth in *Love's Labour's Lost,* a friendly view of him as sharp-witted, about 1593,* and as Ingenioso, a sharper view, in the Cambridge *Parnassus* plays of 1598–1601.† He finished Marlowe's *Dido* (printed 1594) after the death of that evil genius in 1593; or possibly they collaborated, but at what date, if so, is unknown, and critics give Nashe only a few passages. One critic has tried to discover in the anonymous *A Knack to Know a Knave* (1592, printed 1594) the comedy Nashe wrote with Greene.

The Unfortunate Traveller (entered 8 September 1593) he dedicated to Southampton, between two trivial works (*Terrors of the Night* and *Christ's Tears*) dedicated to Sir George Carey's daughter and wife; but when the work was reissued, he removed the dedication (McKerrow thinks, because his current patron, whoever that was, was unfriendly to Southampton). Shakespeare made some use of the novel in *1 Henry IV*, and of *Pierce Penniless* later in *Hamlet,*‡ and it appears that Nashe was associated with the Chamberlain's men, Shakespeare's company, but what the relations of the men were, there is no saying; I myself hear Moth as rather affectionate than otherwise, as an amused sketch of an irreverent tongue.

A letter which survives in the British Museum, to a William Cotton, a long scatological complaint about the state of publishing and the public taste, concludes: "I am merry when I have nere a penny in my purse," but the scanty evidence we have for his short years left mostly suggests misery. *The Isle of Dogs,* a Pembroke's play in which he had a hand with Ben Jonson and probably others, was found seditious in the summer of 1597. The players went to prison and Nashe to Yarmouth, the town which in gratitude then supplies one of the main themes (the chief theme is red herrings) of his final and excellent work *Lenten Stuff* (1599). This year his and

* A recent summary will be found in Richard David's New Arden edition, 1951, xxxix ff.

† See *The Three Parnassus Plays,* ed. J. B. Leishman, 1949.

‡ Cf. the 1957 reprint of McKerrow, v. Suppl., 38, and K. Muir, *Shakespeare's Sources,* 1957.

Harvey's books were ordered seized and new ones forbidden to be published. We learn of his death only from an epigraph in Charles Fitzgeffrey's *Affaniae*, 1601.

1960

Shakespeare at Thirty

We must be content, then, in speaking of such subjects and with such premises to indicate the truth roughly and in outline . . . In the same spirit, therefore, should each type of statement be received; for it is the mark of an educated man to look for precision in each class of things just so far as the nature of the subject admits . . .

—Nicomachean Ethics

I am able to make from the springboard the great leap whereby I pass into infinity, my back is like that of a tight-rope dancer, having been twisted in my childhood, hence I find this easy . . .

—Fear and Trembling

SUPPOSE WITH ME A TIME A PLACE A MAN WHO HAS waked, risen, washed, dressed, fed, been congratulated, on a day in latter April long ago—about April 22, say, of 1594, a Monday—whether at London in lodgings or at a friend's or tavern, a small house in the market town Stratford some hundred miles by miry ways northwest, or at Titchfield House a little closer southwest, or elsewhere, but somewhere in England at the height of the northern Renaissance; a different world. Alone at some hour in one room, his intellectual and physical presence not as yet visible to us although we know its name, seated or standing, highlone in thought. He is thirty years old today and few enjoy this jolt from decade to decade. It would be an error to imagine him very young. He has been married almost twelve years, has (at least) three children, and Elizabethans age fast. He follows several occupations or trades; "professions" we call them, just as we call each other upon no evidence "gentlemen," but in this age they stand low; in two of them, moreover, his future must look at the moment to William Shakespeare problematical. In the third he is now sensationally settled and he may not know that he is about to abandon it.

He is first an actor; this must be how he has chiefly got his living so far. In a book soon to appear students agree that it is he who will be described as an "old player," and possibly he has been a player for fifteen years. He may thrice have been alluded to in print as one. Let us put aside the two earliest "contemporary allusions" given by Sir Edmund Chambers (who does not believe in them either) as referring not to Shakespeare but to John Lyly ("Willy"), Michael Drayton ("Aetion"), and substitute for them George Peele's vapid couplet in *Edward I*, a chronicle-history published in 1593, wherein Queen Elinor says rather gratuitously and very awkwardly to Baliol, just named King of Scots by Longshanks:

> Shake thy spere in honour of his name,
> Vnder whose roialtie thou wearst the same.

This phrase is known elsewhere and the text of this play is morbidly corrupt; nevertheless, I follow hesitantly the late A. W. Pollard in thinking we appear to have here a punning compliment by the playwright to the actor of the part, especially in view of testimony (1610) that Shakespeare had acted kingly parts. Then from another University Wit, Robert Greene, we learned that in 1592 Shakespeare was a player who, intolerably, had set up also as playwright. And from an apology for Greene by his associate, the playwright-to-be Henry Chettle, that same year, we heard an opinion of Shakespeare's acting: it is "excellent." John Aubrey later will tell us that he "did act exceedingly well"—and all this is worth more emphasis than it has received, owing to a tradition that he wrote better than he acted. An unilluminating tradition, for he also wrote better than anyone else has ever acted.

A player then; he plays kings—not Longshanks but Baliol—and other dignified parts (perhaps, as a boy actor, he once took female roles). Those parts that will be indicated are still unconceived, Adam in *As You Like It*, the Ghost in *Hamlet*. In the latter play the Prince will have much to say against some current styles of playing, much to say for "a temperance, that may giue it smoothnesse," and he implies, in part of his advice to the Chief Player, a remarkable opinion of the philosophical and social importance of acting, which it will not be very daring in us to suppose that his creator will then hold also: "oresteppe not [says Hamlet] the modestie of nature: For any thing so ore-doone is from the purpose of playing, whose end both at the first, and nowe, was and is, to holde as twere the Mirrour up to nature: to shew vertue her feature, scorne her owne Image, and the very age and body of the time his forme and pressure . . ." The history of theatrical apologetics contains no encomium or admonition more intense and lofty. But this sentiment, like the style, may lie veiled seven years in the future. So far William Shakespeare must have been apprentice and then "hireling" (not "sharor," or part-owner) in whatever his company or companies were, rising to six shillings a week. Actors, by an ancient statute often renewed, are legally vagabonds—men who if caught masterless are to be branded and put to forced labour—except as they have status being servants to some nobleman or gentleman who protects a company. Just now we do not know that Shakespeare is a member of any company. The theatre is still in such ill repute that a young gentleman has vexed his mother by settling this month in Bishopsgate near the Bull Inn, where plays and players may corrupt his servants. Some private feelings of Shakespeare upon this occupation of his I postpone a little. But he must wonder as he reflects here late in April of 1594 whether he is going to be able to continue to be an actor at all. For a year and a half London's worst plague in generations has forbidden any playing except for one month in winter and a few court performances. Opening hopefully this month, the Rose had to close on the tenth, a Privy Council order of yesterday has again restricted access to court, and Shakespeare does not know that the plague is at last over now for nearly ten whole years. Of course the companies survive by travel in the provinces during plague time. But this disorganization, notable already from 1588 on, has deepened since 1592. Shakespeare can hardly suppose that an entirely new period of stability is at hand. Indeed, he has taken up, during this period of protracted theatrical adversity, a new occupation.

For second he is a poet. I do not mean that he wrote early in his twenties perhaps a large number of sonnets, which he has not printed and will not print for fifteen years more: nor that he writes songs. This is private expression, diversion, not occupation. The Elizabethan poet, too, has status only when attached; as the poet who greeted Elizabeth for the Earl of Hertford in the entertainment several years past at Elvetham, amid fantastic pageantry, was booted, lest he be imagined "a loose and creeping poet." With the 1,200-line *Venus and Adonis*, published a year ago with a dedication to the dazzling young Earl of Southampton, Shakespeare became a professional poet. He seems not to have known Southampton much. "Right Honourable," he wrote, "I know not how I shall offend in dedicating my vnpolisht lines to your Lordship . . . onlye if your Honour seem but pleased,

I account my selfe highly praised, and vowe to take advantage of all idle houres, till I haue honoured you with some grauer labour. But if the first heire of my inuention prove deformed, I shall be sorie it had so noble a god-father; and neuer after eare so barren a land, for feare it yeeld me still so bad a haruest . . ." Poets dedicated often at random, fishing. A few months after, Thomas Nashe dedicated his novel *The Unfortunate Traveller* to Southampton, imitating Shakespeare ("these vnpolisht leaues of mine") but with so little success that in a reprint of this year (1594) he has withdrawn the dedication. Shakespeare's stress upon a coming work suggests, behind conventional modesty, both self-confidence and calculation; a sort of threat, even, being implied (if you do nothing about this honour, you will not hear from me again). His experience must have contrasted with Nashe's, for he is now engaged on the "grauer labour." One reason for our pitching on the present date is that for the first time in his professional life we know exactly what William Shakespeare is doing. He is finishing a second, longer poem, *The Rape of Lucrece*. Just over a fortnight hence it will be registered for printing with a dedication to Southampton widely different in burden and tone from the first: "The loue I dedicate to your Lordship is without end . . . The warrant I haue of your Honourable disposition, not the worth of my vntutored lines makes it [the poem] assured of acceptance. What I haue done is yours, what I haue to doe is yours, being part in all I haue, deuoted yours . . ." What "warrant" the poet has already received, his silent figure does not tell us. But the assurance of this address is as rare, among Elizabethan dedications spanning a social gulf, as was the self-possession of the first, and I think we must take it that a social and financial status never before, perhaps, very promising, has been by the Earl decisively improved. *Venus and Adonis*, meanwhile, has become one of the celebrated poems of the age; Thomas Heywood, down from Cambridge, is busy with the earliest extant imitation of it (*Oenone and Paris*). *Lucrece* will make its mark instantly. In an elegy upon a lady who died ten days ago, somebody signing himself W. Har. will urge Lucrece's poet (and also Cornelia's Thomas Kyd) to call home from the foreign past their pens for women's virtues and praise Lady Branch. For the wife of the Lord Mayor of London, one of the players' most persistent adversaries, Shakespeare we can hardly expect to respond; but it is instructive that he will never but once or twice respond to such occasions and entreaties, which must have come thick henceforth. Through an age brimming with eulogy and lament, his friends will publish and die, his son will die, Essex fall, Southampton languish in the Tower and emerge, the Queen lie speechless sweating and perish, James be crowned, without poems from Shakespeare. He will begin sometime, probably, a third long one, *A Lover's Complaint*, compose a single magnificent enigmatic occasion-poem, *The Phoenix and the Turtle*, throw off six crude lines of epitaph for a wealthy brewer, perhaps some squibs. These are all and more than we are sure of. *Lucrece*'s dedication promises nothing further. But a change will take place immediately in his affairs; whether at the moment he plans a career as a poet, we can hardly say.

For third he is a playwright, and although there is more to be said for his poems than mid-twentieth-century criticism will find to say, this last is certainly the reason we are looking at him. He sits here as the author of a good many plays, including probably three comedies, *The Two Gentlemen of Verona*, *The Comedy of Errors*, *Love's Labour's Lost*, much of a double chronicle called *The First Part of the Contention between York and Lancaster*, and *The True Tragedy of Richard Duke of York* (known to us misleadingly as the Second and Third parts of *Henry VI*), and *Richard III*. It is most improbable that all of Shakespeare's early work has survived. For excellent reasons, his escaped the general mortality of plays. Of 250 surviving plays from the three decades 1581–1611 that he might have seen or acted in, one sixth are his own; two of his are the only survivors we can place readily in the busy theatrical year 1595. But one of his very late collaborations is known to be lost ("Cardenio") and no doubt some apprentice work is lost to us, particularly in its original form. Tantalizing among many plays mentioned later as his are "Love's Labour's Won" (part or most of which may survive under another title), "Iphis and Ianthe" (a subject from one of his favourite works, the *Metamorphoses*, and a form of title he liked), and "King Stephen" (a reign, fully treated by Holinshed, which has points in common not only with John's but with those of Henry VI and Richard II). He has doubtless, like other authors, started things and laid them aside. Some of his casual work survives in plays by other men. He has written at least two scenes (ii. 4, iv. 2) into a stage success, known to us unfortunately as *1 Henry VI*, worked up by Greene and Nashe to capitalize on the popularity of the "Contention" plays by dramatizing the earlier part of Henry's reign; he may have helped an imitator with *Edward III*; and he has lately done a general job of revision, with mocking enthusiasm, on somebody's bloody *Titus Andronicus*. The point of revising plays is that double admission can be charged for plays billed as "new"—an elastic term—and the special point in plague time is that the impoverished com-

33

panies can seldom then afford wholly new plays. Plays in fact have
been swapping about desperately, as companies go on the rocks and
have to sell playbooks, costumes, anything. For the same reason, plays
are coming this year in numbers into printers' hands; normally, of
course, the company that has bought a play from its author wants its
use exclusively and so objects to its printing. *Titus* was registered for
printing two months ago, on the day of its last performance by
Sussex's men (it had belonged earlier to Derby's men, and to Pembroke's). Ten days ago without his knowledge began a raid on work
dominantly Shakespeare's, with the registration of a mutilated version
of *1 Contention* (or *2 Henry VI*), constructed probably from memory by a minor actor with Pembroke's men last autumn, when that
company broke up, for sale to a printer. A similar, vulgarized "report" of *2 Contention* (*Richard Duke of York* or *3 Henry VI*) will
follow next year; and meanwhile, ten days hence, will be registered
for print something called *The Taming of a Shrew*, of which the less
said the better, though criticism is finally beginning to agree to regard it as a memorial reconstruction of a lost play which stood behind
the later *Shrew* play part Shakespeare's—the lost play having been
itself perhaps part Shakespeare's.

So nearly half his visible dramatic work to date may have been
botched. How will Shakespeare feel about it? Philistine biography has
an easy answer: he will be indifferent, or concerned at most with the
financial loss represented in case he is still associated with any of the
companies involved. Why not otherwise take authentic versions (of
the long poems) to his own printer, Richard Field? In passing: the
poet's relation with Field, a Stratford contemporary who married
well, may just now be deteriorating; it is John Harrison the elder
who will enter *Lucrece*, and though Field will print it for him, he
will also transfer to Harrison next month *Venus and Adonis;* Field,
for that matter, seldom prints poetry for himself. But the real reproof
is different and double. Companies own plays, not authors, and anyway, the printers of the pirated versions now control the copyrights.
Shakespeare could be wild and helpless. Note also that no *original*
work of his is yet involved. Later, when his power has increased and
original work is infringed, more often than not we will find him
active enough when this sort of thing happens. I have been trying so
far to avoid general conceptions or preconceptions. But now that the
complacent image of an Apollonian Shakespeare has threatened to
disturb our patient inquiry into the situation of this gifted veteran
thirty years old, it seems time to draw nearer. It is a question whether

we have not found him angry and helpless—but active as well—already.

His manifest public career begins for us with an onslaught by the dying Greene two years ago. Greene was a vain, irritable, redheaded character of thirty-four who when young had written a series of mellifluous romances, which are still half readable and which strongly engaged Shakespeare—their mark is early plain on *The Two Gentlemen*. Greene plastered his title pages with his university degrees. Interested by the triumph of Marlowe's *1 Tamburlaine* in 1586–7, he took up playwriting. Then he turned to realistic pamphlets on sharp practice in London, having deserted his wife for the sister of an important thief named Cutting Ball. Presently he underwent a spectacular and unevenly convincing repentance, displayed in various new pamphlets; of which it is the snarling close of one of the last, written shortly before his pathetic, almost desolate death of a surfeit of wine and pickled herring, that we care about. In order to estimate the force of Greene's attack on Shakespeare, we must take note of several conditions: Greene's fame, the publicity of the affair (such that Barnabe Riche, in a work registered soon before Shakespeare's birthday now in 1594, renews the attack), Shakespeare's highly probable sensitivity upon the educational score, the social score—and just possibly also upon the score of his name. The name seems to have been a Middle English formation, after the Norman model, for some blustering warrior or overactive sergeant of the law: an imperative nickname.* It is immaterial that the first known Sakspere, a William from a village south of Stratford, was hanged in 1248 for robbery, and that the first known Warwickshire Shakespeare was a felon who fled the country. But it is not immaterial, either, that just a century before our date a Merton College Shakespeare changed his name to Saunders "*quod vile reputatum est,*" or that the poet himself may have had recourse as a boy to one of his grandfather's variants, Shakeschaft. Greene, who felt himself deserted by the actors, his inferiors (though it is not clear what they owed him and he had even on one occasion cheated them by a double sale of a play), was warning Marlowe and other university playwrights away from them, "those Puppets (I meane) that spake from our mouths, those Anticks garnisht in our colours." The worst of them, Greene pursued, is "an vpstart Crow, beautified with our feathers, that with his *Tygers hart wrapt in a Players hyde* suppose he is as well able to bombast out a

---

* Earlier speculation has been superseded by J. Hoops of Heidelberg in *Studies for William A. Read*, 1940; even Henry Bradley's.

blanke verse as the best of you: and being an absolute *Iohannes fac totum*, is in his owne conceit the onely Shake-scene in a countrey." Quite apart from the impudent parody of one of Shakespeare's lines in *2 Contention* ("Oh Tygres Heart, wrapt in a Woman's Hide"), here was a congeries of contempt and slander that might enter into the soul. It is far from clear to me that this is not a main slander handled in the sonnets of Shakespeare, particularly the last two of the extremely bitter trio 110–11–12. 110 speaks with self-contempt of his "motley" occupation, but in 111 the emotion has swung to an access of self-pity, with a special complaint:

> O for my sake doe you with fortune chide,
> The guiltie goddesse of my harmful deeds,
> That did not better for my life prouide
> Then publick means which publick manners breeds.
> Thence comes it that my *name* receiues a brand,
> And almost thence my nature is subdu'd
> To what it workes in, like the Dyers hand,
> Pity me then, and wish I were renu'de.
> Whilst like a willing pacient I will drinke
> Potions of Eysell gainst my strong infection . . .

And 112 begins:

> Your loue and pittie doth th' impression fill
> Which vulgar scandall stampt upon my brow,
> For what care I who calls me well or ill
> So you *ore-greene* my bad, my good alow?

Though not much addicted to cryptograms, I feel the suggestion as plausible which sees in the otherwise unknown word "o'er-greene" an allusion to the name of his tormentor, somewhat as in "out-Herod," the meaning of the clause then being: If you wipe out Greene's insult to what *is* ill in me, my occupation . . . In these excruciated poems no resort is had to the veneration for playing that will be expressed by Hamlet; instead, a proud nature seems stung to a writhing assent to what is *true* in Greene's charge. This is Shakespeare helpless, in private with one friend. In public he resented the attack so effectively that, within three months Chettle—whom Shakespeare and Marlowe (he says*) accused of writing the thing himself—had apologized in the Epistle to a book of his own. Not to

---

* Chettle does not name the men, but their identities, which are unmistakable, have not been doubted.

Marlowe, whom he does not care ever to meet. But to Shakespeare, whom Chettle when he was preparing Greene's posthumous papers for the press had not met either, but since has met, and is now "as sory [for not having changed the passage] as if the originall fault had beene my fault, because my selfe haue seene his demeanor no lesse ciuill than he exelent in the qualitie he professes: Besides, diuers of worship haue reported his uprightnes of dealing, which argues his honesty, and his facetious grace in writting, that approoues his Art." Observe how explicit and comprehensive is this witness in repudiation. To Greene's libel of egotism, Chettle replies with his experience of Shakespeare's civility; to Greene's contempt for the actor, with his judgment not alone of Shakespeare's excellence—by implication, of the worth of the profession or "quality." To dispose of what many contemporaries seem to have taken as a charge of plagiarism, owing to a misunderstanding (possibly) of the "feathers" phrase, Chettle then invokes general honourable witness to Shakespeare's character, and not only to this but to the elegance ("facetious" meaning polished) of his work for the stage. Courtesy, professional excellence, integrity, artistry. A most unusual apology, I think; especially when viewed in the light of an independence that refused any amends whatever to the most famous playwright of the moment. It suggests that William Shakespeare had become more favourably known, was more imposing by 1592, than some careful students allow. And it introduces us to his character. "His character," somebody will exclaim like Tesman in *Hedda Gabler*: "But, good heavens, we know nothing about his character!" No; but there is a thing or two more to be said about it all the same.

What is your physical image for this man I don't know. The first authentic image surviving is the fatuous bust at Stratford, perhaps made from a mask but conventionally made as a sepulchral affair and since butchered (let's mean: brought to resemble a butcher) by incoherent repaintings over the stone. The third and last authentic image surviving, engraved by a young Fleming in London, half a dozen years after the man's death, for a collection of his plays in folio, you will have seen there or elsewhere and probably hardly admire. If opposite the present page were placed the second authentic image surviving, which is less well known, I think you would be interested. It is again recognizably Martin Droeshout's "immortal piece of inferior engraving," though the head alone, say, without the vile-drawn dwarf's doublet; but if you looked at it with care, the other two presentments of the man would fade. This is the first state (or

37

"proof") of the Folio portrait, known in just four copies.* Spielmann describes it as that of a frank young English face, with firm delicate features, a gaze calm and observant under fair eyebrows set low. The forehead is bald—perhaps prematurely, perhaps shaved either in a fashion (as were the monks of Iona) or for ease in playing venerable characters; it is broad and massive but lacks entirely the bulbous appearance you are familiar with, and the dark hair grows naturally down from each side of it. There is a slight downy mustache, a small lip-beard above a strong smooth chin. Spielmann speaks also of a "characteristic aspect of large sympathy held in control by critical judgment, the strong reserve of individuality." One sees clearly why Aubrey was told that he was "a handsome well shap't man." Beautifully oval, the forehead wide, high, prominent, the jaws not prominent except as rondure, the chin large but round, the face might alone have inspired Mantegazza's catalogue of the characteristic appearance of intelligence. The nose, however, which dominates it, is singular, a little broader at the nostrils than down the straight, solid bridge. The upper lip is deeply bowed, the lower full. But what is visible of one ear is so misshapen that I wonder how far we can trust Droeshout in detail. Spielmann believes he worked from an outline drawing of the poet, with flat washes of colour, made when Shakespeare was about thirty.

This, then, is the man we have been looking at. Whether Spielmann's impression of "frankness" will do, I doubt. Years of studying the image off and on have not diminished my contrary sense of its enigmatic character. There are faces that seem *merely* reserved. This speaks, it is all but ardent. Yet, proud without assertion, harmonious, formidable, less than any face I have seen does it yield you up any secret. The ambivalent impression is enforced, perhaps, not checked, by the one anecdote transmitted to us about Shakespeare's father. Somebody once saw the "merry cheekt" old man in his shop—he was a glover—and heard him say that "Will was a good Honest Fellow, but he durst have crackt a jeast with him at any time." With a son only "gentle," companionable, "witty," as his contemporaries tell us Shakespeare was, there would have been no question of "daring" to crack a jest.

Now turn back from this face to the second state of the portrait and see what poor Droeshout has done in his attempt to give it proper age and status as the frontispiece to a folio. He has made the skull

* The clearest reproduction I have seen, though small, is that of the Bodleian copy in E. K. Chambers, *William Shakespeare: a study of facts and problems,* 1930.

hydrocephalous by multi-management of light, lifted the hair like a wig, eradicated a mole on the left cheek, stubbled the chin, puffed and hollowed the under-eyes, achieved at last that hard, foxy, *false* appearance which has gravelled us all and sent so many weak-minded persons scurrying about in search of the "real" (the titled) author. I will not suppose that a poet looks like a poet necessarily, whatever that appearance may be. But *if* he does—as Virgil did, we know from the unrivalled mosaic discovered in Tunisia in 1896, and as Shakespeare (it seems) did—it is not only as well to know it but important not to suppose that he didn't. My point, of course, is an analogy. Just as you forget the Stratford bust and Droeshout's rehandling, so it will be helpful if, while recalling as vividly as possible everything you have experienced of Shakespeare's work, you can put out of mind all that you have hitherto known of his character and life. You may know, for example, that Shakespeare was uneducated, his parents illiterate, that he matured very late after a long period in regard to which one guess is as good as another about what he was doing, that he commenced playwright by rewriting other men's plays, that Marlowe was his master, that he followed literary and theatrical fashions, that he did not deal with contemporary events, that he was indifferent to the fate of his work. These are fancies. Some may be true fancies, some false; I think most are false; but all are troublesome because they interfere with the reception of an image which has to be created slowly. At thirty men think reluctantly back over their lives, and we must try how far we can follow him.

Sprung like Virgil and Keats from an unequal match, Shakespeare was the eldest son of a countryman who had married a daughter of his father's landlord, Robert Arden of Wilmcote, moved to Stratford, and prospered.* Mary Arden had brought him some property, not much. He cured and dressed skins, made gloves; sold barley and timber; perhaps he slaughtered and dealt in wool. He was also active in civic life. When the boy was four, John Shakespeare was bailiff or mayor. He signed with a mark and kept the Corporation

* When William, christened on 26 April 1564, was born, nobody knows. The popular birthdate, 23 April, is popular because it is St. George's day, the patron saint of England, and because Shakespeare died on that day in 1616; that a coincidence with the date of death should have gone unnoticed for a century suggests that it is wrong. Evidently he was fifty-two when he died, although there are difficulties even about this. De Quincey fancied that the date of his granddaughter's first marriage, 22 April 1626, memorialized the birthday, and "about April 22nd" is the best we can do. This is Old Style of course; New Style, 3 May or so.

accounts for years; scarcely anyone now thinks he could not write. Marlowe's father was supposed illiterate because he signed his will with a mark, until an excellent signature (prior to the will) turned up in 1937. A mark, originally a cross, was ceremonial. Whether William Shakespeare entered the free Grammar School at five or seven is a mystery for all Professor Baldwin's thousands of pages. The least inhuman inquiry into his schooling is still Baynes's; it consisted of Latin; as Baynes wrote, the most pleasing account we have of the influence of the Stratford country—woodland north, champaign south—on senses and a spirit preternaturally keen. How long the boy lived there is doubtful. When he was twelve his father's way of life altered. Having missed one corporation meeting in thirteen years, that is, before 23d January 1577, during the ten years after this date, he attended just one. Circumstantial argument lately has failed to shake the evidence that his affairs were declining; but some new evidence has made it clear that he was a Catholic. A testament of faith in his name ("calling to mind . . . that I may be possibly cut off in the blossome of my sins"), found under the tiling of his house in the eighteenth century, transcribed and lost, is now known to be a translation—brought to England by Jesuit missionaries in 1580—of an Italian testament composed in Milan shortly before. As of a man who had married near the end of Mary's reign, Catholicism must not astonish us, and many Ardens were Catholics. But the heterodox loyalty helps to explain John Shakespeare's withdrawal from public life; and with regard to his son's training, it is of real importance, as arguing an alternation of Catholic influence at home and Protestant influence at school—the latter being further complicated, De Groot has shown, by an alternation of Protestant and more or less Catholic schoolmasters. The balance of sympathies which is one of the poet's characteristics had thus a deep root. By thirteen or fourteen we may doubt whether William Shakespeare had any more to learn from the one of his masters about whom we know almost nothing, and the tradition that his father—with five younger children to support— withdrew him from school to work at his own trade is plausible enough. To this age, nothing has been transmitted to us about the boy except that he was eloquent at a dramatic stunt called Killing the Calf (you go behind a curtain and act both calf and butcher). He also had now or later, unless Aubrey was misled, a friend his own age as talented as himself who died young.

Now, I think, begin the so-called "lost years." Why it should be thought a conservative estimate that Shakespeare stayed in Stratford until his marriage I have no idea. Throughout life he always returned there from time to time, and very little time is required either for a marriage or the consummation of a marriage. We lose him probably at about fifteen. His marriage, in fact, at eighteen, to a woman twenty-six from a hamlet near Stratford, may have been hasty; six months after the license was issued, a daughter was christened Susanna. A nuptial pre-contract amounting to marriage, such as Shakespeare actually mentions in *Measure for Measure*, has been argued for, and it is true that both practice and law were opposed, in this matter, to ecclesiastical teaching. In any event, from the possibility that he had to marry it does not follow that he was unwilling to. Anne Shakespeare's impressions of the poet have not survived. He did not make a faithful husband, and was seldom at home, but he was a husband of whom, it is not too much to suppose, one could readily be proud, and in time he would flourish. Twins followed the daughter by twenty months, early in 1585, and were named after Hamnet (or Hamlet) Sadler, a baker in High Street, and his wife, Judith. There were no more children. A year or so later he seems to have begun writing sonnets.

About a century after these events, a son of an actor who had been with Shakespeare's company in 1598 told Aubrey that the poet "had been in his younger years a Schoolmaster in the Countrey." This would be as an usher, presumably, not schoolmaster proper, and not necessarily for long. A reflection of the supposed experience had been seen in *Love's Labour's Lost* (where Holofernes strikes one as constructed rather from the point of view of a victim than of a colleague—not to mention his immediate origin in the Pedant of the *commedia dell'arte*). It may be. Failing evidence, this remote assertion is really on no better footing than the numberless demonstrations that he was a soldier, or law clerk, or traveller, or what not. Possible, any of them, but I can imagine nothing more futile than pinning one's faith to a hypothesis which does not even bear upon the fundamental problem: the transition from Stratford obscurity to prominence in the London theatre. Let us reserve our faith or lack of it for frank amusements, like the deer-stealing and horse-holding traditions. Faith is not quite the point in history. I want to indicate the four lines of possibility most attractive in the present state of our knowledge.

The first, and most vivid, is northern. In the autumn of 1581 Alexander Houghton died, a Lancashire gentleman who kept players, leaving to his brother Thomas if he will keep players, if not to Sir Thomas Hesketh, instruments and costumes, and specially commending to them William Shakeshafte and another, who now live with him at Lea, evidently players; and leaving this pair of servants also annuities of two pounds. Chambers, who noticed this will in 1923 (*The Elizabethan Stage*) and forgot it in 1930, has lately, jogged by Oliver Baker, taken up the matter again. The Houghtons, and Hesketh at Rufford, were on close terms with the Stanleys, whose great house, Knowsley, lay just south. Hesketh almost certainly kept players and had them there with him in December 1587. He died a year later. Both the Stanleys—the 4th Earl of Derby and his son Ferdinando, Lord Strange—of course kept players who made up one of the leading English companies, sometimes under one name, sometimes the other. I must enter a little on their history. They played at Stratford in 1578–9 and 1579–80; may have been the unnamed players at Knowsley thrice in 1588–90, when Lord Strange was there; were eighteen weeks at the Rose with Philip Henslowe early in 1592, giving twenty-three plays, mostly old ones by Marlowe, Greene, Peele, Thomas Lodge, Kyd (ten performances of *The Jew of Malta*, thirteen of *The Spanish Tragedy*), but five new ones including "harey the vi," evidently *1 Henry VI* (fifteen performances); for several weeks early in 1593 they were there again, and five men later to join Shakespeare in the most famous company of the age (William Kemp, Thomas Pope, John Heminge, Augustine Phillips, George Bryan) were with them when they were given a special license in May and went on tour. Derby died in September, and next spring, in the week before Shakespeare's thirtieth birthday, his son died (16 April 1594). The company used the countess's name at Winchester on 16 May but in the summer reshuffled (Edward Alleyn, remaining the Lord Admiral's servant, had been at their head for some time) and parted. If the William Shakeshafte of 1581 is William Shakespeare at seventeen, it is clear that he might have passed readily thence to Strange's men, where most critics used to locate him and some still do, and so to London. Perhaps in the present paragraph we have seen Shakespeare lose three or four patrons. This will is the first document ever to appear suggesting, what many have hoped, that he may have been early familiar with a distinguished house; where, they fancy, he acquired the knowledge of books and manners that his plays evince. I see, myself, no difficulty in his reading (as he certainly read widely) almost anywhere, and I think with Granville-Barker that he learnt about life from writing plays about it. But this Lancashire chance is undeniably interesting. It has been reinforced already by Leslie Hotson's discovery that one of the two men chosen by Shakespeare and four of his fellows as trustees in 1599 was not only a native of Rufford but a cousin of Hesketh's widow, and by Alan Keen's showing that a descendant of this man married a relative of the eighteenth-century antiquary William Oldys, whose unfulfilled undertaking "to furnish a bookseller in the Strand . . . with ten years of the life of Shakespeare unknown to the biographers" has hitherto baffled inquiry. The suggestion of Oliver Baker is attractive, that the bequest of a year's wages and the annuity in 1581 may explain the poet's return next year to Stratford and marriage. De Groot's demonstration about John Shakespeare is in the highest degree relevant to all this, Thomas Houghton's widow at Lea being a Catholic recusant (like Southampton's father) and other members of the family suspect. History sometimes really unclouds. The first thirty-five years of George Chapman's life were blank until 1945, when we learned that he was long attendant on a member of the Privy Council, Sir Ralph Sadler, whether brought up by him as Drayton by Sir Henry Goodere, or domesticated later, as was Samuel Daniel at Wilton.

A second line of possibility has opened even more recently. An imperfect copy of Edward Hall's chronicle (the edition of 1550) was discovered some ten years ago containing four hundred marginalia (about 3,600 words) which are claimed as Shakespeare's. They occur mostly over the reigns of Richard II, Henry IV, Henry V. The book was originally owned by Sir Richard Newport of High Ercall in Shropshire, from whose daughter Magdalen, Donne's friend and the mother of George Herbert, it is rather wildly conjectured Shakespeare may have received it, Newport having died in 1570. It wants critical examination, palaeographic and linguistic. Neither Keen's earlier articles nor Moray McLaren's book *By Me* (London, 1949) had much value except descriptive. Keen's last in the *Bulletin of the John Rylands Library*, March 1951, though unreliable, is better. It is the handwriting that is fundamental; a matter for experts. But I will give one example of other indications that require study. Objecting to Hall's use of an authority, the annotator writes: "The Author (if he dyd write it) wrote it in the afternoone." Probably this means: napping. Shakespeare regularly sees the afternoon as the time to sleep (*Hamlet* i. 5. 60, *All's Well*, v. 3. 66, *Tempest* iii. 2. 96) and even uses the phrase "a sleepy Language." I may mention that neither of the copies of Holinshed claimed as Shakespeare's in 1938 by Mme de Chambrun has yet been critically examined: a mutilated 1577 edition in the Folger, "which remained in his sister's family long after the poet's death," and a Stratford-owned, annotated 1587 edition in which the reigns from Richard II to Henry VII are worn thin at the bottom from thumbing. G. B. Harrison was impressed by the case for the latter. Some critics have long thought he used both editions of Holinshed.

The third line was suggested at the end of the last century by Judge Madden and has been developed by Caroline Spurgeon in appendices to their important books (*The Diary of Master William Silence* and *Shakespeare's Imagery*). Shakespeare in *2 Henry IV* knows Gloucestershire remarkably well: games, husbandry, the "sedgie" Severn. By then, if not long before, he had travelled half over England playing; but he names people (who, we find, lived there) at places near Berkeley Castle, which he also knows not only well (in *Richard II*) but *emotionally*, as Miss Spurgeon has made clear with an analysis of his martlet images; and both he and his wife appear to have had relatives there in the Cotswolds. Berkeley's men played at Stratford in the year before he married and again in the year after he married.

The fourth surmise concerns the Queen's men, the most powerful company of the 1580's. Pollard points out that Shakespeare took over later the materials of at least three of their extant plays, handling them not so much like a man who had read the plays as one who acted in them years before, with a strong grasp of situation but negligible verbal congruity. The objection that he might equally have just seen them acted is more satisfactory, I think, with respect to *The Famous Victories of Henry the Fifth* and *King Leir* than with respect to *The Troublesome Reign of King John*. This company mostly broke up on the comedian Tarlton's death in 1588, and the notion receives some support from frequent allusions in Shakespeare's sonnets to the poet's travelling, since it seems likely now that the bulk of these were composed during the years 1586–8.

Through three and a half centuries up to the publication of Hyder Rollins's enormous variorum edition of the sonnets in 1944, hardly anything was discovered about when they were written, and Rollins overlooked the shrewdest suggestion perhaps ever made, that of Fripp's about "o'er-greene," which, a few pages back, I tried to strengthen. This is in accordance with a fatality that seems to dog Shakespearean study. Of "the most expressive man that has existed," the item of correspondence that has survived is a loan-begging letter *to* him, which was never sent. Of England's most effective dramatist, the surviving manuscript is part of a play that was never produced. But from two known circumstances it has never been likely that the sonnets could be much later as a whole than the poet's thirtieth birthday—the last line of Sonnet 94 being quoted in *Edward III* (printed 1595) and Shakespeare's "sugred Sonnets among his priuate friends" being a familiar fact to Francis Meres at some time before September 1598. Into the currently hot controversy (which is weirdly neglecting these two circumstances), I enter here only to explain and a little assist Leslie Hotson's position. Three years ago Hotson took Sonnet 123, of which nobody had ever made any sense whatever, and, proving "pyramid" a regular term for obelisk, argued that the sonnet probably refers to the famous obelisks disinterred by the Pope's order and re-erected at Rome, one each year during 1586-9. Their celebrity was European; strangers just off the ship, we are told, ran to see the first, the marvelous Needle. Not the poet.

> No! Time, thou shalt not bost that I doe change,
> Thy pyramyds buylt vp with newer might
> To me are nothing nouell, nothing strange;
> They are but dressings of a former sight:
> Our dates are breefe, and therefor we admire
> What thou dost foyst vpon us that is ould . . .

The "dated" sonnet so-called (107), about the "mortal moon," had been here and there asserted to refer to the Armada and its defeat in 1588, but assertion is nothing. If the Spanish fleet did not in actuality approach in crescent form, as Hotson supposes, yet that the English thought it did he proves with five quotations calling it a moon (to which, since, others have been added). More cogent still, since 1475 European prophets, Protestants, astronomers had been predicting a doom, a wonder, for '88; and for decades afterward England would rejoice over the catastrophe (designed by some "to be the end of the world"—1631) prophesied and avoided.

> Not mine owne feares, nor the propheticke soule
> Of the wide world, dreaming on things to come,
> Can yet the lease of my true loue controule,
> Supposde as forfeit to a confin'd doome.
> The mortall Moone hath her eclipse indur'de,
> And the sad Augurs mock their owne presage,
> Incertenties now crowne them-selues assur'de
> And peace proclaimes Oliues of endlesse age.
> Now with the drops of this most balmie time,
> My loue lookes fresh . . .

In view of the immediacy of the last six lines, it is useless to deny the possibility that Sonnet 107 was composed in the late summer or early autumn of 1588. Hotson fancies Shakespeare waited until the year ended, but that balmy rain feels like a summer rain and news of the Armada's conclusive dispersal came early in August. Sonnet 123 follows very well in 1588 or 1589; 124—we will see presently—in the latter half of 1589. But except for two odd sonnets (125, 126) these two last end the sequence; all those to Shakespeare's mistress (127–52, followed by two more odd sonnets) having been collected at the end, probably by the 1609 printer, in order to spare the reader as long as possible a story unedifying, the woman being married and also having seduced at one point the poet's young friend. More explicit and savage than those to the friend, these twenty-six belong with Sonnets 40–2. To 107, moreover, is linked backward 106, and to it 105; 104 is the sonnet celebrating three years of friendship with the young man, and I think we may take it, on the present evidence, that Shakespeare wrote most of his sonnets during 1586–8. A few are no doubt later. 110–12 I have placed tentatively in 1592, 125 I should suppose much later. These are misplaced, then. I expect others are. But on the whole the received order is more acceptable than critics (except Chambers) have inclined to allow. The sonnets do not tell a story, still less do they follow a fashion, though a habit of sonnet writing will produce occasional exercises; they reflect interests, pieces of living, two passions. About twenty-five of them contain passages that lodge them among the most beautiful or most energetic short poems in English. Three or four challenge perfection.

But most of them are very moderately good or bad, and I think their mediocrity has been insufficiently appreciated by those critics who feel strong resistance to an early dating for the sonnets. On the other hand, one reason for the resistance is probably the excellence of certain sonnets. The critic cannot imagine lyric verse of this quality proceeding from an author who is simultaneously writing dramatic verse so inferior or no dramatic verse at all that has survived. Here we stumble, I believe, on a misunderstanding of the differences between lyric and dramatic verse. Let the critic consider the superiority of the song "Who is Sylvia?" to almost all the verse dialogue of its play, *The Two Gentlemen*. A similar misunderstanding of the differences between dramatic and narrative verse has led scholars either to set the beginning of Shakespeare's dramatic career much too late, or to fancy *Venus and Adonis* written long before it was printed and to brood painfully over the turgidity of *Lucrece*. Scholars troubled by the poet's allusions to his aging must underestimate either the Renaissance convention or the actual feelings of oldness endured by some young poets, or both. With another reason for resistance to Hotson's discoveries I confess less sympathy. The critic has made up out of nothing long ago, or borrowed, a view which evidence distresses. A man with a distinct idea of what the other side of the moon is like will naturally be disturbed when he arrives. Hotson's case, though itself very difficult, far from being conclusive, and inadequately argued by him, is not only much less unsatisfactory than Professor Harbage's, say, who tries to place in 1603, in the teeth of likelihood, the two sonnets I have discussed; it is the best case we have.

We have arrived, of course, only at some dates, not at identities. Who the dark-haired woman was God knows; her husband was named Will. There has been no small speculation about the identity of the friend, "Mr. W.H.," to whom the 1609 printer dedicated the sonnets as their "onlie begetter." This he was not, but Thorpe was willing enough to keep the woman out of sight. I neglect the considerations positive and negative which ought always to have made it inconceivable that the friend was an earl; since Southampton (and of course Pembroke, forlorn hope) we can dismiss on the score of date. Any gentleman was far enough above an actor. Now we enter the jungle. In the autumn of 1594 will be printed a tedious work in fluent stanzas, ostensibly by one Henry Willoughby, about how various suitors including himself assail with words the virtue of an innkeeper's faithful wife, Avisa. It is implied that she lives in Sherborne, Dorsetshire, where her husband keeps the George, and she may have been a real woman named Avis. I doubt if she was; it has not been noticed that the name "Avice" was considered by some "detorted from *Hildevig*, that is, Lady-defence" (Camden's *Remaines*). Willoughby, when his turn comes, seeks the advice of his "familiar friend," and "old player," "W.S.," who "not long before" fell in love himself and is just over it. Shakespeare, if this is he, gives some unexceptionable advice, in dull stanzas. The whole work is so earnest and dull that it is hard to see it as aggressive, but aggressive it must have been, considering much hocus-pocus impossible to describe briefly, an even duller counterattack by one Peter Colse in 1596, and an order of suppression in 1599. I am not sure "Henry Willobie" is an actual Henry Willoughby who went up to Oxford at sixteen in 1591. But his stated initials are H.W. Now Southampton's initials were H.W. (Henry Wriothesley) and Pembroke's W. H., and Southampton may conceivably be satirized in "Willobie." But as of the Friend of the Sonnets both I believe are irrelevant. But we have seen another W.H. ("W. Har.," actually) addressing Shakespeare in verse in 1594, and there is a limit to the amount of coincidence I am willing to *conjecture*. Some of these friends and poets ought to be the same. If they are not, perhaps we might declare further coincidence inadmissible. Shakespeare's young friend of the sonnets was certainly named Will, and I see "Will" in "Willoughby," and further, without evidence, we can hardly go. Of the "rival poet" nothing can be said except that Marlowe is currently leading Chapman in that ghostly race; from which, I think, Kyd ought not to be excluded.

Hotson's case for a third dated sonnet, 124, is less striking in itself than his others, but more significant still when we link its two parts to two topical features correspondent to them in *The Comedy of Errors*. Again, both religion and politics are implicated; Shakespeare is coming to seem a more allusive poet, perhaps, than we thought him. The scene for the execution threatened at the end of the *Errors*, Baldwin has contended, fits point to point the execution stand set up in Finsbury Fields, near the Theatre and Curtain north of London, where a priest was executed in October 1588 (his initials, I note with horror, were W.H.). If Baldwin exaggerates the psychological correspondence between history's scene and the dramatist's, he makes it appear very possible that Shakespeare's Act V was designed for one of those two theatres at no long interval after the execution, which presumably he witnessed. Now, his subject in Sonnet 124 is the difference between his love and other enthroned things such as monarchs: *their* subjection to change of fortune, weakness-in-power, assassination political or religious, *its* invulnerability—

> It feares not policy that Hereticke . . .

In view of this line, Hotson is undoubtedly justified in referring the couplet to the Jesuit-inspired, devout, futile attempts to cut down Elizabeth:

> To this I witnes call the foles of time,
> Which die for goodness, who haue liu'd for crime.

Yet a sympathy is impressive here behind the theme and verbal condemnation, of interest as our first glimpse of Shakespeare's mature spiritual feeling. We recall his training in balance between the religious parties, as his father had been (and he would be) suspended between social classes, as he stood balanced in some sense, in his twenties, between the sexes (the view, by the way, that he was ever a practicing homosexual is of course untenable). But the earlier part of the sonnet is still more definite than this allusion to Jesuits executed. It uses for metaphor Henri III of France, the "childe of state": whose people rise against him in support of the Duke of Guise in May 1588 ("might for fortunes bastard be vnfathered"), who for the rest of the year endures affably a contemptuous, pro-Guise States General and even news that the Guise intends to kill him ("suffers . . . in smiling pomp"), who murders the Duke and is himself monk-murdered in the summer of 1589—"falls under the blow of thralled discontent,

48

Whereto th'inuiting time our fashion calls . . ." He had named Henry of Navarre his heir, civil war revived, and to this there is explicit allusion in the *Errors*. "I could find out," confides a Dromio, "Countries" in the kitchen wench, and to "Where France?": "In her forehead, arm'd and reuerted, making warre against her heire." A minute later we hear of "Armadoes of Carrects," and anyway this quadruple topicality is irresistible; both sonnet and play ought to belong to 1589.

Shakespeare, then, would seem to have begun writing comedy *at latest* directly after the sonnets. This chronology would account incidentally for what has always seemed to me one of the sonnets' anomalies; he speaks of writing sonnets, of acting, of travelling, of his mistress, of scandal, of a book he gives the friend (77), of a memorandum book the friend gives him (122), but never of writing plays. Perhaps he began in 1588, at twenty-four. Baldwin and Hotson reinforce each other more impressively, of course, by not knowing each other's work. The trouble with this view of Shakespeare's dramatic outset is that it raises as many difficulties as does the "conservative" modern view that he began only about 1590 with *2* and *3 Henry VI*, and in the face of these difficulties the positive evidence is by no means mandatory. I don't believe we can yet say confidently whether he began with comedy or history.

But the conservative view has for a long time been entangled with a most serious error, the clearing up of which does perhaps enable us to form a more satisfactory image of his dramatic outset than has ever been possible before, *if* he did not begin with comedy. I feel sure, that is, that the editors of the Henry VI plays, H. C. Hart and Dover Wilson, are right in regarding them as not originally Shakespeare's, while current authority is wrong in thinking the two important plays are. What is intolerable about the conservative view is that they are patently by several authors, among these dominantly Shakespeare, but the ground plan seems in both *2* and *3 Henry VI* to have been laid by somebody else, probably Greene. The difficulty with this is that they are so greatly superior to plays of the period by Greene or anybody else (except Marlowe's *Edward II*, which follows and imitates them). Consider the superiority alone in theatrical address, the setting up of a story. *2 Henry VI* springs into being as ceremonial, joyous, expectant—the King's bride, whom he has never seen, is about to arrive—everything looks splendid—then a fact, which we feel as odd, is introduced: she comes without dowry—the King pays no attention—but he is shrinking in our sight as the peers grow tall—a qualm—and suddenly, as the author looses the peers, power is pulling exactly seven ways—in Scene 2, power pulls an eighth way—and under this comparison, none of Shakespeare's rivals seem to have a story to tell at all.

I think the key may be found in the length of these plays. One of the things Shakespeare was to revolutionize was play length. Of thirty-six plays belonging to 1590–4, the average length is 2,250 lines; of four by Greene, 2,200. I expect, as originally written, 2 and 3 *Henry VI* were typically inept and strengthless, psychologically primitive, usual-length Greene plays—which Shakespeare expanded into these outsize astonishing dramas (the first over 3,000, the second just under) that gave the theatre after *Tamburlaine* its fresh and true start. Now the hard questions have always been, *why* and *how* the young actor did any such thing. How came he to? Who let him? Who but the other actors? What actor would not have in his part, rather than Greene's inexpressive lines, Gloucester's to the Keeper of his disgraced Duchess:

> Entreat her not the worse, in that I pray
> You vse her well: the World may laugh againe,
> And I may liue to doe you kindnesse, if
> You doe it her . . .

or a weaver's honest testimony to something not relevant, "Sir, he made a Chimney in my Fathers house, and the brickes are aliue at this day to testifie it: therefore deny it not"? It was on the big "parts," especially York's, and the rant, and the comic scenes, that Shakespeare did most work—if that can be called work which seems done so easily—but before he finished he had rehandled or written fresh half the play. Maybe he really just began casually doing it, dissatisfied, like his fellow actors, with the script they had bought; discovering in himself, as he went, feelings that would not let him dismiss even two flagrant impostors without the woman's parting "Alas Sir, we did it for pure need" (which will not soften their sentence), and powers —a diction, say, such that even in this early work he probably uses more words than all his early dramatic rivals taken together—not to speak of an intellect, an imagination, a structural sense, a wit, a sweetness and energy of versification, a syntax, gifts equally for plenitude and concision, all incomparable with theirs. He did much the same to *3 Henry VI*, but with a dwindling interest perhaps (the first play is better), until the figure of Richard rekindled it and drew him then on his own into the masterwork of the opening period. Our taste is uneasy, I think, with the malignant and beguiling Richard; the most sufficient account of the daring manifested in his creation is that of an eighteenth-century Scot, William Richardson. But this daring throws a broad light forward to Shakespeare's achievements—the greater the difficulties, the more active he is—and he was master here already of the unique stroking of presentment that drove Coleridge to one of his deepest conceptions, that of an "ensouling of experience by meditation":

Richard *loues* Richard, *that is, I am I.*

Richard's opening soliloquy, which seems crudely explicit (ugly and therefore unfit for love, I'll be a villain) and yet is so far from being repellent that it fascinates, instead merely hints at what really matters to Richard: his feeling that since wrong has been done him by nature, he is justified in doing wrong—a sentiment which escapes our critical coolness precisely because it is not expressed—unwittingly our similar feeling about ourselves unites with Richard's, and we sympathize and admire. Shakespeare, as Freud put it in an analysis of the speech, "obliges us to supplement, he engages our intellectual activity, diverts it from critical reflections, and keeps us closely identified with his hero."

This work was written, presumably, hard on *Henry VI*, and perhaps in 1592, before playing went under restraint for plague on June 23. Then the English drama reached full psychological stature in Shakespeare before Marlowe, whose *Doctor Faustus* followed *Richard III*. Shakespeare's predecessors in comedy determined the character of his work even less: Lyly as a remote model in elegant prose comedy, Henry Porter with some form of *The Two Angry Women of Abington* about 1589, Peele possibly, others no doubt unknown. *The Comedy of Errors* is a classical farce based on Plautus' *Menaechmi*, with touches in situation from the *Amphitruo;* but it is more complicated and elegant than Plautus and it adds an enveloping action that is romantic. *Love's Labour's Lost* is a classical comedy, likewise observant of the unities of time and place; no source is known for the plot, such as it is. *The Two Gentlemen of Verona* is related rather to the romantic action of the *Errors* and its sources were romantic: a Spanish romance probably through the medium of a lost Queen's men's play, "Felix and Philiomena" of 1585, perhaps a French tale translated by Henry Wotton in 1578, Adlington's *The Golden Asse of Apuleius* (1566), Arthur Brooke's poem *Romeus and Juliet* (1562), etc. This is Shakespeare's emptiest work—his only comedy, for instance, I've not seen performed—and ought for this reason, as well as for its interest in the conflict between love and friendship, a chief theme of the sonnets, to precede *Henry VI* and

Richard III, though it may not have. Whether he began on the classical or romantic side, farcical or comedic, we can hardly yet say. But he developed toward the use of rhyme in comedy; *A Midsummer Night's Dream* will have as much rhymed as blank verse; and it may be instructive that in *The Two Gentlemen* this proportion is less than one tenth, in the *Errors* one third. The *Errors*, at least, cannot be later than 1594 because it was produced in notorious confusion at Gray's Inn at the end of the year. *Love's Labour Lost* is peculiar in everything, partly because a great part of the end of the only version we have was rewritten by the poet about 1598. But the diverse strands of mockery blended in this first triumph of Shakespearean comedy were put at the service of an artistic method he never used again, to the end of polemic.

A cluster of allusions and likelihood seem to locate *Love's Labour's Lost* (the revision apart) late in 1593, perhaps December,* and its special air marks it as designed for private performance. Some ten thousand persons died in London again this year of plague (as if half a million New Yorkers were swept away); playing was restrained. Midway between his long poems, Shakespeare was full in the favour of Southampton; the play must have been done for him, perhaps at Titchfield.† We are within a few months of the point where we began in April of 1594. Now I must invite your attention to some matters that interested the poet. We have seen how he followed French affairs. Despite Navarre's conversion, war dragged on in France between his forces under the young Duc de Biron, Longueville, and others, and the League's under de Mayenne; English troops were now engaged, and I suppose curiosity was active about the French lasciviousness—the King's notoriously, and Longueville had been one of his rivals for Gabrielle the year before, de Mayenne had been prostrate with debauchery at Rouen. The young Earl of Essex stood very high at court, Southampton his intimate in one of the deepest friendships of the age. Essex's rival Sir Walter Ralegh, still in disgrace for the affair with a maid of honour in 1592 that had sent him to the Tower, had retired sulking to Sherborne and was occupied with study and speculation, surrounded by a small group of learned

* Among them allusions to Henri IV's conversion in July (iv. 1. 21–33), to Gabriel Harvey's *Pierce's Supererogation* of this year (iv. 2. 89), to Chapman's poem *The Shadow of Night*, evidently seen in manuscript (Field printed it), for it was registered on December 31 (iv. 3. 346–7, 255), besides plague allusions and "Lord have mercie on vs" (v. 2. 419).

† A garden performance of the comedy a few miles away at Ashford Chace in 1937, by a group from Cambridge, confirmed my impression of its private character, and fadeless radiance.

and literary men of whom the mathematician-astronomer Thomas Hariot was chief. The action of *Love's Labour's Lost* also takes place in retirement. The King of Navarre and three young lords, Berowne, Longaville, Dumaine, withdraw from the world to study for three years, vowing to see no women, fast, watch. Their austerity is to be relieved only by a fantastic strutting Spaniard named Armado, and incidentally a schoolmaster Holofernes, the clown Costard. But the Princess of France with three ladies comes visiting on a political embassy. In secret all four men love, breaking their vows; they discover each other and join forces; after a Farce of the Nine Worthies, Armado, who began the play by accusing Costard of breaking the retreat's laws with a country wench, is found to have got her with child himself; the ladies impose a year's penance upon the lords for vow breaking and part, agreeing to accept them then.

The initial situation is very much that of a musical comedy in which Malenkov, Beria, and Tito agree to give up public life and retire together in silence to study theology.* But this satire is not developed, and I think that recent investigation, however disputable its details, has made good its claim that the general object of the play's satire is Ralegh and his group. Armado must in some degree be a caricature of Ralegh himself. He is melancholy, a "tough signeor" (Ralegh was over forty to Essex's twenty-six), poor, an orator and writer. "His humour," says Holofernes, "is loftie, his discourse peremptorie: his tongue fyled, his eye ambitious, his gate maiesticall, and his generall behauiour vaine, rediculous, and thrasonical . . . too picked, too spruce, too affected, too odd as it were, too peregrinat as I may call it." This is probably a fair Essex-Southampton image of Ralegh. To make him a Spaniard is merely the last straw. Armado cannot multiply one by three—"I am ill at reckning," he explains, "it fitteth the spirit of a Tapster." The mathematical and astronomical satire is intermittent. There may be hits at Hariot in Holofernes, and odd hits elsewhere as at Nashe in Armado's page Moth, perhaps also in Holofernes at Gabriel Harvey of Cambridge and John Florio (later, at least, Southampton's tutor in Italian but incompatible with him politically).

Our knowledge of the make-up and interests of Ralegh's group is

---

* Cf. G. B. Harrison, *An Elizabethan Journal*, 1929, 422. The chief modern discussions of the play's topicality are the introduction to the edition (1923) by Quiller-Couch and Dover Wilson, Frances A. Yates's *A Study of "Love's Labour's Lost"* (1936), M. C. Bradbrook's *The School of Night* (1936), Eleanor Grace Clark's *Ralegh and Marlowe* (1941). A reaction is underway against their exaggerated claims.

imperfect. Shakespeare seems, however, to have taken Chapman's poem *The Shadow of Night* as a statement of its doctrine, and this is his real butt. Chapman called for solitude, contemplation, the Furor Poeticus—

> No pen can any thing eternall wright,
> That is not steept in humor of the Night.

Berowne, throughout a critic of the others' proceedings, is Shakespeare's hero, and he replies directly in the opening scene:

> So ere you finde where light in darknes lyes,
> Your light growes darke by loosing of your eyes.

Of course Berowne is a fearful euphuist, too; he only surpasses the others in self-knowledge and eloquence; and when he is converted to plain speaking, when he rationalizes all their vow breaking with an appeal against affectation and for *experience*, his author is as usual in this play both serious and not serious. Shakespeare's position, as against Chapman's, is a genuine one, but his heart is not in polemic. He might have used Berowne's words to Chapman:

> I haue for barbarisme spoke more
> Then for that Angell knowledge you can say . . .

Shakespeare's playful, imperturbable superiority must sometimes have galled more dogmatic intellectuals. He was interested in creating an exquisite love comedy.

His wit rather than his heart is everywhere, I think, in *Love's Labour's Lost*, except in the revised portions. The first dramatic labour ever fully to engage Shakespeare's *heart* was his next. Here, I suppose, most readers would identify the author with his hero, if anyone, and Mercutio. But among the most personal lines in the play seem to be some unnecessary lines of old Capulet, who has indeed already just welcomed his guests and will shortly welcome them again.

> Welcome gentlemen, I haue seene the day
> That I haue worne a visor and could tell
> A whispering tale in a faire Ladies eare:
> Such as would please: tis gone, tis gone, tis gone.

A moment later among meaningless chat we hear, for no reason, of somebody unidentified and indifferent:

> His sonne is thirtie.

Shortly after his thirtieth birthday in 1594, a company was formed under the protection of the Lord Chamberlain, in which he bought a share; probably by a gift from Southampton, which may have been of £100. In October, Hunsdon was instructing the Lord Mayor to let "my nowe companie" play again at the Cross Keys in Gracechurch Street, and William Shakespeare was one of three payees, with Richard Burbage and Will Kemp, for December performances at Court. Perhaps the ambitious *Romeo and Juliet* was his first play for the Chamberlain's men—as his one other tragedy before *Hamlet* will be written five years hence for the opening of the Globe. Shakespeare's field has strangely cleared: Lyly had long ceased to write for the stage, Peele was ill and to die, Greene and Marlowe and Kyd were dead. And so, on to his wilderness of dramatic literature, or garden, or palace, to be created in the six years coming—*Richard II, 1* and *2 Henry IV, Henry V, King John,* comedies of the *Dream,* the *Merchant,* the *Shrew, Merry Wives, Much Ado, As You Like It, Twelfth Night,* and *Caesar;* and beyond.

1953

Notes on Macbeth

IF A DRAMATIST IS UNFREE IN COMPARISON TO OTHER KINDS of authors, Shakespeare was specially unfree, writing as he did for a particular company (in which he was also an actor) and a repertory company at that. Further, when he wrote *Macbeth*, the company was called the King's Men, and his plays had to please not only the London public, the nobles who would occasionally command a performance, the young lawyers of the Inns of Court, and the provincial audiences the company played for when they went on tour in the summer, but the Court and the King himself.

It is certain that in *Macbeth* Shakespeare made an extreme effort both to interest and please King James. The play is very short, for one thing; the King tended to sleep during long plays, and his taste was well known. For another, the play is laid in James's country—he had succeeded to the English throne only two years before, in 1603. It is elaborately attentive to certain of his special interests, such as witchcraft (on which he had written a book); and its major spectacle—the procession of the Scots kings at iv. 1. 111.—is addressed directly to James's vanity and pride of family: these are the King's actual ancestors. Among all these limitations upon the dramatist's freedom—some imposed, some voluntary—it may seem that an artist could not do his own work at all. Yet scarcely any work in world literature strikes one as more characteristic or freer than *Macbeth*. This freedom is above all a freedom of *language*. It is through his incomparable language, more than any other feature of the work, that Shakespeare communicates his vision. This is also the feature that a spectator cannot study at all—he can only feel it and only feel part of it correctly: thus, when he hears

> violent sorrow seem[s]
> A modern ecstasy

it is hard to know what he will think, but he will not be very likely to know that "modern" meant for Shakespeare and his actor and his

56

audience, not "up-to-date" with admiring connotations, but "ordinary, commonplace" with bored and (here) despairing connotations. In the sketch that is possible here of some of the play's salient qualities and meanings, language is the topic we take first.

In the witches' scene that begins Act IV (Hecate's little speech and the extra witches and their song were very probably added to the play after Shakespeare's death), one of the witches says:

> By the pricking of my thumbs,
> Something wicked this way comes.

There is an allusion here to the ancient superstition "that all sudden pains of the body, which could not naturally be accounted for, were presages of somewhat that was shortly to happen." But she might also have said: "It is suggested to me, by a sensation of prickling in my thumbs, that an evil man is on his way here." The difference between Shakespeare's intense two lines and this rather general, unconcentrated alternative is, first, a difference in the quality of the sound, as there is a difference between what you hear at the beginning of Beethoven's Piano Sonata, Opus 111 and what you hear from a jukebox. The word "wicked" keeps the sound of "pricking" going; the reader's experience of the pricking of the witch's thumbs intensifies. In other ways, too, the two lines are built very closely into each other: "*Some*thing" half rhymes with "thumbs," and the four short-*i* sounds that measuredly follow (-*thing, wick-, -id, this*) carry on the two short-*i* sounds of "pricking" as well as they convey powerfully the sense of movement, something coming, marching. There is an unusually intimate association between the lines, and perhaps we ought to understand the word "by" has quite a different sense from the way we first took it (By means of this sensation, I know, etc.): In accordance with the pricking of my thumbs, something is on its way here, obedient or at any rate *consonant* to my sign. One gets an impression of a fated *assignation* entirely lacking from our paraphrase of the witch's couplet. This sense is greatly strengthened by the alliteration in the second line: "wicked this way"—as if there were something very natural about the wicked man's coming the witches' way, as indeed there is. One thinks of the two ways, of good and of evil, of the Sermon on the Mount (Matthew 7:13–14); and one does not think of them by accident, for the porter in ii. 3. winds up his Hell discourse with "I had thought to have let in some of all professions, that go the primrose way to the everlasting bonfire." This play is certainly about Good and Evil, and we learn so partly from the aural organization of this couplet.

A second difference takes us outside the couplet—as indeed the word "way" has taken us already. The combination of the concept "thumb," in this witch context, and of the particular rhyme that binds the couplet, reminds us irresistibly, if we are careful readers, of four lines earlier in Act I (i. 3. 28–31.):

> FIRST WITCH. Here I have a pilot's thumb,
> Wrack'd as homeward he did come.
> THIRD WITCH. A drum! a drum!
> Macbeth doth come.

The same rhyme (here thrice repeated) heralds each of his interviews with the Weird Sisters, and each time there is a thumb. Now this pilot is the second of the adventuring figures (the first being the sleepless sailor) in whom the dramatist is foreshadowing the fate of his hero: Macbeth, for *his* wife's greed, is to suffer from lack of sleep, and he is to be wrecked as he comes home, both in the literal sense home (where he will do the murder) and in the metaphorical sense (as he achieves the crown, what he aims at, home). The calling up, in Act IV, of this foreshadowing passage, deepens the drama of the couplet, making present, for its suggestiveness, the moral wreckage that had been foreshadowed. But in addition to this general usefulness, there are two or three specific points that claim our attention. It is not possible to be certain about the first one, because we do not know how clearly Shakespeare differentiated his witches in his mind or whether his speech prefixes for them have been faithfully preserved. According to those we have, it is the first witch who has a pilot's thumb and the second whose thumbs prick; but in the light of the fact that presently Macbeth will be saying, "Had I three ears, I'd hear thee"—a striking speech that will interest us again later—there is an eerie chance that Shakespeare was thinking of *three* thumbs pricking, one of them not joined to its body.

Macbeth is announced, at his first coming, by a military drum; it is open, public; he is a hero, a man with a name. At his second coming he is announced by the pricking of a witch's thumbs; his resort is secret, and he comes not as a hero but as a tyrant; we must imagine as suggested also a terrible diminishment, from the booming of a drum to a slight physical manifestation, corresponding to a removal of the real scene from the objective world to the subjective. But this is not all, or even the main thing. It is as "Macbeth" that he first comes, to be saluted by three prophetic titles. It is *with* his three titles that he next comes, but not called by them, or even described as a man, but only as "something wicked." His nature has changed—not his characteristics merely, but his essential nature. He has become, perhaps, a demon; and the form, and sound, and allusive value of the couplet help to suggest this as no paraphrase could do.

A modern critic speaks of the exquisite line about wintry trees, in Shakespeare's Sonnet 73,

> Bare ruin'd choirs, where late the sweet birds sang,

as suggesting marvellously the devastated monasteries and chantries of post-Reformation England, where the choirs of monks had sung for centuries. If a line in a short lyric poem can give, in addition to doing superbly its practical, literal work, this sort of perspective, it need not seem surprising that the analysis of a couplet in a play takes us into complex problems of characterization and theme. Macbeth himself opens the question that leads at last to "something wicked" when he says to his wife (i. 7. 46–7),

> I dare do all that may become a man;
> Who dares do more is none.

This is variously glossed by the commentators as "superhuman," "subhuman," "devilish"; but the meaning is clear: that there is a possibility other than the human for Macbeth—the demonic. His next formulation of this subject, at iii. 4. 59–60, is a little different. "Are you a man?" she asks him as he stands appalled at the Ghost of Banquo:

> Ay, and a bold one, that dare look on that
> Which might appal the Devil.

The daring here has expanded, is "more"; and the claim that he is still a man does not convince. Then we hear "Something wicked this way comes" and we know where we are. Later the non-human diabolic terms applied to Macbeth, "hellkite," "hellhound," confirm our sense, and one's impression of his standing, or boiling, outside human life is crowned by his horrifying expression,

> Whiles I see lives,

not men but *lives*, as if he had not one himself or only one so different that for human lives he could just say "lives" (like targets merely for his sword) and aim at destroying them (v. 8. 2.).

A separation of the critical elements in *Macbeth* into plot, characterization, imagery, and theme is highly artificial. All are interwoven; the play is a tissue of suggestion. The reason for this is that man's nature is complex. The *ambiguity* of Macbeth's nature is perhaps the play's major subject. This is the shortest of Shakespeare's tragedies; it is barely half the length of *Hamlet*. It follows that the intellectual and artistic work that is being done in the play is being done, even more than is the case in the other tragedies, in terms not of statement but of suggestiveness.

At the same time, it is useful to describe the essential action, because it is that to which everything else contributes and on which everything else depends. The action is extremely simple. A man is tempted, falls, suffers, his nature changes, and he is killed. Such a statement does not tell us very much about the play. But it does suggest to us at once the fundamental difference between *Macbeth* and a mystery novel. Here there is no question of suspense about who has done the deed; the suspense is about how *Fate* will work itself out. And of course Macbeth is not the only person in the play.

Elizabethan Englishmen, including King James, did not feel as we do about the supernatural. They regarded it as a serious topic—just as the American philosopher William James did, for that matter, three hundred years later. The witches are fundamental to the play. Technically, they form an enveloping action, oracular in nature. But the element they represent, the supernatural, reaches and operates inside the action also; so that our description of the plot can hardly leave it out.

In fact we must begin with it. Act I consists of: an initial statement about the fundamental ambiguity of nature ("Fair is foul, and foul is fair") by the witches; an external war which turns out also to be a civil war, owing to the treachery of the Thane of Cawdor; a prediction to Macbeth, the hero of this war, that he will inherit the (sinister) thaneship of Cawdor, and then become actually King; a debate within himself, like the civil war, conducted on progressive levels—first silently, as he stands enthralled with the Cawdor news of the Scottish lords, next in soliloquy (i. 7. 1 ff.; the dialogue with his wife at the end of i. v. shows him so taciturn that it is best grouped with the silence and asides of the heath), then in controversy with his wife, winding up first in a declaration that he will *not* go on, then in a statement of their plan. You will have noticed already the alternation of outer and inner struggle. And the feast, or supper, for Duncan, as victorious and kindly King, as kinsman (first cousin to Macbeth), and as guest, in a society where the relation of host to guest was a grave ethical matter—during which the debate between the murdering couple takes place—already symbolizes the concord of the state which is to be wrecked.

The ironic and terrible concord of murderer and victim is symbolized by the banquet in Act III (where the chaos of the state is openly dramatized). These are the fruits. Meanwhile, the uncertain weather of Act I (moral weather for the witches, made physical weather by Macbeth in his first line, "So foul and fair a day I have not seen") has settled for *night* in Act II, which is about the deed. It begins with Banquo's ambitious, troubled dreams about the Three Sisters, and its supernatural phenomena are the apparitions of the dagger and the voice—one leading to the deed, the other forecasting its consequences.

In the murder scene several points need emphasis. The succession of short, nervous questions exchanged between husband and wife, directly following the murder, suggests the uncertainty of the new world they have just entered by committing the murder. But this is only the most tense passage of this sort; critics have remarked on the fact that no other play of Shakespeare's is so *full* of questions—of doubt, of mystery. Then the terror of the offstage deed needs expressive outlet somehow, and gets it in Macbeth's terrible, crescendoing speeches about the voice. *This* is the new single certainty: that sleep is gone. Macbeth clearly is hysterical in these speeches (reaction after murder), and the tone lifts so high that relief is necessary. It is provided at once in the Hell soliloquy of the porter. But this is not merely comic relief, of course; it is very rare in Shakespeare to find anything that serves one purpose only; and what is probably the most famous essay in all Shakespearean criticism is devoted to a study of this passage, Thomas De Quincey's "On the Knocking at the Gate in *Macbeth.*" The *noise*, after the terrible silence, like a re-entry into the play of the real world, suspended during the murder, is staggering in the theatre; but a good reader will hear it also for himself in "Knock, knock, knock!" And Lady Macbeth's confident "A little water clears us of this deed" is succeeded by "the primrose way to the everlasting bonfire." The essential irony of the passage is simple: the porter thinks that he is just joking about "hell-gate" and "this place is too cold for hell," whereas the audience sees that with Macbeth's deed Hell has been let into the world.

With Act III we see Macbeth seated in power, and learn at once his sense that he has accomplished nothing at all:

> To be thus is nothing;
> But to be *safely* thus.

He sets at once to his new purpose, the murder of Banquo and Fleance. Note that he does *not* employ, or even fully confide in, Lady

Macbeth, and that he sets a third murderer to watch his original two. These are the beginnings (or continuations, for already Malcolm and Donalbain have stolen away) of the situation of universal distrust which come to a climax in the scene in England in Act IV and the denudation of Macbeth in Act V. After Duncan has been murdered by Macbeth, who can trust anyone? Macbeth is now fully in alliance with the powers of darkness, and fully at the mercy of his own nerves. The very strange tone created for him by the poet in this act partly accounts for one cardinal mystery of this most demonic of tragedies: that he does not lose the audience's or reader's sympathy.

> O! full of scorpions is my mind, dear wife;

he says, and "be thou jocund," and

> Be innocent of the knowledge, dearest chuck,
> Till thou applaud the deed.

This combination of the domestic with the terrible is unbelievably sinister and grotesque. But it is also pathetic, when we hear it in connection with his fierce suffering and hopeless longing:

> Better be with the dead,
> Whom we, to gain our peace, have sent to peace,
> Than on the torture of the mind to lie
> In restless ecstasy.

His strangeness, then, and his suffering, and also the fact that he is not *profiting* from his crimes, help to explain the fact that he does not alienate us.

Notice that the feast of Act I has moved onstage to become the banquet of Act III, so that we now *see* the atrocious linkage made by Macbeth between hospitality and murder. The fact also that it is Banquo murdered, who was declaring, "In the great hand of God I stand," is striking: God seems altogether remote here in the central act—a place of the witches, the tyrant, the murderers, the Ghost.

Act IV is much lower in key than any of the first three acts, as is usual in Shakespearean tragedy. Such tension cannot and ought not to be sustained. First there is the witches' spectacle, hard only on the nerves of Macbeth, an ironic or sycophantic pleasure to its first audience; then the short pathetic scene of the killings at Fife; then the long—very long—scene in England of the tempting of Macduff. Clearly there is nothing high here. But the scenes are not unrelated: the first ruins Macbeth's dynastic hopes, the second completes the ruin of his moral claims, the third looks to the ruin of his security.

The essential subject, then, is still Macbeth. About the long third scene certain points are worth notice. Its length—how *long* it takes for Malcolm to become assured of Macduff's sincerity—is itself a profound instruction in how deeply trust has been corrupted under Macbeth; as Macduff's sturdiness under Malcolm's progressive "revelations" tells us how low hopes have sunk under the tyrant. It is hard, now, for men to believe each other, and they expect little or nothing; the realm is chaos. Against this chaos in the North is set a realm in concord, England, such concord that the King, instead of being himself a thing of evil, is able to cure evil by "touching" (iv. 3. 140 ff.)— as James I had in fact been doing. This manifestation of a *benevolent* supernatural force is set by the dramatist against all the supernatural evil that has preceded it; critics who take the passage as a gratuitous compliment to King James have hardly done it justice. It looks forward, too, to the discrediting of the witches' guarantees (about the wood moving and "no man *born*") which takes place in the final act.

After this long respite—if it is one—from the Scottish horrors, we are returned in Act V *not* to Macbeth directly but to his wife, in the most ghastly scene of all, where truth, after all the deception and pretense, emerges in the delirium of the sleepwalking scene. Except for this deep inward look, and several magnificent speeches, Act V is huddled, exhausted, and external—evil has worn itself out; the great final gestures of Hamlet, Othello, Lear are not possible here, and Macbeth can only die in a warlike parody of himself as the fighting hero we first met in Act I.

Most of us never get to know many other human beings very well—even our closest friends, even our husbands and wives, above all our children, even ourselves. Our experience of them is discontinuous, our attention uneven, our judgment and understanding uncertain. We know people, perhaps, chiefly by their *voices*—their individual, indescribable, unmistakable voices—and the creation of an individual *tone* for each of his major characters is of course one of the clearest signs of a good playwright. In this particular strength Shakespeare is agreed to be peerless. But the playwright has also two immense advantages over life—"clumsy life," as Henry James put it, "about its stupid work." Even when someone *wants* to reveal himself to another person, he is usually not very good at it, and probably most people spend most of their lives in self-concealment; but self-revelation is a large part of the creation of dramatic character. Moreover, in life we seldom enjoy really informed, highly focused comment by others *on* the person who interests us; and this in drama is the rest of the essence—unless we add that *significant* action plays at least as striking a role in the revelation of character in drama as it does in life, while *insignificant*, distracting action is excluded altogether, enforcing a kind of concentration very rare in ordinary experience.

Not much action, after all, occurs in *Macbeth*. There is some fighting, some eating, no doubt some walking up and down. Plays consist of *talk;* and only one person is talking—the author—*through* his characters, *about* them, to the audience. Therefore, there is, as there is not in conversation, one absolutely continuous subject, which is the characters and the action. (It has been convenient to distinguish between the characters and the action or plot, but really this is misleading: the actions of Macbeth are not more meaningful apart from his character than his character would be apart from them.) Everything said, in short, is, ideally, functional—as very few things indeed are in life; so that the connotations of the word "dialogue" are remote from those of the word "conversation." Even when a line of dialogue is so unstylized, or "natural," that it might occur in conversation, it is easy to show that the purpose it serves in its play is quite unlike the purposes of conversation. For instance, Olivia in *Twelfth Night* is the subject of a good deal of dialogue before we see or hear her: we learn that she is young, noble, wealthy, beautiful, and living secluded, in mourning—she is always spoken of, as it were, *upward*, with love, admiration, longing. Then she enters and says brusquely, "Take the Fool away." The purpose of this unexpected remark is to naturalize, so to speak, the large and gracious image one has formed of her—to give it a voice different enough from expectation to show the audience that that image was only the *beginning* of our understanding of her, though not so inconsonant with the image as to contradict it, and to create for her a tone that convinces, makes an illusion of life. (Elizabethan noblewomen no doubt said, from time to time, "Take the Fool away"—meaning nothing but "Take the Fool away.")

We might approach the characters of Lady Macbeth and Macbeth through one of her observations about him in her soliloquy (i. 5. 21–2):

> what thou wouldst highly,
> That wouldst thou holily . . .

Here is a remark unlike any ever made by an actual human being since the beginning of speech—as unlike life as a great work of music is unlike anyone's humming. Its *subject* is life, but the means is high art, *just as* the means—the true means—of "Take the Fool away" was. What is Shakespeare telling us, through Lady Macbeth, about Macbeth and about herself? Macbeth is ambitious, but an idealist. Now Lady Macbeth is ambitious also, as the whole soliloquy sufficiently shows. But the tone of contempt in "holily"—extraordinary word!— tells us that she not only possesses no such double nature herself but complains of it in him. Lady Macbeth's character—about which so much has been written—is very simple. She is unscrupulous, but short-winded. No doubts beset her, except about the steadfastness of her accomplice. Single-natured, she is even willing to lose the nature she has ("unsex me here") in order to accomplish her purpose. But, nihilistic, she has no staying power. Macbeth stays the course. By Act III she has already ceased to matter, weary, plunging toward insanity and suicide. The nature was shallow from the beginning, with its confidence that "A little water clears us of this deed"; only ambition mobilizes it, and only the horror of guilt can deepen it. There are just enough touches of sensibility—her analysis of her husband, and "Had he not resembled / My father as he slept I had done't"—to make her seem lifelike.

Lady Macbeth, in short, has no idea of what she is getting into. Now the reason she is conceived in this way, of course, is that she may throw a contrasting light on her husband, who is double-natured, heroic, uncertainly wicked, both loyal and faithless, meditative and violent, and *does* know what he is getting into. This knowledge of his is the real burden of the great soliloquy in i. 7:

> If it were done when 'tis done, then 'twere well
> It were done quickly;

The first "done" here means "finished," and the lines that follow show that what Macbeth has in mind is far deeper and more savage than any mere not-getting-away-with-the-murder, so to speak. Macbeth believes in "justice," and is afraid of teaching his own assassin (later) what to do; and he believes in eternal life, punishment, and would like to *skip* it ("jump the life to come"). He *believes;* his wife believes in nothing except her own ambition and her own guilt. He is also given to us as "brave," and "deserving" to be so called, and "worthy," and "frank," and he is full of scruples. But he has another nature. He is envious, ambitious, and hypocritical (the reasons he gives his wife, at i. 7. 31 ff., for not proceeding are quite different from the reasons he has just given himself). Therefore, he can be tempted. Shakespeare holds the balance exquisitely even between supernatural *solicitation* to evil (original) and supernatural *encour-*

agement to evil (secondary), as in Macbeth's line to the apparitional dagger:

> Thou marshall'st me the way that I was going . . .

Holding the balance even is really to ask: does it matter? Does it matter, that is, whether man falls in with temptation or just falls? The world is certainly full of temptations, whether created by nature or by the underworld of man's nature.

This duality of Macbeth is what makes the play possible; it also accounts for the ambiguity, the mystery, that characterizes the play throughout. But it only partly accounts for his hold upon the audience's or reader's sympathy. This is primarily a response to the imagination with which his creator has endowed Macbeth. His imagination mediates between his two natures, expressing and accounting for both, and projecting itself also into the future, in a way inaccessible to Lady Macbeth. One minute before she is bleating about "A little water." he has said:

> Will all great Neptune's ocean wash this blood
> Clean from my hand? No, this my hand will rather
> The multitudinous seas incarnadine.
> Making the green one red.

His mysterious brooding has scarcely a parallel elsewhere even in Shakespeare's work. Increasingly, as the play advances, its antithetical subjects are cruelty and his own suffering; hand in hand these move, until the universe seems to consist of nothing else. There is nothing in *Macbeth* so intolerable as the last act of *Othello*, but no other Shakespearean tragedy is so desolate, and this desolation is conveyed to us through the fantastic imagination of its hero.

The course of action adopted by Macbeth, however, changes his nature, as we saw earlier, and the celebrated description of life as meaningless (at v. 5. 19 ff.)—which has been so often and foolishly taken for Shakespeare's own conviction—is that of a man who is sickening to his end, who has ceased to be a man, who has acted himself—so to speak—out of his beliefs.

Duncan's character is fundamental also to Macbeth's fate. His mark is generosity, trust—even to foolishness, as is made plain at once, when he says of Cawdor the traitor:

> He was a gentleman on whom I built
> An absolute trust . . .

Such trust, Shakespeare is suggesting, *invites* treachery; so that, in some degree, Macbeth is merely cooperating. Such foolish trust leads also to the necessity of the depth of morbid *distrust* Duncan's son Malcolm feels obliged to display in Act IV. A certain natural suspicion, we may generalize, is a reasonable attribute in a ruler.

Every reader of *Macbeth* notices the word "blood." From "What bloody man is that?" (i. 2. 1.) to "thou bloodier villain / Than terms can give thee out!" (v. 8. 7.), the noun and its derivatives darken the play. Critics have given statistics for it; all you have to do is count the number of occurrences in Bartlett's *Concordance to Shakespeare's Works*. But more important than statistics are: one particular way in which it is used, and the fact that it is often suggested without being stated. In the witches' dialogue (i. 3. 1–2) we hear:

> Where hast thou been, sister?
> Killing swine.

Though the word does not even occur, the idea or *image* is present even to inundation, a flood of blood, such as spurts from a stuck pig. The same thing is true of Lady Macbeth's ghastly "Yet who would have thought the old man to have had so much blood in him?" (v. 1. 45.), and accounts—along with the coarse insolence of her reference to the King, guest, benefactor, as "old man"—for the power of this celebrated line. We have blood not only everywhere, then, but swarming. Moreover, in a number of other very powerful passages, the audience or reader is compelled to imagine blood for itself even more specifically than in the "swine" passage.

> It will have blood, they say; blood will have blood:

Macbeth mutters to himself (iii. 4. 122). Here the mysterious "It" is explained immediately—murder cries out for retribution—and yet the force of its initial, dreadful vagueness is not dissipated by the explanation. The horrible suggestion is in fact made, by the explanation that anything in the universe not at once identified as something else *is blood;* and iteration of the actual word thrice in one line assists the suggestion. As a man thinks of his wife not by name but as "she" and "her," so Macbeth thinks of *his* topic—blood, the murder—as "it": central, permanent, a point to which other things are referred. The implied picture of his mind makes one shudder. This is psychological. The physical counterpart we hear at v. 2. 16–17, with Angus's

> Now does he feel
> His secret murders sticking on his hands . . .

This can only be blood, as private as the floods of blood just discussed were public, blood ineradicable, intimate (and one thinks of Lady Macbeth's "A little water" and Macbeth's "this my hand will rather / The multitudinous seas incarnadine"); you notice that the verb is practically a pun—what sticks cannot be got rid of.

Now an ordinary play just tells its story, more or less efficiently. Clearly a Shakespearean play is concerned with something different as well: the presentment and enforcing, through imagery as well as through action and character, of a human experience complex and drenched, so to speak, as well as of a view of it similarly complex. Among the most brilliant results of twentieth-century Shakespearean criticism have been the studies of his imagery by Caroline Spurgeon, Msgr. F. C. Kolbe, Wolfgang Clemen, Edward A. Armstrong, and others. These studies have been little hampered by the fact that no satisfactory definition of "imagery" is really possible; thus also have modern astronomers been able to learn a good deal about a universe which they are quite unable to define. We would *like* to take the word to refer to any representation in language of that which makes its appeal primarily to the *senses*. One *feels*, for instance, the word "sticking" as one does not feel, say, the word "as," which is a purely relational term. "Blood" is seen, smelled, felt, can even be tasted, as the word "position," say, cannot. But language, representing or embodying as it does the operations of the human mind, does not lend itself easily to these pigeonholes. Take the word "sleep": is it abstract or sensual? Shakespeare makes it, in *Macbeth*, sensual enough, and we get an elaborate image pattern. Worse still, a clear abstraction, like the word or idea "confusion," can be treated so obsessively and dramatically, as it is in *Macbeth*, that one has an impression that one is experiencing images. For example: "incarnadine" is plainly, or presents plainly, an image, visual, whereas "multitudinous" does not—or does it? The sensing and reflecting aspects of the mind are not so readily distinguished, except at their outer edges.

Just so, the reader responds both emotionally and intellectually to the image patterns. One both suffers and enjoys (understands) the blood image pattern: one recoils emotionally, *and* sees its point—that "blood will have blood," there is nemesis, and this is satisfying, in a world so terrifying and chaotic as the world of Macbeth.

But the blood image pattern is not of course given to us in isolation. There are other patterns, in the absence of which, indeed, the blood pattern itself would have much less than its actual effectiveness and meaning. One critic (Msgr. Kolbe, in *Shakespeare's Way*) connects the blood pattern with the sleep pattern, which not only forms the burden of several overwhelming speeches by Macbeth and of the sleepwalking scene but receives heavy emphasis in speeches by Banquo (ii. 1. 4–10), the witches (i. 3. 19 ff.), and others; and with these two patterns he associates what he calls a dark pattern—one of the most striking things in the play, of which the reader will easily discover examples for himself. These he generalizes very simply as resulting from the nature of the crime: "Duncan's *blood* was shed during his *sleep* in the middle of the *night*." But all this is still preparatory.

Msgr. Kolbe has half a dozen pages of quotation showing that ambiguity, confusion, *resulting* from this threefold nature of the crime, "is even more pervasive . . . than . . . Blood": "Fair is foul . . . broil . . . his country's wrack . . ."

> Shakes so my single state of man, that function
> Is smother'd in surmise, and nothing is
> But what is not . . .

"Unsex me here"—these from Act I alone. He notes, of "Double, double toil and trouble," in Act IV, that "The ingredients of the cauldron form a hell-broth of chaotic incongruities." (The Cambridge editors' brilliant conjecture "and none," for the Folio's "and move" at iv. 2. 22, accepted now by Dover Wilson and Peter Alexander, has really to be studied in this context of Msgr. Kolbe's:

> when we hold rumour
> From what we fear, yet know not what we fear
> But float upon a wild and violent sea
> Each way and none . . .)

These three patterns are then explained by the critic as follows: ". . . in this story of a great Temptation issuing in a great Crime, resulting in a great Retribution, Shakespeare has intensely individualized the sinners and the sin, but has universalized the consequences of the sin." Is a framework discernible for the patterns so far discovered? Msgr. Kolbe finds one in the antithesis throughout between the forces of Sin (witches, demons, spells, damnation, curses, hell, falsehood, doom) and the forces of Grace (angels, mercy, pity, justice, prayer, blessing, providence, truth). Again the reader will want to follow the development of the antithesis for himself in the text. But at least two parallelisms ought to be noted briefly. Behind Macbeth stand the witches, behind Malcolm the "gracious" (the word is from "grace," of course, which then itself occurs, iv. 3. 189.) King of England; and the expression "By the worst means, the worst" near the beginning is exactly balanced by the extraordinary phrase "by the grace of Grace" as almost the last words of the play (v. 8. 72).

Clearly, the study of imagery emerges even more directly and rapidly into *theme* than does the study of plot or of character. The reason for this is that both plot and character tend to be more explicitly formulated in the artist's mind than either theme or imagery. In the case of a play like *Macbeth*, no formulation can ever hope to exhaust either theme or imagery. It will hardly be wrong, however, to suggest that one of the major themes of *Macbeth* is the exploration, in a very gifted and ambiguous and active man, of man's possibilities downward. It is *our* lower nature, as well as our higher, to which we attend in Macbeth; hence our sympathy. One critic (the late Donald Stauffer) once remarked that the King murder obviously symbolizes Macbeth's murder of his own higher faculties. He picks his line, for evil, and is thenceforward committed to it. How briefly evil flourishes, how rapidly it succumbs to exhaustion (leaving out of account altogether, here, the *narrative* element of its overthrow from outside), is one of the dramatist's cardinal points, even in the dark state of mind in which Shakespeare was when he wrote this play. (The evil which in his directly preceding tragedy, *King Lear*, is reserved to definite villains—Edmund, the elder sisters, Cornwall—is here incorporated with his hero and heroine; and his next work was one of almost universal disillusion, *Antony and Cleopatra*.) Macbeth has no emotion left even for the death of his wife (the contrast here is with Macduff's reception of *his* news). Evil dehumanizes and wears itself out.

Needless to say, the image patterns we have glanced at here are not the only ones in the play. Others that have been particularly studied are the clothes pattern, the animal pattern, the disease pattern, the discord-concord pattern. This last pattern is so closely associated with Msgr. Kolbe's confusion pattern that perhaps they ought to be identified. One theme in this pattern is worth special notice: the images of milk. "I fear thy nature," Lady Macbeth says,

> It is too full o' the milk of human kindness
> To catch the nearest way . . .

Two minutes later:

> Come to my woman's breasts,
> And take my milk for gall, you murd'ring ministers . . .

Malcolm, in his pretense to Macduff, says:

> Nay, had I pow'r, I should
> Pour the sweet milk of concord into hell . . .

Here we have a triple association of that which *nourishes* and is bound to the ideas of "kindness" and "concord," with the ideas "fear," "gall," "hell" producing, for the reader, a sense of chaos, of the unnatural, which is fundamental to the play. We begin, as human beings, with milk—we end, in this play, in blood—and the patterns are set against each other in such a way as to suggest that the whole spectrum of human possibilities is being explored with dismay. Images of courtship, procreation, infancy, allied to the milk pattern, intensify the irony, as in Banquo's speech on arriving at Macbeth's castle: "wooingly . . . bed . . . procreant cradle" (i. 6. 6–8.)—the birthing, here, is to be a murder—and Macbeth's

> Pity, like a naked new-born babe,
> Striding the blast,

and Lady Macbeth's terrifying

> I have given suck, and know
> How tender 'tis to love the babe that milks me:
> I would, while it was smiling in my face,
> Have plucked my nipple from his boneless gums,
> And dashed the brains out, had I so sworn
> As you have done to this.

Images—and ideas, as in this solemn undertaking of Macbeth's to do evil—which in nature are wholly separate and opposed, are joined by the dramatist. The interweaving of the consequent patterns is one of the aspects of this tragedy the reader will want to explore for himself.

1960

Shakespeare's Last Word

JUSTICE AND REDEMPTION

THE DRAMATIST'S SCENE FOR *The Tempest* IS AN "VN-inhabited island" somewhere in the Mediterranean, where live the exiled Duke of Milan, Prospero, his daughter Miranda, his slave Caliban, and spirits, servants to him, of whom the chief is called Ariel. This, with the sea about, is his whole realm and he rules it by magic. By chance his enemies from Italy are delivered into the power of his art, punished with a storm and in other ways, and he regains his original kingdom. The play has sometimes been regarded as a comedy of revenge. But one is made to feel that, except in the interest of justice, Prospero does not much desire his original kingdom ("where Euery third thought shall be my graue"); he never even in the past really desired to rule or administer it: he was interested in *study*. It seems fair to regard him as an unwilling ruler in both the first and the last of the story's three periods of his sway; whether he must be thought of as an unwilling ruler also in the second period—that of the twelve years on the island culminating in the afternoon during which the action of the play occurs (from about two o'clock to about six)—is a question I postpone. Revenge, except as the agent of justice, does not quite name what happens. But revenge is an unsatisfactory characterization for a further reason. It is less striking that he punishes his enemies than that he forgives them, and more striking still is the hope that their natures are altered—most of their natures are altered—by their punishments and his forgiveness—punishments, by the way, obviously symbolic: harmless shipwreck in a magic tempest, mental torture in a magic distraction. Yet what we have been saying has at once to be qualified in two ways. First, Prospero does absolutely rule—no other character in drama is so uncompromisingly in charge of all the presented events; and second, he does certainly not impress the spectator or reader as a naturally

72

forgiving man. On the other hand, it is clear that he rules justly, or on behalf of justice; and he is concerned—as once with the education of Caliban—with the spiritual fate of his enemies. Let us take the play, tentatively, as a tragicomedy of justice and redemption, and look into a curious speech of Gonzalo's.

The unwilling visitors to the island are dispersed, you recall, in four places: Ferdinand alone to meet Prospero and Miranda, Stephano and Trinculo to meet Caliban, the sailors (with whom we are not concerned) on the ship still, and last what we may call the Court party—the King, Gonzalo, and the rest. Now Gonzalo's chief topic, considered as one for shipwrecked courtiers, is a little surprising: how society ought to be organized, or disorganized. "Had I plantation of this isle my Lord," he says (that is, colonization)—

> I' th' Commonwealth I would (by contraries)
> Execute all things: For no kinde of Trafficke
> Would I admit: No name of Magistrate:
> Letters should not be knowne: Riches, pouerty,
> And vse of seruice, none: Contract, Succession,
> Borne, bound of Land, Tilth, Vineyard none:
> No vse of Mettall, Corne, or Wine, or Cyle:
> No occupation, all men idle, all:
> And Women too, but innocent and pure:
> No Soueraignty . . .
> All things in common Nature should produce
> Without sweat or endeuour . . .
> . . . Nature should bring forth
> Of it owne kinde, all foyzen, all abundance
> To feed my innocent people . . .
> I would with such perfection gouerne Sir
> T 'Excell the Golden Age.

Now this view is satirized by the others as he develops it, and Gonzalo concedes he spoke mockingly. But this is a respectable, or distinguished rather, sixteenth-century European view of primitive social organization—the dramatist lifted half of it indeed, almost uniquely for him, word for word nearly, from Montaigne's essay on cannibals. Gonzalo, too, is linked with Prospero, not only as the one notably good man among the Court party, but as Prospero's saviour at the time of the usurpation; the Masque of Ceres aims also at the Golden Age when "Spring came to you at the farthest / In the very end of harvest"—that is, a winterless age; and beyond some superficial resemblance between Gonzalo's ironic description and Prospero's actual commonwealth on the island, they present of course radical and imposing differences, by which we may suppose the dramatist to be developing his theme. I take four of these differences.

Clusters of difference they really are, and may form a chain, but the first is absolute. "No Soueraignty," says Gonzalo, and Prospero is an autocrat. The nature of his sway can be suggested by a consideration of some features of his speech. Even among the grand rulers Shakespeare imagined, Prospero commands an utterance of incommensurable solemnity and majesty. When his daughter ventures a question, he answers, robed, erect:

> Know thus far forth,
> By accident most strange, bountifull *Fortune*
> (*Now* my deere Lady) hath mine enemies
> Brought to this shore: And by my prescience
> I finde my *Zenith* doth depend vpon
> A most auspicious starre, whose influence
> If now I court not, but omit, my fortunes
> Will euer after droope . . .

Birth, rule, age, wisdom do not by themselves account for the extremity of this tone; Prospero also is a magician, and sounds it. He speaks himself of his "dignity"; the transition, both in the courtiers and the drunkards, from levity to evil, is in this play an easy one. Then, his ceremonial elaboration is consistent with the most violent or expressive curtness—a curtness of which the next lines of this speech show an overbearing instance:

> Heere cease more questions,
> Thou art inclinde to sleepe, 'tis a good dulnesse,
> And giue it way: I know thou canst not chuse . . .

In the slowing of the final phrase we hear Miranda succumb; we feel the spell as real. The solemnity is executive.

Majesty, activity. Another feature of Prospero's speech worth signalizing is nakedly its power. Consider some lines from his final adjuration to his spirits—

> by whose ayde
> (Weake Masters though ye be) I haue bedymn'd
> The Noone-tide Sun, call'd forth the mutenous windes,
> And twixt the green sea and the azured vault
> Set roaring warre . . .

This hair-raising language is thoughtful, not ornamental. He calls his assistants "weake" but acknowledges them "masters"; whose master he is. He bedimmed (a high-keyed word) the sun at the moment when that feat might be thought most difficult—a fancy borrowed from Ovid, who exaggerates it. Then he called forth (low or neutral key, as for calling dogs) winds that did not want to come (a figure for the reluctant Ariel); however, they come. Then a vast and blazing image: of the ocean and of heaven's arch, and of the space between them—and since a high "azured" is coming, plain "green" is vivid with "sea"; now, into this space, and between these great stages of nature, he "sets"—a detailed, local word, as if he were going to place a salt cellar there—he sets war, and before, or just as you learn "war," it "roars" at you.*

Sovereignty, then, as against Gonzalo's anarchy, and a sovereignty of which the hard characteristics, displayed in the style, are ritual solemnity, activity, all-mastering power. Prospero's sovereignty in the world of the play, the island, is founded upon power, and nothing else. His power is founded, however, and here we reach a second difference from Gonzalo's commonwealth, upon learning. "Letters should not be knowne." Prospero's learning—his magic art, his actual books—these are repeatedly insisted on; he even studies a good deal during the rather short course of the play, and in the end he has undertaken to drown his book. Prospero has also attended carefully, we learn, to the education of Miranda; and he and Miranda have taught Caliban what Caliban could be taught. Prospero, indeed, is a real pedant—this is one of the directions in which a risk was taken with the audience's sympathy for him.

The ruler, in short, works. Everyone works under Prospero's commonwealth, he at ruling, Miranda at her education and Caliban's, Ariel and Caliban at tasks fitting their quality. This marks a third difference between Gonzalo's image of universal idleness and the island fact, and it is unusual in drama. The audience has been working itself all day (or the Elizabethan popular audience was exactly shirking work to attend the afternoon performance) and does not care to see people work on the stage. But much of this work, again, is done onstage, feeble indeed from a theatrical point of view, like the log-bearing. The sole visitor to the island with whom its ruler comes immediately into contact, Ferdinand, is put to work immediately. We must distinguish, of course, between on the one hand the unsuitable work done by Ferdinand, and Ariel's, and on the other hand, that done by Caliban. Ferdinand's is a test of character, imposed to deter-

---

* The word is taken over from the passage in Golding's *Ovid,* where its use is commonplace.

mine the quality of his devotion to Miranda. Ariel's is on contract—
another feature of society excluded by Gonzalo; it is performed
partly out of gratitude to Prospero for having freed him from the
pine, partly out of fear of the oak, and partly in reliance upon Prospero's promise to free him wholly in the end. And here we come first
upon what anyone must feel is one of the play's dominant themes:
the impending freedom of Ariel. The work done by these two is
limited in term and teleological: it has an end, which is understood by
the ruler—not necessarily by the subject (in Ferdinand's case not),
but by the ruler. Caliban's labours are another matter.

A fourth difference between Gonzalo's description and Prospero's state let us describe as an error made by Gonzalo when he
speaks of "my innocent people." Neither do most of the Court party,
nor Stephano and Trinculo, illustrate any such conception of human
nature as underlies this (ironic, to be sure) optimism; but them we
will come to. On the island already exists a creature able to make
mincemeat of Gonzalo's notion, or the later idea, consistent with it,
of the Noble Savage. Caliban, however, who is certainly one of
Shakespeare's most exquisite creations, crucial to this play, is as complicated as his parentage, and I am anxious not to oversimplify his
character, which is at any rate triple. Upon his first appearance he is
called "Thou Earth, thou," to Prospero's threats he answers only, "I
must eat my dinner," and much of his talk presents nature in its
earthiest form:

> I prethee let me bring thee where Crabs grow;
> And I with my long nayles will digge thee pig-nuts;
> Show thee a Jayes nest, and instruct thee how
> To snare the nimble Marazet: Ile bring thee
> To clustring Philbirts, and sometimes Ile get thee
> Young Scamels from the Rocke: Wilt thou goe with me?

Or

> she will become thy bed, I warrent,
> And bring thee forth braue brood.

But it is clear that this is already very poetic, and the contrast between the tone of this last remark and Stephano's response to it
("Monster, I will kill this man") makes it clearer still that faculties
far higher than those of the butler and jester have not been denied to
Caliban. We are not wholly surprised when the poet places this in his
mouth:

> Be not affeared [he says], the isle is full of noyses,
> Sounds, and sweet aires, that giue delight and hurt not:
> Sometimes a thousand twangling Instruments
> Will hum about mine eares; and sometime voices,
> That if I then had wak'd after long sleepe,
> Will make me sleepe again, and then in dreaming
> The clouds methought would open, and show riches
> Ready to drop vpon me, that when I wak'd
> I cride to dreame againe.

The gulf between him and his colleagues yawns again in Stephano's comment upon this:

> This will preue a braue kingdome to me, where I shall
> Haue my Musike for nothing.

But in Caliban's comment upon *this*—"When *Prospero* is destroye'd" —we are reminded of his third nature, or rather of the disposition that governs, for action and in the commonwealth, both his representative (or lower) and higher natures. This disposition (recognized by Caliban himself in "You taught me Language, and my profit on't, / Is, I know how to curse") is unregenerate and malicious, extending to designs of rape and murder, which require frustration, demand punishment, and make inevitable his status of slave. He is not master of himself, and therefore the freedom of Ariel is out of the question for him: he must be permanently mastered. One of his lines editors take as drunken nonsense. Caliban is fooling around with his name: " 'Ban, 'Ban, Cacaliban." Shakespeare is not fooling around, however. "Ban" means *curse*, and the first two syllables of "Cacaliban" are suggestive: they suggest "cacodeman" (or devil)—a word the poet had applied twenty years before to Richard III, who is *also* deformed. Prospero finally, in Act IV, calls him "a devil." We may wonder whether Prospero's nature—in the dramatist's intention—has not been soured partly by his failure with the education of Caliban—"on whom my paines Humanely taken, all, all lost, quite lost . . ."

We are ready, perhaps, for a more detailed formulation. Sovereignty is implied by society. It should be based on power, and power should be based on learning. Work is necessary, and it should be work done on contract, with its end in view by the ruler, except where the subject is unable to enter into a contract because he cannot be depended upon to fulfill it; such cases exist, and are not incompatible with the possession of considerable and even elevated faculties otherwise than in the matter of self-mastery. Contract is strongest when triply based: on gratitude backward, present fear, and confident hope forward. Mutiny against a just ruler (such as Ariel's in prospect, Caliban's in practice) is the ultimate social crime and gives rise to or accompanies all other evil. Thus, there is no "freedom" upon this island at all. Even Miranda studies and educates Caliban and solaces Prospero. The ruler's work consists in: education (including unremitting self-education), the administration of justice (including punishment), and redemption. Before passing on to this third work of the ruler, of which we have said almost nothing, I want to notice one broad controlling design of justice dramatized.

A singular feature of the structure of *The Tempest* is that the catastrophe occurs in the opening scene, which delivers Prospero's enemies into his power. We do not at the time know this. We see only a storm at sea, rulers on board, a wreck. We learn it during the second scene, suspectingly and slow, then suddenly in the speech that I used to illustrate Prospero's solemnity. But meanwhile we have heard about another "sea-sorrow" twelve years before, of which the near-victims were Prospero and his daughter. Thus, the instant of full recognition of *what* has happened contains a full recognition of *why* it happened. Those tortured by the sea at first were innocent; those who caused that torture are guilty and are now tortured by the sea; justice exists. Deep in the play Ariel makes the vise-like pattern explicit:

> you three . . .
> Exposed vnto the Sea (which hath requit it)
> Him, and his innocent childe: for which foule deed,
> The Powres, delaying (not forgetting) haue
> Incens'd the Seas, and Shores, yea, all the Creatures
> Against your peace . . .

It is owing to this unexampled priority of the catastrophic action, as a German critic has pointed out, that imagery in *The Tempest* has not its normal Shakespearean function of foreshadowing but is used rather to recall, to remind of what has happened (and so, as well, of what it meant). I adduce two morose, disdainful instances of the way in which the persistent sea imagery is linked with the guilty men and with the conception of the ocean as an agent of retribution. When Anthonio is working the inert Sebastian toward the murder of his brother, Sebastian admits:

> I am standing water.
> ANTHONIO. Ile teach you how to flow.
> SEBASTIAN. Do so; to ebbe
> Hereditary Sloth instructs me.

Here the water image is forced into a full sea image by "ebbe." The other, the most elaborate image perhaps in this play very scant in imagery, is declaimed by Prospero about the guilty men in Act V when he releases them from their distraction:

> Their understanding
> Begins to swell, and the approaching tide
> Will shortly fill the reasonable shore
> That now lyes foule, and muddy . . .

Here only the two abstract terms keep the subject in sight, all the rest being contemptuous metaphor; this is mercy with a *vengeance*.

Alonso is punished throughout in his grief for his son, and at last by Ariel's instruction is brought to despair:

> The thunder
> (That deepe and dreadfull Organ-Pipe) pronounc'd
> The name of *Prosper:* it did base my Trespasse—

that terrifying pun—and so thence to repentance. His enmity to Prospero was general, his crime against Milan general. With Prospero's brother an intenser course is necessary. Before he is punished, he is made (by temptation—the others' magic sleep) to re-enact his crime by persuading the dull Sebastian to the murder of *his* brother; and this persuasion has almost the tone of Iago—it is hardly comedic. Even the brutal fool Sebastian, when at last he sees Anthonio's drift, is moved to ask, "But for your conscience":

> ANTHONIO.   Ay Sir: where lies that? If twere a kybe
>   Twould put me to my slipper: But I feele not
>   This Deity in my bosome: Twentie consciences
>   That stand twist me, and *Millaine,* candied be they,
>   And melt ere they mollest. Here lies your Brother,
>   No better than the earth he lies vpon.
>   If he *were* that which now hee's *like* (that's dead)
>   Whom I with this obedient steele (three inches of it)
>   Can lay to bed for euer: whiles you doing thus,
>   To the perpetuall winke for aye might put
>   *This* ancient Morsell: this Sir Prudence, who
>   Should act vpbraid but course: for all the rest
>   They'll take suggestion, as Cat laps milke,
>   They'll tell the clocke to any businesse that
>   We say befits the houre.

This enforced, hell-like recapitulation—it is the plotters who are lapping the poisoned milk set out—is *justice* with a vengeance. Are we drifting back to "revenge"? An element of vindictiveness disconcernible in Prospero ought not to make us lose our heads and see him as a vindictive rather than as a just man. Besides the twelve years of barbaric exile, take the nature of the crimes: intended murder and, far worse to an Elizabethan or Jacobean, usurpation and intended usurpation. The usurpation, moreover, had been, was to be, by worse rulers against better—self-deprecation is not one of Prospero's foibles —and his native state, Milan, thus became basely tributary. But I think we are bound to confess a sense that Prospero finally forgives his enemies rather from justice (the sense that they have suffered enough, and repent, and deserve his restored esteem) than from mercy. There exist touches of mercy; but even these are apt to be accompanied by *rational* resentment and rational, rather than emotional, redemptive operation:

> Thogh with their high wrongs I am strook to th' quick
> Yet, with my nobler reason, gainst my furie
> Doe I take part: The rarer Action is
> In *vertue*, then in vengeance . . .

And what reconciliation can be heard in this?—

> For you, most wicked sir, whom to call brother
> Would even infect my mouth, I do forgive
> Thy rankest fault . . .

—to which Shakespeare wisely gives Anthonio no reply. The general view taken of human nature here? Not high, not high. To see in the last plays, as recent critics do, a sort of ministry of reconciliation seems to me to sentimentalize them and falsify our experience of their reality. Everybody does by no means kiss and make up—not even in *The Winter's Tale*, which (as villainless) I should call the most charitable of them.

Now virtue for a ruler consists in the production of virtue in himself and his subjects—or, where it exists already, the encouragement, refinement, and maintenance of it, as in Prospero himself, in Miranda, in Ferdinand, in Gonzalo. But where it does not exist, it must be produced in whatever degree is practicable, according to the nature of the subject; and this brings us to the fates of Alonso, Anthonio, Sebastian, of Stephano and Trinculo, of Caliban.

Take the first group. Without insisting upon my term "redemption," I think we need not hesitate over the fact, which is that Alonso, Anthonio, and Sebastian are redeemed—reclaimed, ransomed, delivered, from their guilt, and by Prospero, in a sequence of deliberate operations. This makes the situation essentially different from the one in *As You Like It*, where, also, a duke is exiled by his brother to a sort of utopia, his daughter is with him, the usurper comes and is converted—there is even, also, a *second* wicked brother who comes and reforms. The imagination of this author used the same materials again and again, all down its mature working life; but it used them differently. The illuminating and nailing difference, between the conventional comedic reformations in the Forest of Arden and those on the enchanted island, is the thematic hammer in *The Tempest* of the word "free," the central word in the play. This is Shakespeare's word. It first appears as "Libertie," in Ariel's demand—which, with Prospero's promise, alluded to throughout and at last performed, is our metaphorical and dramatic instruction in the play's prime theme. But the constant words are "freedom," "free." Alonso, Anthonio (maybe), and Sebastian, are set *free* from their old selves, from their guilt. Even Caliban, whose nature forestalls freedom, is freed, at any rate, from his illusions about Stephano and Trinculo, and undertakes in his final speech (one of Shakespeare's oddest and most attractive notes) to "be wise hereafter, / And seek for grace." How is it that Stephano and Trinculo have or can have no part in this general redemption?

Possibly it is because they are drunk. Amusingly as here their antics are handled, drunkenness is not much a comic topic in Shakespeare's mature plays—in *Hamlet, Othello, Measure for Measure*. The drunkenness of Stephano and Trinculo images their self-slavery and the moral stupidity that allows them to fall in with the suggestions of Caliban's malice. Their crime, too, like that of the men from the top of society, intends not murder only but usurpation—Stephano is to be King in Prospero's place. Irrational, self-set outside reason, they stand beyond the reach of the ruler's redemptive design. *They* think they are "free," of course, as Caliban imagines he is with his new master. "Freedome," he cries, "high-day, high-day freedome, freedome high-day, freedome." The catch sung by Stephano and Trinculo, adapting a proverb already employed in *Twelfth Night*, certainly embodies one of the dramatist's most daring and schematic ironies: "Flout 'em and cout 'em: and Skowt 'em and flout 'em, / Thought is free."

The theme rules without irony the final line of the play, when Ariel hears at last:

> To the Elements
> Be free, and fare thou well . . .

and in the final line, the final word, of the epilogue, Prospero asks the
audience to set *him* "free." Probably we are right to wonder whether
Prospero *is* not himself in some way freed in the play or by its
action. Prospero we have evidently to see in at least two characters;
as the exile, injured and vindictive, and as the great Magician and
Judge—God onstage—who rights the wrongs sustained by the exile
(himself) and also redeems the exile's enemies, so far as their natures
permit. Then clearly Prospero is set free, in both the rules: free from
vindictiveness (strongly conveyed, the sense of this, in the fifth act)
and from the sense of injustice, and free from his overwhelming
power. Perhaps those men only who have exercised formidable
power can feel fully what it means to wish to be free of it; but
everyone understands both fatigue and the desire to be free of the
responsibilities of power. But to be free of unruly and discreditable
desire is the heart of the play's desire, and even in this does Prospero
participate, released from the intoxications of hatred and might.

The scene, wonderful in production, where Ferdinand and
Miranda are discovered "playing at Chesse," brings them, too, within
the conclusion of this theme. Here is a game, as against the work they
formerly did. No ordinary game: an exercise ancient, orderly, and
intellectual. We remember Prospero's harsh adjuration to them *not*,
before marriage, to

> Giue dalliance
> Too much the raigne; the strongest oaths, are
> To th' fire ith' blood . . .

and we *see* them holding in check their desires, and perhaps we
remember Hamlet's crying

> Giue me that man
> That is not passions slaue, and I will weare him
> In my harts core, I in my hart of harts . . .

Nobody, I suppose, who had not himself *been* passion's slave could
have made the longing envy in these lines so central in his most
personal play and their sense so necessary in the design of his final
play.

THE FREEDOM OF THE POET

The Tempest was produced at Court on 1 November 1611. (It may help us through an account unavoidably a bit intricate if you will bear in mind that we are interested henceforth in this year 1611.) This was either its original production or an early one: it makes use of two West Indies shipwreck pamphlets of 1610 besides a letter of the same year, and Trinculo's "dead Indian" is no doubt one of the five American savages—only four of whom then returned—brought to London in 1611 itself by the Earl of Southampton and another. William Shakespeare was forty-seven years old. Apparently he had planned to retire two years before and changed his mind; we infer this from a memorandum of September 1609 by a cousin living in the poet's main house at Stratford, New Place, saying he "perceived I might stay another year at New Place." Also in 1609 were published: the last play that appeared during his lifetime, *Troilus and Cressida*, and his *Sonnets*, which for contemporaries ranked as his "works." I have an idea, considering his whole publishing history and these present circumstances, that he may have been responsible for the issuance both of the first, which judges so diverse as Goethe and Keats have thought his profoundest, most characteristic work, and the second. It looks as if at forty-five he meant to retire but stayed on for two years, writing *Cymbeline*, *The Winter's Tale* (seen by a playgoer on 15 May 1611), and then *The Tempest*. He was wealthy. He had perhaps stopped acting some years before, though he may still have been producing. His company, the King's Men, could rely on younger dramatists, and many of his own plays remained so popular that they were competing with each other. He was tired, conceivably, after two decades (at least) of activity hardly by anyone ever paralleled. His memory may have been failing: so we infer from a lawsuit of 1612, when his testimony about a financial agreement was crucial and he said he could not remember, though it was the dowry of a marriage in which he had been the go-between himself; it's interesting that the good Gonzalo is a "lord of weak remembrance." All this comes to a constellation of motives powerful indeed, apart from what drew him to Stratford—business affairs, a granddaughter now three, his younger daughter, Judith, still seriously unmarried *at twenty-six*, and the orchard that had filled his plays with orchards for five years after he acquired it. Now for an entire year and a half *after* this production of *The Tempest* nothing connects him with his theatrical company; he never again wrote a whole play; and it's likely that only the double strain of 1613 for the company (he was still a principal shareholder, of course)—first of Francis Beaumont's withdrawal, then the demands made on them in connection with Princess Elizabeth's wedding to the Elector Palatine—summoned him back to their assistance, collaborating in three plays with John Fletcher. Everything obliges us to suppose that, at the latest, directly after making *The Tempest,* he entered upon the retirement for several years actively contemplated. And few critics have decided not to hear in the play what Victor Hugo calls "the solemn tone of a testament."

But before pursuing this, let me examine a little the impression it gives of its author.

Solemn and testamental it may be—and it shows that what he was most rereading or remembering was Ovid and the *Aeneid* and *The Faerie Queene*—but it goes in for a good gay final flick at George Chapman, with whom Shakespeare seems to have had a long difference or feud. "Temperance," says Anthonio, "was a delicate wench." In Chapman's comedy *May Day,* of a year or so before, his character Temperance is a foul-mouthed bawd. Most of the other objects of the courtiers' satire have not survived or not been recognized, but *The Tempest,* like Shakespeare's other work, is much and immediately indebted to its theatrical environment. There is a deep influence from the court masque, especially Daniel's *Tethys Festival* of 1610. It picks up phrases from the last act of Fletcher's recent *Faithful Shepherdess.* The Wild Man Bremo in the old play *Mucedorus,* revived by Shakespeare's company in February 1610, is the frantic original of Caliban, and it would not surprise me to learn that Caliban was born when the poet heard the character called Envy in *Mucedorus* speak some lines probably new at this production:

> From my foule Studie will I hoyst a Wretch,
> A leane and hungry Meager Canniball,
> Whose lawes swell to his eyes with chawing Malice:
> And him Ile make a poet.

Memories of a lifetime spent in the theatre were swarming also: Gonzalo's speech out of Montaigne, by *Isaiah,* is indebted as well to primitive-society speeches not only in *Mucedorus* but in the twenty-year-old *Selimus.* Nor is the style Olympian, outside Prospero. I would illustrate it—admitting its variety, and ignoring *character*—with the line about "turfy mountains, where live nibbling sheep." The beauty of this I account for thus: one thought the gorgeous "turfy" was finished, just a piece of diction, and then the related, even more actively visual and physical "nibbling" brings "turfy" back to life and incidentally completes the presentation of a pastoral

world in one line, thick with excellent life. Nor is the form Olympian, but concise as this style, and methodical. *The Tempest,* unlike most of Shakespeare's dramatic work, especially unlike the romances sprawling through time and space that he had just been writing, is a work expressly obedient to the Elizabethan understanding of the classical unities; and it is hard to agree with Dr. Johnson that the regularity of its plan is "an accidental effect of the story, not intended nor regarded by our author." Prospero looks at his watch too often. It was a demonstration.

Was Shakespeare specially proud of this work? It stands first in the collection of thirty-six of his plays that appeared a few years after his death; that's editorial. But Shakespeare's younger friend Ben Jonson was already by 1613 editing his own plays for a collected volume. Shakespeare lived three years longer, dying in the year Jonson's folio appeared. When his long-time associates Heminge and Condell prefaced the Shakespeare folio they had put together, they "confessed" the "Wish" "that the Author himselfe had liu'd to haue set forth, and overseene his owne writings; But . . . it hath beene ordain'd otherwise, and he by death departed from that right . . ." The priority of *The Tempest* may be as well due to him as to them. Now authors like their last works best, notoriously. But I want to make two points. This was one of the least didactic major poets who ever lived. *The Tempest* is the extreme exception in the canon, only *Measure for Measure* approaching it, and our whole earlier discussion may be held to support the view that Shakespeare might have held it dear as an embodiment, at a high level enough of compression and expressive art, of his maturest feelings about human organization and duty. That that is not why *we* value it is immaterial. My other point is also biographical.

The duke of *Measure for Measure,* who, so much in tone, insistence on chastity, and arbitrary management, resembles Prospero, pretends to relinquish his power, and devotes much intrigue to getting married a protégée of his named Mariana. This was in 1604, midway through Shakespeare's tragic period: for all we know, he was dreaming already of retiring, and his elder daughter, Susanna, ought already to have been married at twenty-one. A year or so later, King Lear, who resembles in eccentricity and hauteur both that duke and Prospero, though he surpasses them in irascibility, does relinquish his power, having married off satisfactorily two of his daughters; both of Shakespeare's legitimate daughters were now marriageable. By Prospero's year, only one had still to marry, like Miranda, and besides I must point out a curious fact: Prospero does not wholly retire. He only retires from his *art*. When looking well ahead toward retirement, it may seem to a man that it can be complete; when a man in Shakespeare's situation gets to that point, he sees that it cannot. Investments have to be protected and extended, family matters arranged, and so on; he even returned to dramatic writing. But back to Miranda. Her father produces for her a stainless prince, sees them betrothed, and watches them hawklike with distrust (at the same time one has an impression of him leaning forward waiting for progeny—even Caliban, in both his lustful passages about her, envisages progeny).

Now unless Shakespeare's daughters were freaks, and if they were, they were good matches; yet they married, Susanna at twenty-four, Judith at thirty-one—grave ages for this period. Their father must have been choosy, very, and, while being choosy, anxious. With reason: backward, remembering that their mother at twenty-six had married him at eighteen and borne Susanna in six months (not to speak of his own later infidelities); and forward, as things turned out. He had got a physician, Dr. John Hall, as husband for Susanna, but for Judith he had to wait until two months before his death, when she married a vintner so rapidly that they were excommunicated. But his sufferings over Susanna must have been keener still, for a young gentleman asserted in 1613 that this "witty" woman (as she is described) "had bin naught with Rafe Smith" and her successful action for slander—he did not appear—tells us rather that her father was influential than that her accuser was a liar. The intense anxiety of Prospero upon this topic of unchastity is one of the clearest features of his creator. Dis's rape of Proserpina—the classic plot on a virgin—must have been familiar to William Shakespeare all his life; suddenly in *The Winter's Tale* and again in *The Tempest* it inspired passages, energetic and of ravishing beauty, the beauty of pain.

It is remarkable—in a work rich with the happiness of the exercise of supreme art—how often, and with what longing, *sleep* is invoked. "Tis a good dulnesse, and giue it way." "Do not omit the heavy offer of it," one says to Alonso drowsy. Caliban's visionary cadenza on sleep and dream you remember. This longing—for release, for freedom—it is which resolves, I think, a genuine difficulty that I cannot truly remember any critic to have noticed: the coarse discrepancy, to appearance, between Prospero's reassurance, "be cheerefull Sir," to Ferdinand, and his celebrated, magnificent, apparently disillusioned and frightening forecast of universal dissolution that follows.

But there is no discrepancy, and it is neither disillusioned nor frightening, this forecast—though not Christian either. It is radiant and desirous.

be cheerefull Sir,
Our Reuels now are ended: These our actors
(As I foretold you) were all Spirits, and
Are melted into Ayre, into thin Ayre,
And like the baselesse fabricke of this vision
The clowd-capt Towres, the gorgeous Pallaces,
The solemne Temples, the great Globe it selfe,
Yea, all which it inherit, shall dissolue,
And like this insubstantiall Pageant faded
Leaue not a racke behind: we are such stuffe
As dreames are made on; and our little life
Is rounded with a sleepe . . .

? 1962

II

The Development of Anne Frank

WHEN THE FIRST INSTALLMENT OF THE TRANSLATED TEXT
of *The Diary of Anne Frank* appeared in the spring of 1952, in *Commentary*, I read it with amazement. The next day, when I went into
town to see my analyst, I stopped in the magazine's offices—I often did,
to argue with Clem Greenberg, who was a sort of senior adviser to
what was at that time the best general magazine in the country in spite
of, maybe because of, its special Jewish concerns—to see if proofs of
the *Diary*'s continuation were available, and they were. Like millions
of people later, I was bowled over with pity and horror and admiration for the astounding doomed little girl. But what I *thought* was: a
sane person. A sane person, in the twentieth century. It was as long
ago as 1889 when Tolstoy wound up his terrible story "The Devil"
with this sentence:

> And, indeed, if Evgeni Irtenev was mentally deranged, then all people are mentally deranged, but undoubtedly those are most surely mentally deranged who see in others symptoms of insanity which they fail
> to see in themselves.

Some years later (1955), setting up a course called "Humanities in
the Modern World" at the University of Minnesota, I assigned the
Diary and reread it with feelings even more powerful than before but
now highly structured. I decided that it was the most remarkable
account of *normal* human adolescent maturation I had ever read, and
that it was universally valued for reasons comparatively insignificant.
I waited for someone to agree with me. An article by Bettelheim was
announced in *Politics*, appeared, and was irrelevant. The astute
Alfred Kazin and his wife, the novelist Ann Birstein, edited Anne
Frank's short fiction—ah! I thought—and missed the boat.

Here we have a book only fifteen years old, the sole considerable
surviving production of a young girl who died after writing it. While

decisively rejecting the proposal—which acts as a blight in some areas of modern criticism—that a critic should address himself only to masterworks, still I would agree that some preliminary justification seems desirable.

It is true that the book is world-famous. I am not much impressed by this fact, which I take to be due in large part to circumstances that have nothing to do with art. The author has been made into a spokesman against one of the grand crimes of our age, and for her race, and for all its victims, and for the victims (especially children) of all the tyrannies of this horrifying century,—and we could extend this list of circumstances irrelevant to the *critical* question. Some proportion of the book's fame, moreover, is even more irrelevant, as arising from the widespread success of a play adapted from it, and a film. That the book *is* by a young girl—an attractive one, as photographs show—must count heavily in its sentimental popularity. And, finally, the work has decided literary merit; it is vivid, witty, candid, astute, dramatic, pathetic, terrible,—one falls in love with the girl, one finds her formidable, and she breaks one's heart. All right. It is a work infinitely superior to a similar production that has been compared to it, *The Diary of "Helena Morley,"* beautifully translated by Elizabeth Bishop in 1957. Here is a favourable specimen of the Brazilian narrative:

> When I get married I wonder if I'll love my husband as much as mama loves my father? God willing. Mama lives only for him and thinks of nothing else. When he's at home the two spend the whole day in endless conversation. When papa's in Boa Vista during the week, mama gets up singing wistful love songs and we can see she misses him, and she passes the time going over his clothes, collecting the eggs, and fattening the chickens for dinner on Saturday and Sunday. We eat best on those days.

Clearly the temperature here is nothing very unusual, and no serious reader of Anne Frank, with her extraordinary range and tension, will entertain any comparison between the two writers. But I am obliged to wonder whether Anne Frank has *had* any serious readers, for I find no indication in anything written about her that anyone has taken her with real seriousness. A moment ago we passed, after all, the critical question. *One finds her formidable:* why, and how, ought to engage us. And first it is necessary to discover what she is writing about. Perhaps, to be sure, she is not truly writing about anything—you know, "thoughts of a young girl," "Jews in hiding from the Nazis," "a poignant love affair"; but such is not my opinion.

Suppose one became interested in the phenomenon called religious conversion. There are books one can read. There is one by Sante de Sanctis entitled *Religious Conversion*, there are narratives admirably collected in William James's lectures, *The Varieties of Religious Experience*, there is an acute account of the most momentous Christian conversion, Paul's, by Maurice Goguel in the second volume (*The Birth of Christianity*) of his great history of Christian origins. If one wants, however, to experience the phenomenon, so far as one can do so at second hand,—a phenomenon as gradual and intensely reluctant as it is also drastic,—there is so far as I know one book and one only to be read, written by an African fifteen hundred years ago. Now in Augustine's *Confessions* we are reckoning with just one of a vast number of works by an architect of Western history, and it may appear grotesque to compare to even that one, tumultuous and gigantic, the isolated recent production of a girl who can give us nothing else. A comparison of the *authors* would be grotesque. But I am thinking of the originality and ambition and indispensability of the two books *in the heart of their substances,*—leaving out of account therefore Book X of the *Confessions*, which happens to award man his deepest account of his own memory. I would call the subject of Anne Frank's *Diary* even more mysterious and fundamental than St Augustine's, and describe it as: the conversion of a child into a person.

At once it may be exclaimed that we have thousands of books on this subject. I agree: autobiographies, diaries, biographies, novels. They seem to me—those that in various literatures I have come on—to bear the same sort of relation to the *Diary* that the works *on* religious conversion bear to the first seven books of the *Confessions*. Anne Frank has made the process itself available.

Why—I asked myself with astonishment when I first encountered the *Diary*, or the extracts that *Commentary* published—has this process not been described before? universal as it is, and universally interesting? And answers came. It is *not* universal, for most people do not grow up, in any degree that will correspond to Anne Frank's growing up; and it is *not* universally interesting, for nobody cares to recall his own, or can. It took, I believe, a special pressure forcing the child-adult conversion, and exceptional self-awareness and exceptional candour and exceptional powers of expression, to bring that strange or normal change into view. This, if I am right, is what she has done, and what we are to study.

The process of her development, then, is our subject. But it is not possible to examine this without some prior sense of two unusual sets of conditions in which it took place: its physical and psychological context, first, and second, the qualities that she took into it. Both, I hope to show, were *necessary* conditions.

For the context: it was both strange, sinister, even an "extreme situation" in Bettelheim's sense,* and pseudo-ordinary; and it is hard to say which aspect of the environment was more crippling and crushing. We take a quicksilver-active girl thirteen years old, pretty, popular, voluble, brilliant, and hide her, as it were, in prison; in a concealed annex upstairs at the rear of the business premises her father had commanded; in darkness, behind blackout curtains; in slowness—any movement might be heard—such that after a time when she peeks out to see cyclists going by they seem to be flying; in closeness—not only were she and her parents and sister hopelessly on top of each other, but so were another family with them, and another stranger—savagely bickering, in whispers, of course; in fear—of Nazis, of air raids, of betrayal by any of the Dutch who knew (this, it seems, is what finally happened, but the marvellous goodness of the responsible Dutch is one of the themes of the *Diary*), of thieves (who came),—the building, even, was once sold out from under them, and the new owner simply missed the entrance to their hiding place. All this calls for heroism, and it's clear that the personalities of the others except Mr Frank withered and deteriorated under conditions barely tolerable. It took Anne Frank herself more than a year to make the sort of "adjustment" (detestable word) that would let her free for the development that is to be our subject.

But I said, "as it were, in prison." To prison one can become accustomed; it is *different*, and one has no responsibilities. Here there was a simulacrum of ordinary life: she studied, her family were about her, she was near—very near—the real world. The distortion and anxiety are best recorded in the dreadful letter of 1 April 1943. Her father was still (sort of) running the company and had briefed his Dutch assistant for an important conference; the assistant fell ill and there wasn't time to explain "fully" to his replacement; the responsible executive, in hiding, "was trembling with anxiety as to how the talks would go." Someone suggested that if he lay with his face on

* Bruno Bettelheim's well-known article, "Behavior in Extreme Situations," in *Politics*. I am unable to make anything of his recent article in *Harper's*, weirdly titled "The Lesson of Anne Frank," which charges that the Franks should not have gone into hiding as a family but should have dispersed for greater safety; I really do not know what to say to this, except that a man at his desk in Chicago, many years later, ought not to make such decisions perhaps; he also complains that they were not armed. Some social scientist will next inform the Buddha of *his* mistake—in leaving court at all, in austerity, in Illumination, and in teaching.

the floor he might hear. So he did, at 10:30 a.m., with the other daughter, Margot, until 2:30, when half-paralyzed he gave up. The daughters took over, understanding scarcely a word. I have seldom, even in modern literature, read a more painful scene. It takes Anne Frank, a concise writer, thirteen sentences to describe.

Let's distinguish, without resorting to the psychologists, temperament from character. The former would be the disposition with which one arrives in the world, the latter what has happened to that disposition in terms of environment, challenge, failure and success, by the time of maturity,—a period individually fixed between, somewhere between, fifteen and seventy-five, say. Dictionaries will not help us; try Webster's Dictionary of Synonyms if you doubt it. Americans like dictionaries, and they are also hopeless environmentalists (although they do not let it trouble their science, as Communists do). I ought therefore perhaps to make it plain that children do differ. The small son of one of my friends would cheerfully have flung himself off the observation tower of the Empire State Building. The small son of another friend was taking a walk, hand in hand, with his father, when they came to an uneven piece of sidewalk and his father heard him say to himself, "Now, Peter, take it easy, Peter, that's all right, Peter," and they went down the other end of the slightly tilted block. My own son, a friend of both, is in between, Dionysiac with the first, Apollonian with Peter. I think we ought to form some opinion of the *temperament* of Anne Frank before entering on her ordeal and thereafter trying to construct a picture of her character.

The materials are abundant, the *Diary* lies open. She was vivacious but intensely serious, devoted but playful. It may later on be a question for us as to whether this conjunction "but" is the right conjunction, in her thought. She was imaginative but practical, passionate but ironic and cold-eyed. Most of the qualities that I am naming need no illustration for a reader of the *Diary:* perhaps "cold-eyed" may have an exemplar: "Pim, who was sitting on a chair in a beam of sunlight that shone through the window, kept being pushed from one side to the other. In addition, I think his rheumatism was bothering him, because he sat rather hunched up with a miserable look on his face . . . He looked exactly like some shriveled-up old man from an old people's home." So much for an image of the man— her adored father—whom she loves best in the world. She was self-absorbed but un-self-pitying, charitable but sarcastic, industrious but dreamy, brave but sensitive. Garrulous but secretive; skeptical but eloquent. This last "but" may engage us, too. My little word "industrious," like a refugee from a recommendation for a graduate student, finds its best instance in the letter, daunting to an American student, of 27 April 1944, where in various languages she is studying in one day matters that—if they ever came up for an American student—would take him months.

The reason this matters is that the process we are to follow displays itself in a more complicated fashion than one might have expected: in the will, in emotion, in the intellect, in libido. It is surprising what it takes to make an adult human being.

For one reason in particular, which I postpone for the present, I am willing to be extremely schematic about the development we are to follow. I see it as occupying six stages, surprisingly distinct from each other, and cumulative.

1. *Letter of 10 August 1943:* "New idea. I talk more to myself than to the others at mealtimes, which is to be recommended for two reasons. Firstly, because everyone is happy if I don't chatter the whole time, and secondly, I needn't get annoyed about other people's opinions. I don't think my opinions are stupid and the others do; so it is better to keep them to myself. I do just the same if I have to eat something that I simply can't stand. I put my plate in front of me, pretend that it is something delicious, look at it as little as possible, and before I know where I am, it is gone. When I get up in the morning, also a very unpleasant process, I jump out of bed thinking to myself: 'You'll be back in a second,' go to the window, take down the blackout, sniff at the crack of the window until I feel a bit of fresh air, and I'm awake. The bed is turned down as quickly as possible and then the temptation is removed. Do you know what Mummy calls this sort of thing? 'The Art of Living'—that's an odd expression."

I make no apology for quoting this remarkable passage, as it seems to me, and the crucial later ones, at length, because here there are so many points to be noticed, and because later the excessive length itself of an outburst may prove one of its most significant features. Of course the passages are interesting in themselves, but it is their bearing, in analysis, on our investigation that counts; though I take the reader probably to be acquainted with the *Diary*, a detailed knowledge of it can hardly be expected.

We notice first, then, that this "idea," as she calls it, really is "new"—there has been nothing like it in the diary hitherto—one has an impression, considering it, that she has up till now (over a year) merely been holding her own under the ordeal, assembling or reassembling her forces; and also that it addresses itself strongly to the future. Moreover, it is by no means simply an idea: it is a *program*, and a complicated one, and as different as possible from people's New Year's resolutions ("I will," "I will not," etc.). She describes, and explains, what she *is doing*. Her tone is sober and realistic, the reverse of impulsive.

Now for the burden of the program. It takes place in the Practical Will, and aims at accounting for the two *worst* problems with which her incarceration (let's call it that) confronts her. It has nothing incidental about it. These problems are meals and rising. Meals, because the exacerbated interplay of these huddled persons then is more abusive and dazing even than at other times, and because the fare is so monotonous and tasteless. Rising, because she is rising to what? the same fear, darkness, slowness, privation, exasperation as on all other days; the tendency of profoundly discouraged men to take to their beds and stay there is familiar, and got dramatic illustration—even to many deaths—in the dreadful record of our fighting men as captives in Korea. The steps taken by her against these problems are exactly opposite but verge on each other. She uses first a refraining (that is, a negative) and then her imagination (that is, a positive). I must comment on both procedures. This girl's imaginativeness—the ability to alter reality, to create a new reality—was one of her greatest mental strengths: it is here put twice, solidly, at the service of her psychological survival and tranquillity. The food, and getting up, change under her hand, in a process which *inverts* what we call daydreaming. As for the refraining, one subsidiary point seems to me so important that I want to reserve it for separate consideration, but I hope that the reader will not undervalue the main point: her decision to keep silent. Examples of garrulous persons undertaking silence are certainly not unknown, but they are spectacularly rare, as programmatic and experimental. The one comparable case that I recall is described not in the journal of a young girl but in the journal of a Nobel Prize winner, one of the greatest modern men of letters. W. B. Yeats recorded, late in life, that he once decided, attending his club, to be silent for once; and observed—to his improvement in humility—that every argument he was tempted to use was sooner or later mentioned and developed by someone else. Yeats's *motive* was different from and lighter than Anne Frank's, but that we have to go so far upstairs—or is it upstairs?—for an analogy may help to retard our tendency to underestimate this girl's character as it here begins to form and unfold.

Third, the program is *submitted to her mother*. Whether my

word "submitted" is quite right will be questionable. I use it tentatively, looking to an evaluation of the decidedly strange tone of her comment on her mother's comment. Her mother, clearly impressed by her daughter's account of the new administration—as who would not be?—applies an adult label; one, by the way, far from stupid. Anne Frank responds with the automatic doubt of a child about adult labels, say: children are concrete, non-categorical, and no child was ever more so perhaps than this girl. But I cannot feel that we have accounted for the sentences—in terms either of what has been taking place in the diary or in terms of what is to come. I hear *scorn* in her characterization of the mother's formula—"that's an odd expression" (I do *not* hear respect, and the expression is not neutral); and I confess to surprise that she told her mother about the program at all, much less submitted it to her,—she has not been in the habit of doing anything of the sort. I take it that the referral, the telling, contained an element of competitiveness, even aggression—as if to murmur, "You are not mastering your own ordeal in this way"; and that this element emerges even more plainly in the final, almost contemptuous comment. Independence comes hard-won and is not friendly. I hardly think, however, that we can form an opinion about these suggestions except in relation to the second and third stages of the development.

The subsidiary point is this: the refraining is described as embarked on *first* in the interest of *others*—and this will interest us later.

2. Three and a half months later, 27 November: "Yesterday evening, before I fell asleep, who should suddenly appear before my eyes but Lies!

"I saw her in front of me, clothed in rags, her face thin and worn. Her eyes were very big and she looked so sadly and reproachfully at me that I could read in her eyes: 'Oh, Anne, why have you deserted me? Help, oh, help me, rescue me from this hell!'

"And I cannot help her, I can only look on, how others suffer and die, and can only pray to God to send her back to us.

"*I just saw Lies, no one else* [my italics], and now I understand. I misjudged her and was too young to understand her difficulties. She was attached to a new girl friend, and to her it seemed as though I wanted to take her away. What the poor girl must have felt like, I know; I know the feeling so well myself!

"Sometimes, in a flash, I saw something of her life, but a moment later I was selfishly absorbed again in my own pleasures and problems. It was horrid of me to treat her as I did, and now she looked at me, oh so helplessly, with her pale face and imploring eyes. If only I could help her!"

There is as much again as this, in the same strain, but this will have to do.

If we had *only* this letter on this topic, I don't think we should be able to interpret it, but even so, certain observations might be made. We are dealing here with a *vision,* and a vision heavily charged with affect; nothing earlier in the *Diary* resembles it, and this very cool-headed girl seems overwhelmed. It seems, in short, to demand interpretation, as a dream would. Second, the *reason* given for the remorse (in the fourth paragraph) strikes one, I think, as inadequate; one suspects that an operation of the unconscious has thrown up a screen, if Lies is the real subject. But I have to be doubtful, third, that Lies is the real subject, in the light of the phrases that I have taken the liberty of italicizing. Why should the girl so stress the identity of an individual seen in a vision? I once as a young man experienced an hallucination of a senior writer whom I wildly admired, the poet Yeats whom I mentioned earlier, and it would never have occurred to me, in describing it, to say "I just saw Yeats, no one else." We seem bound to suppose that the emotion—passionate remorse—is real, but that both its cause (to which it is excessive, and violently so) and its object are not real—are, as we say, *transferred.*

These doubts are confirmed by a very similar letter of a month later, 29 December: "I was very unhappy again last evening. Granny and Lies came into my mind. Granny, oh, darling Granny, how little we understood of what she suffered, or how sweet she was," and so on and so on, and then back to an agony over Lies.

Now the actual circumstances—the girl friend's fate being doubtful, and the grandmother having died of cancer—were tragic. The question is whether they account for the strangeness and extremity of these outbursts, *at this point,* of love-and-remorse; and I feel certain that they cannot. Clearly, I would say the real subject is the mother—for whom the friend and the grandmother, also loved and felt as wronged, make eminently suitable screens. But how has Anne Frank wronged her mother? This emerges, *at once,* in the next letter. What I think has happened, in this second stage of the development, is that the girl is *paying beforehand,* with a torrent of affection and remorse, for the rebellion against her mother that then comes into the open.

3. 2 January 1944: "This morning when I had nothing to do I turned over some of the pages of my diary and several times I came

across letters dealing with the subject 'Mummy' in such a hotheaded way that I was quite shocked, and asked myself: 'Anne, is it really you who mentioned hate? Oh, Anne, how could you!' . . .

"I used to be furious with Mummy, and still am sometimes. It's true that she doesn't understand me, but *I don't understand her either.*" "I can't really love Mummy in a dependent childlike way—I just don't have that feeling." Again I have italicized the crucial horizontal mature expression.

Three days later comes the remarkable letter that winds up, to my sense, this first phase of her development, concerned with her mother. The important passages are three. "One thing, which perhaps may seem rather fatuous, I have never forgiven her. It was on a day that I had to go to the dentist. Mummy and Margot were going to come with me, and agreed that I should take my bicycle. When we had finished at the dentist, and were outside again, Margot and Mummy told me that they were going into the town *to look at something or buy something—I don't remember exactly what.* I wanted to go, too, but was not allowed to, as I had my bicycle with me. Tears of rage sprang into my eyes, and Mummy and Margot began laughing at me. Then I became so furious that I stuck my tongue out at them in the street just as an old woman happened to pass by, who looked very shocked! I rode home on my bicycle, and I know I cried for a long time." It is clear that the *meaning* of this experience is not known to the girl, and cannot become known to us, since we do not have her associations; but its *being reported,* and here, is extremely interesting. I notice that censorship has interfered with memory, in the passage I have italicized, just as it interferes with the recollections of dreams, and of course if we were in a position to interpret the account, this is where we would start. But there is no need to interpret. The traumatic incident has served its purpose, for her and for our understanding of her development, *in being recollected:* this is the sort of experience that in persons who become mentally ill is blocked, whereas the fullness here both of the recollection (with very slight blockage) and of the affect testifies to her freedom.

The next passage concerns her periods, of which she has had three, and its unexpressed tenor certainly is that of rivalry, maturity, independence of the mother, while the letter concludes with the one solid passage of physical narcissism in the whole *Diary.*

It is time to say, before we pass into the second phase of her development, that more than a year earlier (7 November 1942) Anne

Frank had defined for herself with extraordinary clarity this part of her task. "I only look at her as a mother, and she just doesn't succeed in being that to me; I have to be my own mother . . . I am always making resolutions not to notice Mummy's bad example. I want to see only the good side of her and to seek in myself what I cannot find in her. But it doesn't work . . . Sometimes I believe that God wants to try me, both now and later on; I must become good through my own efforts, without examples and without good advice. Then later on I shall be all the stronger. Who besides me will ever read these letters? From whom but myself shall I get comfort?" Self-command and strength, virtue and independence: we have seen the struggle for them working itself out through the practical will, the imagination, an agonized vision, a trauma recovered, the physical self. The mother will remain a focus for comparison, and almost that only; not a model.

4. The second phase begins on the night of the day of the traumatic and narcissistic letter, and we hear of it in the letter of the day following—as if to say: Now that that problem's dealt with, let's get on with the next. She has sought out Peter Van Daan, exceptionally for her (he has hardly figured in the *Diary* at all to this point), in the evening in his room, and helped him with crossword puzzles. 6 January: "It gave me a queer feeling each time I looked into his deep blue eyes . . . Whatever you do, don't think I'm in love with Peter—not a bit of it! . . . I woke at about five to seven this morning and knew at once, quite positively, what I had dreamed. I sat on a chair and opposite me sat Peter . . . [these dots are in the original, or at any rate in the English translation] Wessel. We were looking together at a book of drawings by Mary Bos. The dream was so vivid that I can still partly remember the drawings. But that was not all—the dream went. Suddenly Peter's eyes met mine and I looked into those fine, velvet brown [*sic*] eyes for a long time. Then Peter said very softly, 'If I had only known, I would have come to you long before!' I turned around brusquely because the emotion was too much for me. And after that I felt a soft, and oh, such a cool kind cheek against mine and it felt so good, so good. . . ."

The rest of this letter, and the next, give the history of her secret calf-love for Peter Wessel,—of whom we have heard nothing for a year and a half, since the second entry in the *Diary*. The girl does not realize that the dream is not about him, of course. Now, again, we cannot interpret the dream with any assurance, lacking associations; but as Freud observed, some dreams are so lightly armored that they can be read at sight by a person of experience and some familiarity with the situation of the dreamer, and I think this is such a dream. I would not say that the real subject is Peter Van Daan, as perhaps a hasty impression would suggest. Two passages in the letter of the very next day confirm one's feeling that, as in the case of Lies and her grandmother, we are dealing with *two* screen figures and that the real subject is, naturally, her father: "I am completely upset by the dream. When Daddy kissed me this morning, I could have cried out: 'Oh, if only you were Peter!' " But he *was;* notice that it is otherwise hard or even impossible to account for her being "completely upset" by this very agreeable dream, and for the absence of transition from the first sentence to the second,—her unconscious needed no transition, because the subject had not changed. Needless to say, in view of the well-known slang use of the word "peter," the dream has a phallic as well as a paternal level; as one would expect from the narcissism of the preceding day. The other passage is this: "Once, when we spoke about sex, Daddy told me that I couldn't possibly understand the longing yet; I always knew that I did understand it and now I understand it fully." One of the most interesting and unusual features of this girl's mind—using the term "mind" very broadly—is its astonishing vertical mobility, unconscious and conscious and half-conscious. Three letters later (22 January) she recognizes herself the formative importance of her dream: "It seems as if I've grown up a lot since my dream the other night. I'm much more of an 'independent being.' " The unsuitability of her father as object, like the unsuitability of her mother as model, later, in fact, becomes explicit.

5. This stage, comprising her intense and miserable attempt to create a post-paternal love object out of the unworthy (but solely available) Peter Van Daan, scarcely needs illustration. It fails because she cannot respect him (16 February: "I told him that he certainly had a very strong inferiority complex. He talked about the Jews. He would have found it much easier if he'd been a Christian and if he could be one after the war. I asked if he wanted to be baptized, but that wasn't the case either. Who was to know whether he was a Jew when the war was over? he said. This gave me rather a pang; it seems such a pity that there's always just a tinge of dishonesty about him"); and the girl's independence and moral nature are now such that she cannot love where she does not respect. By the end of this month, February, he is already becoming unreal and shadowy: "Peter Wessel and Peter Van Daan have grown into one Peter, who is beloved and good, and for whom I long desperately." This is hardly a conception

to be heard without amazement from anyone in love with another actual human being. But he has *served his purpose*, and it is just two months after the dream, 7 March, that she is able to summarize, with uncanny self-knowledge, the process with which—from our own very different point of view—we have been concerned.

6. "The first half of 1943: my fits of crying, the loneliness, how I slowly began to see all my faults and shortcomings, which are so great and which seemed much greater then. During the day I deliberately talked about anything and everything that was farthest from my thoughts, *tried to draw Pim to me* [my italics]; but couldn't. Alone I had to face the difficult task of changing myself . . . I wanted to change in accordance with my own desires. But *one* thing that struck me even more was when I realized that even Daddy would never become my confidant over everything. I didn't want to trust anyone but myself any more.

"At the beginning of the New Year: the second great change, my dream. . . . [her dots] And with it I discovered my longing, not for a girl friend, but for a boy friend. I also discovered my inward happiness and my defensive armor of superficiality and gaiety. In due time I quieted down and discovered my boundless desire for all that is beautiful and good."

There is much more of interest in this long letter, but with a final self-comparison, later this month, to her mother, I think the process that we have been considering may be said to be completed—though what I mean by "completed" will have to have attention later. 17 March: "Although I'm only fourteen, I know quite well what I want, I know who is right and who is wrong, I have my opinions, my own ideas and principles, and although it may sound pretty mad from an adolescent, I feel more of a person than a child, I feel quite independent of anyone.

"I know that I can discuss things and argue better than Mummy, I know I'm not so prejudiced, I don't exaggerate so much, I am more precise and adroit and because of this—you may laugh—I feel superior to her over a great many things. If I love anyone, above all I must have admiration for them, admiration and respect."

In these passages, and particularly with the crushing phrase "more precise and adroit," we are not dealing any longer, surely, with a girl at all but with a woman, and one almost perfectly remarkable. In the sense that *Daniel Deronda* is more "mature" than *Adam Bede*, the process of maturation never ceases in interesting persons so long as they remain interesting. But in the sense—with which, you remember, we began—of the passage from childhood to adulthood, Anne Frank must appear to us here more mature than perhaps most persons ever become.

Our story, of course, can have no happy ending, and so it would be especially agreeable at this point to draw attention to the brilliant *uses* she made of this maturity during the four months of writing life left to her—the comic genius of the dramatization of "the views of the five grownups on the present situation" (14 March 1944), where a description that seemed merely amusing and acute is brought to the level of Molièrean comedy by a piercing conclusion: "I, I, I . . . !"; the powerful account of her despair and ambition dated 4 April; the magnificent page that closes the very long letter of a week later, where in assessing God's responsibility for the doom of the Jews she reaches the most exalted point of the *Diary* and sounds like both spokesman and prophet. I want, indeed, presently to make some use of this last letter. But it is no part of my purpose in the present essay to praise or enjoy Anne Frank. We have been tracing a psychological and moral development to which, if I am right, no close parallel can be found. It took place under very special circumstances, which—let us now conclude, as she concluded—though superficially unfavourable, in fact highly favourable to it; she was *forced* to mature, in order to survive; the hardest challenge, let's say, that a person can face without defeat is the best for him. And anyway in the end we are all defeated; Hemingway once put it that the only point is to make the enemy pay as heavily as possible for *your* position; this she certainly did. And even on the way, life consists largely, if you aim high enough, of defeat; Churchill spent most of his years out of power. Then we said something of the qualities that went into the development: her temperament. I think that we ought to form an opinion, before leaving her, of the moral character with which she emerged,— where, that is, she aimed.

It would be easy to draw up a list of the qualities she valued, but it may be more helpful to begin with an odd little remark she once, between the passages quoted above under Stage 6, made about her sister. I notice with interest, by the way, that Margot figures hardly at all in the development, and I wonder whether, on this important evidence, the psychologists have not overestimated the role played by sibling rivalry after very early childhood. "Margot is very sweet and would like me to trust her," Anne Frank writes, "but still I can't tell her everything. She's a darling, she's good and pretty, but she lacks the nonchalance for conducting deep discussions . . ." The criticism is given as decisive, and I think it may puzzle the reader until we recall that Socrates' interlocutors were frequently baffled to decide whether he was in earnest or not. She objects, let's say, to an *absence of play of mind*. But I think still further light is thrown on the expression by the formidable self-account that ends the long letter (11 April) I spoke of earlier: "I am becoming still more independent of my parents, young as I am, I face life with more courage than Mummy; my feeling for justice is immovable, and truer than hers. I know what I want, I have a goal, an opinion, I have a religion and love. Let me be myself and then I am satisfied. I know that I'm a woman, a woman with inward strength and plenty of courage.

"If God lets me live, I shall attain more than Mummy ever has done, I shall not remain insignificant, I shall work in the world and for mankind!

"And now I know that first and foremost I shall require courage and cheerfulness!"

Much of what we need to know of her character is to be found here, and deserves comment, but perhaps it may occasion surprise that among these high ideals should be mentioned as climactic "cheerfulness." I am not sure that its placement should occasion surprise, taken with the remark about her sister. We might seek an analogy, one singular enough, too, in the thought of Whitehead. The philosopher once cast about (the passage can be seen conveniently in Morton White's little anthology *The Age of Anxiety*) in an attempt to decide what few concepts were *indispensable* to the notion of life—not merely our life—any life; and he chose four, and he put "self-enjoyment" first. Now he was writing as a metaphysician, while she writes of course as a moralist. But the congruity seems to me remarkable, and for that matter his other three concepts—self-creation, aim (a negative notion, the rejection of all except what is decided on), creative advance—rank very high also, clearly, in her thought. It will be understood that I am not, with these exalted comparisons, claiming philosophical rank for Anne Frank; I am trying to explain what an extremely thoughtful and serious person she made herself into, and how little conventional.

For the rest, the strongly altruistic character of her immense individual ambition, as well as the scorn for anyone of lesser aim, should perhaps be signalized. And I would say finally that the author of the searching expression "my feeling for justice is immovable" has taken full account of all that which makes human justice so intolerably unattainable that Pascal finally rejected it altogether (Fragment 298) in favour of might.

We began, then, with a certain kind of freedom, which is destroyed; we passed through a long enslavement, to the creation of a new kind of freedom. Then this is destroyed, too, or rather—not so much destroyed—as turned against itself. "Let me be myself and then I am satisfied." But this, of course, was precisely what the world would not do, and in the final letter of the *Diary*, and at the end of its final sentence, we see the self-struggle failing: ". . . finally I twist my heart round again, so that the bad is on the outside and the good is on the inside and keep on trying to find a way of *becoming* what I would so like to be, and what I could be, if . . . there weren't any other people living in the world." The italics of the lacerating verb are mine, but the desperate recognition that one must advance ("self-creation," in Whitehead's term) and that there are circumstances in which one cannot, and the accusing dots, are hers. She remained able to weep with pity, in Auschwitz, for naked gypsy girls driven past to the crematory, and she died in Belsen.

1967

Conrad's Journey

I RAISED A DOZEN YEARS AGO, IN THE PREFACE TO A CRITICAL biography of Stephen Crane (1950), the question of why psychoanalytic criticism should have little or nothing to tell us about certain writers, and suggested that I knew nothing about this difficult problem. No one, as far as I am aware, has taken up the matter,—or the related problem of why certain works of a given writer resist psychoanalytic investigation, while others invite or even plead for it. About this second problem it may be possible to say something at the end of the essay. I mention the first only because Joseph Conrad, on the face of it, looks like an author of whom psychoanalytic criticism would have nothing to say. It is true that a Cambridge critic has observed that "Few novelists, in fact, offer such fine material for the psycho-analytical delver: childhood in Poland under the rule of the Czars, a mother who died in exile and a father who was released dying, abandonment of his own country at seventeen, gun-running in the Caribbean, a love affair with the ex-mistress of the pretender to the Spanish throne and a duel for her at eighteen, a British Master Mariner's ticket and the legal adoption of a new nationality at twenty-nine, followed by a career as a writer in which he returns again and again with loving care to the incidents of his past life, looking at them from different angles under more or less thin disguises."* But all this ridiculous sentence tells us, of course, is that its writer knows nothing whatever of psychoanalysis, which is concerned—one would have expected the news to reach even Cambridge, my old university, by now—with the operation of the unconscious.

It is precisely the heavy *explicit* autobiographical bearing of most of Conrad's fiction that makes him appear an unpromising subject for depth-psychological study. But in *Heart of Darkness* we do seem to come on a story inviting such inquiry. Despite its great fame—able critics have not scrupled to call it, on occasion, the

* Douglas Hewitt, *Conrad: A Reassessment*, 1952.

greatest story in the English language—it has always made a curious effect on critic and ordinary reader alike. It seems, for all its dramatic power, curiously *muffled,* both in structure (for which one writer resorts to the word "evasive") and language. It is as if the story were being reluctantly told. The horror of its main narrative theme will in part account for this, but only, I think, in part. There are, too, an extreme inconclusiveness and a refusal-to-vouch-for which are decidedly unlike Conrad in general. One may feel some question also as to whether the political and the demonic aspects of what Marlow, the narrator, learns ever really join forces. It is a weirdly divided story. Is it about Kurtz or is it about Marlow? There is no agreement on the subject; and if we retreat to the position that it is about *both* (as of course in some sense it is bound to be "about" both), the question of its unity hangs fire. In Kurtz we attend to a tragedy of disillusion—or degradation—but is it not after all too horrible for the term "tragedy"? The word seems more appropriate somehow for what happens to Marlow, his tragedy of withdrawal. His tragedy is difficult to describe—everything in the story (or novella, as it properly is) is difficult to describe—but we feel it vividly enough; the impression one gets is of a man floating on his back in the sea, without effort, future, or interest, after some ultimate failure. And yet he has only— for the most part—*seen* what happened. The case of Kurtz is very different: we see the *results* of his evil passion, but not quite it—except on the path, where Marlow blocks him, in a scene which is rather burked by Conrad and can hardly claim to be one of the most convincing things in the story. In the light, or murk, of all these difficulties, we may well decide to look underground a little.

Two warnings, though. I have no slightest intention of trying to "explain" the story; I only hope to tell some truth about it. And the truth is likely to be rather unpleasant. As Freud somewhere says, the wishes of the unconscious seem to well up out of a veritable hell, where incest and murder and other matters are everyday occurrences. It is never possible in such cases, when writing for the general public, to give all one's evidence, and even with regard to the points selected to be made, there will have to be omissions. In any event, it is far from my wish to exhaust the story psychoanalytically.*

Suppose, seizing the bull by all three horns, we look first at a single strange passage.

"For a moment I stood appalled, as though by a warning. Finally I descended the hill, obliquely, towards the trees I had seen.

* There is now a psychoanalytic biography of Conrad by Dr Bernard C. Meyer. I have not seen this. [Note added by author in 1970.]

"I avoided a vast artificial hole somebody had been digging on the slope, the purpose of which I found it impossible to divine. It wasn't a quarry or a sandpit, anyhow. It was just a hole. It might have been connected with the philanthropic desire of giving the criminals something to do. I don't know. Then I nearly fell into a very narrow ravine, almost no more than a scar in the hillside. I discovered that a lot of imported drainage-pipes for the settlement had been tumbled in there. There wasn't one that was not broken. It was a wanton smash-up. At last I got under the trees."

I do not know how this strikes the reader. To me it reads as dreamlike, and I think that if it were handed by one of his patients to a competent analyst he would without hesitation declare it to be substantially a sexual fantasy, governed by guilt and fear. The emotions are partly open (appalled, warning), partly hidden (obliquely, criminals, nearly fell, wanton, *avoided*—and the broken pipes, which are more complex, I postpone a bit). The sexual materials, of course, are all hidden. "I stood" (erection) and "descended the hill" (approach to intercourse) are introductory and comprehensive. Then we have three stages. First the amazing passage about the mysterious "hole"—with which "criminals" may have "something to do"; the writer shies off from this subject, adopting a jocular (that is, disguised) tone and then insisting that he knows nothing about it. The "very narrow ravine" is the second female symbol, and "scar" the third. I scarcely dare mention what I think is probably at work in respect to the pipes. A pipe will be a male symbol—in fact is—especially a pipe put into a "very narrow ravine" or "almost . . . scar" in a passage like this one; not that I remember ever to have encountered another passage like this one in professional literature. But these pipes are broken, *all* broken, lying in the ravine. Here we are probably dealing, in fantasy, with the legend, familiar and widespread in folklore, called "vagina dentata." One version goes as follows: there are brothers, and the eldest marries a beautiful but wicked woman who is genitally equipped with teeth and bites off his phallus; so with the next and the next, until the youngest, marrying her in turn, cagey, inserts an iron bar, stripping out her teeth, rescuing all his brothers' organs—and they all live happily ever after. The legend's content is the male fear of entrusting to mysterious territory a part so valued; and it seems to figure urgently in *Heart of Darkness*—it is *ivory* that Kurtz strips and sends out from the Dark Continent.

It is hard for the critic to guess what an unprejudiced reader will find plausible in what he has said so far. The unconscious is not plausible, though it is unbelievably ingenious at getting represented what it wishes to represent, whether in words or in action, and it is perfectly unscrupulous.

Let me try to put in summary form—aiming rather at the report of an opinion than at persuasion—what I feel the story to be "about," from our present technical point of view. It will disfigure the page, but aid understanding, if I go in for italics.

There is a *penetration* of the Dark Continent (the mother's body; it is also called Hell—here one thinks of Boccaccio's story—and contains ivory and devils, particularly a chief devil, the father-figure Kurtz) by Marlow (the son, the author's unconscious). This is made possible by an older female relative (the first of several mother-surrogates). He follows in Kurtz's footsteps, that is, finds him wickedly in possession, cutting off heads (castration symbol), and *in bed*. His feelings about Kurtz are complex to put it gently. He is fascinated by him, he worships him, he would even like to *be* him. "I will never hear that chap speak after all, and my sorrow had a startling extravagance of emotion . . . I couldn't have felt more of lonely desolation somehow, had I been robbed of a belief or had missed my destiny in life." He is also filled by Kurtz with disgust and horror, as well as contempt (it is impossible not to hear a sexual insult in the play made with the name, as meaning Short). He even wrestles with him; notably on the path, when Kurtz is on his way to a woman, at night. This rescue, and the overall rescue operation with the steamboat, are to be understood with the same ambivalence as his feelings; rescues are well known in analytic symbolism to stand for *punishments*, the fantasied punishment here being for (1) priority with the mother, (2) engaging in those nasty (sexual) activities at all—a child's sense of his parents' hypocrisy when he learns that *they*, too, "do that" is familiar and plays a large part in the dramatization of the grand hypocrisy of Kurtz. The son-figure is intensely aggressive, in short, and the father-figure is vilified and destroyed—though with the tortured feelings of the lament just quoted. How far the son succeeds in his mother-mission it is not easy to form an opinion about. Sexuality has been by the author almost completely censored out of Marlow. But I think I would say that in the symbolism he is successful—he *makes the journey;* for which he then punishes himself by *withdrawal* (sexual and spiritual), several times figured in the representation of him as an idol, and specifically a Buddha.

This marvellous work, then, embodies at its deep level both a struggle against and a submission to an imperfectly mastered Oedipus complex, like *Hamlet* and some other interesting productions of the human spirit. It is pleasant to record that Joseph Conrad, so far as I can discover, was never in any degree aware of this fact—if it is a fact.

You expect, in these cases, a wealth of contributing subordinate material, and it is not lacking here. Its proper disposal and considera- tion would occupy fifty pages; so I will give it one or two para- graphs, again not to secure assent but for clarity,—though, as Conrad himself once wrote, "The inner truth is hidden—luckily, luckily."

Of the mother-surrogates in the story, we've mentioned only the aunt (for the sexual permission, dramatized) and the native mistress (for depravity); assimilated to the latter, I think, is also the Intended (for exculpatory ignorance of the father-figure's real nature); the major surrogate is the great river itself, the Continent. The one son- surrogate I have identified, unless the Russian is one, is the helmsman, Marlow's only true intimate in the story (they are identified by the symbolic shoes), whose death it turns out that Kurtz has caused, ordering the attack. The father-surrogates are the manager and the bricklayer, who both praise him, who have candles (these phallic symbols, which abound—staves, rivets, and so on—are of interest chiefly as testifying to the phallic anxiety of the son-figure, his fear of being bested or even, as we saw, there injured). I hope the multipli- cation of these will not seem superfluous—in the unconscious work- ing, I mean. Many absorbing details might be noticed, but one will have to do. When the brickmaker shows Marlow's woman, painted, we may think of Mr Bloom, in the penultimate chapter of *Ulysses*, showing Stephen his wife's photograph; a hidden invitation is implied in both cases.

Perhaps enough has been said of the directly sexual symbolism, except that there are indications here and there of the journey's having for the son-figure two further significations so far unmen- tioned: a travel back in time to the womb (which is frequently bound up with Oedipal strivings, and which we ought in this case probably to connect with Marlow's evident death will) and a re-creation of a Primal Scene. The evidence for the latter is too elusive for confi- dence, but my impression is that it would prove on analysis to be what is called a "concocted" scene, not a real one.

Some readers, it is borne in on me, may very well imagine liter- ary critics as sitting industriously about in a passionate search for hidden meanings—psychoanalytic, religious, whatever. Without at all wishing to deny the possibility that Critic A or even Critic B may at some time have done this, the idea is so distasteful to my sense of reality that I would like to spend two words doubting it. In my own very limited experience with psychoanalytic criticism—I have come on detailed findings in this direction in only five authors, I think—no such search was ever instituted. Naturally one reads an author who interests one as carefully as one can, with a mind as wide as possible; but most authors in most of their works really neither need nor repay this sort of study. It is only when one finds oneself *obliged* by one's overwhelming impressions to set to this work that one does it. I emphasize the verb because this work is hard, and unwieldy, and cannot be judged except by other experts, as a rule, and is generally unwelcome. In short, it is done reluctantly. Why then is it done at all, and in particular why have I written this essay?

I was about to say that I hardly know. But before attempting after all to answer the question, I would distinguish between studying something and writing about it. A friend who was going to be away briefly from the university where we both then were once asked me to give two or three lectures on Campion's lyrics for him; I was pleased, fond of him and fond of Campion, whose work I thought I understood pretty well after years of intermittent attention. After a few hours' work for the first lecture, I was unable to ignore the fact that for the first time I understood Campion's "deep" subject. It had nothing to do with the lectures, and I have never written it out. (The present essay came into being in much the same way: an invitation, surprised never-used notes, and four or five years later a writing out.) But here we must distinguish again between writing out and printing. One does not necessarily print what one writes out, but still there is a tendency to do so; and what I had found out in my opinion at any rate about Campion was not creditable to him personally, and as I say, I was fond of him and did not write it out lest I print it. (His subject, I had better observe at this point, is almost wholly different from Conrad's in *Heart of Darkness*.)

We can now make some replies to the question about the reason for the existence of the present essay. One works out of a desire to *know*—or perhaps boredom or habit—but I think the first cause is paramount. Just to know for oneself. Then, as to writing out and printing, I feel myself that we should trade all accessible information on important works of art. (Campion did not quite make it; Conrad did.) Then, the creative process is so obscurely apprehended that it would seem to be our duty to contribute to that apprehension if we can; and as a corollary to this we should help the psychologists if we can.

But in the present case I had yet another motive. I *think*—this is an impression only—that *most* of Conrad's works will yield little or nothing to this sort of examination. I wondered: Why this one? and why this one *when* it was created? Well—

There is no satisfying full-scale biography at this writing, and so I am relying on Gerard Jean-Aubry's *The Sea-Dreamer*, 1957. I will be as candid as usual. I had never looked until recently at a biography of Conrad, although I had had to read letters and memoirs of his. Well: I *hoped* that the biography would inform me, in electric-blue letters (visible only to me), of Conrad's father's death just before the composition of the story. It is true that astonishing events in art and science sometimes follow directly on the paternal deaths for the producers: the final recension of *Hamlet*, the basic labour for the work that began modern psychology, *The Interpretation of Dreams*,—to drop a notch: Housman's main body of poems (1895–6). So I hoped. And I *feared* that I would find nothing. And the hope and the fear were stupid.

I found something. I got the impression from Jean-Aubry and other available accounts that the depth-inspiration we have been looking into came perhaps rather from the presumable time of conception of the tale than from the period of its composition. Conrad was an orphan; now years already deep into his first real story, about Almayer; there had just been a visit to childhood scenes, the first in twenty-three years, reactivating feelings about his parents? as well as his childish ambition to go to Africa; there was an adorable aunt, just met, in Belgium, and her husband died two days later. The journey— and he calls it so in the story—was a nightmare, his only freshwater exploit, when he had to sail as *Second* Officer under Captain Koch, in the *Roi des Belges*. We know little or nothing of Kurtz's origins, unless he may have been based on a dying agent named Klein, or been a damnified syncopation of Klein and Koch. (Conrad's biographer speaks of a resemblance between Klein and Kurtz as "confirmed" by the author's use of the Klein name four times in the manuscript, now at Yale. I cannot have this. We know nothing of the dying agent except that he was an agent and he was dying and in the Interior and named Klein; where Kurtz came from, *so far*, remains a mystery. Conrad *hated* Koch.) The captain's frustration, disappointment, rage— and then a protracted serious illness both in Africa and back in Europe—may just possibly have helped in the familial reactivation. He had got his official command, according to Jean-Aubry (170), solely through Captain Koch's illness. And this is all that we can say about it.

This hesitant study has had nothing to propose for our understanding of the correlation of literary and psychological values. It was intended as a contribution, crude but sincere, to a science (or art) unborn.

1962

The Mind of Isaac Babel

THE DAZZLING STORY, "IN ODESSA," ONE OF SEVERAL BY
this Russian author collectively entitled *Benya Krik the Gangster,* is
likely to bewilder a reader at least as much as it pleases or amazes him.
In some ways it sounds very offhand. Benya's extortion note is not even
given in full, for instance; the author just says "and so on," as if one
received that sort of letter every day. On the other hand, the story's
style is extremely elaborate, and its two principal events—the holdup
and the funeral—seem to bear a formal relation to each other: the complication involved in the holdup is resolved by the funeral or funerals.
But the story's stylized and formal character may itself seem incongruous with its bloodthirsty material. To tell the truth, it has somewhat the air of a horse opera: an exchange of fantastic letters, a crazy
holdup, sudden killings, a powerlessness of the police, a funeral like
something out of Chicago in the 1920's. Its theatrical quality is even
insisted on by the author—"So began an opera in three acts!" he has
the old man say of the holdup. Moreover, what sort of instruction is
this for a rabbi, a learned man, to be giving a spectacled schoolboy?
Why is a gangster held up to admiration? This story gives rise to all
sorts of questions.

The part of Benya Krik's career described in "In Odessa" might,
for example, have formed the subject of a simple anecdote, but told in
that way (how he got started as a gangster, his first job, and its
consequences), it would have borne little relation to the story we
have; it would have raised no questions. It is no exaggeration to say
that the slick writer wishes to make the reader forget himself and the
serious writer wishes to make him *think.* Of a popular story we never
dream of asking *what it is about,* whereas this is what deeply concerns us with respect to serious imaginative writing. The popular
story or narrative is just about itself; the question never comes up.
Part of the strangeness of Babel's story must be a way of guarantee-
ing—by the author—that this question *will* come up.

The material of the story might be thought of like this. We have Benya Krik, twenty-five, reaching at the stars, but the son of a teamster (the locale is a traditional society where a son follows his father's trade) and in addition a Jew, in Czarist Russia. Part of his life story is recited by an old man (Reb Arye Leyb) sitting on the wall of the Second Jewish Cemetery, to a disciple, a schoolboy, "I," who has asked him why, of three magnificent gangsters, Benya is supreme. The old man answers the boy's question. Benya, tortured by longing, went into business; he offered his services, as a crook, to Froim Grach. It is to be noted that he was not so rash, despite his energy and ambition, as to try to set up in business for himself. Evidently crime was highly organized. Grach, who runs a lawless outfit or gang under the patronage of an "elder" of the Jewish community, holds a conference and decides to take Benya on—to fix Tartakovsky. Madly rich, Jewish too, but wicked, Tartakovsky now is given a character sketch corresponding to the one we had of Benya. His insolence is beyond anything, he employs half Odessa in his stores, and he has been held up nine times.

Benya writes him an extortion note. Tartakovsky replies paternally, reproachfully. The letter goes astray, and Tartakovsky's place (apparently his main store) is held up by Benya with four masked assistants. While the loot is being packed, another gangster turns up late and drunk—one Savka Butzis—and for no reason shoots a clerk named Muginstein. As the gangsters run off, Benya threatens Butzis with the same fate.

Benya goes to the hospital to see (and threaten) the head doctor, ordering all special care for the clerk at his expense, but Muginstein dies. Then Benya goes, "in broad daylight," riding in a red automobile, with a music box playing from *Pagliacci*, to visit Muginstein's mother, Aunt Pesya. Finding Tartakovsky there, he argues him into promising her five thousand down and fifty rubles a month instead of the "miserable hundred bucks" Tartakovsky had sent her. He himself then apologizes to Aunt Pesya, who is lying on the floor, saying to her, "If you need my life, you can have it, but everybody makes mistakes, even God," and he tells her about the money settlement, and promises her son an absolutely exceptional funeral. (Nearly all peoples of the earth, except Americans, place great importance upon funerals; our general squeamishness about death doesn't let us.) This overwhelming funeral takes place. "Odessa never saw such a funeral, and the world will never see another like it. That day policemen put on cotton gloves." At the climactic moment, when the coffin is placed on the steps of the cemetery chapel and the cantor begins the service,

Benya shoots up in his blaring car. In the sudden stillness, a vast wreath is carried to the hearse by four men from the car. The same four carry the coffin after the service. Benya steps on the grave mound and makes a speech: ". . . Gentlemen and ladies, what did our dear Josif get out of life? A couple trifles. What was his occupation? He counted other people's money . . . There are those who know how to drink vodka . . . and there are those who don't know how to drink it, but drink all the same . . . That is why, gentlemen and ladies, after we have said a prayer for our poor Josif, I will ask you to accompany to his grave Savely Butzis, unknown to you, but already deceased . . ." Another coffin is placed in a grave, and Benya has the cantor and sixty choir boys do the whole service over again—"Savka had never dreamed of such a service," as the old man says. A beggar sitting on the wall watching says: "A King."

Such—in three crude paragraphs which gravely and inevitably misrepresent the actual story—is what takes place. Notice that they correspond to the story's introduction, complication, and resolution. The conflict between Benya's character and his circumstances, producing his visit to Grach, and the community between Tartakovsky's circumstances (wealth) and character (insolence, making it certain that he will resist demands), make up the introduction. In one sense, the complication has begun already, since it is obvious that, Benya being what he is, some of Tartakovsky's money is going to pass into his possession, and complication flows from character and circumstances as much as or even more than it does from accident. Still, it seems fair to regard this as the introduction, setting the scene. About the complication—the letters and holdup—Babel's employment of the haphazard helps strongly to produce, by contrast, the feeling of inevitability. A letter is posted but not delivered. A gangster comes late (so that he does not know that all is going well) and drunk (so that he is given to convulsive physical actions). A clerk happens to be in front of the bullet. After these accidents, the four-stage resolution has the effect of a sequence of things *fated*, proceeding—in a degree even more complete than everything that has gone before—from Benya's character. He works to save Muginstein, he makes sure that the bereaved mother is really compensated (so far as compensation is possible in life), he arranges a magnificent funeral, and he avenges him. At the end of a good story, something—an action—has *completely* taken place.

We have made too little of the fact that the whole thing is told by an old man to a boy as they sit on a cemetery wall. This frame action is part of the story, of course. No view of what the story is about could satisfy us which did not take this into account. And now we are in a position to begin saying what the story is about—its subject, substance, and theme.

The story answers the boy's question about the reason for the difference between Benya Krik, "the King," and two other superb criminals. What qualities above all *matter* in life, that is. Arye Leyb replies with a tale of Benya's beginning and how he came to be called "King." His energy was indispensable, of course; a high degree of energy marks one difference between achievement and failure or mediocrity. So was his daring; all four parts of the resolution involve daring—his openly visiting the hospital, the mother, the funeral, and his not only murdering Butzis but acknowledging the deed, as it were. But these qualities are not the real point.

His sense of responsibility is the real point. The world is not chaotic for Benya Krik; it makes sense. He makes it make sense. The major elements that require notice are his imagination, his kindness, and his justice. Benya's imagination, if it needs illustration, is seen vividly enough in his car and in the funeral grandeur. Could a king be responsible—*be* a king—without imagination? the story asks, and answers: Certainly not. In his kindness, voluntary, to Aunt Pesya, Benya strikes one as a sort of Robin Hood, extracting from the rich for the poor; and his references to classes of people in his speech on the grave mound enforces this feeling. His justice, which is what matters most, is primitive, but it is the oldest of all Jewish justice: an eye for an eye, a death for a death. Benya simply takes the law into his own hands, as he should do, being a king. Now it is proper that the old, who are wise, should instruct the young, who are ignorant: the old man and the boy sit on the wall. What is a fitting subject for such instruction? The center of life, which one of them has passed, the other not attained; and *in* the center of life, a man as a focus of power, whether for good or for evil, perhaps especially if for *both*, as most men are in some degree and a king in the highest degree. Yes, the qualities and responsibilities proper to a king, discoursed on by age for youth; and this is Babel's subject. It is not of course his whole subject, and we have not taken into account his irony, which is basic and persistent.

This story is tragic, yet funny, yet not funny. The world it describes, or rather creates and presents, is an atrocious one, lacking altogether, outside the figure of Benya Krik, in the compassion and justice that he brings into it. The context is Czarist Russia, with its special persecution of the *whole* Jewish community, inside which the action takes place. "That was when the thugs from the Sloboda district were beating up the Jews on Bolshaya Arnautskaya Street." "That day policemen put on cotton gloves"—the special force of this brilliant sentence lies in one's sudden vision of the *usual* aspect of their hands: fists, clubs, whatever they used, as in Detroit in the 1930's. There is not much of this; not much is needed, and in general the Jews—that is, all the people of the story—are seen as too *low* to be of concern, even malignant concern, to the Russian society in which they live ("You can spend the night with a Russian woman, and the Russian woman will be satisfied by you" is an early, savage pointer to this broad assumption made by Babel). This fate of the Jews is crucial. "A terrible mistake has been made, Aunt Pesya. But wasn't it a mistake on God's part to settle the Jews in Russia, where they've had to suffer the tortures of hell?" The nerves of the story are singing with pain on this topic; *therefore*, Benya continues, like Danny Kaye: "Would it be bad if the Jews lived in Switzerland, where they'd be surrounded by first-class lakes, mountain air, and nothing but Frenchmen? Everybody makes mistakes, even God." The grotesquerie and comedy are defensive, one way of treating the intolerable.

But on the whole we are, in this story, among Jews only. Their world is an atrocious place just in itself. "Tartakovsky has the soul of a murderer, but he's one of ours . . . it was his own Moldavanka people who made trouble for him. Twice they kidnapped him for ransom, and once during a pogrom they staged his funeral"—the phrase "during a pogrom" placed in this sentence shows how little Babel conceives the agony of the Jews to be due merely to persecution from above. They suffer because they are human beings. Businessmen with murderous souls confront gangsters who are in business ("the firm of Lyovka Byk and Company") under the aegis of an *elder* (a respected community leader). Benya himself is a gangster, and kills. That the entire narration takes place by a cemetery, and is told by one who has escaped from the war of life to one who has not entered upon it yet, testifies to the fundamental gloom of the story. At the beginning, we hear of the "green peace of the graves," directly after hearing of the three furious gangsters. Men are victims, not of fate, but of other human beings. Life is wolfish; God is a blunderer.

There is little religious faith in this story, but there is a deep and vivid love, all the same, for this community (of which, of course, Babel had once been a part), with all its errors and crimes. This love is clearest in a paragraph cataloguing, as with tender pride, all those who attended the funeral—among them "the milkmaids from the Bugayevka district, wrapped in orange shawls" who "stamped their feet like gendarmes on a holiday parade, and their wide hips gave off the odors of the sea and of milk." His ridicule issues not from contempt for them but from his tragicomic personal vision of their responsibility for their own misery or a large part of it. Here is the reason for the *Pagliacci* music—the clown who sings while his heart is breaking. Babel's pity, rich and hopeless, fills the story. His love and pity are unsparing, however, toward the reality of their life. The last words spoken by the helpless Muginstein before he is killed are a lie, and the author emphasizes this disconcerting fact. Even Arye Leyb mocks the boy for his weak sight, for the impossibility of his ever becoming Benya Krik. The story, which is *written* almost as a fantasy, is sharply realistic at this level.

The subject of a complex, ambitious story such as "In Odessa" is more readily identified, and can be more briefly described, than its substance. Its theme is more difficult still. Why is a gangster held up to admiration? The first answer is that exalted human qualities, even in a gangster, form a proper matter for transmitted wisdom. Implicit in this answer is a certain humour—that it is to a *gangster*, in an oppressed race, that we have to be looking for these qualities. Of course this is ironic. If the *boy* alone admired Benya Krik, we would learn nothing; boys do in fact make heroes of gangsters. But Reb Arye Leyb admires him, too. We hardly feel either of them to be a fool, or vicious, and our second answer to the question shows that it is not only ironic but also *natural* that they—and through them, we—should admire Benya, who is a superior product in an amusing but disgusting world. To say the least of it, he refuses to drown. Stifling, in danger of spiritual death, trapped between his circumstances and his desires, he goes to Froim Grach: "Take me on, Froim. I want to be cast upon your shore. The shore I'm cast on will gain by it." The image is that of shipwreck. All the others *are* shipwrecked, lost in their evils, stupidities, sufferings. *He* finds himself, both in the qualities that are proper for success in this savage world and in the qualities that would be proper (*are* proper, as is recognized by Arye Leyb) in another, higher world. He respects himself and feels for others and believes in justice. This second answer (substance) gives a much less optimistic account of things, it will be noticed, than the first subject did, but both are comparatively realistic. The third answer, in terms of *theme*, is ideal and imaginative, and is the true motor of the story's power. A reader does not have to "know" consciously just what it is that he is responding to, any more than most of us do in music—hearing Mozart's Quartet K. 499, for example—or seeing, entering, rounding the cathedral, say, at Seville.

A short way to put the third answer might be this: Babel is seeking, and creating, *sources of authority*. We live, in this story, in a world where authority has broken down. People are at each other's throats, and gouging. The American government's attempts in recent years, backed by the press and by a solid quantity of public opinion, to disinfect the leadership of the Teamsters' Union, which have ended so far in complete failure (Mr. Beck being succeeded by Mr. Hoffa, who is far stronger), are one of a thousand examples that could be cited of this twentieth-century breakdown; the weakness of the Weimar Republic invited Hitler; *six* more or less democratic regimes, brand-new, in backward countries in Asia and Africa, became military dictatorships in the single year 1958. But already it is clear that the jungle atmosphere at the bottom is produced by power vacuums at the top—into which jungle elements move. Babel's story is complicated partly because it was written *in* Soviet Russia *about* Czarist Russia, or the Jews under it in one of the country's great southern cities, Odessa.

Jungle from breakdown. What authorities, in the story, seem to be valued? A reader notices four: the "elder," the rabbi—these are inside the community—the police (representatives of the Czarist regime), God (the Jewish God). The elder, Lyovka Byk, is head of a "crook" firm. The rabbi, Arye Leyb, sits on a cemetery wall, apparently waiting for death, without influence upon anything except his small, bespectacled disciple. The police are powerless against Benya (and of small assistance, apparently, to others—witness Tartakovsky's having been held up nine times). God makes mistakes. Therefore: *false authorities.* (1) Benya Krik, with his simpleminded, straightforward illusion of the existence of democracy (his conversation with Muginstein at the holdup). (2) Communism, which is parodied by Benya in the funeral oration when he says of Muginstein, "He perished for the whole working class." These are the authorities, one reigning when the story was written, one imagined into the earlier time, an authoritarian crook, paralyzing the authorities, astonishing and delighting the community, doing his will, compelling the imagination of old and young with utopian dreams. "Explain it to me, Muginstein," says Benya during the holdup, "as to a friend: he gets a business letter from me; why couldn't he get into a trolley for five kopecks then, and ride up to my place and have a glass vodka with the family and a snack, taking potluck? What kept him from having a heart-to-heart

talk with me? 'Benya,' he could have told me, 'thus and thus, here is
my bank balance, wait a couple of days, let me get my breath, give
me a chance to turn around . . .' What would I have answered? Hog
don't meet hog, but man meets man. Muginstein, do you get me?"
The democratic dream is seen in this touching passage—the loot is
being packed—as central to the nature of man, post-animal. Men are
equal. Benya believes this, in the teeth of all evidence, and Muginstein
agrees (not truthfully) and is killed. The author's contempt, in this
story, for both democratic and Communist theory is plain. (Not
surprisingly, his work proved unacceptable to the Soviet Union, and
they killed Babel twenty years ago.) What then does he believe in? It
does not follow, from his dislike for two of the ruling political philos-
ophies of our century, that he believes in anything. Increasingly, as
the world progresses, people believe in nothing. Perhaps Babel is a
nihilist?

   Real authority, imagined. There are two sources of real authority imagined: one of action, Benya Krik; one of reflection, Arye
Leyb. Benya is created as a folk hero. He is made a practical man (he
does not try to set up in "business" for himself, a tactic frowned on
by organized crime), but essentially he operates in another sphere.
He does not give charity like Robin Hood. We were wrong there.
Money is not the point. He *does glory* (if we may put it this way)—
Muginstein's funeral and Savka Butzis's—and he *does justice*—the
atonement of Butzis's killing for Muginstein's. Note the rising order
of the functions, first glory, then justice. These are what he gives
them, and is King. The inability of the police to operate against him
is magical; at this high creative level of the story, magic is allowable,
and he even sways the police (in cotton gloves) to presence at the
funeral—this because of the special Jewish demands made upon
leaders, an absolutely fundamental topic. He is a source of authority
and of fixing-things-up, such as we need because God is hardly to be
depended on. It is true that he only does a *bad* justice—such is clearly
the author's thought—but this is because he has to work in a wicked,
submerged world where that is the only sort of justice (death for
death) that is possible. He is only human; he makes mistakes. Or is he
human? for God Himself makes mistakes. So much, with one very
important reservation, for Benya. He is the King that history has
denied the exiled, dispersed, persecuted, and suffering Jews. This is
what, ironically, this marvellous story is really up to.

   But he *becomes known* to us through the recital of his kingship
by Arye Leyb to a boy. Not only must there *be* a king, but he must
be recognized and named as such and his deed transmitted from gen-

eration to generation as a topic of traditional racial wisdom. Arye Leyb is the second great source of authority in the story. Note that he makes the boy *wait* for instruction; nothing could be more unlike the hurry-scurry, empty give-and-take of American popular education than the tone of the framework of this story. "A man who thirsts for knowledge must be patient. A man who possesses knowledge should be dignified." Note that he himself qualifies his authority as a teller in a way suggesting that he alone can ("I wasn't at that session. But it is said that they did hold it"); for the boy his authority is absolute. Observe his saying at the end: "Now you know everything"—as if convinced that he has communicated an essential and all-encompassing secret of wisdom completely. In its own way, this story is a wisdom-work, like the greatest of all Jewish wisdom-works, the Poem of Job embodied (with later additions and corruptions) in the Old Testament *Book of Job*. Both poem and story are ironic and rebellious, but whereas one submits in the end to God's power (the sixth-century B.C. poem), the other imagines—only imagines—a different authority and power. Note the monumental strength of the narrator's assertion of authority: "Fill your ears with my words. It was with my own eyes that I beheld all I beheld, sitting here on the wall of the Second Jewish Cemetery . . . It was I who saw it, I, Arye Leyb, the proud Jew who is neighbor to the dead." Pride is what the two sources of authority, the agent (Benya Krik) and the interpreter (Arye Leyb), have in common, the pride denied to the Jews for two thousand years.

In reading any literary work of another time and place, it is necessary to think ourselves into the knowledge and frame of mind available to the contemporary reader of that work, as far as we can. We can never do this completely; but no work of art is ever thoroughly understood anyway, even by the artist. As with all other things in life, we make out with approximations, a truth recognized in physics by one of its major twentieth-century laws, Heisenberg's Principle of Indeterminacy. We do it as well as we can, partly with learning, partly with imagination. The matter of learning whole national and racial attitudes, for example, requires imagination. Japanese streets have no names, or had none until the American Army arrived and nearly went crazy; only an intersection had a name. Indians (in India) express approval by shaking their heads—a custom disconcerting to Western lecturers until they accustom themselves to it. These habits are indicative of attitudes toward experience different from ours. Now the Jews' particular respect for learning is fairly well known, even though, living in American conditions, many Jews have discarded it and adopted instead our American contempt for learning. But readers who are not Jewish (and the writer cannot claim to be, any more than he is Russian, whether Czarist or Soviet) will have small idea of the *degree* of the Jewish feeling for learning and authority which is taken for granted in this story. An anecdote that best conveys this feeling, perhaps, is a funny one by the greatest of living Jewish philosophers, Martin Buber. The scene is a city in Central Europe where Buber was lecturing before World War I. After the lecture, "I went into a coffee house with some members of the association who had arranged the evening. I like to follow a speech before many, whose form allows no reply, with a conversation with a few in which person acts on person and my view is set forth directly through going into objection and question.

"We were just discussing a theme of moral philosophy when a well-built Jew of simple appearance and middle age came up to the table and greeted me. To my no doubt somewhat distant return greeting, he replied with words not lacking a slight reproof: 'Doctor! Do you not recognize me?' When I had to answer in the negative, he introduced himself as M., the brother of a former steward of my father's. I invited him to sit with us, inquired about his circumstances of life and then took up again the conversation with the young people. M. listened to the discussion, which had just taken a turn toward somewhat abstract formulations, with eager attentiveness. It was obvious that he did not understand a single word; the devotion with which he received every word resembled that of the believers who do not need to know the content of a litany since the arrangement of sounds and tones alone gives them all that they need, and more than any content could.

"After a while, nonetheless, I asked him whether he had perhaps something to say to me; I should gladly go to one side with him and talk over his concern. He vigorously declined. The conversation began again and with M.'s listening. When another half hour had passed, I asked him again whether he did not perhaps have a wish that I might fulfill for him; he could count on me. No, no, he had no wish, he assured me. It had grown late; but, as happens to one in such hours of lively interchange, I did not feel weary; I felt fresher, in fact, than before, and decided to go for a walk with the young people. At this moment M. approached me with an unspeakably timid air. 'Doctor,' he said, 'I should like to ask you a question.' I bid the students wait and sat down with him at a table. He was silent. 'Just ask, Mr. M.,' I encouraged him; 'I shall gladly give you information as best I can.' 'Doctor,' he said, 'I have a daughter.' He paused; then he continued,

'And I also have a young man for my daughter.' Again a pause. 'He is a student of law. He passed the examinations with distinction.' He paused again, this time somewhat longer. I looked at him encouragingly; I supposed that he would entreat me to use my influence in some way on behalf of the presumptive son-in-law. 'Doctor,' he asked, 'is he a steady man?' I was surprised, but felt that I might not refuse him an answer. 'Now, Mr. M.,' I explained, 'after what you have said, it can certainly be taken for granted that he is industrious and able.' Still he questioned further. 'But Doctor,' he said, 'does he also have a good head?'—'That is even more difficult to answer,' I replied; 'but at any rate he has not succeeded with industry alone, he must also have something in his head.' Once again M. paused; then he asked, clearly as a final question, 'Doctor, should he now become a judge or a lawyer?'—'About that I can give you no information,' I answered. 'I do not know the young man, indeed, and even if I did know him, I should hardly be able to advise in this matter.' But then M. regarded me with a glance of almost melancholy renunciation, half-complaining, half-understanding, and spoke in an indescribable tone, composed in equal part of sorrow and humility: 'Doctor, you do not *want* to say—now, I thank you for what you have said to me.'

"This humorous and meaningful occurrence, which apparently has nothing to do with Hasidism, afforded me, nonetheless, a new and significant insight into it. As a child, I had received an image of the zaddik and through the sullied reality had glimpsed the pure idea, the idea of the genuine leader of a genuine community. Between youth and manhood this idea had arisen in me through knowledge of Hasidic teaching as that of the perfected man who realizes God in the world. But now in the light of this droll event, I caught sight in my inner experience of the zaddik's function as a leader. I, who am truly no zaddik, no one assured in God, rather a man endangered before God, a man wrestling ever anew for God's light, ever anew engulfed in God's abysses, nonetheless, when asked a trivial question and replying with a trivial answer, then experienced from within for the first time the true zaddik, questioned about revelations and replying in revelations. I experienced him in the fundamental relation of his soul to the world: in his responsibility."

To this *extreme* sense of the Jewish need for authority, and the Jewish people's sense of storytelling, let us now connect the things omitted earlier about Benya Krik and Arye Leyb. One of the strangest remarks in Babel's story is one about Benya. One of the gangsters was packing the loot, Muginstein had his hands over his

head, and "in the meantime Benya was telling stories from the life of
the Jewish people." This remark means, probably, to identify the
unusually laconic folk hero, a doer, with the theme of traditional
wisdom that belongs otherwise (but Benya's speech at the funeral,
explaining his justice, is a second instance) to the frame of the story.
The statement about, or rather by, Arye Leyb that we have not
considered is the most exalted, perhaps, in the story: "And now I
shall speak as the Lord did on Mount Sinai out of the burning
bush . . ." Here we have actual divine authority claimed, in simile,
for the revelation (as we had better call it) of Benya Krik's arrival at
the funeral(s)—the manifestation of his glory, his presence, and his
justice. A Law is announced. What Law? A New Law, like Paul's in
the New Testament? No, the same Law as Moses's—put *back* into
force, as if the abrogation of the Old Law announced by Paul had
failed (Czarist Russia was a strongly Christian society), and in order
to have *any* Law it was necessary, with Benya Krik and his interpreter Arye Leyb, to re-establish the old.

At this point we may see our account of the story's meaning as
sufficiently full. How does this meaning reach the reader emotionally,
so that he is moved, impressed, perhaps changed even, without being
able to say exactly what it is that has worked on him? Identification is
probably the chief means, and Buber's anecdote gives us a fine example by way of contrast. The reader does not identify himself, in
any *serious* sense, with either Buber or his anxious interlocutor. The
identification that occurs in serious works of the imagination takes
place at deep levels in the mind or spirit. The identification is very
incomplete—few people still sane have ever felt for a moment that
they *were* Hamlet or Don Quixote—but may be profound and last-
ing, because learning has accompanied it: the learning what it is like
to be, or to pretend to be, someone else. In Babel's story, primary
identification of course is with Benya—but we do not reach Benya
directly. The explanation of his royalty comes to us from the old man
and we hear it with the ears and excitement of the boy. (It is impossible not to feel, by the way, that the author has put himself into the
story, to some extent, in the figure of the boy.) The double remove
from the figure of the hero allows the story's mythical and magical
qualities free play; we are less disposed to criticism, as we listen with
the boy's open ears to the old man's authority. Any very strong
personal identification with Benya is forbidden; it would be undesir-
able, considering the stature the author wishes to secure for him. We
can identify with Tartakovsky only in his helplessness before Benya
and his feelings upon attending his own "funeral"; on this note also,

the villain as victim, his character disappears—he is said to have re-tired. When he is his usual self (playing, for example, *from above*, on Benya's sympathies, as in his letter), we attend to him with perfect objectivity. The actual victims, again, we reach indirectly: Mugin-stein, during the holdup, is "as green as green grass" as he says, pathetically, "I am in charge here," and just before he is shot he is more or less forced by Benya (who feels that everyone shares his own folk-democracy) to tell a lie. This is not very much to go on, though it shows us that identification is not a product only of charac-terization but of imagery. With Savka there is no identification at all. But of Aunt Pesya we learn that at her son's great funeral she "trem-bled like a little bird"; here is unquestionably a moment of feeling with her. In this story of an oppressed people, it is natural that identification should be through weakness. But perhaps it is true that we are more inclined to identify with weakness and suffering than with strength and joy, because most people's lives are so much more fully characterized by the first two qualities than by the second two.

It is as much by means of style and tone and imagery as by what is said that an author's personal vision is communicated. Two of the most obvious elements of style in Babel's story are clearly the man-agement of pace and the richness of imagery. The tranquil setting of the narration—the man and boy at peace on the cemetery wall—con-trasts sharply with the furious, jocular rapidity of the narrative itself, with its violent content. This is emphasized, of course, by the cere-monious dialogue of man and boy in contrast with the unceremonious action described. But the contrast is not simple, because the element of ceremony enters also into the action, with the funeral, Benya Krik's apology to Aunt Pesya, and his funeral oration. The otherwise jerky action is also raised to a poetic level, and drawn out of its squalid urban setting to be seen against the general background of nature, by the imagery—like a little bird, as green as green grass. This dimension of the story's style allows Babel to be much more offhand than he could otherwise be without losing stature and significance for his action.

Tone, a term closely related to style, describes something which is a product of style but not quite the same thing and not lending itself readily to short definition. It corresponds rather to the tone of a man's voice in conversation—unmistakable, but not to be identified exactly with any combination of nameable elements. What adjectives shall we apply to Babel's tone here? Jaunty and dubious. He needs both these qualities at once, because they affect each other; neither would be the same in isolation. The combination is one of the richest of all literary tones and one of the oldest. There is a passage in the Babylonian epic of *Gilgamesh*, some four thousand years old, which has a tone remarkably like Babel's in this story. The hero is approached by the Lady Ishtar and offered all sorts of things to become her lover. He remains unmoved. "Lady," he replies, "you speak of giving me riches, but you would demand far more in return. The food and clothing you would need would be such as befits a goddess; the house would have to be meet for a queen, and your robes of the finest weave. And why should I give you all this? You are but a drafty door, a palace tottering to its ruin, a turban which fails to cover the head, pitch that defiles the hand, a bottle that leaks, a shoe that pinches. Have you ever kept faith with a lover? Have you ever been true to your troth? When you were a girl there was Tammuz. But what happened to him? Year by year men mourn his fate!" and so on. The blunt and poetic realism of the two works, their tone, the heroes' refusal to be surprised or overtaken, have much in common.

Finally, something must be said about point of view. Most stories are told from the point of view of an omniscient narrator, the author, who writes in the third person and knows everything. The advantages of the omniscient-narrator technique are obvious; it is the method, for example, both of the epic of *Gilgamesh* and of *War and Peace*. But except in very powerful hands it tends to lack immediacy, becoming something more resembling a report than a presentation. Babel's method is very different. It is first-person narrative, the second most usual way of telling a story. But to say this hardly describes it adequately. Because of the doubling of this technique in the story, it really resembles drama to some extent. The whole story is told by the boy. But since so much of what he tells us is exactly what the old man tells him, the story has the effect of a conversation—losing in scope what the *author* might have been able to tell us that the boy and the old man do not know, but gaining in directness. This is not only because the old man speaks with the special authority of personal knowledge but because we do not even hear him directly except with the pricked ears of ignorance and longing.

1960

The Monk *and Its Author*

"*The Monk*" IS ONE OF THE AUTHENTIC PRODIGIES OF ENG-
lish fiction, a book in spite of various crudenesses so good that even
after a century and a half it is possible to consider it unhistorically; and
yet it has never quite become a standard novel. Several reasons for this
must be its intermittent unavailability, its reputation for eroticism, its
not being reinforced by excellence in Lewis's other imaginative work,
so that it has had to stand alone. But the chief reason must be that it
has long suffered from a prejudice against the Gothic novel in general,
which I am anxious not to combat except as it affects our experience
of *The Monk*. Deservedly forgotten—all but two or three exemplars—
save by enthusiasts and specialists, this grotesque school helped usher
in the English Romantic movement and debauched taste without ever
really participating in the glories of the movement, unless in the book
before us. Here we might take refuge in the notion that *The Monk* is
only incidentally a Gothic novel, and owes its excellence to other
qualities; that it is good in spite of being to some extent a Gothic novel.
But I don't think this is true. *The Monk* seems to me exactly a Gothic
novel, in a sense to be elucidated. What I propose is to consider the
book critically, without making any allowances whatever for it. It has
found no considerable modern champion, as even *Vathek* found
Mallarmé; a frailer work, but Oriental not Gothic. But though nothing
could recommend itself less obviously to current critical taste than
Lewis's masterpiece, it is clear that in certain respects we are better
placed with regard to it than his contemporaries were. We will not be
offended by it; and time has other advantages. When Coleridge discussed *The Monk* in *The Critical Review* of February 1797, a novel
more strongly resembling it in central feeling than any yet existing,
Wuthering Heights, lay fifty years in the future, and he neglected to
note the influence, strange, tenuous, but saving, of what he later beautifully described as the "self-involution and dreamlike continuity" of
Samuel Richardson.

Somehow *The Monk* ought not to have been good at all. Its author was a witty diplomat, aged nineteen, its locale the Spain of the Inquisition and romantic Germany, its mode the Gothic mode that had been originated, unpromisingly, by Horace Walpole's *The Castle of Otranto* thirty years before and appeared to have just reached its highest development in Mrs Radcliffe's *The Mysteries of Udolpho* (1794). This lachrymose, spineless, more or less insufferable romance Lewis much admired and aspired to imitate. Well, we read at once of "hurry and expedition," and to the end of his novel a "loud and audible" youthful diffuseness will recur. The author's immediate, art-less, extensive revelations of precedent action do not promise much by way of address. The aunt who fancies herself admired is tiresome. Even Ambrosio does not begin well. We probably resent the secret of his character's having been delivered up to us at once in the initial epigraph given by Lewis, which is about Angelo's apparent character in *Measure for Measure*. In Chapter 2, when we come on him alone, the note of spiritual pride is struck so emphatically that his hypocrisy seems almost laughable. Shakespeare at least—we say to ourselves—had the instinct to make his paradigm a truly virtuous man up to a point. Now our conception of what Lewis is up to is quite wrong, and this second chapter, occupied with the Monk and "Rosario" up to his fall, gradually becomes impressive. But the two long chapters that follow, devoted to Raymond's adventures with the robbers and his and Agnes's story, though they are very well, are perhaps less impressive; and so with the fifth, which resumes the Lorenzo-Antonia story and conducts Raymond and Agnes to her "burial." I have scarcely ever read an excellent novel which for so long fails to declare its quality. Up to the sixth chapter, or halfway through the book, it is charming and interesting in varying degrees, eminently readable, but hardly remarkable. Then it becomes, with great suddenness, passion-ate and astonishing.

Ambrosio has been so long neglected that one has almost forgot-ten him, in the Bleeding Nun and other events. Now he emerges dead-center again, and upon his direct satiation with Matilda we realize that we are not dealing with Shakespearean pastiche at all; the devel-opment is a novelist's, it has more in common with one strain in *Anna Karenina*. An inexperienced author has been learning as he proceeded. The ambitious, complex pages that follow, generalizing Ambrosio's character as it has issued from his powers and weakness in the govern-ing monastic environment, are a product of genius. They cite Angelo again, but it was solely Angelo's temptation and fall that interested Shakespeare, who besides had other fates at heart in that strange comedy. Lewis is interested in the *progress* of Ambrosio. His enlargement takes over Antonia from Lorenzo, the Raymond-Agnes story dwindles to her miseries under the nuns (as these counterpoint the monkish corruption of Ambrosio's progress), and henceforward he dominates the book. Matilda, too, is an engrossing character, and the alterations of the two in Chapter 6 might be studied with advantage by a modern chronicler of passion. But Ambrosio is the point; the point is to conduct a remarkable man utterly to damnation. It is surprising, after all, how *long* it takes—how *difficult* it is—to be certain of damnation. This was Lewis's main insight, fully embodied in his narrative, and I confess that such a work as Thomas Mann's *Doctor Faustus* seems to me frivolous by comparison. In romantic art, as in snake venenation, overtreatment is the lesser error; but you have to be treating a man who has been bitten. Mann's book has admirable essays in it, wide and profound experience, an art subtle to decadence, but maybe the main thing is not there. In *The Monk* the main thing is there.

Discriminating thus its principal intellectual and spiritual substance, we hardly have behind us the authority of Coleridge. Coleridge thought *The Monk* an "offspring of no common genius" and allowed it to possess "much real merit"; the tale of the Bleeding Nun was "truly terrific"; but the book contained "abominations." It violated equally nature and morality. One of his objections, concerning Ambrosio's pursuit of Antonia, is too curious to be neglected. It is "contrary to nature," the great critic asserts, for a mortal, fresh from his impression of the Devil's presence and employing for the first time the witching myrtle, to be "at the same moment agitated by so fleeting an appetite as that of lust." I am less confident about this than Coleridge; but the question being not altogether a literary one, the reader must seek his own counsel. It seems to me that it is just in the presentment of the Monk's flickering affections and lusts that Lewis is most steadily natural. Very striking is the turn of motive that he first *loves* Antonia. Coleridge himself found the character of Matilda, in whom the same problems occur, "exquisitely imagined, and as exquisitely supported."

Coleridge was distracted, of course, by what he calls "a libidinous minuteness" in *The Monk*, and by the "impiety" for which he cited with horror the passage satirizing the use of the Bible as reading for young people. Neither of these qualities, supposing they existed, is likely to trouble a generation familiar with the lively early work of Henry Miller and the superior, more offensive, far more fantastic books of Jean Genet. But the question why authors write thus is a real one. To a high degree in these extreme modern cases, and to some degree in Lewis, no doubt a personal assertion is being made; but an aesthetic restlessness so closely accompanies the assertion that to treat the matter as merely psychological will not do. The aim of a rebellious narrative art is always in some fashion to represent life better.

Lewis was even following a prescription. The Gothic novel was broadly thought of, even while it flourished, as designed to answer a craving for the gloomy, the ancient, the weird, which Walpole not so much revived as made fashionable. But it had a more particular end. *The Castle of Otranto* itself is an anomaly. This concise and frigid tale seems to exist simply as proof that a celebrated production by a literary craftsman of the first order of talent, a work obviously inspired and also laboured, a work of formidable psychoanalytic interest and permanent literary-historical interest, can be yet so deficient in literary merit as later to be barely readable. It is Walpole's programmatic formulation, prefatory to the second edition, rather than his example, that is instructive. His book, he tells us, was "an attempt to blend the two kinds of Romance, the ancient and the modern. In the former, all was imagination and improbability: in the latter, nature is always intended to be, and sometimes has been, copied with success. Invention has not been wanting; but the great resources of fancy have been dammed up by a strict adherence to common life. But if in the latter species Nature has cramped imagination, she did but take her revenge, having been totally excluded from old romances." The despairing vacancy here posited of the novelist of the Age of Reason confronting contemporary subjects will not seem strange to the American writer confronting many nervous persons at the end of a day's abstract work collected in a fireless, carefully empty room, smoking cigarettes and drinking martinis; envying, perhaps, abductions, duels, not to mention spectres and the Old One's agents. Walpole thought it possible to reconcile the two kinds of romance. "Desirous [he says to himself] of leaving the powers of fancy at liberty to expatiate through the boundless realms of invention, and thence of creating more interesting situations, he wished to conduct the mortal agents in his drama according to the rules of probability; in short, to make them speak, think, and act, as it might be supposed mere men and women would do in extraordinary positions."

This reconciliation or adjustment Walpole was unable to effect, and knew it, gracefully: "If the new route he has struck out shall have paved a road for men of brighter talents, he shall own with pleasure and modesty, that he was sensible the plan was capable of receiving greater embellishments than his imagination or conduct of the passions could bestow on it." But the ability to see what *can* be profitably done is nearly as rare as the ability to do it. Walpole had both prepared for, and explained, the achievements of Lewis and, later, Maturin. A Gothic novel, then, is not so precisely a matter of a haunted castle, though this property was almost invariable, as it is an attempt to marry two modes of literary conduct; an analogy being observable in the term "free verse," where, when that which is being so characterized is not nothing, our emphasis ought to lie, rather than upon the word "free," upon the word "verse." In a style unpretentious and surprisingly adequate, Lewis makes credible a chain of deepening terrors and enchantments intended to exhibit, to test, his characters. Hear Matilda, in the wildest situation imaginable, on the point of death from poison, and determined to save herself in some mysterious way: " 'I have been expecting you with impatience,' said she; 'my life depends upon these moments.' " We believe her. Lewis does not always succeed. His prioress (so called) of St Clare wants credibility. It has been rightly pointed out that the Fiend's claim about Matilda's nature at the end is inconsistent with all that has gone before, a blunder of Lewis's. There is implausibility in the long illnesses produced at will to forbid communication among the principals that would prove awkward for the plot. But on the whole, especially with Ambrosio, he contrives with the Strange to deepen interest while maintaining the Natural. Since the passions are his motor subject, it is necessary that they should be realistic; this "impassioned realism" is what distinguishes radically *The Monk*—I agree with Montague Summers, Mrs Radcliffe's chief modern advocate— from Mrs Radcliffe's work, even from *The Italian*, which shows his influence; and so his book was bound to give offense.

Its supernatural elements are more likely to trouble the reader now; not, I think, very likely. They are strongly done, for one thing. But the book is poetic, for another. I allude not only to the far from contemptible poems irregularly introduced, though these help to determine its character. I mean the general colouring of its inspiration. Lewis mistook and misrepresented, for example, the procedure of the Spanish Inquisition, but he pursues Ambrosio to the wall and behind the wall to the next wall and beyond that to the abyss. At the same time, he is as alive to the inconstancy of human purpose as he is to its obsessive character, and some of his highest effects are simple indeed, as when the Monk, eager to damn himself by reading a certain passage in the Bible backward—the Inquisition's officers are at his cell door—can't find the page.

Monk Lewis was a famous person in his age, and is for us now a more shadowy figure in the biographies of his contemporaries than the author of *The Monk* ought to be; besides, at the end of his life he wrote another book which is remembered. But Mrs Baron-Wilson's adulterated, childlike *Life and Correspondence* of 1839 has never been replaced by a proper biography. From this, however, and his writings, and additional accounts by a Finnish student (Eino Railo in *The Haunted Castle*, 1927), the tireless Dr Summers (in *The Gothic Quest*, 1938), and lately by William B. Todd (in the University of Virginia's *Studies in Bibliography*, 1949), it ought to be possible to reconstruct an image.

Lewis, born in London 9 July 1775, was the eldest child of parents, both from prominent families, who separated permanently while he was still at the Westminster School. His father, a proud cold man, Deputy-Secretary at War, moved the separation. Sir Thomas Sewell's youngest daughter repaired briefly to Paris, keeping her elder son's affections close. Of his childhood little is known except that he was her pet. At Stanstead Hall, Essex, where he often stayed, the way each evening to his bedroom lày past a haunted chamber. He loved to stage plays. He was precocious enough to resent at fifteen, in his first term at Christ Church, Oxford, the rejection of a farce he had had submitted to the manager of Drury Lane. This he may have recast after a year or so as *The East Indian* (which was eventually produced as a benefit play by Mrs Jordan). Meanwhile, he had written another play, *Felix*, "two volumes" of a novel burlesquing Richardson, and begun a romance modelled on *Otranto*. What he studied at Oxford besides Greek and Latin is uncertain; designed by his father for a diplomatic career, he spent vacations on the Continent. He learned German thoroughly at Weimar during the second half of 1792, translated poetry, and met Goethe. The next year he passed some time with Lord Douglas at Bothwell Castle, translating Schiller, but stayed partly in Oxford, trying to get poems published, writing squibs for newspapers, and dealing by correspondence with his difficult mother.

Mrs Lewis was a beautiful woman, myopic, merry, musical, devout; having been motherless, untrained rather and naïve; greatly admired, she was "all gentleness and complacency, even to a fault," and it appears that her husband had been jealous. The boy's letters show him surprisingly dignified, incisive, fair, though affectionate. One passage is pathetic. "You have put me," he writes to her, "in the most distressing and embarrassing situation in the world: you have made me almost an umpire between my parents. I know not how to extricate myself from the difficulty. I can only believe neither of you to be in the wrong; but *I* am not to determine which is in the right." To his younger brother (crippled by an accident, soon to die) and two sisters, as to both parents, Lewis was scrupulously attentive, solicitous, generous. He was rational, however, and opposed a marital reunion baselessly moved by her. What money he could he gave her; all his literary efforts, he said, were for her benefit—she was in reality well off, but extravagant. For the rest, he was somewhat vain, gay, something of a snob, intensely kindhearted, very ambitious. Physically he did not resemble her. "Mat [observed Walter Scott] had queerish eyes—they projected like those of some insects, and were flattish on the orbits. His person was extremely small and boyish—he was indeed the least man I ever saw, to be strictly well and neatly made." Of his imagination's positive life up to this point the extant materials tell us: nothing.

His father got him made attaché in the British embassy at The Hague, whither he went in May of 1794. He was almost nineteen and the Dutch society bored him. It was indeed so boring, he complained, that an Irishman, Lord Kerry, though fifty-odd and presumably acquainted with boredom, one evening became so dangerously bored that with one terrible yawn he dislocated his jaw. Inspired by the current *Mysteries of Udolpho*, which he fancied "one of the most interesting books that has ever been published," Lewis had taken up again his *Otranto*-like romance, and he wrote a farce, *The Twins*. But against such boredom graver measures were wanted and he began a new work, which in the middle of a long letter to his mother on 23 September he was able to mention as finished. "What do you think of my having written, in the space of ten weeks, a romance of between three and four hundred pages octavo? I have even written half of it out fair. It is called *The Monk*, and I am myself so pleased with it that, if the booksellers will not buy it, I shall publish it myself." Notwithstanding the notorious freedom of authors' statements of this sort, I think it plausible enough that he had really written in this time the whole book more or less as we have it, especially in view of his dating of its prefatory poem (28 October 1794) and the casualness of his next reference (22 November): "For my own part, I have not written a line excepting the Farce and *The Monk*, which is a work of some length, and will make an octavo volume of 420 pages. There is a great deal of poetry inserted, a few lines of which I will send you . . ." On the other hand: he left very shortly for London (apparently resigning his post) in order to publish *The Monk;* and though a tradition exists of publication in the summer of 1795, and there may in fact have been prepublication copies that year, *The Monk* was not properly issued until March 1796; so that 1795—a year when we know nothing about him—may have seen a good deal of verbal revision, or even expansion, and this may explain the puzzling delay. The poem sent to his mother ("Inscription in an Hermitage," Chapter II) contains a dozen variants from the published text.

The book created a sensation instantly. It was denied all originality—unreasonably, because apart from the avowed groundwork of a story in *The Guardian* (No. 148) and legends, it drew only on a story by a Weimar professor, another German story, two French plays, all these slightly, and its debts to Smollett and Walpole, as to Mrs. Radcliffe's shabby villain Montoni, were slight; but its power was admitted and everybody read it. It was attacked, defended, parodied, plundered, dramatized, opera'd, adapted, translated, imitated. The boy's vanity, however, brought down on him gratuitously what was most outraged in the uproar. On coming of age in July 1796 he was returned to Parliament for Hindon (taking the seat, oddly, of the author of *Vathek*), and when a second edition was called for in October, he not merely put his name on the title page but added "M.P." This was oil to fire. That a LEGISLATOR should calmly avow this mass of immorality and impiety exasperated many besides Coleridge. It seems likely that Lewis and his publisher, Joseph Bell, were indicted by the Court of King's Bench and required to recall the third edition and purge it (*nisi*). Lewis at any rate did expurgate it. The degree of submission required, and of resentment, may be estimated from a long letter he had to write in 1798 to his father, who had been profoundly disturbed. "I perceive," he says, "that I have put too much confidence in the accuracy of my own judgment; that, convinced of my object being unexceptionable, I did not sufficiently examine whether the means by which I attained that object were generally so; and that, upon many accounts, I have to accuse myself of high imprudence. Let me, however, observe that TWENTY is not the age at which prudence is most to be expected." No doubt timidity, thus precipitately acquired, is a poor qualification for an artistic career; but timidity was one element of many in a situation increasingly unpropitious.

So Monk Lewis—as he was known henceforth, to his indifference (he disliked his given names, Matthew Gregory)—became a lion. He seems to have been personally a modest one, but the position, at best, encouraged the sort of social-literary trifling at which he was too good. He passed much time with the Duke of Argyle at Inverary Castle, strolling, poetizing, composing songs, directing theatricals. On a poor lunatic met one day he wrote a ballad, "Crazy Jane," that swept the kingdom, producing a fashionable "Crazy Jane hat" and long afterward supplying a hint, I suppose, for Yeats's great poems. His musical melodrama *The Castle Spectre* (14 December 1797) had a prodigious run at Drury Lane and sold seven editions in a year. As Wordsworth observed, it fitted the public taste like a glove. The old comedy *East Indian* and *Adelmorn the Outlaw* took less well, but when after the turn of the century he shifted to Covent Garden, *Alfonso* (1802) again was a hit, and if his monodrama *The Captive* was not, at least it drove four members of the audience into hysterics. Cold and dull it reads now. He published a satirical dialogue, *Village Virtues* (1796), a translation of Juvenal, *The Love of Gain*, translated Kotzebut, adapted Schiller, Zschokke (*The Bravo of Venice*, 1804, a short novel vigorous and absurd), Kleist, everybody. I must not pretend to have explored every page of this stuff, but one impression is very strong: no literary development took place after *The Monk*. What matters about all this work is not that it is bad but that it is *pointless*. Some of it is not bad. *Alfonso* is a respectable, over-wrought, neo-Jacobean tragedy; wanting any real excellence unless perhaps the scene in Act II between the king and the old friend he has wronged, it is still one of the best English tragedies of the nine-teenth century and not inferior to most of Massinger. But there was no point in it. Of course there was some personal point: Act III reconciles two fathers with their children, and the author had to wait ten years for a deathbed reconciliation with his father when they were estranged over Mr Lewis's mistress. There was no artistic point, no pressure, no direction. Lewis probably knew this. "Very possibly," he introduces the print of *Alfonso*, "*nobody* could write a *worse* Tragedy; but it is a melancholy truth, that *I* cannot write a *better*." He was twenty-six, a celebrity several times over. But the remnants of abstract literary ambition were not enough. His father, even during most of the estrangement, allowed him a thousand pounds annually (half of which he gave to his mother). He had no political ambition, he never addressed the House. He had taken the measure, he thought, of fame—too early, but with reference to a truth: "In my opinion," he remarks to his mother, "the acuteness of *pleasure* in this world bears no proportion to the acuteness of *pain*." Under these uninspiring circumstances, and given a dreadful facility at both prose and verse, not to add music, perhaps only the strictest conception of what he wanted to do as an artist would have enabled him to accomplish more. This he neither had of himself nor was advised to, apparently, by anyone. At thirty-three he threw in the sponge, in the preface to *Venoni* (1808): "The act of composing has ceased to amuse me; I feel that I am not likely to write better than I have done . . ."

Now we must go back a little. As of the fertile mediocrity into which Lewis descended after *The Monk*, we may seem to have had only too much explanation for what hardly needs explanation at all. But it will be observed that neither was his head turned by fame, nor was he crushed by notoriety; the talent of his mediocrity itself remained vivid; and Lewis was formidable for two things not yet discussed: his verse, and a final celebrated book as different as possible from his first. With timidity, adaptation, and shallowness, ease, an awkward mid-ground always between the amateur and the professional, want of aesthetic, our explanation is still incomplete.

There was a frustration deepening to paralysis. His hopeless passion for Argyle's youngest daughter (who, marrying first in 1796, produced nine children, then, as Lady Charlotte Bury, nine fashionable novels, the *Diary of a Lady-in-Waiting*, and a cookbook) was probably invented by Mrs Baron-Wilson. He may have had by somebody a daughter who perhaps, long afterward, as Mary G. Lewis, herself published verse and novels. But Lewis was, like William Beckford, homosexual, though unlike Beckford he never married and escaped public disgrace, and in this role, as with each of his parents, he was tortured, his favourite (William Kelly, son of an indigent lady novelist, fourteen when they met in 1802) proving wild and unfaithful in a degree for which other intrigues seem to have given him scant consolation. The sensibility upon which these problems scraped was extreme. The student of Lewis's life almost believes him when he remarks to his mother, during the protracted agony over his father's mistress, "I am so constituted, that I believe I never felt a painful sensation which I could afterwards efface from my memory, however strongly I may have wished to do so." He learned to congratulate himself upon avoidance or mitigation of anguish. Some of his reflections during his father's illness, but before the reconciliation, which all but killed him, are among the most melancholy ever set down: "as it is now above nine years [he writes] since I have had any intercourse with him that carried with it any kindness, his loss will alter none of the habits of my life; I shall have but few remembrances of his affection; I shall not miss his place at the table, nor the morning welcome, nor the affectionate good-night." Before his second journey to Jamaica, he scrawled an agitated command to his London agent that should anything happen in his absence to his mother—with whom, since his father's death, his relations had been even closer—he should "on *no* account" be informed. Yet this was after he had brought his life under final, stoical control. From the earliest years onward, one receives a persistent sense of a wounded personality.

The loss to poetry was not less, probably, than the loss to the novel. A poet who was praised by Coleridge—who was the poet of Shelley's youth—of whom Scott said, in maturity, that "he had the finest ear for the rhythm of verse I ever met with—finer than Byron's"—ought to have imposed himself. Lewis was, in fact, extremely promising as a poet and all his life retained an unusual power of metrical expression. He was perhaps, poetically, as accomplished a writer as one can be, short of overwhelming achievement. But there was a facility that often makes him sound like Auden—

> Beauty, does nature's hand bestow it?
> It swells your pride, and plain you show it;
> Though wealthy cit, and airy poet
> Your charms pursue,
> Church—physic—law—you're fair; you know it,
> You'll none, not you!

besides a failure of either steady poetic aim or the disconcerting personal intensity that makes poets "immortal"; instead, he wrote a large proportion of the most popular ballads of his time. None of what has survived surpasses the poems scattered through his first and his last books. "Alonzo the Brave and Fair Imogine" (in Chapter IX) is his most famous piece; but one in his last book, singled out by Coleridge, is his finest poem, "The Hours." This I must quote.

> Ne'er were the zephyrs known disclosing
>   More sweets, than when in Tempe's shades
> They waved the lilies, where, reposing,
>   Sat four and twenty lovely maids.

> Those lovely maids were called "the Hours,"
>   The charge of Virtue's flock they kept;
> And each in turn employ'd her powers
>   To guard it, while her sisters slept.

False Love, how simple souls thou cheatest!
　In myrtle bower, that traitor near
Long watched an Hour, the softest, sweetest!
　The *evening* Hour, to shepherds dear.

In tones so bland he praised her beauty,
　Such melting airs his pipe could play,
The thoughtless Hour forgot her duty,
　And fled in Love's embrace away.

Meanwhile the fold was left unguarded—
　The wolf broke in—the lambs were slain:
And now from Virtue's train discarded,
　With tears her sisters speak their pain.

Time flies, and still they weep; for never
　The fugitive can time restore:
An Hour once fled, has fled for ever,
　And all the rest shall smile no more!

The ear is certainly exquisite, and the pathos of loss communicated in the first lines of the last stanza so deep that this poem written at sea on his first journey to Jamaica, in 1815, would be worth keeping if he had composed nothing else.

On his father's death in 1812 Lewis inherited a large fortune and increased his benevolences, but did not change his style of living—a cottage at Barnes, rooms in the Albany. He was free from the insistent passion for a visibly picturesque that created Strawberry Hill, Fonthill Abbey, Abbotsford. He "did much good by stealth," said Scott, "and was a most generous creature." He was "pestilently prolix and paradoxical and *personal*," said Byron, who was fond of him and whom Lewis advised as he did Scott—"a good man, a clever man, but a bore, one may say, a damned bore." Worrying over the condition of the slaves on his West Indian estates under their overseers, he undertook presently the exhausting, hazardous voyage to Jamaica and was there during the first months of 1816, refusing all social life, doing everything in his power to improve and secure their safety and happiness. He kept a journal during this visit and during his last one, the following year, which was published after his death as *Journal of a West India Proprietor*. This attractive, sensible, humane, and witty book Coleridge praised very highly, and rightly. It was last reprinted in America in 1929. It is almost the work of a new man; Lewis had made his peace with life. "Our captain," he wrote on the first voyage out, "is quite out of patience with the tortoise pace of our progress; for my part I care very little about it . . . whether we have sailed slowly or rapidly, when a day is once over, I am just as much nearer advanced towards 'that bourne,' to reach which, peaceably and harmlessly, is the only business of life, and towards which the whole of our existence forms but one continued journey." But he avoided England, leaving it quickly after his return, to trade ghost stories with Byron and Shelley at the Villa Diodati, passing some months in Italy near a sister, and returning to Jamaica. On the voyage back he had yellow fever, and died after terrible suffering (14 May 1817), and was buried at sea. The weights slipped, and the coffin danced off behind the ship toward Jamaica.

Lewis's work, good and bad, exerted a considerable influence over the writing of several countries during the first half of the century. Even his verse has a monument in that graveyard, literary history, as the good Saintsbury testified. "Both by precept and example," Saintsbury writes in the *History of English Prosody*, "he was, at an early date, and long before the great work of the great school appeared, the champion, both of exact versification in a good sense, and of widened and strengthened versification as well . . . It is quite certain that ["Alonzo the Brave and Fair Imogine"] showed the way to something like a new use of the anapæst; that Lewis was a perfect master of easy metre years before Moore and decades before Praed and Barham; and that, in his time and place, he was really important prosodically."

As for his prose, and particularly *The Monk*, its influence is visible in Mrs Radcliffe's *The Italian*, Maturin, and a host of mediocrities like Charlotte Dacre, but touched also Scott, Shelley, even Wordsworth, Southey, Landor, and reached abroad to Hoffmann, Scribe, Hugo, Sue. The elements of this influence—the haunted castle, the criminal monk, suspense and terror, incest and eroticism, the Wandering Jew—have been duly catalogued by Railo and others. The conception of the Byronic hero owed something, certainly, to Lewis's synthesis. Probably Railo has not gone too far in extending the supernatural influence to Poe and *The Marble Faun*.

But with the mention of Poe, it is clear that Lewis's real importance in the extraordinary pageant of the novel in English is symbolic. He helped to recover poetry—I say recover, because the Elizabethan novel was poetic. The school in which he labored deserved Miss Austen's ridicule, but Lewis did not. Most of our critical admiration (just now) is devoted to her line, the prose line, but there is another line, and Lewis reopened it. Perhaps, in a more concrete way, too, he helped the century to two of its greatest masterpieces in the other line. Of Emily Brontë's reading not much is known, but Mrs Gaskell gives us one glimpse of her making bread in the kitchen with a German book open before her, standing against the edge of the kneading trough, and it is almost certain that she knew Hoffmann, who had learned from Lewis and whose "Die Majorat" her plot resembles. And it was his reading of *Wuthering Heights* that exploded Hawthorne's spirit for *The Scarlet Letter*. Little enough of the criminal monk survives in the Rev. Arthur Dimmesdale, but something, though, and in his hypocritical physician (oddly) more. To have played a part in the long, strange process that made possible these works is Lewis's honourable final claim.

What essentially distinguishes these greater novels from *The Monk*—wherein their immense superiority consists—is a nice question. Decidedly, it is not style. Emily Brontë and Hawthorne wrote better than Lewis did. Emily Brontë, I think, wrote better than she is usually supposed to have done, and Hawthorne less well. "Their voices came down, afar and indistinctly, from the upper heights where they habitually dwelt. Not improbably, it was to this latter class of men that Mr Dimmesdale, by many of his traits of character, naturally belonged." When we read this, we see where part of Henry James's style came from, but we also see a wonderful author in one of his frequent naps. "He told his wife the same story, and she seemed to believe him: but one night, while leaning on his shoulder in the act of saying she thought she should be able to get up to-morrow, a fit of coughing took her—a very slight one—he raised her in his arms; she put her two hands about his neck, her face changed, and she was dead." Writing can hardly be better than this, and *The Monk* of course never comes near it, but that is not the difference. Nor does the difference consist in a "perfection" or consistency of execution. To tell the truth, if you have not read *Wuthering Heights* lately (but that would be a pity), what you remember as the book is only the first half of the book, and even so Mr Lockwood is a notorious bore. As for Hawthorne's echolalic allegorizing, no sensible reader has ever pretended that there is not much too much of it. Lewis's uncertainty and unevenness do not register his place. The difference is one of weight, size, drive of conception. We really cannot say much about what deeply matters in stories, novels. They had stronger minds than

Lewis, tougher hearts, a superior intuition of necessity—the "dark necessity" invoked by Chillingworth when he refuses to pardon. Lewis had this intuition, too, but in a form less terrifying and affecting; but then he had it.

1952

The Freedom of the Don

DANTESCA, SHAKESPEAREAN, CERVANTINA—THE WORDS point to worlds. The poet of the *Iliad* once seemed to men to have handled everything, but clearly neither he nor the poet of the *Mahā-bhārata* can for us lay claim to the universality of the representation indicated in our three overwhelming epithets. The world of Job is condensed and vertical. Even the world of Tolstoy, comparatively to these three, lacks overtone; I mean the world of *Anna Karenina, War and Peace, Master and Man, The Death of Ivan Ilyich*, where nothing corresponds to the comic and disastrous overworld of the *Iliad*, the cosmic arrangements of the *Commedia* and the *Mahābhārata*, the supernatural dimension in Shakespeare—or the what in *Don Quixote?* But that will be our subject in the pages that follow. The Fourth Gospel ought probably to have been considered here, if it were not so hard to assess the artistic merit of works purely doctrinal.

Universality, I would observe, makes small claim on our admiration these days. Authors high in modern favour, like Henry James, Kafka, Jane Austen—I do not know who is higher in favour than these, by the way—are extremely special, and of course this is what we value them for. Emma with her plans, the intensely unsatisfactory but miserable Joseph K., Densher with his problems, seem to meet perfectly our sense of things. I think anyone who has read the whole of *Don Quixote* (in the one translation into English in which it can be read, J. M. Cohen's*) will agree that the works of these fascinating

---

* Putnam's is admired; compare, at the brutal climax of the Tale of Foolish Curiosity, I, xxxiv, for "*Rindióse Camila; Camila se rindió*," Cohen's "Camilla gave in; she gave in" with Putnam's fatuous "Camilla surrendered, yes, Camilla fell." I hope this example will serve to discredit Putnam forever. On the other hand, it is unfortunate that Cohen decided to give *no* notes; later in the same chapter one is sharply needed on "your captor . . . not only possesses the four S's"—put by Lope de Vega (I pretend to no learning: I am using the matchless 2,000-page variorum Fourth Centenary edition published at Madrid by Ediciones Castilla, with Clemencin's magistral commentary—I wish there were such an edi-

authors fit elegantly or agonized into a corner of it; yet I have been reading the literary magazines—*The Dial, Hound & Horn, Symposium, The Southern Review, Partisan, Kenyon, Hudson,* and the rest—for half a lifetime without ever coming on a piece about Cervantes. Perhaps nothing more needs to be said about him or his work? No one would say so of Shakespeare or Dante—with Auerbach's essay "Figura" and Armstrong's *Shakespeare's Imagination* before us. Writers at this level are inexhaustible; agreed. But is Cervantes really at this level? Is there not a rude drop from "Dantesca, Shakespearean" to "Cervantina"? And to what extent can we call Cervantes universal? For Spain, yes; a place violently unreal, between Europe and Africa. Dante did not speak for Italy—there was no Italy. Shakespeare with his Romans and Britons, and Greeks even, did not speak only for England; many of his glories pretend to be Italian. Moreover, they deployed, these two, hundreds of individuals, whilst Cervantes is concerned with, truly, at most two.

Suppose we begin to try to get at the questions so far posed by considering one Shakespearean character and one Dantesque.

Parolles, in Act IV of *All's Well That Ends Well,* is taken captive by troops of his own side, blindfolded, foxed with nonsense language, and invited to spill his guts, which he immediately does: about the secrets of the army and the characters of his superiors, who are listening. He is unmuffled then, discredited as scarcely any other literary personage has been, and left alone, with "I am for France too; we shall speak of you there." He should be speechless, he should kill himself, the earth should open and swallow him. No.

> Yet am I thankful: if my heart were great,
> 'Twould burst at this. Captain I'll be no more;
> But I will eat and drink, and sleep as soft
> As captain shall: simply the thing I am
> Shall make me live.

Toward the close of the brawling, savage fifth canto of the *Purgatorio,* paralleling Francesca in Canto V of the *Inferno,* a new voice speaks, without introduction:

> "Deh, quando tu sarai tornato al mondo,
>   e riposato della lunga via,"
> —seguitó il terzo spirito al secondo,

---

tion of any English book—but what English book deserves it?) as "*solicito, sabio, secreto, y solo.*"

"ricorditi di me, che son la Pia;
Siena mi fe', disfecemi Maremma:
salsi colui ch' innanellata, pria

disposando, m'avea con la sua gemma."

(Pray, when thou shalt return to the world, and art rested from thy
long journey,—followed the third spirit after the second,—remember
me, who am La Pia; Siena made me, the Maremma unmade me: as he
knows, who, first plighting troth, had wedded me with his own ring.)
—Okey's version, altered.

The lightest sound in the world, "Deh," "Please . . ." Solicitude.
(The damned have cared only for themselves.) A succession of tiny
vowels, in the self-identification. The terrible line of her beginning
and her end (her husband, wanting either her fortune or to marry
someone else, apparently immured her in the Roman marshes where,
malarial, she died) that has been imitated in English poetry from the
Earl of Surrey to Pound and Eliot. Then a piece of syntax as involved
as the emotions are complex. Being *to be saved*, she cannot lie, she
must acknowledge the truth of her murder, but she pushes *back*
through that horror to the twin supreme moments of her trust and
happiness, the betrothal and wedding; we are out of Hell.

Now it will hardly be denied by the candid reader that Don
Quixote—never mind Sancho Panza yet—does not come to us, is not
given to us, with the incandescent contestless *reality* of Parolles and
La Pia.

To them there are no alternatives. They are, were, and will be
Parolles and La Pia. With the Don the situation is rather different.
We do not know, and carefully never learn, exactly who he is, even.
Cervantes's first joke is on his first page: "Our gentleman was verging
on fifty, of tough constitution, lean-bodied, thin-faced, a great early
riser and a lover of hunting. They say that his surname was Quixada
or Quesada—for there is some difference of opinion amongst authors
on this point. [The reader begins, here, to feel weak.] However, by
very reasonable conjecture we may take it that he was called
Quexana. [The reader snorts with dismay.] But this does not much
concern our story [the reader does I do not know what]; enough
that we do not depart by so much as an inch from the truth in telling
it." This cool reprise on the opening sentence ("In a certain village in
La Mancha, which I do not wish to name"), with its elaborate and
indifferent insolence to the chapter head (". . . del famoso hidalgo
Don Quixote . . ."), puts the reader rather on his own. Toward the

146

end of the chapter, after the signal ordeal of the naming of Rocinante
(a minor riot: "rocin" is one of a large number of Spanish attacks on
degrees of inferior horseflesh—put with "ante" it means "He used to
be a hack before his new dignity" and "The first and foremost of all
the hacks in the world"), which has taken four days, "he next decided to do the same for himself, and spent another eight days thinking about it. Finally he decided to call himself Don Quixote. And that
is no doubt why the authors of this true history, as we have said,
assumed that his name must have been Quixada and not Quesada, as
other authorities would have it." In Chapter 5 he is *called* "Master
Quixada," and there the mystery is left. *For his mission,* he—or somebody—assumes a nonexistent identity.

The end, dreaded by the reader, of this great work spares him
after all. Don Quixote does not die. How could he? "When the priest
saw that he was no more he desired the clerk to draw up a certificate
that Alonso Quixano the Good, commonly called Don Quixote de la
Mancha, had passed out of this present life and died a natural death
. . ."

This clowning, even here at the end of Part II, is wholly serious.
There is a repudiation of the creature inconceivable as by Dante or
Shakespeare of Parolles or La Pia. I conclude that Don Quixote does
not exist, and never did.

That there *is* no such person we may take to constitute our first
insight, and what I mean by this will be clear later on. It is the *role*
that is real—a role, above all, aesthetic and theological; whereas in
Dante and Shakespeare it is the persons who are real, all else subsidiary though important. I want to approach the role first rather
through Talk than through Adventures.

But it will be as well at this point to mention some of the vast
and standard Cervantine topics that I plan to ignore entirely, in order
to hope to get something said critically. I am ignoring, then, the
fascinating life of this great man, whose elaborate life-failure (mutilated as a soldier, enslaved, repeatedly caught in attempts to escape, a
hack writer, a discredited and repeatedly imprisoned minor official,
pleader for New World posts—four at least—which he never got,
father of a bastard daughter whose fortunes engaged him to the end,
miserably married, sonless, poverty-stricken always, despised even by
the risen sun Lope de Vega, neglected by his patrons—proud, honest,
heroic, modest, gay) is unmistakably reflected in the Don's failures;
critics are almost unanimous in seeing Cervantes as one of the most
personal of writers—as far beyond Dante to one side as the Shake-

speare of the plays, and Homer beyond him, are distant from them on the other side. (If my reader, by the way, is familiar with the eight topics I glance at here, I apologize; but I wonder whether he is; I would agree with the latest English study—Aubrey F. G. Bell's *Cervantes*, 1947—that this author is by English-language readers "more often praised than read" and that "Those who read the whole of *Don Quixote* are comparatively few"; the enormous libraries of commentary are certainly a closed book to most Americans, even most Americans of cultivation.) Secondly, the waning of Spain's imperial glory—its overreaching—is plainly figured in the novel, and I say nothing of this level of significance (Part I in 1605 came seventeen years, a very long time, after the ruin of the Armada). Nor are we going to be concerned with the embodiment of the Counter Reformation in the work, which is said to be that huge movement's literary masterpiece, and is. I ignore, fourthly, the literary-historical aspect of *Don Quixote:* its status as satire, a very ambivalent one, I would remark, of chivalric romances; this brings it into relation with the pastoral satire *As You Like It,* very closely contemporary (1600? though that adorable play, as we have it in the Folio, is almost certainly a rehandling of the mysterious *Loues Labour's Wonne* of perhaps 1593—F. N. Lee's argument in *The Times Literary Supplement* several years ago was conclusive), and has great interest in itself, but not for us. And fifthly, I say nothing of the Shakespearean connection generally (the best study of which is still Fitzmaurice-Kelly's, 1916, and the best known, Turgenev's on the Don and Hamlet), except to notice that the fantastic coincidence of their deaths on the same *day* (though not the same date, owing to national lag in calendar revision), in Stratford and Madrid, is meaningless, like so many other coincidences; Shakespeare, after his retirement, read Cervantes's Part I, and based a lost play, *Cardenio,* on one of its tales, but since his knowledge must have been only of Shelton's grotesque translation (1612) and the play is lost, we can make nothing of this. The empty coincidence, though, of the two best minds of Europe sinking away in a day, reminds one of another such: the deaths on a day, and that day the fiftieth anniversary of the birth of the nation of which they were the surviving architects, of Thomas Jefferson and John Adams. God amuses himself. Then man amuses himself: both the facts have been forgotten. Both the Don and Prospero are moral and social reformers, and both have resort to magic (it is the Don's enemy, Prospero's recourse); an absorbing study could be directed here, on the doorstep of Descartes. Sixthly, we can spare no pages to the celebrated bifurcation of the mysterious Spanish spirit (if anyone is interested in this spirit, I can recommend wholeheartedly Américo Castro's *The Structure of Spanish History* and the British critic V. S. Pritchett's *The Spanish Temper*) in the master and servant—the Don ideal, alacritive, imperious, Sancho Panza earthy, lazy, obedient; *Don Quixote* used to be recommended as a traveller's companion for Spain, or prologue to travel; now that travel is so easy, a few months in Spain might be recommended as a prologue to *Don Quixote*. Spanish temperament, whether in Toledo or Madrid or Salamanca, or (if these are Spanish) Barcelona and Seville, is better experienced than described, though Pritchett has made a cunning, Castro a noble, attempt. I may note, though, that notwithstanding the largeness of the work, it exactly, as the Spanish epic, confutes the national prolixity, being almost unbelievably concise. (So is the poetry of Lorca and the poetry of St. John of the Cross: I can think of no other Spanish master who does not suffer from diffuseness, even Lope and Jiménez.)

Not that, seventhly, we can undertake the study of the work as an epic. Tillyard* puts the considered view as well as anyone when he accuses the work as a whole—while recognizing its "true epic range and a superb quality of prose style" and praising especially the "weight and density" of the first quarter of Part II—of being "governed by no powerful predetermination," of being non-"strategic," improvisatorial. I think critics have made too much of this matter of the Don's casual beginning. He only comes to life, they say, when Sancho joins him. But this is quite wrong, for already at the burning of the books (I, 7) he is being dealt with in a truly Shakespearean (that is, *inward*) way: the priest and barber "wall up and close the room where he had kept his books . . . they might say that an enchanter had carried them off, room and all"; then comes an amazing passage: "This was quickly done, and when two days later Don Quixote got up, the first thing he did was to go and look for his books; and when he failed to find the room where he had left them he went all over the house searching for it. Finally he went to the place where the door used to be, and felt for it with his hands, and ran his eyes over everything again and again, without saying a word." The double remove, here, from reality, and his unexpressed grief, and wonderment, bring the moment fully, I would say, within epic requirements; it seems to me respectably comparable with the tearful rapprochement, ironic as it is, of Achilles and Priam. In short, it seems to me that the speed and inworking and theme, from the beginning, show the hand and full attention of the immortal master of

* *The English Epic and Its Background*, 1954.

narrative. Whether, as I was saying, the mastery is *epic*—and it may be observed that Tillyard's thoughtful, wide-ranging book neglects all mention of both the Hindu epics, and *Gilgamesh,* and *Popul-voh*—cannot here be considered. Nor, finally, are we concerned with the obvious "lesson" of the work—"directed" (as Bell puts it) "not against those who leap but against those who do not look before they leap, those who prefer theory to practical experience"—although it will be impossible to ignore the massive instruction to humility. This word occurs again and again in Cervantist criticism, with reason, and we may use it as a lever for Sancho's story about the goats.

Two passages in "The Colloquy of the Dogs" will serve to impose it. "As you well know," Berganza barks, "humility is the basis of all the virtues, which cannot exist without it," and Cipión: "human decency, Catholic doctrine, an extraordinary wisdom, and, lastly, a profound humility that is the basis upon which the entire edifice of a holy life is reared" (Putnam's version of *Three Exemplary Novels,* 1952). If any virtue is more "basic" in Cervantes's thought, it has yet to be discovered.

Sancho's crazy tale may seem to have little to do with it. Immobile in a meadow in blackness, you remember, horrified by the roar of waters and "a sort of clanking of iron and chains" (I, 20), the two suffer the Tremendous Exploit of the fulling mills. Sancho offers to divert his master with a story, and relates a brainless, extravagant, contradictory, and above all self-interrupted nonsense about a goatherd or "shepherd" who first loves a shepherdess and then doesn't, and who in escaping across a river into Portugal has to rely on a fisherman whose little boat will carry only one man and one goat. There are three hundred goats.

> "The fisherman got into the boat and took one goat over, came back and fetched another, and came back once more and took another. Keep an account of the goats which the fisherman is taking over, your honour, for if you lose count of one the story will end, and it won't be possible for me to tell you another word of it. I'll continue now and mention that the landing-place on the other side was very muddy and slippery, which delayed the fisherman a good deal in his journeys backwards and forwards. But, all the same, he came back for another goat, and another, and another."

> "Take it that they are all across," said Don Quixote, "and do not go on coming and going like that, or you will never get them all over in a year."

> "How many have got over so far?" asked Sancho.

"How the devil should I know?" replied Don Quixote.

"There now, didn't I tell you to keep a good count? Well, there's an end of the story. God knows there's no going on with it now."

"How can that be?" replied Don Quixote. "Is it so essential to the tale to know exactly how many goats have crossed that if you are one out in the number you cannot go on?"

"No, sir, not at all," answered Sancho. "But, when I asked your worship to tell me how many goats had got across and you replied that you didn't know, at that very moment everything I had left to say went clean out of my head, though there were some good and amusing things coming, I promise you."

The rest of this dialogue is equally delicious, but there is enough here for our purpose.

The fundamental subject is *submission to the artist*. There is a contract: he will do his part *if* the auditor does his, and only if; an imaginative collaboration then has its effect, and the auditor will be delighted. The Don does not understand this at all. With characteristic pedantry he thinks he is being penalized (in not hearing the rest of the story—the attack involved here is on the theory of the arrogance of the artist) for not knowing the exact number; whereas it was his insolent indifference to the whole matter that dried up the well of Sancho's invention. (That the story was an ancient one, Oriental, is immaterial.) We generalize then further that without a responsive and responsible audience the artist cannot create. A mere piece of outrageous drollery is very deep. I would like to gloss this a little more.

I once went to see a Chaplin film that I had missed in its first run—*Modern Times*—at a small cinema on Third Avenue (as it then was) in New York that apparently never closes, in the morning. Perhaps three other people were there, and the film seemed to me an almost hopeless failure. I was so puzzled by this experience that I went later to see it again, when the auditorium happened to be full. I found it marvellous, and understood that one laughs very differently alone from the way one does in a crowd; and that *while* crowd-laughing one can neither hear nor even see; and that Chaplin's genius allowed for this, so that on my desolate morning I was both hearing and seeing things I was not supposed to. The timing—Mozart once in a letter complains of a pupil that she cannot understand the thing *most necessary* in music, time—had been put wrong by me, the audience.

My other gloss is philosophical. The Buddha was approached by a Brahmin bearing gifts in both hands. He said to the Brahmin, "Drop it!" and the Brahmin let fall the gift in his right hand. He came nearer. "Drop it!" said the Enlightened One, and the Brahmin let fall the gift in his left hand. He came closer, with empty hands. "Drop it!" the Buddha advised, and the Brahmin understood.

SLAPSTICK AND THE SUPERNATURAL

The Buddha's point was the abolition-of-self, a central tenet in Buddhism, which would let the Brahmin understand that, even after abandoning his gifts, the self-personality that imagined the gifts and procured them, as from one self (his) to another's (the Buddha's), survived. The Christian counterpart is humility. The reader must be humble, as the author is. We are now in a position to say something of the mystery that began the last section of this essay: Who is humble? *No one.* The role is not filled. But the explanation is so far only aesthetic. We must look at the Adventures.

That they *are* adventures, and numerous, unforeseeable, is one of their glories. Hamlet has no adventures, nor sullen Achilles, and Dante's are formal, bound in an ordained frame. It is Sherlock Holmes who has adventures—the cases are called so: we do not know what will happen, except that Holmes will win (not always, exactly) and the Don will lose (only not always—but the winning, as with Andrew, at first proves sometimes highly ambiguous). We are free of a grand scheme. But are we free of *meaning*, as in Conan Doyle's stories? I am very doubtful about this, and I think any study we may go in for of the Adventures can pretend successfully to a different footing from the New Criticism reading-into superfluity of explanation to which I object as strongly as the reader can. Cervantes was a moralist. In the prologue to the *Exemplary Novels*, he says: "There is not one of them that does not afford a useful example. If it were not that I do not wish to expand upon this subject, I could show you the savory and wholesome fruit that is to be had from each of them separately and from the collection as a whole" (Putnam's translation, *op. cit.*, p. 5).

Let's start with the Windmills.

It might be asserted that this is the most famous adventure in literature (I, 8)—for what reason it is hard, offhand, to say. The Don sees thirty or forty windmills, thinks them giants (an error less remarkable than one might suppose, windmills in this province being far shorter than our image of windmills), attacks them, and is sent "rolling badly injured across the plain" (Cohen's translation, 1950, p.

69—from now on, unattributed page numbers are to this translated edition). The whole thing takes a page and a half. How has it seized the imagination of the world?

I do not know, unless mere absurdity will explain the seizure,— but world literature is full of absurdities; and I would hardly dare, without the *Exemplary Novels* prologue text, and my general experience of literature of the first rank, to presume that an explanation is *necessary*. As it is, I suppose Cervantes has something in mind.

Windmills grind wheat, from which is made bread.

It is that simple, I think. The Knight, committed to the Christian ideal ("Man shall not live by bread alone") and as usual *overreaching* it, attacks the means of ordinary—that is, un-Christian—life, and suffers accordingly. I hope, if this explanation seems phantastic, that it may be helped by a cry of the Don's niece in the preceding chapter (p. 65): "Wouldn't it be better to stay peacefully at home, and not roam about the world seeking better bread than is made of wheat . . . ?" Don Quixote seeks the better bread and is therefore inevitably the enemy of the lesser or apparent bread. If there is a more unrewarding task than explaining jokes and allegory, I do not know what it is. Of course, the fact that it *has* to be explained is part of the *aesthetic* point: the reader must cooperate, in order to reach the exemplary and theological. And the more work we can persuade the reader to do, the better. And if the man laughing over the windmills refuses to pass on to Matthew 4:4, so much the worse for him. He won't hear the story.

I pass on to the sheep armies (I, 18) he attacks. *Men* are sheep; to be led, not attacked—"Feed my sheep." But men are *sheep*, dopes, and in that character requiring attack by an idealist. The Christian and the realistic post-Reformation reformer merge. The aged anti-militarist, too. Rachel Bespaloff contends that in Tolstoy and Homer (the poet of the *Iliad*, she means) alone are combined "a virile love of war and a horror of it," and she has left out Cervantes.

I put him in. Her book, though, on "Homer," has more to say to Cervantes's final works—particularly with Hermann Broch's initiatory comment—than many technically devoted works. This is a very strange author. He needs comment, which he seldom gets, from outside.

The Adventure of the Wine-skins. Maybe this is the second of the most famous of these ridiculous adventures. He is asleep, the Don, dreaming of a battle with a giant. Then he shocks the wine-skins, and is in trouble all over. He is said by the author to be "the architect of his own dishonour" (p. 320). I doubt that we would understand his problem. He spills blood all over. But this blood has already been explained: "What this fellow takes for blood must be the wine spilt on the floor." We seem to be dealing with an *anti*-sacrament. The transubstantiation that the Don believes in has *not* taken place. He is deluded, and his vocation false.

The role, the vocation, exists—unfulfilled. True virtue is dead, and what we confront instead is a mad impostor. The fact that he happens to be adorable is irrelevant to the theology.

SANCHO'S PROVERBS

The mission of the Ideal is not unaccompanied, as we know. Crazy, but methodical, learned (even pedantic—"that is, if I decide to imitate Roland in my penance rather than Amadis," I, 25, p. 205), ceremonious, the Don has with him a walking Tilley, or Tilley on a mule.

Two further meanings of the Adventure of the Wine-skins would run: (theological) I hope! I am a priest; (practical) man must be sober, so I destroy the wine. Sancho has, at the outset anyway, no such illusions. He is firmly based in a family, about which he worries, and he wants money. He seems real. He is devoted but self-seeking; fatalistic (like a Spaniard) but opportunistic; skeptical (as against his master's mad trust) but hopeful (for his Island).

He seems real, apart from the interaction that genuinely occurs in all intimate life associations—husbands and wives come to resemble each other; Thomas Hardy's second wife's handwriting could not be distinguished from his by his closest friends—and is in this novel better represented than anywhere else in literature: the Don displays cunning, Sancho gets wilder than his master. Credulity and incredulity trade faces, roles.

What makes me wonder whether the servant is more real than the master is his role. The role can be described very simply as folk wisdom. He spouts proverbs, proverbs issue from him at all times of the day and night, he drives both the Don and their reader mad with proverbs. The German term for this, "*Sprichwörtermanie*," is better than any we can invent: proverb-madness? He is a *spokesman*, that is to say, as the Don is a spokesman (but acting it out) for the Ideal. The Christian imagination has set the Christian Hope against the reluctant and imperfect Folk, and made them cooperate—toward failure, blows, agony.

Morris Tilley in his great work (*A Dictionary of the Proverbs in England in the Sixteenth and Seventeenth Centuries*, 1950) shows better than anyone else has ever done the part played by proverbs in the Shakespearean achievement. But even he, who knew more than any other man ever will about the dramatist's use of proverbs, nowhere isolates a character as particularly addicted (my own guess would be that on count no one would surpass Iago, the *application* of the proverbs being almost always ironic). He does, however, notice characters in special situations as stringing together proverbs in somewhat the way Sancho does: John of Gaunt, dying; in *Richard II*, ii. 1., the proverbs here being used for authority; Friar Lawrence in *Romeo*, ii. 6.; Polonius of course to Laertes in *Hamlet*, i. 3.; and Tilley contrasts the real authority of Gaunt with the fatuous authority of the others, proverbs serving in each case as the vehicle.

Perhaps we get here an insight as sharp as we could desire into the double function of Sancho's proverbism: he is *asinine* and *wise*. In both aspects, I observe, there is a correspondence to the Don—who also is theoretical and formular (the folk wisdom, folk solutions, folk warnings corresponding to the chivalric romances), and who also is wise with inherited wisdom.

The inherited or innate wisdom emerges largely, for Sancho, in his governorship (II, 45–53). This is governed, by the way, by the proverb matter, which, having hung fire as an overt topic for some seven hundred pages, boils to the surface in the chapters of the Don's advice to the squire on his coming responsibilities. The Don is here shooting forth proverbs himself as bad as Sancho, yet he is scrupulous to warn:

"Also, Sancho, you must not interlard your conversation with the great number of proverbs you usually do; for though proverbs are maxims in brief, you often drag them in by the hair [this is a proverb, of course], and they seem more like nonsense."

"Let God look after that," answered Sancho, "for I know more proverbs than a book, and so many of them come all together into my mouth when I speak that they fight one another to get out . . . But from now on I'll take care to bring in only those that suit the gravity of my office. For in a well-cooked house the supper is soon cooked; and a good bargain doesn't hold up the business; and the man who sounds the alarm is safe; and giving and taking need some sense."

The serene and delirious irrelevance of Sancho's wisdom is nowhere vivider.

"Go on, Sancho," said Don Quixote. "Cram them in, thread and string your proverbs together; no one will stop you. My mother scolds me and I whip the top. [This must be the same proverb as Tilley T439,

155

first recorded in the Fletcherian part of *The Two Noble Kinsmen* (1613), v. 2. 49.] I tell you to refrain from proverbs, and in one moment you have brought out a whole litany of them . . ."

As usual, the apparent subject is not the real one: it is not the proverbs but the *in*application of them; as it is not the Don's energy, courage, goodness, but his maladministration, or overapplication, of these admirable qualities. Notice the word "litany" for Sancho's theology. The aristocracy—in the novel's pretense—has its highfalutin', and useless (Don Quixote practically never does any actual good and often does positive harm, in loosing the galley slaves, in "saving" Andrew), or even dangerous, understanding of Christianity; the people have their monotonous, shrewd, thieving prayers. A reader who supposes, though, that we are engaged with a satire on religion is wide, wide of the mark (I have caught the proverb mania). The Don is a Catholic, and so crudely is Sancho, to prove that Europe held no other Catholics three or four generations after the Augsburg Confession; and their creator died as a Franciscan Tertiary. Shakespeare is said, much later, to have "dyed a Papist"—his father's old religion. Cervantes was one.

So Sancho goes off to rule his island.

We notice at once the parody of Spanish world administration and, inversely, of what Gerald Brenan, in *The Face of Spain*, morosely describes as the "incurious, melancholy, Iberian way" (p. 189). The squire had taken on the knight's powers and initiative. One can hardly wait.

But one has doubts, though. The first genuine appeal the Don ever received (p. 400—a careful study of p. 47, on Andrew, will reveal the truth that he received there no appeal) is refused by him, on two legal grounds—though he continues then as a peacemaker. How will Sancho make out?

He is given brain-breaking cases and makes out beautifully. He is starved—all foods are dangerous—and tortured by an application of dolts, mostly spurious or instructed, until he cries out governors and judges should be made of brass! As his "tormentors assembled and planned together the means of making an end of his governorship," Sancho hands down decrees which last after him. "He decreed that no blind man should sing miracles in rhyme unless he could bring unquestionable evidence that they were true, as most of their tales were, in his opinion, fictitious and brought discredit upon the genuine ones." I have not ventured to italicize Cervantes, but I hope the last phrase is heard. The Christian world of miracles is real, and the

Reformation is untrue (though their attack on false miracles is just).

Sancho's apotheosis comes—everything in the story is indirect—not in his own adventure, but in the correspondence that Cervantes has with his love handed us between Sancho and the Don and Sancho's wife: "I received your letter, my beloved Sancho, and I swear to you as a Catholic Christian I was within an inch of going off my head with delight. Yes, indeed, when I learnt that you are a Governor I thought I should fall dead on the spot from pleasure; for they say that sudden gladness kills like a great grief, you know. [She has been inoculated, plainly.] And your daughter Sanchica wetted herself without noticing it, out of pure joy . . . Send me some strings of pearls, if they are in fashion in your isle . . . I await an answer to this and a decision about my going to Court; and with this, may God preserve you more years than me—or as many, for I should not like to leave you in this world without me." She still thinks him, that is to say, a hopeless fool, incapable of making out alone; but the dazzle-seizure of the husband's new honours has never been so well represented, and the coarseness which is regularly characteristic of this great author is illustrated well enough. That love—love—is also implied at the first level, and the third, at the end of the maniacal letter, is Cervantes's secret.

Sancho makes out better in his mission than the Don does in his; reality is preferable to appearance. But much better? "All right, let me be armed," he says (II, 53). ". . . Then they put a spear into his hand, and he had to lean on it to keep on his feet . . ." Later: "Make way, gentlemen, and let me return to my old freedom . . . I am a Panza, and we are all stubborn. If once we cry odds, odds it must be, even though it's evens, and in spite of all the world . . ."

All through the latter part of the book, one does not know (as if one had a choice) whether to laugh or cry, and does both. The servant, originally "free," undertakes service, where he suffers, and glory, where he suffers far more, and then is to be restored to his original nothingness, "in search of his master, whose company gave him more pleasure than the governorship of all the isles in the world" (II, 54).

Quest, let's call the subject. It was Hamlet's also, and Oedipus', and King Lear's for freedom from the responsibilities of power, and Dante's in the *Commedia*. Capaneus can declare *"Qual io fui vivo, tal son morto"* (What I was alive, am I still, dead); but the saved are different. What is the quest for?

Here we may pause to ask whether it matters what the quest is for. It is a very odd thing that, as of great works of art, it does not seem to signify what the subject or purpose is. Judaizing Galacians, chivalric nonsense—the author's power of mind, intensity of feeling, greatness of spirit, breadth of experience, depth of imagination, make or not the work. The irresolute ambition of a medieval Scots noble?—*Macbeth*. A magician stranded?—*The Tempest*. Man trying to get home?—*The Odyssey*. Whales? a Puritan adultery?

It does not seem to matter. But here it matters. For the object of this quest is freedom, and this is the topic not only of the *Epistle to the Galatians*, and the controversy between Luther and Erasmus (which Luther won because he made Erasmus—Erasmus—look like a window shopper) in the previous century, but of all art of which I have any knowledge. How is the Don's freedom arrived at, and in what does it consist?

Sancho seeks leadership—as Arlova, the Communist hero's mistress or (more important) secretary, once says to him in *Darkness at Noon*, "You can always do anything you like with me." These are the masses.

The Don provides it (freedom from inactivity—the proverbial Spanish vice). Then he suffers, in reverent parodies of the crucifixion, in vigils, in beatings. Throughout he *sees:* on p. 204 (of Cohen's translation) we understand at last: he is not taken in: he *sees what is* (what we see); but he also sees what is not—and it is in accord with the second that he acts,—and indeed isn't that what all Christians do? and all decent men? and everybody?

Then he is set free from that responsibility.

?1960

III

The World of Henry James

VOLUMINOUS, UNEVEN, FRIGHTENING TO THE ASPIRANT, this master calls more than most for simplification of counsel—a note on what to read, merely—which he seldom gets, and for my brevity in which I shall not apologize further. The indispensable fiction of Henry James is in *The American* and *The Portrait of a Lady*, of the early period; "The Liar," "The Aspern Papers," "The Pupil," some of the stories of the Artist, and *The Spoils of Poynton*, of the middle period; *The Ambassadors*, *The Wings of the Dove*, and all five stories in *The Finer Grain*, of the last period. There is a good deal of invaluable criticism in the *Hawthorne* and in essays—which want selecting and re-printing together—scattered through four other books; his critical prefaces to his selected works (collected ten years ago in *The Art of the Novel*) are best taken singly, with strict attention, with salt, each after the work to which it refers. The finest of the half dozen descriptive books is *The American Scene;* of the volumes of reminiscence, *Notes of a Son and Brother*. These are the works, therefore, which should be read first. They should be read (for pleasure as well as for understanding) in something like this order; no comment on James should be read until one is well along, and no accident of republication or advertising should be permitted to seduce one from this progressive experience of his major achievement. Certain of his other books are delightful or powerful in their ways, but they can wait. Many readers, indeed, will feel that they do not have so much time even as this to spend; and I shall not try to persuade them, except to say that, utterly as his world seems to have been clubbed down, he is the great novelist of our own time whose experience speaks most directly to us; the experience of others is nearer, but they have not his authority or size. There is another reason. The whole major work of James constitutes in a sense a procedure nearly as single and inevitably developing as one of his late productions: the gradual revelation of an unique subject— the Social Fate, with its initiations, loyalties, sacrifices, salvations, becoming the Personal Fate; and if this is to be experienced at all, it must be experienced at large and ought to be experienced in an order.

This will be advice hard to follow for most readers without access to large libraries. James's books have become increasingly difficult to buy in his native country; the New York Edition of the Novels (all but eight) and Tales (all but forty) never was adequate and now [1945] is out of print, like most of the single volumes. What is really wanted from the current James "revival," along with the misrepresentation and cant, is a cheap—volumes separately obtainable—full edition of his fiction, such as the British have long had in thirty-five volumes, but including, of the "dramatic" fiction there omitted, his horrifying novel *The Other House*. Short of this, F. O. Matthiessen's collection of stories* with the Artist for subject is a fair model of how the short fiction should be made available again. He prints eleven stories, in James's final text: one of the earliest good ones, "The Madonna of the Future"; "The Author of Beltraffio" and "The Lesson of the Master," two of the finest of the eighties; three short masterpieces, "The Real Thing," "The Death of the Lion," "The Next Time" (supremely good-natured and pathetic, this last, as the "Lion" is one of his most bitter); and three of special charm to Old Jamesians, "The Middle Years," "The Figure in the Carpet," and "The Story in It"; also "Greville Fane" and "Broken Wings," not dull but slighter. The only remarkable omission is the brilliant fable from *The Finer Grain* " 'The Velvet Glove,' " where Artist and Aristocrat confront each other for a last astonishing time. Other tales which could be placed in this category (notably—for readers who are curious—"The Liar," "The Coxon Fund," "The Private Life," "The Great Good Place") are excluded as being properly "psychological" or—the last two—"supernatural" tales. Matthiessen's introduction contains some matter that will be new to most readers, particularly on James's controversy with Wells, a type here of Journalism (what James elsewhere calls "the great new science of beating the sense out of words"). But the best critical study of this phase of his art is R. P. Blackmur's essay "In the Country of the Blue" (printed in the Henry James number of *The Kenyon Review*, Autumn 1943); and it is to this that readers should turn for generalization when they have read the stories.

With the so-called *Great Short Novels* we enter unhappily on a

* Henry James, *Stories of Writers and Artists*. Edited with an introduction by F. O. Matthiessen, 1944.

more characteristic form of the "revival." If Philip Rahv* had done his simple duty as an editor and printed these ten tales as James left them, we could have been grateful to him for a very useful volume, although we would have had certain reservations. Aside from the over-praised, inevitable "Daisy Miller," there is too much of the early "international" short fiction: "Madame de Mauves," "An International Episode," "The Siege of London," "Lady Barberina" (the first and last of these the best). The selection of the others is admirable: "Beltraffio" (the better version is in *Stories of Writers and Artists*), "The Aspern Papers," "The Pupil," "The Turn of the Screw," and "The Beast in the Jungle." All this work is misrepresented in the catchpenny title. Some of James's other *nouvelles*, far from "great," are yet better than some of these; and a *nouvelle* is not any sort of novel, but a "tale" more fully developed than the usual English short story. James even refers to "The Pupil" as one of "the considerable group of shorter, of shortest tales"; *Washington Square, The Sacred Fount*—these are short novels. It is also misrepresented by Rahv's revivalist assertion in his opening sentence that James "is now generally regarded by discriminating readers as America's greatest novelist"—which is in my experience certainly not true—and his talk, for example, about James's "exciting and original" plots, in spite of which his comments introductory to most of these tales carefully give them away. But Rahv has not done his duty. He has reprinted the tales in their original versions; and since New Directions, reprinting *The Spoils of Poynton* recently, also used the original version, a service of clarification is in order.

When James revised the novels and stories selected for the New York Edition (1908), the labour constituted for him a reseeing of his subjects as well as a correction of his style. It was performed at the height of his power, and the seriousness with which he viewed his achievement may be judged by his declaring, of a young man who had asked for advice, that if he did not somehow obtain access to the revised edition "he forfeits half, or much more than half, my confidence." It differed from work to work, being heaviest in the early stories and novels and decreasing as he approached recent work—"The Turn of the Screw" (1898) has only some hundreds of changes; but its general effect over the half dozen productions I have examined can be summarized. By way of *correction:* punctuation is halved, syntax tightened, repetition avoided, relatives omitted; names

* *The Great Short Novels of Henry James*. Edited with an introduction and comments by Philip Rahv, 1944.

disappear into pronouns or "his friend," "so special a subject"; "to be," "to have" strengthen into action verbs; everything feasible is colloquialized. By way of *reseeing:* general ("a fine texture") becomes particular ("the marks on a piece of fine porcelain"), vivacity is wooed ("pay her" becomes "fork out," "go away" becomes "cut sticks"), sensuous detail is added ("with long, vague faces," "in elegant ringing gold"); tone is appropriately heightened ("standards" to "desperate proprieties") and lowered ("a sharp spice" to "a small strain"); faults in probability are corrected; point-of-view is sharpened; characterizing images are introduced; gradations of judgment and awareness flower; pace is quickened and slowed; rarely, decided alteration occurs in emphasis, character, even action—large passages are omitted or replaced or added. No critic would find every change for the better. The late style of James does its work, sometimes well, sometimes badly—worst, unquestionably, on the earliest work in the New York Edition, where yet the gains are so formidable that I am doubtful whether a story exists of which the primitive coherence of the first version is really preferable to the richness of the later. If so, the original can be found in the libraries. An editor has no choice but to give work to the public in the author's final form. Rahv's excuse for not doing so, beyond a vague reference to "authorities on James," is archaeological: to let the reader "gain a direct impression of the development of James's style"—as if a public capable of interest in the development of James's style would not by the same token be much more interested in the finished products of his art. New Directions also refers to "James authorities"; but the truth is that most of the few writers on this subject have decided for the revision. *Henry James: The Major Phase** contains as an appendix an elaborate account of the effects of the revision of *The Portrait of a Lady*, which will be read best in connection with James's remarks in his prefaces to *Roderick Hudson* and *The Golden Bowl*. In *The Spoils* (ed. of 1908, p. 150), James says that Owen struck Fleda as "all potent nature in one pair of boots." "Potent" was not in the original version, but to omit it now is like emasculation.

Matthiessen's book is the fullest study so far of the late novels, developing the familiar thesis that James's highest, finest, most characteristic work is contained in them. It is best on *The Wings of the Dove*, which clearly he prefers to the others, although to my sense he glosses over too much in forty pages the grave faults of this most pathetic, perhaps most beautiful, of James's novels; and very good on

* By F. O. Matthiessen, 1944.

The Ivory Tower. The obsessive imagery of the late style is treated with unexceptionable care, unless one feels that he scants its sometimes unmistakable dream character, as when Milly rises to her feet in the park and looks about her "at her scattered melancholy comrades —some of them so melancholy as to be down on their stomachs in the grass, turned away, ignoring, burrowing . . ." There are extremely interesting quotations from James's unpublished notebooks (of which an edition is promised), especially this on *The Portrait of a Lady:* "The obvious criticism of course will be that it is not finished—that it has not seen the heroine to the end of her situation—that I have left her *en l'air.* This is both true and false. The *whole* of anything is never told; you can only take what groups together. What I have done has that unity—it groups together. It is complete in itself—and the rest may be taken up or not, later." In general, however, despite these and other virtues, Matthiessen's exposition in this book is so often questionable that it is difficult to recommend. I must take up briefly, for readers familiar with James's late work, some crucial matters as to which I should be sorry to see Matthiessen's opinion prevail.

"The burden of *The Ambassadors* is that Strether has awakened to a wholly new sense of life. Yet he does nothing at all to fulfill that sense." This judgment, expressing Matthiessen's main dissatisfaction with this novel and accounting perhaps for his preference of *The Wings,* appears to me unreasonable. The subject of *The Ambassadors,* as of *The Wings* and *The Golden Bowl,* is the Personal Fate— "the fate that waits for one, the dark doom that rides." It is Strether's fate to have awakened "too late" to the possibilities of life in him; but too late only for most, the best of his years. So late, so unexpectedly, but with what equipment and how fully, he *lives* indeed during his European months; absorbed, excited, "mad," he controls, betrays, is betrayed, is loved, loves. When Maria Gostrey says to him, " 'The wonderful and special thing about you is that you *are,* at this time of day, youth,' " Strether's reply is always the same: " 'Of course I'm youth—youth for the trip to Europe . . . I never had the benefit at the proper time, which comes to saying that I never had the thing itself. I'm having the benefit at this moment.' " The book contains his life; at the end, in every way now old, and "right" by renunciation of that for which he is anyway too late, he goes back to America. Matthiessen complains that he "leaves Paris and Maria to go back to no prospect of life at all." But he has *had* it. Madame de Vionnet's last words, in the magnificent interview which effectually closes his "life," are "'. . . I want everything. I've wanted you too.' 'Ah, but you've *had* me!'" Strether declares "with an emphasis that made an end."

Matthiessen's criticism of *The Golden Bowl* is even less acceptable, and his account bristles moreover with misreadings of detail, reaching a climax when he asserts of the silken halter by which Maggie images her father's control over and punishment of his wife: "James's neglect of the cruelty in such a cord, silken though it be, is nothing short of obscene." This is strong language. The cord, of course, precisely symbolizes cruelty—cruelty perhaps in the interest of "justice," but flat cruelty, culminating in Charlotte's positive exile. Small wonder that the book is for this critic more or less "hollow of real life." He misses the whole irony turned unobtrusively by James upon his precious Americans. They have good faith, yes, but they are selfish—selfish for each other, as a pair selfish, Maggie a bad wife, Adam a bad husband. The Prince, too, has his good faith (which does not exonerate him); the situation of his adultery is irresistibly produced by the conduct of his wife and his father-in-law. Maggie indeed, in her blind way, is shown by James as recognizing this. The speech that she imagines Charlotte in anguish addressing to her is one of the supreme revelations of the novel:

> You don't know what it is to have been loved and broken with. You haven't been broken with, because in *your* relation what can there have been, worth speaking of, to break? Ours was everything a relation could be, filled to the brim with the wine of consciousness; and if it was to have no meaning, no better meaning than that such a creature as you could breathe upon it, at your hour, for blight, why was I myself dealt with all for deception? why condemned after a couple of short years to find the golden flame—oh, the golden flame!—a mere handful of black ashes?

Justice is strange in these books; nothing is simple in them; I have charges to make against *The Golden Bowl* myself, capital ones. But I hope I have cleared it by suggestion from Matthiessen's charges.

His final chapter, called "The Religion of Consciousness," is the least satisfactory of all, with curious defects in understanding (for instance, of William James), but its materials are accurately chosen and it has the value of calling attention to the essay "Is There a Life After Death?" (1910), one of James's most arresting personal statements. Matthiessen misrepresents this by having James "virtually" say, "'The soul is immortal, certainly—if you've got one; but most people haven't'"—without reference to James's qualification of his view ("The probability is, in fact, that what we dimly discern as waste the wisdom of the universe may know as a very different matter") and without reference to the fact that the sentence quoted was invented by James only as a remark put into the mouth of the hero of his early raving melodrama, "A Passionate Pilgrim," when he revised the story. Behind this chapter lurks an important subject— which might be seen as "the aspirations of the secular"—and I am sorry it is not better. I am sorry the whole book is not better, for its author occupies an influential position in our critical life, working honourably to stem the illiterate tide which, as James foresaw and feared, is now mainly having its way.

1945

Stephen Crane

THE RED BADGE OF COURAGE

THE WARS OF MEN HAVE INSPIRED THE PRODUCTION OF some of man's chief works of art, but very undemocratically. Napoleon's wars inspired Goya, Stendhal, Beethoven, Tolstoy; a prolonged bicker of 1100 B.C. inspired the poet of the *Iliad*, who celebrated and deplored three centuries later a little piece of it near its end; the Wars of the Roses resulted in Shakespeare's giant effort, again long afterward; the Athenian empire's ruin was adequately dramatized by a participant, the greatest of historians; Picasso made something of the soul-destroying civil war in his native country. But what came of Cromwell's war? Or of the atrocious conflict between North and South in the United States?—thirty years after it ended came a small novel by a very young man called *The Red Badge of Courage*. The immediate literature of the Civil War has been beautifully studied of late in Edmund Wilson's *Patriotic Gore*, but no one, I think, would claim for that literature any such eminence as belongs, after now almost seventy years, to Stephen Crane's novel. A critic seems to be faced, then, with alternative temptations: to overrate it, as an American, because it chronicles our crucial struggle, or to underrate it, in the grand perspective of the artists just mentioned, because it appears to assert neither the authority of the experienced warrior nor the authority of the historical artist—Tolstoy having both, Thucydides both. Crane was no scholar and had seen no battle. Yet some authority has got to be allowed him, and identified, for his work has not only brilliantly survived but was recognized instantly abroad—in England—as authentic; professional military men were surprised to learn that he was not one.

It is hard to see how anyone, except a casual reader, could overrate *The Red Badge of Courage* for patriotic reasons, because, though the book does indeed handle parts of the battle of Chancellorsville, it is not really about the Civil War. For instance, it shows no interest in the causes, meaning, or outcome of the war; no interest in politics; no interest in tactics or strategy. In this book, these failures are a merit, in opposition to the supreme fault of *War and Peace*, which is philosophical and programmatic. Here we have only parts of one minor battle, seen from one ignorant point of view, that of a new volunteer. One would never guess that what has been called the first modern war was being studied. All the same, as from the weird diagrams of Samuel Beckett, the helpless horror of modern man emerges: we learn, as we learn from few books, about the waiting, the incomprehension, rumour, frustration, anxiety, fatigue, panic, hatred not only of the enemy but of officers; about complaints of "bad luck" and the sense of betrayal by commanders. This is a losing army. Since every intelligent man has to be at some point afraid of proving himself a coward—which is what the ordeal of Crane's protagonist is about—the story presents itself to us initially as making some claim to universality; and the claim is strengthened by Crane's reluctance to divulge the name of the hero (it is Henry Fleming) or the names of the only other two people who matter—the tall soldier (Jim) and the loud youth (Wilson)—or the identity of the regiment, or the geography. By *leaving things out* the author makes his general bid for our trust.

But of course he has put in things, too, and our problems are where he got them and how he put them. The main things he put in are: reflection and action. Much of the book really is battle. Crane had read *Sevastopol*, Tolstoy's short novel, and declared that he learned what war was like from football—after starring in baseball at the two colleges he briefly attended, he coached a boys' football team in New Jersey. One of the staff at his military academy, a major-general, had seen action at Chancellorsville and liked to talk about it. Crane had played war games as a child, and talked with veterans, and read (with disappointment and contempt) magazine articles on the war. Later, after witnessing substantial parts of the Greco-Turkish war, he said, "*The Red Badge* is all right." I don't know that we can say precisely how he learned what he knew, except to recognize in him an acute visual imagination and an inspired instinct for what happens and what does not happen in conflict. Here is a short passage:

He expected a battle scene.

There were some little fields girted and squeezed by a forest. Spread over the grass and in among the tree trunks, he could see knots and waving lines of skirmishers who were running hither and thither and firing at the landscape. A dark battle line lay upon a sunstruck clearing that gleamed orange color. A flag fluttered.

Other regiments floundered up the bank.

Some of the features of Crane's *style* appear: his convulsive and also humourous irony ("expected," as if he would not see it but he saw it, and "firing at the landscape"), its violent animism ("squeezed"), its descriptive energy ("knots and waving lines"—like an abstract expressionist painting). But a Tolstoyan sense also of futility and incomprehension is swiftly conveyed, and this is only partly a product of the style. He is inventing, he is experimenting. Crane himself goes in for this language—he several times speaks of "experiment" and says of the youth, "He tried to mathematically prove to himself that he would not run from a battle." In the action, then, the fantastic and the literal cooperate. The reflective aspects of the novel are another matter.

The scene of this extremely simple novel is laid in a single mind. It starts with soldiers speculating loudly about whether there is going to be a fight or not. Then "a youthful private" goes off to his hut: "He wished to be alone with some new thoughts that had lately come to him." This has the effect of understatement, putting so flatly the youth's debate with himself about his honour, but it is literal, besides introducing the theme of intense isolation that dominated Crane's work until the later story, his masterpiece, "The Open Boat," where human cooperation in face of the indifference of nature is the slowly arrived-at subject. Here his youth broods in private, having crawled into his dilemma, or hut, "through an intricate hole that served it as a door"—and the rest of the book provides a workout of the plight. On the first day he does well, and then runs away. A Union soldier clubs him in the panic retreat; Crane's ironic title refers to the "badge" of that wound; the youth is taken for a good soldier. He witnesses the death of his boyhood friend, the tall soldier, a true hero. Returned, by the kindness of a stranger, to his regiment, he is cared for as a combatant by the loud youth—toward whom he is also enabled to feel superior in that, scared, earlier, Wilson entrusted him with letters to be sent in the event of his death and has now, shamefacedly, to ask for them back. Next day he fights like a hero or a demon. Such is the story. Perhaps many readers take it as a novel of development, a sort of success story, and this view is encouraged by the climactic passage: "He felt a quiet manhood, non-assertive but of sturdy and strong blood . . . He had been to touch the great death, and found that, after all, it was but the great death. He was a man," and so on.

It is possible to feel very uncomfortable with this way of looking at the book.

For one thing, pervasive irony is directed toward the youth—his self-importance, his self-pity, his self-loving war rage. For another, we have only one final semi-self-reproach for his cowardice and imposture: "He saw that he was good . . . Nevertheless, the ghost of his flight from the first engagement appeared to him and danced. There were small shoutings in his brain about these matters. For a moment he blushed, and the light of his soul flickered with shame." I find it hard to believe that Crane is here exonerating his hero, without irony. Finally, we have very early on an indication of his pomposity (his mother's "I know how you are, Henry"), and there is pomposity in his final opinion of himself as a war demon. That would suggest a circular action, in the coward middle of which he appeared to reveal his real nature, or in fact did reveal it, by running. The irony embraces, then, all but the central failure.

It is easy to feel uncomfortable with this view, too—the more particularly because the apparent wound of the first day is indeed a real wound, and its silent pretension is later justified. On the other hand . . . The irony never ends. I do not know what Crane intended. Probably he intended to have his cake and eat it, too—irony to the end, but heroism, too. Fair enough. How far did he fail?

Again I invoke, as praiseworthy, that which is not done. The youth is frantically afraid of being found out (he never is found out), but except in the passage just quoted, he never suffers the remorse one would expect. Intimate as Crane is with his hero psychologically, still the view he takes of him is cold, unsentimental, remote. This certainly preserves him from any full failure (though there have been many good readers from the day the book was published to now who have not liked it, because they regarded it as artificial and sensational).

The coldness leads to a certain impersonality, and it is a very striking fact that some of Crane's deepest private interests find no place in the novel—are deliberately excluded. Three of these are worth singling out. In his earlier novel, or long story, called *Maggie*, laid in New York's Bowery, Crane dramatized a distinct social philosophy—environmentalist, deterministic, and convinced that "the root of slum-life" was "a sort of cowardice." Yet his indifference to society in *The Red Badge* is complete, and it will not do here to say, "Of course it would be," for an army *is* society.

So with the matter of personal philosophy. We happen to know Crane's views perfectly, because he put them at length in letters to a girl (Nellie Crouse) by whom he was fascinated in 1895–6. We have time for a passage: "For my own part, I am minded to die in my thirty-fifth year [he died at twenty-eight, in 1900]. I think that is all I care to stand. I don't like to make wise remarks on the aspect of life but I will say that it doesn't strike me as particularly worth the trouble. The final wall of the wise man's thought however is Human Kindness of course"—and, exceptionally for him, Crane capitalized the two words. Now it might have been supposed that, bringing his hero through to maturity in *The Red Badge*, he would have got down to work in this area. But no. It seems impossible not to conclude that the splendid burst of rhetoric with which the novel concludes is just that, *in part*—a burst of rhetoric—and that Crane retained many of his reservations about his hero. As the wisest of modern British novelists, E. M. Forster, once observed, novels almost never end well—character desires to keep on going, whereas remorseless plot requires it to end. I hardly remember a better instance. Yet the last page is confidently and brilliantly done:

> It rained. The procession of weary soldiers became a bedraggled train, despondent and muttering, marching with churning effort in a trough of liquid brown mud under a low, wretched sky. Yet the youth smiled, for he saw that the world was a world for him, though many discovered it to be made of oaths and walking sticks. He had rid himself of the red sickness of battle.

But *then* comes a sentence in which I simply do not believe: "He turned now with a lover's thirst to images of tranquil skies, fresh meadows, cool brooks—an existence of soft and eternal peace." In short, we are left after all with a *fool*, for Crane knew as well as the next man, and much better, that life consists of very little but struggle. He wrote to Miss Crouse of "a life of labor and sorrow. I do not confront it blithely. I confront it with desperate resolution. There is not even much hope in my attitude. [Perhaps I may mention that at this point Stephen Crane was an international celebrity.] I do not even expect to do good. But I expect to make a sincere, desperate, lonely battle to remain true to my conception of my life and the way it should be lived . . . It is not a fine prospect." The shutting out of his hero from his personal thought redeems for me, on the whole, the end of the book.

The absence of interest in religion in *The Red Badge of Courage* is more surprising still than the other indifferences, whether seen in a critical way or in a biographical way. Henry Fleming, orphan of a farm widow, was seminary-trained. What emerges from the training is scanty indeed. "He would die; he would go to some place where he would be understood. It was useless to expect appreciation of his profound and fine senses from such men as the lieutenant." This is a fine and funny passage, not deeply Christian. Then there's the famous passage about the wafer, long quoted as a war cry for modernism in American fictional art. Unutterably wounded, upright, the tall soldier had sought a private ground away from the retreat, in a field mysteriously chosen, followed by the youth and a tattered soldier, for his dance of death.

> As the flap of the blue jacket fell away from the body, he could see that the side looked as if it had been chewed by wolves.
> The youth turned, with sudden, livid rage, toward the battlefield. He shook his fist. He seemed about to deliver a philippic.
> "Hell—"
> The red sun was pasted in the sky like a wafer.

Pasting is a failingly temporary operation, I suppose—for the pagan god of the sky?!—handed us here as an overpowering rebuke to the youth's rebellion. A wafer is thick nourishment, too, is it not? Disdain and fury against the prerogatives of majesty seem to be the subject. But I notice two points. Even here it is hard to decide just how far Crane is with the youth and how far critical of him. And revolt, in a seminary youth, should have been better prepared: one would welcome a *trace* of his Christian history, pro or con; what Crane never provides. Shortly afterward we hear: "He searched about in his mind for an adequate malediction for the indefinite cause, the thing upon which men turn the words of final blame. It—whatever it was—was responsible for him, he said. There lay the fault."

Crane did not here believe in evil. Henry Fleming is not evil, nor is anyone. A strange setup for an ambitious novel. Determinism is in control ("It . . . was responsible for him") or is it? for the next little words are "*he said*"—which may be a repudiation. Again we are in the seesaw.

It is not a bad place to be, so long as one trusts the writer.

Crane's religious history I'll do briefly. He could not help being the son of a clergyman and of a madly missionary woman: "that cooled off [he told an interviewer] and when I was thirteen or about that, my brother Will told me not to believe in Hell after my uncle had been boring me about the lake of fire and the rest of the sideshows." "I cannot be shown [he said at another time] that God bends upon us any definable stare, and his laughter would be bully to hear out in nothingness." I think we may conclude that neither this personal opinion nor the fierce scorn of Christianity that flashes in many of Crane's brilliant poems has anything really to do with the purely naturalistic framework—from this point of view—of *The Red Badge of Courage*.

With the word "naturalistic," however, we turn to some consideration of the artistic affiliations of the novel. All the categorical terms that have been applied to Crane's art are slippery, but let me deny at once that he was a Naturalist. The Naturalists—Frank Norris, say, and Theodore Dreiser—are accumulative and ponderous. Crane's intense selectivity makes him almost utterly unlike them. Crane himself, when hardly more than a boy, allied his creed to the Realism preached—in revolt against the slack, contrived, squeamish standards of popular American fiction in the nineties—by his first admirers, William Dean Howells, then the country's leading critic, and a younger writer, Hamlin Garland. But Crane's work does not resemble theirs, either, and he seems to have meant, in his alliance, only that art should be "sincere" (one of his favorite words) and truthful. Like many another young genius, he regarded most writers as frauds and liars—and, in fact, perhaps most writers *are* frauds and liars. But epithets so vague as "sincere" and "truthful" tell us very little. The best term is undoubtedly that of his close friend, the far greater novelist Joseph Conrad (though whether a *better* writer it is probably too soon to say), who observed in a letter to a mutual friend that "He is *the* only impressionist, and *only* an impressionist."

If we can accept this characteristically exaggerated but authoritative judgment, we are in a position to make some reservations. Conrad and Crane, when they met in England in 1897, recognized immediately an affinity; Conrad was soon charged by reviewers with imitating Crane (a charge he denied to Crane), and in truth parts of *Lord Jim* are much indebted to *The Red Badge;* yet Conrad clearly did not regard himself as an impressionist. Next, there exist in Crane's work obviously realistic and fantastic elements—as in Conrad's and in their friend Henry James's, also domiciled in the south of England at this time—two Americans and a Pole re-creating English fiction, which was languishing, so far as form was concerned, in the powerful hands of Thomas Hardy and Rudyard Kipling. The power of *experiment* came from abroad, as later from Joyce and Hemingway and Kafka—and in poetry from T. S. Eliot and Ezra Pound.

Finally, his use of irony enters so deeply into most of Crane's finest work—all the five last authors named are ironists—that the simple term "impressionist" will hardly do, and my uncertain feeling is that Crane is best thought of as a twentieth-century author. Authorities date modern American literature, some from *The Red Badge* in 1895, some from the reissue the following year of *Maggie*. This is no occasion for an exposition of the nature of irony, in relation to Crane—which in any case I have attempted elsewhere—but maybe something of that will emerge from a summary study of his style. By way, though, of winding up the impressionist reservations, let me enforce Conrad's label with a quotation from Crane: "I understand that a man is born into the world with his own pair of eyes and he is not at all responsible for his vision—he is merely responsible for his quality of personal honesty. To keep close to this personal honesty is my supreme ambition." Ill, dying indeed, hard-pressed with guests and fame and need for money, working incessantly, he said to a journalist visitor during his last year of life: "I get a little tired of saying, Is this true?" He was an impressionist: he dealt in the way things strike one—but also in the way things are.

This famous style is not easy to describe, combining as it does characteristics commonly antithetical. It is swift, no style in English more so, improvisatorial, manly as Hazlitt; but at the same time it goes in for ritual solemnity and can be highly poetic. I illustrate. For speed: "For a moment he felt in the face of his great trial like a babe, and the flesh over his heart seemed very thin. He seized time to look about him calculatingly." Here we are already into something like the other category, illustrated in the opening sentence of the novel: "The cold passed reluctantly from the earth, and the retiring fogs revealed an army stretched out on the hills, resting." Here's a high case of the animism I have referred to. The colour of the style is celebrated—maybe he got it from a theory of Goethe's; but the style is also plain, plain. Short as it is, it is also unusually iterative; modern and simple, brazen with medieval imagery; animistic, de-human and mechanistic; attentive—brilliantly—to sound: "As he ran, he became aware that the forest had stopped its music, as if at last becoming capable of hearing the foreign sounds. The trees hushed and stood motionless. Everything seemed to be listening to the crackle and clatter and ear-shaking thunder. The chorus pealed over the still earth." Adverbs are used like verbs, word order deformed: somebody leans on a bar and hears other men "terribly discuss a question that was not plain." But the surest attribute of this style is its reserve, as its most celebrated is its colour. Crane guarantees nothing. "Doubtless" is a favorite word. The technique of refusal is brought so far forward that a casual "often" will defeat itself: "What hats and caps were left to them they often slung high in the air." Once more we hear a Shakespearean contempt, as in *Coriolanus*. In a paradoxical way: if he won't vouch for what he tells us—if he doesn't push us, trying to convince—he must have things up his sleeve which if we knew them would persuade us. As for colour: "A crimson roar came from the distance"—the mildest example I have been able to find. His employment of it here is not only not naturalistic—what roar was ever red?—but is solely affective, that is, emotional; like his metaphorical use, in the novel, of devils, ghouls, demons, spectres. Crane made use of a spectrum. A final item is his rueful humour: "He threw aside his mental pamphlets on the philosophy of the retreated and rules for the guidance of the damned."

On that note we might end, except for a poem written by Stephen Crane several years after the novel called "War Is Kind," one of his major poems, and one of the best poems of the period in the United States of America.

In the novel there is little of the pathos of which he had already shown himself a master in *Maggie,* and little of the horror informing his best later war stories. They come to life in the poem. Crane makes a sort of little bridge between Tolstoy—supreme—supreme?—and our very good writer Hemingway. But these superior gentlemen do not compete. One of the best remarks ever made about the poet of the *Iliad* is that he shared with Tolstoy and with Shakespeare both a virile love of war and a virile horror of it. So in his degree did Crane, and before he had seen it.

1965

"THE OPEN BOAT"

To HIS TITLE "THE OPEN BOAT," STEPHEN CRANE appended this subtitle, "A Tale Intended to be after the Fact: Being the Experience of Four Men from the Sunk Steamer *Commodore.*" The shipwreck, of which the men's experience in the boat is the aftermath, actually occurred early in 1897. When Crane got ashore safely with the captain and the cook, he wrote a long dispatch to his New York paper (he was a reporter) about the shipwreck, which they published.

His dispatch does not describe the experience in the boat. Now the story is said by him, in the subtitle, to be "after" (in accordance with) the *fact, "being* the *experience* of," and so on. Shall we expect then to hear the true story of the ordeal? It would certainly seem so, and a very interesting article by Cyrus Day of the University of Delaware has lately appeared,* studying the story from this point of view: as a full and veracious account of what took place between the foundering and the landing. Day inquires into the ethics of the captain's having left his ship at all, into the specifications of the dinghy, the speed of the wind at the time of the wreck and afterward (using U.S. Weather Bureau records), the distance from land, Crane's seamanship as an author, the oiler's and the captain's actual seamanship (apparently), and other such matters. He emerges with a rather dim view of most of these topics and appears to feel that he has discredited the story.

But all this has nothing really to do with the story at all, important though it certainly may be from a *biographical* point of view. It is a little as if we called in a fashion expert, expert in color, to determine whether the sides of the face of the mistress of the Elizabethan poet Thomas Campion, whom he calls "Rose-cheekt Laura," have been accurately described. The author's *intentions* do not matter very much; it is what he does that counts. He says "*Intended* to be after the Fact"—a word that recognizes, of course, the impossibility of exact correspondence between any event in nature and any literary account. He also says "A *Tale*," using a word of which the connotations are (as the dictionary says) "a false story," "a mere story"; a word rather like the American word "yarn," meaning a tall tale told by a sailor, partly incredible. Crane used language with great precision. In short, whether we ignore his intentions or take them into account, we may disregard the question whether much of the story is *true*. Imaginative art *takes off from* reality, becoming something else.

The opening sentence reads: "None of them knew the color of the sky." Why are we told first a fact so flat and odd, a negative fact? Perhaps we are being told this *instead* of something else we expected to hear. You may say, "But the story begins with this sentence!" No, it began with its title, and subtitle, and it is in the light of both that we read the first sentence. An expectation *has* been disappointed, for when one hears of an open boat, and four men in it from a sunk steamer, perhaps the first thing one thinks of is the excellent view they unfortunately have of the sky and their deep interest in the weather it foreshadows. "Completely wrong," Crane is saying. "You

---

* "Stephen Crane and the Ten-foot Dinghy," *Boston University Studies in English* (1958), iii.

know nothing about the matter." The men are watching the sea, with anxiety about the waves, presumably (we do not *know* yet—the sea may even be calm), and watching the horizon, with an equal anxiety to see it (we do not know yet how far out they are). The line, thus, is far more *businesslike* than anything one expected. It has the effect, shall we say, of bringing the reader's gaze—as if taking him by the back of the neck—*down* from the skyey expectations of the title and subtitle to what is *level* (this word then occurs immediately) and a matter of human efficiency. Crane's opening sentence is *anti*-heroic, that is to say, standing as it does like a blunt sentry, in the forefront of what looked to be an epic of the sea. Anti-heroic and ironic, in view of the "big" opening (high-keyed, exalted) that the reader presumably expected.

But it is a curious fact that this very prosaic though active sentence makes a line of formal verse. It is an iambic pentameter, what is called a heroic verse, with trochaic substitution in the opening foot. No doubt the line is not so intense or highly coloured as the first line of a poem on this subject might be, but the character of the rhythm, being formal, is antithetical to the sentence's anti-heroic muscular meaning and tone. This author desires to take possession of the reader, on several fronts simultaneously, at once. In this first sentence, the reader, made aware that the men are watching the sea, immediately understands the true scale of the experience to come. The quality of the thought of the sentence, at the outset, forces the reader to begin to think *with* the men. What looks like an impersonal declarative sentence is really in its effect personal, questioning, psychological. At the end of just a page or so, this process of obliging the reader to enter the boat (and share the men's experience) has gone so far that Crane can say "the faces of the men must have been gray" and we are inside—though *not* yet with the correspondent, only with all four.

Clearly, Crane's opening sentence, by *not* being about the sky but about—what? well, something else—introduces a complication. The longer second and third sentences are not only explanatory but *resolving*, and the resolution comes in almost the rhythm of the complication: "and all of the men knew the colors of the sea."

A wave has passed. Almost at once a second wave begins. "Many a man" is mock-heroic in tone (burlesquing heroic style) and the bathtub carries on the low-comedy sense. But the effect of the sentence is not comic. This dry, gay, senseless remark—as one critic has said—enables Crane to contrast, as in a flash of lightning, the most comfortable and sheltered situation conceivable (a bath in one's own bathtub) with on the other hand the sinister wilderness of wave and wind, where a man *owns* ("ought to have") nothing except, precariously, his life. But there is something more. A bathtub exists to fill with water—and with this sinister glimpse of the dinghy shipping water (we have not even been openly told yet that she is), the second complication is over. The wave is about to break, and in the famous sentence that follows, it does break: "These waves were most wrongfully and barbarously abrupt and tall . . ." The sentence itself appears to swell and tower like a wave in the ear and mind, after the light, odd little sentence preceding: its long, mournful middle sounds ("most wrongfully and barbarously") are succeeded so rapidly by the extremely surprising, fast word "abrupt" and the even shorter, also sinister "tall," that it is a little as if a comber had loomed and broken over oneself. But the key word is "barbarously." The men are here in a world that has nothing to do with bathtubs. Civilization has been obliterated for them, and their ordeal is going to be primitive, barbarous. Notice, finally, that the tone has risen so very high in the part of the sentence we have been studying that Crane, in order to be able to get on with his narrative, drops his tone sharply in its second half, to make a technical remark; which has also the effect of saying that the barbarous is being confronted, at any rate, with skill.

So much for the opening paragraph, which is certainly one of the fastest, subtlest, toughest operations in American prose. Then each of the four men in the boat has a little paragraph to himself. The first thing to be observed about the four of them is negative: we spoke of "skill," and it immediately follows that not one of the four men is a proper sailor. Instead, we have men (in poor condition, as it will turn out) from the galley, the engine room, the passenger cabins, and the bridge—and the man from the bridge is injured. It follows that they will not be able to summon much except courage and endurance to save themselves. The author is clearly an author strongly given to irony.

Crane's treatment of the first man, the cook, is the reverse of heroic. There does not seem to be anything wrong with him and yet he is not doing anything; his costume is undignified, so is his speech, so is his fatness, so is the evident fear with which he regards the two inches of gunwale. This general impression is somewhat neutralized, however, by the last thing we hear, that he "invariably gazed eastward over the broken sea." This tone is more elevated than that of the rest of the paragraph, his intensity is communicated, and, after all, he does seem to be exercising a role: he is lookout.

The mock-heroic tone partly characteristic of the opening paragraph makes the semi-clownish cook the perfect character, of the four, to introduce first. What is our surprise, then, to hear far *less* about the oiler—almost nothing except that he is steering with a thin little oar and raises his body sometimes to avoid water. Is he going to prove even more insignificant in the story than the cook? Or is the author holding his fire, as with the cook there seems no reason to think he may be doing? All we can note at the moment is surprise.

Of the correspondent we hear, if possible, less still. He is rowing, watching, wondering "why he was there." But is this less? Surely with "wondering" we enter briefly the mind of the correspondent, as we never did the cook's mind, much less the oiler's. The notion of an explanation for the ordeal begins, with this verb, to reverberate in the story. It is suggested to us that at least one of our main points of view—notwithstanding the general tact of Crane's third-person narrative—is going to be that of the correspondent.

It is obvious, instantly, that one of the things Crane has been doing with the others is holding his fire in order to do a proper job on the captain. Injured, shipless, he is lying down (the others squat or sit), and the quality of his reflection and memory (of his foundering ship) is conveyed by Crane in language which has none of the irony that has characterized the opening page down to this point. The others are anxious, working. He is withdrawn. One realizes at once that his situation is not going fully to be that of the others: in a sense, his defeat has already taken place, fate can do nothing worse to him. He still gives orders—his "profound dejection and indifference" do not extend to an abandonment of his duty to the others; but he gives them in a voice "deep with mourning, and of a quality beyond oration or tears," and one does not receive an impression that the captain's fate is going to be the major concern of this story.

Whom, then, does it seem the story is going to be about?—at the end of this first page, that is; for a good reader is sensitive to as many as possible of an author's announcements and foreshadowings (*and omissions*, which is often the way announcements are made and suggestions conveyed).

The cook? Hardly. Of course, the author may have surprises in store for us; but a good author does not work in terms of surprises so much as of expectation, discussed later. It is unlikely that Crane will have misled us to that extent. The cook—just as we know him so far (and do we ever learn more?)—does not seem fitted to be either the hero or the victim of a tale one of whose keynotes is set by the august paragraph about the captain. We have to say hero *or* victim, naturally, because we do not know how the story will turn out. But it is unlikely to turn out either a simple tragedy or a simple escape story—

considering the complexities of tone we have been examining on its first page.

The oiler? Conceivably; for we know nothing about him yet; the author may be making us wait, and it is a little striking that the first thing we learn, after the four characterizing paragraphs, is the oiler's name. Those paragraphs have already made it apparent that we are in the hands of an author who does not lightly reveal his characters' names: he is concerned, rather, with their roles, perhaps with their fates.

The correspondent? Conceivably; but, if so, in a very different way from the way the story will be about the oiler, if it proves to be. The correspondent, as one would expect, reflects and inquires.

Or all four? A study of the story's form will take us further, but how intense and elaborate is the initial impression made just by one paragraph and a little cast of characters.

The ordeal dramatized in the story has three parts, each growing out of, and superseding, the part preceding (this is true even of the first part, as will be clear in a moment), and each having a theme different from what one expected. The seven sections into which Crane has divided his story, that is, we may see as three waves. Each gathers, swells, breaks, and is followed by another, until the final word of the story brings the movements to a conclusion. But then this word itself shows that the three movements were one movement only. Far more than is the case even with most really good stories, "The Open Boat" reserves its true meaning to its actual final word.

What would the title, and the initial line of explanation ("A Tale," etc.), lead us to expect the story to be about? Hardship, certainly; fear; the relation between man and nature. But the first wave of the story (Sections I–III) is not about these things, essentially. It is about comradeship—the relation between man and man—and its basic tone is optimistic. At first no land is visible at all, then II ends with a "pin" appearing on the horizon, and the words "serenely" and "cheerful" are applied to the men. Section III strengthens this feeling at its close with the exquisite iteration "Slowly the land arose from the sea . . . Slowly and beautifully the land loomed out of the sea," and the men light cigars. The climax of this wave comes at the beginning of III, with "the subtle brotherhood of men that was here established on the seas." A man, that is to say, in his ordeal, is not alone; he may trust other men, and must, and does, and finds that they will help him. This is a *preliminary* conclusion, in the light of the rest of the story, but two things are to be noted about it at once. In the first place, it is, for this author, an unusually *hopeful* way of seeing man's situation. In Crane's earlier works, *Maggie* and *The Red Badge of Courage*, and in his later stories, such as "The Blue Hotel," men are seen as either completely alone or as *collaborating into disaster*. In the second place, this brotherhood is not arrived at easily or at once. As against the cliché that men in adversity stick together, Crane is careful to show these men quarrelling toward the end of Section I; so that the establishment of brotherhood comes as an achievement.

The second wave (Sections IV–VI) is concerned powerfully to question both this brotherhood and the nature of the ordeal itself. Its tone is very dark; all three of its sections end in gloom.

Already in part one, it was clear that the brotherhood was established against an enemy, the Sea, which is envisaged as animal: "There was a terrible grace in the move of the waves, and they came in silence, save for the *snarling* of the crests" and "There was a preparatory and long *growl* in the speech of them." The nature of this enemy is now to be explored. But the brotherhood itself—to deal with this first—is seen as both partial and incompletely operative. It does not include the men on the shore, who can only stand and wave, not help. So, are men able to help their fellow man in crisis, after all? Moreover, the brotherhood does not spare the correspondent his agony in the night—though we have to qualify this statement with a reminder that the captain *is* awake and with him, without his knowing it until later. Men must undergo their crises of rage and fear essentially alone.

To move now toward the nature of the enemy: man's fear is of death, but his rage is directed, rather, toward what is going to cause his death—that is to say, nature. But is nature man's enemy? To the extent that it is going to cause his death, one would think so. But in that it *cannot receive rage*, it is not after all an enemy: "he at first wishes to throw bricks at the temple, and he hates deeply the fact that there are no bricks and no temples." The final formulation of the truth about nature is reserved to the third part of the story: here it is enough to know that *nature is not an enemy*, so far as man's *expression of emotion* is concerned. Therefore, in one of Crane's subtlest passages (in Section VI), the rage and fear are transformed into *self-love* and *self-pity*. Nature does not hate man but does not love him either, and does not pity him; and so if he needs these emotions, he must supply them himself. There is irony, of course, even in this view, but it is a tenderer irony than most of Crane's, and the paragraphs about the soldier of the Legion dying in Algiers form one of his most beautiful achievements. (Technically, they get their effect by holding back and holding back in order to accumulate enormous pressure on the simple word "sorry" in the final sentence, making it ring in the mind.)

The dramatization of nature, in the correspondent's mind, as the shark, then, was false or misleading, and in the third part of the story we hear what nature *is:* she is "indifferent, flatly indifferent." Emotion directed toward her—anger or entreaty—is wasted. What is wanted is something very different; *understanding* of her. With this conception, however, we are approaching the word with which the story ends, and before entering on that final subject, it is necessary to understand the death of the oiler.

The oiler's death is the price paid by the men for the salvation of the other three. He dies as a sacrifice. Nature is indifferent, but the arrangements of nature—so to put it—exact tribute. From the narrative point of view, it has to be the oiler who dies because of the disqualifications of the other three. The cook is lacking in dignity, the correspondent is the perceiving mind, and the captain is already injured (a sacrifice must be in perfect condition). But somebody must die; man (the four men in the boat) does not escape scot-free from ordeal; and so the oiler perishes.

And now for the word "interpreters," toward which the entire story has been moving.

This unexpected and dramatic word lifts the story explicitly to a plane that has earlier only been implied. The experience, and *only* the experience, of nature's most dangerous and demanding ordeals, fits man to do what it is most his duty and power to do: to *explain* —explain what nature is, what man is, what matters. The whole story, then, has in some sense been a metaphor, and the ordeal of the boat only an instance of what can happen to man and what it means, what qualities the experience of nature requires. The best imaginable comment on Crane's word "interpreters" is the splendid passage with which William Faulkner closed his Nobel Prize address in 1950: "I decline to accept the end of man. It is easy enough to say that man is immortal simply because he will endure: that when the last ding-dong of doom has clanged and faded from the last worthless rock hanging tideless in the last red and dying evening, that even then there will still be one more sound: that of his puny inexhaustible voice, still talking. I refuse to accept this. I believe that man will not merely endure: he will prevail. He is immortal, not because he alone among creatures has an inexhaustible voice, but because he has a soul, a spirit capable of compassion and sacrifice and endurance. The poet's, the writer's, duty is to write about these things. It is his privilege to help man endure by lifting his heart, by reminding him of the courage and honour and hope and pride and compassion and pity and sacrifice which have been the glory of his past. The poet's voice need not merely be the record of man, it can be one of the props, the pillars to help him endure and prevail."

1960

Enslavement:

Three American Cases

THEODORE DREISER

FOR DECADES THEODORE DREISER LOOMED LARGE AS ONE OF the few world figures in our fiction. Then his immense fame so deteriorated, especially after his death in 1945, that four years later, when a detailed biography was produced by Robert H. Elias, an influential book reporter could question whether Dreiser was a subject of general interest to the public at all. Now with the posthumous study by one of America's most respected literary historians, the late F. O. Matthiessen of Harvard,* the question is conclusively answered. Dreiser's shifting, sombre, dubious life is hardly one to be dealt with briefly (as it has to be in this account), but that it has to be dealt with, and that it is of great general interest, there is no longer any doubt.

The earlier part of that life has been handled impressively by Dreiser himself in several books (*Dawn, Newspaper Days, Twelve Men*) very like his novels and not much less interesting. Small wonder if Matthiessen's opening chapters are somewhat perfunctory, but it is to his credit that even here he helps to clarify Dreiser's story.

Born in Indiana in 1871, Dreiser was a German immigrant's son. His father was a strict Catholic and his mother loving and easygoing. His education was wretched by any standard and he proved to have small gift for language, and very modest ability as a newspaper reporter. At twenty-seven, as Matthiessen says clearly, he showed exactly no promise of becoming a writer of note. When presently he wrote his first novel, *Sister Carrie*, he had to be prodded by a friend, Arthur Henry (as Louis Bouilhet prodded Flaubert into *Madame Bovary*). And when it was virtually suppressed upon publication in 1900, Dreiser sank into a depression that lasted three years and wrote no more fiction for ten.

* *Theodore Dreiser.* American Men of Letters Series, 1951.

Instead, upon recovery, Dreiser became an optimistic and extremely successful director of popular magazines, soliciting from other writers, including Mencken, just the sort of emasculated trash he had despised. For six years he rode the facile American waves. Then, at thirty-nine, he wrote *Jennie Gerhardt* and, behold, he had learned nothing and forgotten nothing and was just the same and nearly as good as before.

Matthiessen emphasizes, without attempting to explain, the mystery of Dreiser's resumption of his talent and integrity after an entire decade of wasted or degraded activity. He says very little, however, about a mystery more cardinal still—namely, Dreiser's blank failure thereafter to develop as an artist. Four long novels followed, and then, at last, two others—one better, the rest worse, but all essentially like the early novels.

It has not escaped notice that Dreiser wrote like a hippopotamus. His ineptitude, in fact, has been so long familiar that perhaps we have not been sufficiently surprised that an important author, writing badly over a lifetime, should continue to do so without an effort at redemption or amelioration. Probably the two mysteries are related, and we might try to approach them through a consideration of Matthiessen's chapters on the individual novels.

The usual decline of an author's reputation following his death was dramatized in Dreiser's case by an increasingly feeble or contemptuous response to the posthumously issued novels, *The Bulwark* (1946) and *The Stoic* (1947). The critical chapters here ought to help arrest this decline.

Matthiessen is hardest on *The Genius*, which he calls Dreiser's poorest novel, the one "least rewarding to reread." This strikes as very severe a man who has read it four or five times just for pleasure —never, I confess upon reflection, with admiration precisely, but with the febrile, self-indulgent eagerness Dreiser is apt to induce. But Matthiessen is right, of course, or if not quite right, he has only forgotten *The Stoic*.

Matthiessen is nearly always right. He attributes Dreiser's formidable descriptive power to a freshness of eye and obstinate memory fused with a deep sense of changingness which made it seem historically important to preserve appearance. He analyzes handsomely the debts to Balzac and Spencer, and the devices, such as they are, used by the novelist to organize his materials. He remarks that "one of the reasons why Dreiser's characters often take on a grave magnitude lies in their refusal to be hurried, a refusal on his part as well as on theirs."

He denies genuine stature to Frank Cowperwood and does not conceal a progressive weakening through the financial trilogy. He notes that Dreiser's naïveté above a certain social level is simply the price we pay for the marvellous keenness of longing represented in his characters for successive levels of luxury and achievement far above them, but still below most of his cultivated readers. Matthiessen is right above all in insisting on the word "rhythm" as a key to Dreiser's method.

It is well to have this position—which looks like a critical haven—stated by someone as scrupulous, as cautious as Matthiessen, who had seldom much to say on his own as a literary scholar and stuck close to his texts. He describes Dreiser's style as a matter of "the groping after words corresponding to a groping of the thought, but with both words and thought borne along on the diapason of a deep emotion"—of a "deep grounding, at its best, in the rhythm of his emotions." This seems to me to be profound, the only way, indeed, of accounting for immense effects achieved by means so banal and shabby.

The question, then, is to identify the emotion or emotions. Here we can be in no doubt. Matthiessen speaks in other passages of Dreiser's most recurrent theme as that of "the outsider." Yet is the theme really a figure? Is it not rather the feelings that swarm, hardly distinguished, through the figure of the outsider—the bright, vague longing or aspiration or *yearning* that every reader will probably recognize as Dreiser's central and characteristic emotion?

This emotion is American. We remember it less broodingly in sharper, more polished works by Dreiser's contemporaries, in the early novels of Sinclair Lewis, in *The Great Gatsby*. The objects vary—money and fame and love—but the clustered, helpless emotions persist without change even through their gratification—because it was the emotions and not their objects that mattered.

What distinguishes Dreiser from his contemporaries is a kind of stupidity, a kind of un-self-consciousness, that forbade him ever to employ these emotions until they had passed thoroughly under the mastery of his elephantine memory. He could deal only with the past. Not surprisingly, therefore, he displayed no promise, and he could not be corrupted. We recall Mencken's mature description of him as "granitic, without nerve," with no cunning but with a "truly appalling" tenacity.

There was no question of "integrity" at all. He could be discouraged, and so do nothing, or he could be busy with other things, and so not write. Yet once his imagination came into play at all, it brought up the one fixed emotion, and the tides of a real life, long past, billowed through him again.

Stupidity is a weapon, for an artist, almost as powerful as intelligence—as a social man can be protected against bores by a mild deafness. The same stupidity, or un-self-consciousness, prevented Dreiser from ever improving his style. Probably the notion never occurred to him, and thus no artifice ever arose to interfere with the almost unconscious *overwhelming* way in which his finest work sweeps the reader with it. A test of Dreiser, as of any large writer, is how he handles what matters most.

The magnificence of his supreme achievement has not always been distinguished from the merely fascinating readability of his early novels. His masterpiece—I would agree with what I take to have been Matthiessen's opinion—is *An American Tragedy*, and the center of it is the murder (legal and moral up to a point, and then only moral). The darkening rhythm of these phantasmal scenes has hardly been surpassed in fluidity since *Life on the Mississippi*. "And then, as planned that night between them—a trip to Grass Lake . . . And yet . . . And then . . ." The prose is artless and unlike Mark Twain's except that both embody freely American plain speech; the comparison is between their perfect attention to the nervous rhythms of their heroes' desires. It is worth mention, too, that "no" style may on occasion be preferable to some aspects of Melville's lengthy and deplorable affair with Shakespeare.

One of Matthiessen's shrewdest remarks about this wonderful book is this: "As Clyde plots murder in spite of himself, Dreiser goes to the opposite extreme from the writer of a detective story. Everything that Clyde does is so inept that he is discovered at once." But, all the same, the kind of interest that Dreiser's work evokes and satisfies resembles more the interest we take in a detective story than the interest we take in Hemingway or Jane Austen. It is a little feverish.

Some readers will remember a devastating passage in E. M. Forster's *Aspects of the Novel* where the author is relating the action of some novel by Walter Scott. "And then?" he says, and tells you what comes next. "And then?" "And then?" But suddenly the novel was over, and you must not—says Forster acidly—ask that question too often. In Scott, no doubt, one follows an artificial series of events, and in Dreiser a natural, but the kinds of interest gratified are the same: a gossip interest, an "And then?"

Greater writers, frankly, do not evoke this interest so keenly or simply—although it has become fashionable, as storytelling decays among us, to pretend that they do. One does *not*, that is, rush on from chapter to chapter of *Anna Karenina* just to see what *happens*.

One great author who admittedly does evoke this interest is Dostoevsky, and it is with Dostoevsky that Dreiser must be compared. He poorly stands the comparison when his major work is placed against one by no means the Russian's greatest—*Crime and Punishment*. As Matthiessen says, Clyde Griffiths is no Raskolnikov, and Dreiser knew no such heights of understanding as those upon which Dostoevsky created his ultimate chapters.

An English view will enforce the abyss of difference. H. G. Wells, who ought one day to be recognized as a judge of modern fiction with few peers, described *An American Tragedy* perfectly as "a far more than life-size rendering of a poor little representative corner of American existence, lighted up by a flash of miserable tragedy . . . It gets the large, harsh superficial truth" and is "one of the great novels of this century." Dreiser commanded pathos without the tragic dimension. Perhaps he insisted too much upon personal ideas.

Still, Dreiser at present has other interests for us. Matthiessen's second real achievement is the careful study in his concluding chapters of Dreiser's politics and philosophy. Thoroughly grounded himself in American radical thought, and sympathetic with the broodings of an inquirer, Matthiessen has unravelled as well as anyone could the tangled paths by which Dreiser approached simultaneously a membership in the American Communist Party and a cloudy position somewhere in the universe of neo-Christian mysticism. A long comparison with Clarence Darrow is more helpful here than were the frequent comparisons earlier with Whitman, Melville, and others.

The whole painful discussion, which does not avoid, for example, Dreiser's slow development away from anti-Semitism, is relevant to Matthiessen's tragic death last year and ought to be read by everyone interested in either man. "Contemplating for ourselves," Matthiessen writes, "the extremes to which both Darrow and Dreiser had gone in their skepticism, we are faced with the grave question of how long positive values can endure only as the aftershine of something that has been lost."

An essential horror in life, in modern life, which Dreiser did not ever really face in his fiction, faces us quietly in these last chapters, and we can only mourn two honest men.

1951

❧❧❧

DREISER'S "THE TITAN"

THE CHARMING REMEMBERED NOVELIST WILLIAM DEAN
Howells knew something of the business world, and Sinclair Lewis
knew more. It might seem that, of the very small number of successful
novels by Americans devoted to America's principal activity to date,
The Rise of Silas Lapham and *Babbitt* are those to which Dreiser's
Cowperwood series—in particular *The Titan*—ought to be compared.
But it won't do, though to say why is not easy.

The three authors are obviously dissimilar (American "realists");
what I am thinking of is certain differences among the books. If more
local points in novels were noticed in novels—the novels that matter
—criticism might improve. Rereading *Babbitt* some years ago, for no
special reason, I found myself indifferent to the apparent satire that
brought it general fame but much impressed by its *poetic* quality.
The products of the American business world glow and shine for
George F. Babbitt and his creator. We come on something similar at
a vivid point in *Lapham*, when the rough, rich paint manufacturer
declares, "deeply moved," to a young man of superior position he is
thinking of taking on, "It's the best paint in God's universe"; the
young man is impressed, and so was I. Now for all its energy and
seeming dedication, *The Titan* lacks this glamour of faith in business,
and comparison fails.

Perhaps now we can make the reasons clear. Though not wholly
free of idealistic elements, Cowperwood can make no show of decency alongside Howells's and Lewis's heroes because he is not dealing with the real world as they are. Our position here is paradoxical
but helpful. Paint and real estate are real things, real business. Finance
is not; it is abstract. When Cowperwood hurls himself, in his "genial"
way, on the growing city Chicago, it seems next door to accident that
he fastens first on the gas companies and then on the street railways as
means to his ends. *Means.* So strongly is the insignificance of the facts
of the means conveyed that it is with a tiny surge of definite surprise
that one learns casually, late in the book, that one of his enormous
New York backers, surveying the Chicago scene from Wall Street,
feels that Cowperwood "knows a lot about running street-railways"
and, elsewhere, that Cowperwood himself had personally gone so far,

years before, on his visits to New York, as to inspect the new elevated line *physically*—just in case he should ever want to build one of
his own. One never thinks of him as running a business—providing
gas or transportation—but only as operating out of businesses. But as
means to what end? Money? But he came from Philadelphia with
money, and though it is true that he finally leaves Chicago enriched
to the tune of twenty million, there are ways to make money outside
the dangerous and speculative world of high finance. Besides, I get a
definite impression that he does not value money itself, and so we are
still left with the matter of end. Sex? Love? Well, money is an
element in his successes here, but one feels that like most of Dreiser's
other heroes he could have had plenty of women without money.
Political power? Not in itself. Social position? But in Chicago, with
his Philadelphia reputation following him, he cannot have it, recognizes this without a tremor (though: *he wanted it*), and operates
harder than ever.

What Cowperwood aims at is control—control of the fastest-
growing, most involved services of a great crude city, control of his
bankers and associates, control of his enemies, financial and political,
control of his passive and helpless wife (men of his sort in Dreiser
never seem to have children: Cowperwood's two are rarely mentioned), control of big physical establishments, control of certain
women (especially those theoretically least available), control of
works of art. This is not a businessman but a predator, comparable to
nobody in *Lapham* or *Babbitt*—although we may think of the novels
as comparable in artistic merit, all being second-class in my view,
following on *A Hazard of New Fortunes* (along with parts of *The
Landlord at Lion's Head*), *Arrowsmith*, and *Main Street*, and—more
clearly still—*An American Tragedy* and *Sister Carrie*. Thank the
Lord for second-class novels, or what would we read after the age of
twenty-one, and how insufferable would be a criticism that devoted
itself solely to first-class novels (the fifty-two or eighty-six there
are). It is an advantage, moreover, when not dealing with masterpieces, that it is easier to be candid. Nobody, perhaps, has ever
thought Vronsky a successfully realized character; but who wishes to
admit this fact?

Treacherous, brutal, corrupting, insolent, ego-sane as Dreiser
presents his hero, we might reasonably inquire what means he has
taken to recommend him, and how far they succeed, and here we
come on tangles. I think his inventor has taken very few means indeed—I will mention some presently—to recommend Cowperwood

to the reader. His point of view seems to be both lordly and helpless: lordly ("Take him or leave him") and helpless ("Can I help it if human nature—one human nature—is like this?"). These two qualities go far to describe Cowperwood himself, the man of imperious will who yet continually *wonders* why he *has* to do what he does. Several of Dreiser's favourite terms are already in play—"wondered," "Life was very strange," "necessary" ("As in the past they had made it necessary for him to work against them by bribery and perjury")— and he is also fond of "inconsequential" and "nebulous," and all these words come to us with a bearing practically programmatic, as if some vague "mood" philosophy of human life were being laid out or imposed.

I am prepared even to wonder whether Dreiser's failure to understand his hero, which so far we have considered as deliberate, may not be merely inadvertent. On one page we are notified, as if we needed to be, that "His greatest weakness, if he had one, was that he could but ill brook opposition of any kind." And twenty pages later: "Cowperwood, individual, reliant, utterly indifferent to opposition of any kind," etc. I believe this is called eating your cake and having it, too, and it reminds me of the most important American novel yet written about a businessman—a real businessman—by that most improbable adept in the subject, Henry James: I mean *The American*, where an honest critic will have to confess that too much is *put into* Christopher Newman for credibility, especially during the first half of the novel. But there we are dealing with a masterpiece: how shall we exonerate Dreiser?

A standard plea would be Whitman's "Do I contradict myself?" and so on. Remaining, to some extent, within the American scene, I prefer—and I think Theodore Dreiser would—a remark by a great master of pity, one of the human areas in which Dreiser perhaps was feeblest. There was until lately an English lyric poet named Ralph Hodgson, much admired in the early 1920's, hero of a delicious tribute by T. S. Eliot, who felt more for animals' maltreatment by man in his left little finger than all the rest of even his own race felt put together; and wrote about nothing else for sixty years—"The Bells of Heaven" being one of the little masterworks of the age. At around eighty, in "retirement" on an Ohio hillside, thought long dead, he published a splendid new collection and was interviewed. "I don't try to reconcile anything," he said. "This is a damned strange world."

Cowperwood is not a villain, in his master's view. Let's begin with that. Nor is there anything tragic about his defeats. One does not even suffer them. His second marriage is a horror. The wife claws his current mistress (a very good scene) in his own house, and there is a problem of propriety, since the mistress may die. His bought men in politics do not stay bought—Kerrigan and Tiernan, I would say in passing, are the most effective ward leaders in American literature, handled with something rare in Dreiser, humour, as well as complete understanding. He is finally wrinkled out even of the street-railways scene, and heads for New York and Europe, refreshed. With a larger fortune.

When Silas Lapham's paint is to be replaced by one equally good that costs less, one's heart hurts. Not in *The Titan*.

And yet Dreiser looms a far more formidable novelist than Howells. The general rage that went up when Lewis won the Nobel Prize—that overrated literary encomium—instead of Dreiser, I am happy to echo. (I am also glad that Dreiser cuffed Lewis physically—although any reader of Mark Schorer's biography of Lewis must feel intermittent sympathy with him—on a famous and absurd occasion in New York.) Dreiser remains one of the commanding writers we have had, for the readers who can bear him.

Alfred Kazin, a critic of bulky temperament, who understands the fantastic Dreiser as well as anyone, once committed himself to the following proposition: "Dreiser's success in handling social fact is due not merely to his doggedness and repetition but to the fact that his main characters are never shown in the round, are never complex" (*Major Writers of America*, edited by Perry Miller, vol. II, 1962). This stricture, masquerading as an encomium, I would say is false. It is easy to agree that Dreiser is often dogged and repetitious, but I would no more think of praising him for these weaknesses than I would praise the author of *Love's Labour's Lost* if that flashing play could be thought to possess them. Surely the truth is that Dreiser's power is felt in his strokes, like any other author's: for instance, the few sentences in which we learn that it was Cowperwood's habit, often, when returning home alone late at night, to go and sit in his gallery in front of one or the other of his art objects, and wonder. Dogged? Repetitious? In the fact of the immense assemblage of the primary materials of this ambitious novel—Money, Society, Sex, Politics, cunningly interacting—that is but a touch, only a strong one.

As for "never shown in the round," I have to be skeptical. Strength and geniality are Cowperwood's chief notes; need for control; need for women; amazement at art; blunt male egotism ("he could not forgive her for not loving him perfectly, as had so many others"); ruthless cunning—how complex does Kazin desire a character to be? But I would say more.

To put differently a matter adumbrated earlier, it is an oddity that an artist with Dreiser's views, or un-views, about life should have chosen for his most extensive character presentment a man of commanding activity and almost blind faith in his own destiny. (It is true that Cowperwood's career has its origin in the actual Philadelphia-Chicago-London career of the tycoon C. T. Yerkes, but I think no critic has pretended that Cowperwood is a portrait of Yerkes, and in any case the question is irrelevant to our present concern, since Cowperwood is plainly Dreiser in temperament and thought, just as plainly as the artist-hero of *The Genius*, Eugene Witla.) When *The Bookman* once asked Dreiser for a credo, he wound up with a comprehensiveness unusual even for him and struck us out: "I can make no comment on my work or my life that holds either interest or import for me. Nor can I imagine any explanation or interpretation of any life, my own included, that would be either true—or important, if true. Life is to me too much a welter and play of inscrutable forces to permit, in my case at least, any significant comment. One may paint for one's own entertainment, and that of others—perhaps." Follows a genuinely Whitmanian, anti-Whitman, peroration that seems to me one of the most moving moments of this wonderfully candid and mysterious man: "As I see him the utterly infinitesimal individual weaves among the mysteries a floss-like and wholly meaningless course—if course it be. In short I catch no meaning from all I have seen, and pass quite as I came, confused and dismayed." (This is 1928, quoted in Robert H. Elias's reprehensible biography of 1949.) An antithetical reciprocity, or the modulation in the superman Cowperwood to this antiphilosophy, now and then seems to me to account for much of his attractiveness. Who fails to sympathize with a leader in despair?

At the same time, a composure hard to parallel, in Cowperwood, is pleasing. Without parallel, I mean, face to face. I have sometimes thought that our highest admiration ought to be reserved for those authors who find things for their characters to say when (manifestly) not only is there nothing to say, but even if there were, no human being could find out what it might be. Nowhere in Dreiser will we discover anything approaching the depth of Parolles' "Simply the thing I am / Shall make me live," but for similar composure under intolerable circumstances, consider an interview of Cowperwood's with Mr Haguenin, editor of the *Press*, whose daughter he has seduced—to public knowledge. Mr Haguenin bitterly reproaches him for his conduct, in a long tirade, and severs all business relationships with him:

> Cowperwood, who had listened very patiently and very fixedly, without a tremor of an eyelash, merely said:
> "There seems to be no common intellectual ground, Mr. Haguenin, upon which you and I can meet in this matter. You cannot understand my point of view. I could not possibly adopt yours . . ."
> He turned and walked unconcernedly out, thinking that it was too bad to lose the support of so respectable a man, but also that he could do without it.

For years I've thought this one of the high points of the novel. It is certain that Cowperwood attracts us, if he does, by the same "appetite for the wonders of life" and "that instinct for the essential and vital which invariably possessed him," a certain sprightliness, that must have attracted Dreiser, in conception, to him. But I have never been quite clear as to what Dreiser really thinks about this hero to whom he devoted three long novels. His admiration is obvious, his irony far less so—if it were not for one episode, one might deny him irony entirely. This is the masterly account—in two parts, very brief —of Cowperwood's entrapment and blackmailing of the mayor, Sluss (a blonde chaser). For somebody—author, Cowperwood himself, the reader—it ought to exhibit his magnanimity, for he does not ruin Sluss publicly, as he could with impunity do (he only destroys poor high-minded Sluss's principles and peace of soul). But the truth is that Sluss exposed would be of no use to him.

It is time to say something of Dreiser as a poetic writer, as a chronicler of American urban life (many consider him, with whatever misgivings, the most impressive we have), and as a philosopher. The first two matters may be taken together, and some quotations prefaced with the observation that it is when Dreiser girds up his poetic loins that he becomes intolerable. "To whom may the laurels as laureate of this Florence of the West yet fall?" he wildly inquires (I am quoting exactly). "This singing flame of a city, this all America, this poet in chaps and buckskin, this rude, raw Titan, this Burns of a city!" How flatulent it seems beside the invocation of Saul Bellow at the beginning of a novel about Chicago that better evokes it: "Chicago, that somber city." (Chicagoans are so touchy that perhaps the present writer should explain that he has four or five reasons for being grateful to Chicago and nothing much in particular against it.) Intent as he is on it, Dreiser's evocation of the Chicago of the

1880's and later is not one of *The Titan*'s most luminous features; Philadelphia, in the first volume of the trilogy, *The Financier*, is handled more freshly.

As for his ideas, perhaps Dreiser took them too seriously, confused as they were and remain. He never decided between Chance and Determinism—and why should he?—but he continually redecided and never knew quite on which side to place his magic "chemic" formula by which he hoped to explain to himself the mysteries of human life. Man sees woman: chemistry. Small wonder that he wound up half-Communist, half-Christian; dogmas, both, quite irreconcilable with the body of his published work. I am not objecting to his inconsistency but to his lifelong misconception of the role of ideas in imaginative work. It is true that he was uneducated, but even this, in my opinion, did not save him.

Something, but as little as possible, needs to be said about Dreiser's women. Women! At all points they strike one as emerging from his heroes' ears until one sits merely awaiting, with exasperation, the emergence of the next one, and as for the real women, it took him a very large work indeed (*A Gallery of Women*) to memorialize merely a few. He sweats over them, too—his anxiety that we should be hypnotized by Berenice is patent, and indeed she is one of his best portraits. But the whole topic does not represent Dreiser at his happiest. His interest in them, I think or rather feel, peaks with his hero's and flags with his hero's, and there is a want of objectivity which is fatal. A good instance is Aileen in *The Titan*, whose deterioration to smoking—smoking!—and liquor and adultery is grotesquely unconvincing. (Her lover, Polk Lynde, comes over poorly, too—a caricature—Dreiser is numb with young men above a certain station in life.)

Here then are two reasons for the comparative failure: the pattern, destroying drama, and subjectivity. The major reason I feel to be a little different, and since at this moment in time it may seem strange to accuse an author of want of delicacy, I want to take a counter-illustration from *The Rise of Silas Lapham*. The stupid beautiful sister and a well-bred young man are left alone briefly while a party is inspecting the half-finished house her father is building. For four pages, while a Jane Austen-ish conversation is taking place, Irene, to dissimulate her intensity (young Corey has no interest in her whatever—he is polite), follows shavings on the floor with her parasol. Finally he helps her get one, and Howells writes: "To a girl everything a young man does is of significance; and if he holds a shaving down with his foot while she pokes through it with her parasol, she must ask herself what he means by it." Returned home with her sister, she bursts into storms of tears and smiles. It must be clear, even from this barren outline, that Dreiser would never have attempted such a scene and could not if he had tried. His women are mere objects. Perhaps, for all his experience, he really knew very little of women.

In summing up Dreiser's contribution to American letters, difficult though it may be to evaluate accurately, perhaps we should turn to Sinclair Lewis. I do not recall a more generous, more noble paean of praise to a fellow worker than Lewis's statement to the Swedish Academy in 1930, when he accepted the Nobel Prize, which Dreiser had so begrudged him: "Suppose you had taken Theodore Dreiser," said Lewis nervously. "Now to me, as to many other American writers, Dreiser, more than any other man, is marching alone. Usually unappreciated, often hounded, he had cleared the trail from Victorian Howellsian timidity and gentility in American fiction to honesty, boldness and passion of life. Without his pioneering I doubt if any of us could, unless we liked to be sent to jail, seek to express life, beauty, and terror."

1952

F. Scott Fitzgerald

"In the Twenties, his heyday, he was a kind of king of our American youth"—so a writer of Fitzgerald's generation remembered him when he died five years ago. It would be pleasant to leave him there, among the fast cars, the bloom of youth, the beat of jazz, ruling from Princeton and Long Island and the Riviera his incoherent kingdom. This would be pleasant and historical; but we cannot do it. We have serious business with one or two of his books, and perhaps with the lesson of his shade,—what he calls back to us, if we care to attend. The king is extremely dead, his subjects are dispersed. We had better be critical, which is to try to save.

Some very good readers will wonder whether anything is worth saving. We may agree that this king went in heavily and childishly for fireworks, beautiful in the immediate darkness, a mess of wire and cardboard in the morning. We want something better than lips which are stated to be thrilling and daydreams drifting over fatuity. But there can be no doubt that in *The Great Gatsby* we have something better. This short novel, published in 1925, still has readers; three publishers flourish it on their current lists; there is a widespread impression that it is Fitzgerald's best novel. Undoubtedly it is. An impression less widespread, which I wish to encourage, is that it is a masterpiece.

The word need not be pretentious or invoke wild rivalries with Hawthorne or Stendhal. Let us mean by it a work of the literary imagination which is consistent, engaging, and dramatic, in exceptional degrees; which exhibits largely mastered a human subject of the first importance; and which seems in retrospect to illuminate the whole physical and spiritual situation of which it was, by the strange parturition of art, an accidental product. One easy test will be the rapidity with which, in the imagination of a good judge, other works of the period and kind will faint away under any suggested comparison with it. Now a small work may satisfy these demands as readily as a large one, and *The Great Gatsby* satisfies them, I believe, better than any other American work of fiction since *The Golden Bowl*.

Fitzgerald's general subject in it is the irresponsible world of American wealth in the early twenties, into which he thrusts up through the ambiguous levels of our society his elegant young roughneck Jay Gatsby, born James Gatz. Most of his scenes picture the semi-activities of the rich on Long Island and in New York, stretching to include Tom Buchanan's journeys into the lower middle class to meet his mistress, and Gatsby's continuing criminal associations. All these parties and meetings are imaged with a clear honesty and an exact feeling for relation. But his precise subject is the impact of this world upon the two outsiders who venture into it, and particularly upon Carraway, Fitzgerald's narrator, the history of whose disenchantment during one summer the novel practically is. Carraway stands with less distortion for the author himself than, probably, any other character he created,—the initiated but detached Middle Westerner, the moralist; and the closeness with which Fitzgerald's cleaves to his narrator's perception partly accounts for the great difference in control between this and his later novels. *The Great Gatsby* is in Chekhov's sense a purely graceful book ("When a man spends the least possible number of movements over some definite action, that is grace"). Not a page could well be lost from it without disturbance to Fitzgerald's achievement of the rapt immobility of Gatsby fixed upon his far object, and Carraway's advance toward nausea. To Carraway the nature of the wealth-world can be revealed. He can suffer through his mistress, through his cousin Daisy and her husband, Tom, and return to the Middle West, summing up like an evening bell: "It was all very careless and confused. They were careless people, Tom and Daisy—they smashed up things and creatures and then retreated back into their money or their vast carelessness, or whatever it was that kept them together . . ." Gatsby can be physically destroyed, and he is; his is one of the three deaths Tom and Daisy cause. But no revelation of their world can be made to him. Gatsby has had a prior and very different revelation.

He is described at the outset as possessing "an extraordinary gift for hope, a romantic readiness," "some heightened sensitivity to the promises of life," and it is clear that this is the quality that drew Fitzgerald to his creation. But how far and how strangely he insisted upon it does not appear to have been understood. When Gatsby and Daisy have been reunited, Carraway recognizes in Gatsby's bewilderment "the colossal vitality of his illusion. It had gone beyond her, beyond everything. He had thrown himself into it with a creative passion . . . No amount of fire or freshness can challenge what a man can store up in his ghostly heart." The theme recurs blankly when Carraway attempts to warn him: " 'I wouldn't ask too much of her,' I ventured. 'You can't repeat the past.' 'Can't repeat the past?' he cried incredulously. 'Why of course you can!' " And finally in a profound moment as Gatsby is speaking to Carraway of Daisy's feeling for her husband, whether at the beginning of their marriage she did really love Tom: "Suddenly he came out with a curious remark. 'In any case,' he said, 'it was just personal.' What could you make of that, except to suspect some intensity in his conception of the affair that couldn't be measured?"

These passages will locate for us, I think, the obsession which dominates Gatsby, the man and the book, and provides the permanent theme of Fitzgerald's serious fiction. Carraway is not permitted to understand it fully, but I have no doubt that Fitzgerald himself did and wished his reader to do so. In the introduction he wrote in 1934 for a reprint of *Gatsby* occurs this startling claim: "How anyone could take up the responsibility of being a novelist without a sharp and concise attitude about life is a puzzle to me." It was not intended, probably, as a claim, but a claim it is; and although Fitzgerald looked on himself as a moralist (and plainly is one), this seems to me less a reference to morality than to an attitude or pattern of the most general kind, a "figure in the carpet," as James called it. What is the "figure"?

It is not an idealism, and not Hope, though it is kin to these. It is hardly even an attitude toward experience, although it is a way of taking Life. It is a view of Life in which the creature's supreme admiration is commanded by that which the artist knows to be *wrong*, in which the supreme allegiance is forced to be felt—producing "creative passion"—toward a hopeless error. It insists that the enthusiast be *impersonal* or selfless, and *certain*. It is as if a young artist, a young man, saw every road blocked and sent his characters forward singing. There is helpless irony in the mounting of such a theme, owing to an incongruity between what the hero is made to be obsessed by, his impersonal devotion and confidence, and what the author knows, his own despair. But this irony is not tragic in Fitzgerald; it is as unhappy and tender as a farewell. The superior knowledge has no condescension or rebuke. Carraway knows, for instance, that Gatsby's chance for Daisy is long past, but there is only love in his witness to Gatsby's fantastic vigil,—or there is envy. This feeling is as idiosyncratic and as literal as some of Wordsworth's feelings, and as difficult to understand for the same reason: most people are familiar with the attitude in some diffused form but cannot imagine that anyone really believes it in a strict form. What Fitzgerald valued was a beauty and intensity of attachment, which his imagination required should be attachment to something inaccessible. For the wholly inaccessible he admitted two modes, the never existent and the already past. He drove his characters sometimes toward the first, as in certain of the stories which are actual fantasies, but regularly toward the second, as in *Gatsby*. And his finest work is saturated with the desperate or ecstatic nostalgia, the firm hope and the firmer despair, of the superb conclusion of this novel.

And as I sat there brooding on the old, unknown world, I thought of Gatsby's wonder when he first picked out the green light at the end of Daisy's dock. He had come a long way to this blue lawn, and his dream must have seemed so close that he could hardly fail to grasp it. He did not know that it was already behind him, somewhere back in that vast obscurity beyond the city, where the dark fields of the republic rolled on under the night.

Gatsby believed in the green light, the orgastic future that year by year recedes before us. It eluded us then, but that's no matter—to-morrow we will run faster, stretch out our arms farther. . . . And one fine morning—

So we beat on, boats against the current, borne back ceaselessly into the past.

Any reader in 1925 (one would suppose, but it is hard to hear new music justly) should have been astonished by *Gatsby*, not least a reader who had followed the author from the beginning. Nothing in Fitzgerald's earlier books strongly suggests the access of rein and understanding shortly to come. They are fluent and gaudy, vague and self-indulgent, a little embarrassing now. Suddenly he was able, not yet thirty, to lay out and execute a masterpiece. He was happily married, widely admired, and had made money. One might have expected such a career of production as American artists rarely have achieved. What happened then?

After almost ten years he published *Tender Is the Night*, a novel diffuse, lush, uncertain, and badly designed. There are admirable things in it, a few scenes, some description, some epigrams; but it is hard to believe that anyone ever found it as a story anything but a failure. Perhaps Nicole is all right. The other characters are not, and one hears a personal insistence in the degeneration of Dick Diver and Abe North which seems external, morbid. It would wreck a firmer book than this. Episodes, too, almost uniformly disagreeable, are hurried in and out without reason—simply, one guesses, because they *happened* once. The style alters senselessly from section to section, as if the book were a series of exercises. Most of the second half can hardly be read as continuous narrative. All the talent of Carraway's summer has gone to bits.

Six years later Fitzgerald left *The Last Tycoon* unfinished when he died. Resisting the inclination to exaggerate the merit of post-humous work, as James's *The Ivory Tower* has been overpraised and Stephen Crane's *The O'Ruddy* would be if it were read, one must testify that Fitzgerald had gone far enough with it to demonstrate a reassembled gift. His film producer, Monroe Stahr, comes from the imagination that made Jay Gatsby: "He had flown up very high to see, on strong wings, when he was young. And while he was up there he had looked on all the kingdoms, with the kind of eyes that can stare straight into the sun . . . he had stayed up there longer than most of us, and then, remembering all he had seen from his great height of how things were, he had settled gradually to earth . . . You could say that this was where an accidental wind blew him, but . . . I would rather think that in a 'long shot' he saw a new way of measuring our jerky hopes and graceful rogueries and awkward sorrows, and that he came here from choice to be with us to the end." The opening chapters are excellent, the writing compact as well as rich, the symbols working plainly and quietly, as in Stahr's name, as in the suicide of Mr. Schwartz beside the mysterious Hermitage. There is no doubt that we suffered in losing the novel's completion. To try to measure the loss is futile, although I should note that Fitzgerald was having extraordinary difficulty already with his point of view,—perhaps ill-chosen, a producer's daughter—as he had had in *Tender Is the Night* for similar reasons; and that he appeared in Chapter VI to be moving toward areas of his subject imperfectly familiar to him though necessary to his conception. Both these books will have to be kept afloat, if at all, by *The Great Gatsby*.

Then there are the magazine stories, of which he collected the least trivial from time to time into volumes. Claims have been made for some of these, without much justification, unless perhaps for "The Rich Boy." The two most ambitious strike me as about equally false: "May Day," banal, fundamentally disordered, and "Absolution," which (besides relying unduly upon Joyce's profound story "The Sisters") at its climax imposes shamelessly upon the little boy the obsession which I have called the permanent theme in Fitzgerald. This is accomplished, or attempted, with a brazen rhetoric perfectly characterized by the author in another place—the *Gatsby* introduction—when he speaks of "the large false face peering around the corner of a character's head."

It is little to show for fifteen years of the fullness of such a gift. The fullness?—hardly. If the similarity of Gatsby's story and Stahr's suggests to us that the gift was a limited one, we should remember that not only did Fitzgerald not *develop* it beyond 1925 but he hardly exercised it at all thereafter. The whole story is not clear in the articles and letters and notes printed by Edmund Wilson in *The Crack-up;* one would like to see it told one day. But enough is clear there to show that during most of these years he could not use his gift because he no longer had it. He had sold it for money. He got a good deal of money for it,—$400,000 in fifteen years, he estimated in 1934. And he missed it a good deal before the end,—six months before his death he wrote to his daughter: "I wish now I'd *never* relaxed or looked back"—but said at the end of *The Great Gatsby:* "I've found my line—from now on this comes first. This is my immediate duty—without this I am nothing."

No man knows another's temptations well; I am not concerned to judge his long apostasy, but merely to look at some of its results, because no other recent history known to me exhibits so sharply the difficulty and danger an artist undergoes who must do his work in a culture essentially confused in the way and to the degree that ours is. A division between intellectual and popular culture, between the million semiliterate and the hundred more or less educated, between the standards of *Collier's* and the standards of *The Dial*, is a natural division. But it is unnatural—it is essentially confused—that either should submit to, or wish to usurp, the standards of the other; and this is our desperate case.

Fitzgerald, for instance, appears to have lived his whole life in the well-heeled infantile world of American popular writing. I cannot pause to describe this world; a representative spokesman for it is John O'Hara, who contributes a vacant gossip by way of introduction to a recently published selection of Fitzgerald's writings. Fitzgerald did not share all of its attitudes (for example, its jealous hatred of intellectuals) and his judgment remained to some degree independent of it (for example, he notes about a book of his friend O'Hara's, "He just began chewing with nothing in his mouth"). But he accepted its standards, made his friends in it, castrated his work for it, and took its rewards. When halfwits in editorial offices cracked the whip, Fitzgerald danced. And yet he somehow believed—perhaps at intervals only—that he was really on the other side. In one of his weakest sketches for *Esquire*, the Author, showing a visitor about his house, takes him finally to the attic, where are piles of old *Dials* and *Little Reviews*, clippings, letters, and says, "This is the loot. This is what one has instead of a bank account." It is true that his $400,000 had been spent when he wrote this, but the capacity for self-deception is surprising and must be due to Fitzgerald's knowledge that his best work *was* really on the other side. In the popular world work is dead in a month; Fitzgerald had been forgotten before he died; he must have needed the hope that his work would cross the line and be accepted, where alone acceptance is meaningful, on "the other side."

Meanwhile, there was Fitzgerald among the formula boys. What did it cost him, besides the ability to practice his art? It cost him, first, the criticism that might have saved him: by shaming him from his bad work, stiffening his conscience, protecting him against his abasements. The old association with Wilson and Bishop seems to have been his only link. When Eliot wrote to him that he thought *Gatsby* "the first step that American fiction has taken since Henry James," the praise was agreeable but the encouragement fell into a vacuum. Fitzgerald prostrated himself always, apparently, before Hemingway—even in *To Have and Have Not* he discovered "pages that are right up with Dostoievsky in their undeflected intensity." The attitude hurt his work, and nobody of responsible judgment was close to show him Hemingway's feet of clay—coyness, random brutality, fatuousness—or the superiority in certain ways of his own highest work. "Trollope kills me by his mastery," Tolstoy thrust into his diary while he was writing *War and Peace;* then he added, "I console myself that he has his and I have mine."

It cost Fitzgerald, second, his sense of reality. He could not write, and publish, what he felt, so at intervals for years he abandoned the realm of truth altogether: he wrote fantasies, one his intolerable play *The Vegetable,* the rest stories, of ghosts, diamond mountains, men growing young. Here he could construct his own laws, and his own conscience, for feeling; not even his own reproaches would reach him. It cost him, last, his faith in art. The papers printed in *The Crack-up* witness again and again to his sense of "a rankling indignity, that to me had become almost an obsession, in seeing the power of the written word subordinated to another power, a more glittering, a grosser power." By this he meant the film, but artistic power is subordinated in other passages to "great animal magnetism" and to "experience," or is found inadequate in itself. On this heresy followed lacerations. A long misery for Fitzgerald, the last years of the thirties,—alcohol, poverty, Hollywood, despair, illness. Then the miraculous return of nerve just before the end: the organic style again of "There was an eager to-do in the eastern sky, and Wylie could see me plain—thin with good features and lots of style, and the kicking fetus of a mind," and the creation of Stahr.

What he calls back is clear enough after all: ". . . without this I am nothing."

1946

THE CASE OF RING LARDNER

IT IS A DISCONCERTING FEATURE OF MUCH AMERICAN LITerary art that either it's so closely bound up with the world of popular entertainment that the boundaries between are not easy to fix, or else —as of poetry, say (Ogden Nash allowed as an exception)—it has no relation to that world at all. In France, England, other countries, there is both less reciprocity and more. A man like Noël Coward seeks his level quicker, after initial hesitation (in a play like *The Vortex*), and though an artist like Cocteau may operate also as an entertainer, no doubt is raised, by him or by anyone else, about his *being* an artist. The arts are less glumly separated from the life of the more or less educated citizenry, and at the same time their status is clearer. Here, matters are more ambiguous. A thing like Norman Corwin's *On a Note of Triumph* is not only praised by Walter Winchell and sells at least fifty thousand copies; it is also hailed, with happy illiteracy, in *The New York Times Book Review* ("Even if he had written this one, five or ten years after V-E Day, its values would be the same. His writing has some of the quality of universal truth") and woofed up by Carl Sandburg, an actual poet, as "vast . . . terrific . . . certainly one of the great all-time American poems." We might be in Palmer Stadium. Pictures fly around of Corwin, portentous, brooding like Beethoven, and—God's truth—his thoughtless concoction was declared to be "the Eroica of this historic year."

Now these windy views do not fail to occur, though they are less frequent, in London, Paris, and Rome; but they are not taken seriously there, except by the author and his cronies. Here almost everybody takes them seriously, until some fresher fantasy has supervened. Some of our artists take them seriously; Hemingway and Faulkner, two of the most ambitious writers living, describe themselves as hunters and farmers. Moreover, we impose our view on the world; Pearl Buck wins the Nobel Prize. Oscar Hammerstein 12th makes a bulkier literary figure than J. F. Powers. The situation is not new, either. It goes back nearly a century. Cooper, Poe, Hawthorne, Melville were men of letters, and we have had others. But for a long time we have also, in figure after figure, faced this double anomaly of the artist who pretends not to be one and the entertainer who pretends to the status of an artist (or has it pretended for him).

With a man of letters, criticism has only to address itself to the perplexing questions of whether he is any good, and where, and how good, and in what ways. Plainly, if you are obliged to decide, in the first place, whether your subject is an artist at all, criticism will be more difficult. The extreme uncertainty of our criticism of our own literature, which is to be attributed partly to senses of inferiority and dependence, vanity, and remorse therefor, must be due as well to a sneaking down-with-him attitude toward the self-confessed deliberate artist and a sneaking admiration for the guy who entertains us without undemocratic pretensions—this admiration then translating itself naturally into the hope that after all he may prove *also* to be the real literary thing.

I offer these desultory remarks as prelude to some consideration of a borderline character named Ring Lardner. Nobody over thirty-five will have to be told who he was, but I don't find that younger people read him any more, except in short-story courses, where they run into "Haircut" or "Champion," and in any case they will know nothing of his extra-literary personality, which was so engaging to the rest of us during the twenties and early thirties. An extra-literary personality is so important to an entertainer, though unimportant to art, that we might begin with it, assisted by Donald Elder's biography.* This is comparatively artless, and too long—Elder's reluctance to cut a letter, no matter how trivial, is positively Byzantine; but it is full, shrewd, and surprisingly candid for a work produced so soon after its subject's death, and under the continuous assistance of his surviving family. I shall be quarrying shamelessly for a bit.

The outline of the life is very much what one expected. Niles, Michigan, 1885, to years of baseball reporting in Chicago, to New York and general celebrity and then literary recognition; a wife and four sons; loads of dough, monumental boozing; fading reputation, broken health, the protracted decline that his friend F. Scott Fitzgerald imaged in the musician Abe North of *Tender Is the Night;* death in 1933 at forty-eight, not old, not young, apparently unfulfilled. An American pattern, in short. Nor will it surprise anyone to learn that this famous clown was a very gloomy guy indeed, suspicious as W. C. Fields, silent as a pharaoh. But the filling in of the outline takes us into what one would not have expected.

Was it in the cards that this man who elected to spend most of his life with athletes and show people and assorted idiots, who presented himself weekly to millions, in dialect, as a "wise boob," should have been the precocious, petted ninth of nine children born into a cultured family of long-established wealth? Each child had its own nursemaid, and the house had its own tennis court and baseball diamond. One foot was deformed from birth, corrected by a surgeon, and he wore a brace until he was eleven; Elder connects with this his irrational admiration for athletes. But he would not have gone to school anyway: his mother, whose rather wild, deeply religious personality appears to have been eight feet high (with his father Lardner was never close at all), taught the three youngest children, until a tutor did. He entered what we *amusingly* call high school at twelve, played football, was graduated at sixteen.

At this point the family fortune collapsed. He spent part of a year at the Armour Institute in Chicago headed toward engineering. Then for four years he did practically nothing, in Niles: amateur theatricals, the gas company. By a fluke, a job on the South Bend

* *Ring Lardner,* 1956.

Times, two years; then he was lifted to Chicago. Here he worked on the *Inter-Ocean, Examiner*, and *Tribune*, accompanied the White Sox, became a sports expert, took over an established column, began to publish in *The Saturday Evening Post*, perfected his mask, made one of his two abortive trips to Europe (a place nonexistent for Lardner, who had no historic sense whatever, no interest in politics or society, no interest in ideas), and succeeded in forming no relation with the enthusiastic remodelling of both verse and prose then supposedly taking place in Chicago—being himself intensely conservative and provincial, as he was to the end, with no visible quarrel of any kind with Niles.

This was one trouble. It let him be courteous, generous, modest, fastidious, romantic, scrupulous, chivalrous, and proud; but it left him worrying, deadpan, restless, suffocated—and bored. He was one of the most heavily armoured men, and one of the most exposed, that even this country can ever have produced. That is, Lardner was wise; he never let anybody get close. So if somebody ripped his heart out, it was not a friend. All the lies told about him were by acquaintances and strangers. On the other hand, among the things he never recovered from were the Black Sox scandal of 1919 and his disappointment later in Jack Dempsey. When he moved East in the fall of 1919, it was not to write about sports but to do a syndicated weekly column about anything, by the "wise boob."

Nearly all of his best writing was still to come; not that it is bulky. But I should say that he went to pieces with great rapidity—at a pace dissolved into Elder's narrative—for already during 1922–4, when he and Fitzgerald were neighbors in Great Neck (they never saw each other much after), it was the younger man's sense that Lardner was "getting off"—doing his work conscientiously but not enjoying it. Fitzgerald badgered him to collect his stories, supplied the title *How to Write Short Stories*, badgered Scribner's to bring them out (with the incongruous aid of Sir James Barrie, this came about); some of his uninteresting earlier books were reissued; and all this probably cheered Lardner more than Elder (who is rather chary about Fitzgerald altogether) is eager to allow. Fitzgerald wanted Lardner to organize himself and undertake a large work; so did Edmund Wilson; these notations belong later in this article, but have to be mentioned because Lardner must have recognized in himself an entire incapacity for anything of the kind, and in his silent way suffered. He was doing a comic strip, an exasperated fake autobiography, all sorts of things. *The Love Nest* came out in 1926. Elder sees him this year at his height, making some $30,000, his column in 157

papers. The consumption of bourbon is not recorded. He found he
had tuberculosis.

Now comes a phase unpredictable or gruesome. He gave most of
this up, and attacked Broadway. The ruling passion of Lardner's life
was music. He had perfect pitch, and taught himself six instruments.
The music that interested him was not what we call classical music or
"serious" music, and was not jazz—as Elder says, he was somewhat
behind the times; he was interested in *popular* music: popular songs
and, for he was also stage-struck, musical shows. It is a peculiarity
that all his life he often wrote intimate letters in a sort of parody
verse, precisely the kind of thing he appears to mock in "The Mays-
ville Minstrel"; he was strongly interested in what he thought of as
poetry, though it goes without saying that he disliked all real poetry.
Music, drama, and poetry came together for him, and for years he
contributed lyrics to Ziegfeld's shows. He did *Elmer the Great* for
George M. Cohan in 1928, and Cohan redid it. There were various
unproduced scripts, and the "nonsense" playlets that I'll say something about later. At last in 1929, with George S. Kaufman, he had a
hit in *June Moon*. He wrote a film script for $7,500 in four days. He
only published some dozen songs, however, and in general all this
aspect of his career was a failure. He was in and out of hospitals all
the final years—Florida, Arizona, California, New York—not only
with dipsomania but recurrent attacks of tuberculosis, a heart ail-
ment, digestive disorders, probably pernicious anemia. *Round-up*,
collecting thirty-five stories, came out in 1929. There is no interesting
fiction after 1926, but his humourous stuff remained sometimes astonishing, as "Large Coffee" (you can find this one in the Whites' *Sub-
treasury of American Humor*) and the parodies of "Night and Day"
which I remember in *The New Yorker* and am glad to see that Elder
quotes:

> Night and day under the fleece of me
> There's an Oh, such a flaming furneth burneth the grease of me.
> Night and day under the bark of me
> There's an Oh, such a mob of microbes making a park of me.

Anybody who can still hear the daffy croon of Tony Wons reciting
will be glad to know the cheer that Lardner made up for him:

> Tony Wons! Tony Twice!
> Holy, jumping . . .

These last things appeared in the midst of an intensely bitter and earnest crusade that Lardner carried on against the stupidity and especially the pornography of the lyrics of popular songs; he was so pathologically squeamish—as he was throughout his life about dirty stories (though it's true that he hated funny stories of any kind, and never told them) and indeed about anything sexual—that he even had doubts about "Tea for Two." He was extremely pedantic, in this as in other things, and was only less stern against ill grammar than against innuendo. His final work was about a drunkard, sympathetically portrayed, in the toils of family constriction. It is not likely that it would have been any good; he always lost all his irony when he wrote for the stage, and his energy anyway by now was so low that it had taken him six months to write a twenty-page story.

It is impossible to read the account of Lardner's life without admiration for his courage and dignity, and sympathy for his misery. The question is whether in it—never mind his work yet—one can perceive the sense of *purposefulness* that is obvious and strong in the lives of, say, Dreiser and Fitzgerald (drunkards, too, and popular and acquaintances of Lardner), or the drive toward *expression* visible in them.

Purposefulness, I think, is just what one does not see; except for the desire to escape (from familial protection and suffocation, intolerable frustration, boredom), which took the forms of alcohol and silence. He was a boozer from way back; began as a kid and improved. Some of the legends seem to be true, such as that of his sixty-hour vigil in one chair at the Friars Club. Apparently, seldom quarrelsome, seldom tiresome, he held liquor very well. That was unfortunate; and it must be remembered medically that he was drinking during the most devoted years Prohibition liquor. He went on the wagon again and again, like the man who found it so easy to stop smoking that he had done it fifty times; he telephoned friends and explained what a heel he was; he tried a psychiatrist. But on the whole he was very deliberate and unashamed, and so stubborn while drinking that he once, taken to hospital, refused to have an injury treated there but repaired to a club before he let a doctor come. Monumental remorse, often referred to, darkens the last years—for talent drunk up. Self-punishment, self-loathing. It is grievous to read that during the final months, at home, in East Hampton, "Sometimes he was observed alone, with his face in his hands, sobbing." And he had no recourse whatever: no satisfaction in his achievement; no discernible belief or even religious sense, an overmastering hatred of humanity in general, and all its works; no freedom. "He awoke a certain feeling," Sherwood Anderson wrote of him as he was at his most successful and happiest. "You wanted him not to be hurt, perhaps to have some freedom he did not have."

I said no freedom, but actually he had the freedom (and pride and grief) of silence: a profound reticence, a refusal to be known or speak out. Thomas Hardy's poem "He Resolves to Say No More," written at the very end of his long, expressive life, gives wonderful voice to this genuine impulse of artists. But as a lifelong characteristic, which is what it was in Lardner, nothing could promise less for the production of interesting work. He suffered from a lifelong drive toward *in*expression. It is under this reservation that we have to look at what he got done.

There are varying accounts of Lardner's characters, the world they inhabit, what he thinks of them, and so on; Constance Rourke has several good pages on his method; critics have argued at length about whether his work is by really a humourist or a realist or a satirist or whatever. But let us be inductive, and examine the kind of story in which his characters occur. He is certainly best known now for his stories—the eleven given by Gilbert Seldes in *The Portable Ring Lardner* and a few others; so that we are bound to try to decide whether or not we agree with E. B. White that he was "not essentially a writer of fiction." I take "The Love Nest" more or less at random, as one of his most familiar, one written during the half dozen years (1921–6) when he was most effective in story writing, and one he liked enough himself to make the title story of a collection.

"The Love Nest" goes like this. A writer named Bartlett is doing a piece on Lou Gregg, president of Modern Pictures, and the great man takes him in a Rolls out to his mansion for overnight, "to see us just as we are": his wife, Celia, a former actress, and their three little girls. Gregg offers Bartlett a drink and is surprised when the butler tells him a barely opened bottle of bourbon is only half full; it's happened before; he blames the servants (but the reader doesn't). Celia entrances. Much "sweetheart"-ing between the loving couple, Celia refuses a drink ("Lou objects to me drinking whisky, and I don't like it much anyway"), Gregg remembers that he has to go out for the evening, two of the girls are brought down and exhibited, Gregg takes them upstairs. Celia is to show Bartlett around what she calls "our love nest," but asks if he minds her having a drink instead, and has two. After dinner Gregg leaves. She has various drinks, wants to dance, explains that she is drunk half the time, married Gregg only out of ambition, would now "change places with the scum of the earth just to be free instead of a chattel, a *thing*." She goes to bed, Gregg returns, and the men retire. In the morning Celia sleeps late but calls downstairs, "Goodbye, sweetheart!"

What can we say about this story except that it is undeveloped and manages to be both trite and implausible? About Bartlett we learn nothing except that he is single and does not dance, and the mystery is why we learn even these things; as a writer he is not convincing—a man after a story would not so readily give up being shown around the place; he has no tone, never comments. Gregg is even more primitively presented and less convincing—he is boastful, and that is all; according to Celia he is cruel, but we are given no evidence of it. Celia is managed worst of all: she has got through half a bottle either the night before or today and yet shows no signs of it; and yet two drinks and perhaps a sneaked one or two and a cocktail make her absent-minded and red-faced at dinner (almost the only physical image in the story, put as follows: "Her face was red"). Her husband does not know she drinks, or he does (in fact he would). But he doesn't, or he wouldn't ask in front of Bartlett about the bottle (compare "no matter what he had on me, he'd never let the world know it"). But he must, from the dinner exhibition and "She's had a lot of headaches lately"—or his stupidity ought to be more impressively conveyed. The author desires to have his cake and eat it, too; he simply doesn't care about an impression of life. Lardner's friends and Elder make much of his conscientiousness. That must be as a journalist, chiefly, for what this story displays is gross carelessness, indifference.

Now for the medium. The story is written in dialogue, which has either no tone at all or is too strident to be convincing or has this tone: "I mean nobody would ever thought Celia Sayles would turn out to be a sit-by-the-fire. I mean she still likes a good time, but her home and kiddies come first. I mean her home and kiddies come first." Two paragraphs are exceptions to this law. One tells us about the red face. Here is the other:

> While the drinks were being prepared, he observed his hostess more closely and thought how much more charming she would be if she had used finesse in improving on nature. Her cheeks, her mouth, her eyes, and lashes had been, he guessed, far above the average in beauty before she had begun experimenting with them. And her experiments had been clumsy. She was handsome in spite of her efforts to be handsomer.

As I say, this is the only *writing*, so to speak, in the story, and it must be clear that the paragraph is equally feeble and pretentious, the sort of thing you'd strike out of an apprentice's story, besides having nothing characteristic about it and nothing resembling it elsewhere in the story. It is just a little Jamesian attempt (compare "My dear, you're looking very well for him—within the marked limits of your range") that failed.

Why was this story written, apart from a check from *Cosmopolitan?* It cannot have sprung from a wish to create or even to report, life. For instance, if Celia is as afraid of her husband as she says she is, she would never dare confide in Bartlett, especially Bartlett, a writer; or, unprincipled, with a life with her husband obviously so unsatisfactory, she would head for Bartlett—the nervous taking up, only to put it aside, of her sex life (men's pawing her) is about as close as Lardner ever came—not close enough—to this subject. The story is a fake, pretending to deliver more both in narrative and in character than it can deliver, except insofar as it produces a journalistic effect of *exposure*. You think big producers have happy marriages?— Don't give me that. Lardner's stories convey a perpetual effect of going behind an appearance—perpetual, and cheap, because the appearance is not one that could have taken in an experienced man for five minutes: the revelation is to boobs. How shall we describe then the strength of the emotional impulse behind the story? I should say that it had roughly the force of what we used to call in the third form a gripe.

To compare such a writer to Swift (as people have done, and I will come back to this), even to take him seriously, may seem ridiculous. But we are dealing with a very considerable reputation, established now in the literary histories; and "The Love Nest" has nothing funny about it—we are thinking of him now just as a story writer; and, though perfectly characteristic, it is not one of his five best stories. It has the advantage for us, however, that it is not a baseball story. The notion of Lardner's having any permanent interest as a baseball writer has got to be abandoned. Fitzgerald wrote: "During those years, when most men of promise achieve an adult education, if only in the school of war, Ring moved in the company of a few dozen illiterates playing a boy's game. A boy's game, with no more possibilities in it than a boy could master, a game bounded by walls which kept out novelty or danger, change or adventure . . . A writer can spin on about his adventures after thirty, after forty, after fifty, but the criteria by which these adventures are weighed and valued are irrevocably settled at the age of twenty-five. However deeply Ring might cut into it, his cake had the diameter of Frank Chance's diamond." Surely there is something wrong with this view.

In the first place, I do not believe it philosophically, any more than I believe Yeats's pronouncement is true, that "A man's mind at twenty-one contains all the truths that he will ever find." Neither allows for the self-transformations that many men active emotionally and intellectually achieve during their thirties. In the second place, Fitzgerald's view is nonsense both in the light of the facts and of what Lardner did. Yogi Berra is a boy? Lardner wrote about big leaguers largely: not boys, men, in danger every second of demotion to the minors, or focuses of national attention. They *were* nowhere, and they *will be* nowhere. Here they are, in continuous crisis, dramatized in the key plays Lardner describes so well. Now take a man who had always a dim view of life, and trusted nothing: this precariousness makes a good subject. It is the subject in fact of his only really fine baseball story, "Harmony," one of his few affecting and well-constructed stories, the kind of dramatic depthwork he only two or three times attempted. His two best stories are not about baseball: "The Golden Honeymoon," a beautifully modulated thing about the persistence of rivalry and pettiness into an area where everything ought to be solved, and "Haircut," which deserves its fame, as the simpleminded and incredible "Champion" does not. His two other good stories, "Some Like Them Cold" and "I Can't Breathe," are not about baseball, either.

Much of the semi-novel *The Big Town* is still readable, though unimportant; and the ends of certain stories—"Anniversary," "Ex Parte," "Now and Then"—are good, corroborating Lardner's not altogether joking account of his method of composition ("I write three thousand words about nothing; that is a terrible struggle. Then I come to, and say to myself, 'I must get a punch in this.' I stop and figure out the punch, and then sail through to the finish"). But the five stories are really what matter. It will be noticed that four of them are first-person, and the fifth a series of letters, and I think we must agree that White is right: Lardner was only in appearance a fiction writer. His gift was for mimicry, burlesque, parody. He had no invention, little imagination, a very limited sense of style, and almost no sense of structure. His best work is accidents of talent. He was a humourist of course; but only two of the five stories are at all funny, and he is not likely to keep on being known as a humourist. Humourists—except one very special kind I want to say something about in a moment—do not interest posterity as humourists unless they have also all sorts of more important gifts as well, such as Mark Twain had. Humour dies fast. Lardner was a realist, too, and interesting to his contemporaries as that, but this value has vanished already; after just thirty-odd years it is hard to imagine the initial effectiveness of *You Know Me Al.* As a satirist he is unimportant. There was not enough power of mind, and no imagination of a *different* past or future condition for the object satirized. A comparison with Swift makes one's critical sense reel.

But two things remain to be said. He *was* as bitter as Swift. There is no doubt about it. But so are countless denizens of Skid Row, and what does it matter to anyone except a social worker, a relative, a friend? But Lardner had some power of expression, and it matters. He was fitted by disposition—God knows why—for investigations of Hell, like Andreyev's; and he couldn't make it. Besides the desire for silence, one must certainly suspect here also a failure of courage, selflessness, ambition. That's one thing.

The other is that he had a special gift for what looks like nonsense. You see this most clearly in his little plays, of which my own favorite has always been *Clemo Uti—"The Water Lilies."* Its cast is:

Padre, a Priest.
Sethso ⎱ both twins.
Gethso ⎰
Wayshatten, a shepherd's boy.
Two Capitalists. (Note: The two Capitalists don't appear in this show.)
Wama Tammisch, her daughter.
Klema, a janitor's third daughter.
Kevela, their mother, afterwards their aunt.

Scene for Act I: The Outskirts of a Parchesi Board. People are wondering what has become of the discs. They quit wondering and sit up and sing the following song:

> *What has become of the discs?*
> *What has become of the discs?*
> *We took them at our own risks,*
> *But what has become of the discs?*

Wama enters from an exclusive waffle parlor. She exits as if she had had waffles.

214

Acts II and III are thrown out "because nothing seemed to happen."
IV takes place in a silo. Two rats have got in there by mistake. One
of them seems diseased. The other looks at him. They go out. Both Rats
come in again and wait for a laugh. They don't get it, and go out. Wama
enters from an off-stage barn. She is made up to represent the Home-
coming of Casanova. She has a fainting spell. She goes out.

> KEVELA. Where was you born?
> PADRE. In Adrian, Michigan.
> KEVELA. Yes, but I thought I was confessing to you.

Act V winds up: Two queels enter, overcome with water lilies.
They both make fools of themselves. They don't seem to have any self-
control. They quiver. They want to play the show over again, but it
looks useless. SHADES.

Now there is genius here—"genius limited and yearning," as
B. H. Haggin once said of Gershwin, but genius—which ought to have
taken Lardner into even better and firmer and more confident studies
of irrelation, which might have brought him into the small, fascinating company of the great fantasists Lear and Carroll, who were, in
fact, he once confessed, his favorite humourists. Elder canvasses various critics' views of these playlets and plumps for Gilbert Seldes's
that they are an "attack of sheer lunacy" and "had no purpose at all."
But surely what they are about is the failure of communication in the
modern world, and especially in the modern American world, which
is all Lardner cared about. They remind one of Peter Fleming's remark that in Europe conversation is like tennis—you hit the ball to
the other man and he hits it back—whereas in America everybody
goes on hitting his own ball. They are the work of a man who found
it only too easy to communicate at a superficial level and who refused
to communicate at any deeper level. Besides irrelation, you need relation. The trouble is that to mock the intellect successfully you have
to be right in there yourself. But Lardner's scorn and hatred for
everything "highbrow" is one of his chief marks. Unfortunately,
everything good in the end is highbrow. All the artists who have ever
survived were intellectuals—sometimes intellectuals *also*, but intellectuals. The popular boys cannot understand this. When Shakespeare
mocked Chapman and Raleigh and their school of intellectual art, he
did it with a higher brow than theirs. Hemingway studied Turgenev
and everyone else he thought useful. Lardner never studied anybody.
One of the weirdest sentences in Elder's book is about "Dryden, who

probably had a greater influence on his earlier career than any other writer." Of course, this is *Charlie* Dryden, a sportswriter.

The differences between entertainment and art have less to do with the audience and the writer's immediate intention than with his whole fundamental attitude toward doing what he does at all. Inverting the common notion, art for the artist we might oddly regard as a means, entertainment for the entertainer an end. Elder, who quotes approvingly from a piece by T. S. Matthews called "Lardner, Shakespeare and Chekhov," seems to have no idea of this, and I doubt if Lardner had: the notion of art is "a self-discipline rather than a self-expression," as Auden has put it. Of this crucial sense there is no trace, I believe, in Lardner's work. He was not interested, he found it hard enough to hang on, he wanted just to be let alone, and he got what he wanted. The few fine stories come like reluctant fugitives from a room almost perfectly soundproofed. His art did nothing *for* Lardner.

1956

Hemingway's

"A Clean, Well-Lighted Place"

THIS SHORT, ALMOST DESPERATE, AND BEAUTIFUL STORY IS an unusually fine example of a very special kind of story which is not anecdotal at all. If you were asked by somebody, "What happens in this story?" you would have to reply, "Nothing." Now *nothing* is exactly what the story is about: Nothing, and the steps we take against Nothing. The fact that there is no plot is part of the story's meaning: in a world characterized by "Nothing," what significant action could take place? The two waiters are only very gradually distinguished from each other; their voices in the beginning are choric, just two men talking, any two men. Of the old man in the café we learn very little, and of the barman at the end, nothing. The older waiter is clearly the most important person in the story, but we do not really learn very much about him, either. You could hardly say that the story is *about* him. The part usually played by plot and characterization is left in this story largely to setting and atmosphere.

Hemingway's style is famous for its simplicity—short, common words, short sentences—and is said to be realistic or naturalistic. Is it realistic? "I am of those who like to stay late at the café," the older waiter says. "With all those who do not want to go to bed. With all those who need a light for the night." Surely this is elaborately rhetorical, nobody actually talks this way, and one of the reasons (though only one) for the Spanish setting of the story is the author's desire to achieve from time to time this highly poetic and unnatural tone (as he can do by pretending to be translating from Spanish into English) without its seeming inconsistent with the curt talk, rapid description, and coarse and bitter material of the story. Hemingway's style is very complicated; even where it appears simple, it is not very simple. Look at the first two sentences:

It was late and every one had left the café except an old man who sat in the shadow the leaves of the tree made against the electric light. In the day time the street was dusty, but at night the dew settled the dust and

217

the old man liked to sit late because he was deaf and now at night it was quiet and he felt the difference.

Then we learn that this old man tried to kill himself last week, even though he has plenty of money; in short, he is *in despair*, and the phrase is used by one of the waiters. That is why he is drinking himself drunk, as he does every night. Even in themselves Hemingway's opening sentences are rather stylized—the rhythms are insistent, alliteration is employed (dew . . . dust . . . deaf . . . difference), even rhyme (night: quiet), and "late" is repeated in a choric way. But as the opening of *this* story, which is to come to a climax in a violent parody of the Lord's Prayer, clearly these sentences have already begun the symbolism which is the reason for the story's being. It is *late*, not only on this evening, and in this man's life, but *in a tradition*—a religious tradition, specifically the Christian tradition (we are in a Catholic country, Spain); so late that the tradition cannot support or console, and suicide invites. There is thus a second reason, besides the physical debility that awaits all of us at the end of life, for the old man's being deaf: he is deaf to the Christian promises, he cannot hear them. He is *alone*, isolated, sitting in the "shadow" left by nature in the modern artificial world. All the light desired in this story is artificial, as if nature had abandoned man, and anything he may want he has to get for himself—precariously and briefly.

We are now in a position to hear better the first little conversation between the waiters:

"He was in despair."
"What about?"
"Nothing."
"How do you know it was nothing?"
"He has plenty of money."

This is not just a sour joke, though it is that, too. We have to hear "Nothing" also as *something very positive*, the name given in this story to the modern condition of moral vacancy and meaninglessness which the old man feels, and so he tried to kill himself, and the older waiter feels, and so he suffers from insomnia: "It was a nothing that he knew too well. It was all a nothing and a man was nothing too. It was only that and light was all it needed and a certain cleanness and order. Some lived in it and never felt it but he knew it all was nada y pues nada y nada y pues nada" (nothing and then nothing and nothing and then nothing).

It is *feeling* this condition of nothingness, not the nothingness itself, which is Hemingway's real subject. His deep sympathy with the two sensitive men, the old man and the older waiter, is the story's strongest feeling. Neither is a passive victim. The old man has his "dignity"—a key word for Hemingway. When the younger waiter says, "An old man is a nasty thing," the older waiter, without sentimentalizing or denying the general truth of this (very unpleasant) remark, defends the honour of this particular old man with precise observation: "Not always. This old man is clean. He drinks without spilling. Even now, drunk. Look at him." And when the impatience of the younger waiter has pushed him out, he walks away "unsteadily but with dignity." It is not much, human dignity, in the face of the human condition of nothingness, but it is what we can have.

The older waiter's symbol for it is *light*—here a man-made device to hold off the darkness, not permanently, but as late as possible, and *in public*, as if man's essential loneliness were less intolerable where the forms of social life have to be observed, where one's dignity is called on. (The specific danger of being alone is, of course, suicide.) He formulates this, as it were, on behalf of the old man, and only gradually do we become aware that *his* plight is similar, he is an *older* waiter. In the beginning, as we saw, the two waiters are hardly differentiated. The view that money is all that matters in life, the little conversation about the soldier and the girl, cannot even be assigned to one or the other; it is just waiters' talk—waiters we think of as automatically cynical, like taxi drivers. (What is the purpose of the incident of the soldier and the girl? This shows us two people who *do* have a program, something to do that they want to do, as the younger waiter does and the two older do not; and it also establishes a context for this café in which nearly the whole story takes place— that context is war.) The older waiter begins to become distinct when he points out the cleanness of the old man. He is "unhurried," unlike the younger waiter, having no place to go. But his nerves do not strike one as being at all good: his coarse joke ("You have no fear of going home before your usual hour?") proceeds from some deep irritability, which is then partly explained by his "No. I have never had confidence and I am not young." More and more distinctly he has become the story's spokesman, the younger waiter being unfitted for this role by his insensitivity (in one of his very rare value judgments, Hemingway implies that he is "stupid") and the old man by being too completely isolated. In the three-sentence speech quoted near the beginning of the story, he takes on himself the open role of spokesman, and he sees himself also as a custodian of certain values ("It is not only a question of youth and confidence although those things are very beautiful. Each night I am reluctant to close up because there may be some one who needs the café").

Light, cleanness, order, dignity: to hold the Nothing at bay. The reason these things are necessary is that everything else has failed. The parody of the Lord's Prayer has a deliberate effect of blasphemy, and thus explains why these symbols have been used—and why this story, for that matter, has come into existence. Notice how brilliantly the narrative is handled. Turning the light off in the café, he continues the conversation with himself. We are given no indication that he is moving, much less going somewhere else. The parody ends: "Hail nothing full of nothing, nothing is with thee. He smiled and stood before a bar with a shining steam pressure coffee machine." Without our knowledge he has been moving, while blaspheming, and the Lord's Prayer has brought him—where? Precisely where you cannot be with dignity, standing at a bar. Religion is a cheat. You might as well worship this sudden apparition, the shining steam pressure coffee machine, as the Christian God or *nada*.

When the barman asks what he wants, he answers, *"Nada,"* meaning, "Nothing is all that is possible, so that is what I'll have." The barman does not understand, of course (*"Otro loco más"* is One more lunatic, another joker). The lack of understanding of the barman is the point of the end of the story. Insensitive, like the younger waiter, the barman leaves the older waiter isolated with his knowledge that all is *nada*, that this bar is unpolished, that a bar is not a dignified place, and that he himself will not sleep. The last two sentences of the story come like a lash, ranging him again, in his loneliness and desperate need for dignity, with the large class of human beings ("I am of those who . . .") who feel and suffer man's desertion by God—an invented God. (One of Hemingway's little poems takes a different tone with the same theme:

> The Lord is my shepherd.
> I shall not want
> Him for long.)

This essential human ordeal is for all men, but it is only recognized, the story suggests, in age; so that this is what our journey is toward. This, miserably, is what wisdom is of: *nada*. Perhaps no story in English has ever been built so obsessively around one word (the volume of stories in which it originally appeared was called by Hemingway *Winner Take Nothing*).

The angry desolation of the story has its roots in Hemingway's disillusion during the First World War, best expressed shortly in a famous passage of his novel *A Farewell to Arms*. An Italian and the hero are talking, and the Italian says, "We won't talk about losing. There is enough talk about losing. What has been done this summer cannot have been done in vain." "I did not say anything. I was always embarrassed by the words sacred, glorious, and sacrifice and the expression in vain. We had heard them, sometimes standing in the rain almost out of earshot, so that only the shouted words came through, and had read them, on proclamations that were slapped up by billposters over other proclamations, now for a long time, and I had seen nothing sacred, and the things that were glorious had no glory and the sacrifices were like the stockyards at Chicago if nothing was done with the meat except to bury it. There were many words that you could not stand to hear and finally only the names of places had dignity. Certain numbers were the same way and certain dates and these with the names of the places were all you could say and have them mean anything. Abstract words such as glory, honor, courage, or hallow were obscene beside the concrete names of villages, the numbers of roads, the names of rivers, the numbers of regiments and the dates." In the light of this passage, it is clearer why the older waiter has such difficulty in saying what it is that he hates—*nada*—and what it is that he sets against it—dignity—and why he has to use symbols to express his malignant dissatisfaction with the Christian universe.

1960

A Note on Augie

ONE MIGHT EXPECT A CONSENSUS OF THE REVIEWERS OF A book to decide whether it is any good or not. For most books they do this well enough, and the books are immediately forgotten, forever. But for a few books, although they try to do this, all they can truly speak to is the book's importance; its degree of excellence or badness may be matter of debate for years or decades. The reviewers of Saul Bellow's new novel, *The Adventures of Augie March*, whether admiring, like Lionel Trilling and Robert Penn Warren, or disapproving, like Maxwell Geismar and Norman Podhoretz, appear to have established it firmly as important. Making small attempt, then, to estimate its merits, let us inquire a little into its relation to its tradition. It looks like a naturalistic novel, undoubtedly. But there are radical differences between it and the naturalism, say, of Dreiser and James T. Farrell.

If we compare with *Augie March* other well-written novels like *The Naked and the Dead* and *Lie Down in Darkness*, we notice that its style is far more individual: it is almost as intensely individual as Hemingway's or Faulkner's. Whether this style is Bellow's or Augie's is at present Bellow's secret; he has certainly not employed it before. His next book might be supposed to let us into the secret. But considering the fact that nobody yet knows whether the style of Mark Twain's masterpiece was Huck's or his, perhaps we may never know. Now a powerful and singular style has been at work in American naturalism before—namely, Stephen Crane's—but that was a long time ago. The later men have just drudged along. We have to consider the general effect of this on language. Dreiser's verbless maundering off toward some invisible period has done our language no good. I would guess that the effect of the sharpness and acrobatic freedom of *Augie March* ought to be salutary, as Crane's naturalism was.

A second difference is related to style, but transcends it. The book is dominated by a recurrent allusiveness to masters of Greek,

Jewish, European, and American history, literature, and philosophy. Sometimes their deeds or opinions are mentioned, sometimes they rule the imagery. We might call them Overlords, or Sponsors. ("If you want," Augie says at one point, "to pick your own ideal creature in the mirror coastal air and sharp leaves of ancient perfections and be at home where a great mankind was at home, I've never seen any reason why not.") The Overlords have a double use. They stand as figures of awe and emulation to Augie (one of whose favourite authors is plainly Plutarch)—corresponding in this to the heroes of his actual experience, such as Einhorn. And they create historical depth, the kind of legendary perspective that our naturalism has deeply desired; a portrait on the scale of Einhorn's would be impossible without them. Replacing the vague merciless forces invoked by Dreiser, they remind me of the marvelous vast heads of statues in some of Watteau's pictures, overlooking his lovers. They are bound to irritate some readers as pretentious or hand-to-mouth, or a mannerism, because they are a new element, a new convention, in our fiction; new conventions are likely to irritate at first.

Along with these differences goes a decisive change in theme from the naturalism we have known, which dealt as a rule with success, and was likely to be tragic. Augie does not aim at success, and his story is a comedy, having for theme the preservation of individuality against the pressures in American life (modern life) toward uniformity, the adoption of socially acceptable roles: pressures exactly toward success, or at any rate security. The pressures are dramatized by Bellow as "recruiting," everybody's attempts to get Augie to serve their ends. Augie is all risk, he always consents; but then he always withdraws, because, experimental and aggressive, he is trying to refuse to lead a disappointed life. The insistence upon having one's own fate we might relate to the divorce now between parents and children, in (as W. H. Auden has put it) "a society where the father plays as minor a role as he plays in America." Augie has no visible father (he is illegitimate) and can hardly follow in his father's footsteps.

The novel, then, because of the recruiting, has the form of a theme-and-variations, and because of the search for a fate good enough, it has also the direction of a "pilgrimage"—Bellow's word late in the book. The first is more important than the second, but I don't quite understand Clifton Fadiman's regarding it as "undirected." Another critical mistake seems to me to be Warren's when he wishes that Augie "had been given the capacity . . . for more joy and sorrow." Surely he suffers and rejoices enough for several books. Possibly Warren read *The Adventures of Augie March* too much in the light of Bellow's earlier, constricted novels, which strike me as interesting now chiefly in relation to this one. Both the stunning wit and the emotional range are new here to Bellow. Wit has not been a characteristic of our twentieth-century naturalists, either. At the same time, notwithstanding these differences, *Augie March* does clearly belong on the Dreiser side, inclusive and tidal, as against Hemingway's and, in its insistence that what is widespread shall also be intense, may help to foster a fresh dimension for naturalism.

1953

IV

"Song of Myself":
Intention and Substance

THE ARBITERS OF CURRENT TASTE—POUND, ELIOT, AUDEN, others—have generally now declared themselves in favour of Whitman; but always reluctantly and with a certain resentment or even contempt. I am not able to feel these reservations myself, but I think I understand their origins and will try presently to suggest what these are. I like or love Whitman unreservedly; he operates with great power and beauty over a very wide range, from small pieces like "A Noiseless, Patient Spider" and "I Saw in Louisiana a Live-Oak Growing" up through "Out of the Cradle Endlessly Rocking"—a poem in which a profound experience crucial to the poet's vocation is rendered as fully as in the Cliff passage in the First Book of *The Prelude* and nearly as fully as in "Resolution and Independence" (Wordsworth comes first to mind as being far the greatest poet of his century in England, as Whitman was here)—up through this range, I say, to *Song of Myself*, which seems to me easily his most important achievement and indeed the greatest poem so far written by an American. It is not by any means an easy poem to understand. It is hard, frequently, to see why the poet is saying what he is saying, and hard therefore also to see what he is saying. All I mean to do here is to construct a crude approach that may prove helpful to the discovery of answers to the questions that these difficulties inspire.

Though I wish so far as possible to avoid the paradoxes that writers on Whitman too readily indulge in, I note, as an initial problem, that this poem of fifty pages is the work of a man who agreed with Poe "that (at any rate for our occasions, our day) there can be no such thing as a long poem" ("The same thought had been haunting my mind before, but Poe's argument, though short, worked the sum and proved it to me"—this in 1888). Now "long" is a relative term, and the author of *The Faerie Queene*, for instance, may well not have considered *The Rape of Lucrece* (at 1,850 lines) a "long" poem. But clearly this is not what Whitman has in mind. What I think he does have in mind comes up sharply in another passage: "It is not on 'Leaves of Grass' distinctively as *literature*, or a specimen thereof, that I feel to dwell, or advance claims. No one will get at my verses who insists upon viewing them as a literary performance, or attempt at such performance . . ." He did not, that is, think of *Song of Myself* as a *long* poem, because he did not think of it as a poem at all. Our problem has become a question: What then did he think of it as? The question is quite unanswerable in this form, unless we say that he thought of it as a work of *life* (as I feel sure he did), but we can get on by inquiring what it was intended to *do*, what purposes it was desired to serve. Declared purposes, first; here we have many statements from him—too many—of which I am going to take four that seem to me indefeasible. The first is national, the second religious, the third metaphysical, the fourth personal. And although *he* is talking about *Leaves of Grass*, in quoting him you will understand *me* to be referring to *Song of Myself*, the epitome of his book, where it stands first.

First: "One main genesis-motive of the 'Leaves' was my conviction (just as strong today as ever) that the crowning growth of the United States is to be spiritual and heroic. To help start and favor that growth—or even to call attention to it, or the need of it—is the beginning, middle and final purpose of the poems." Nothing could be more comprehensible and explicit, and nothing more incomprehensible or repugnant to most cultivated readers a century later; though not, as it happens, to me. But in what way *Song of Myself* was designed to "favor that growth—or . . . to call attention to . . . the need of it" is not yet clear.

For the second intention, not less fundamental than the first, I must quote rather a long passage—in which Whitman had to coin a word, "germenancy," corresponding to "growth" in the first.

When I commenced, years ago, elaborating the plan of my poems, and continued turning over that plan, and shifting it in my mind through many years, (from the age of twenty-eight to thirty-five,) experimenting much, and writing and abandoning much, one deep purpose underlay the others, and has underlain it and its execution ever since—and that has been the Religious purpose. Amid many changes, and a formulation taking far different shape from what I at first supposed, this basic purpose has never been departed from in the composition of my verses. Not of course to exhibit itself in the old ways, as in writing hymns or psalms with an eye to the church-pew, or to express conventional pietism, or the sickly yearnings of devotees, but in new ways, and aiming at the widest sub-bases and inclusions of Humanity, and tallying the fresh air of sea and land. I will see, (said I to myself,) whether there is not, for my purposes as poet, a Religion, and a sound Religious germenancy in the average Human Race, at least in their modern development in the United States, and in the hardy common fiber and native yearnings and elements, deeper and larger, and affording more profitable returns, than all mere sects or churches—as boundless, joyous, and vital as Nature itself—A germenancy that has too long been unencouraged, unsung, almost unknown . . . With Science, the Old Theology of the East, long in its dotage, begins evidently to die and disappear. But (to my mind) Science—and may be such will prove its principal service—as evidently prepares the way for One indescribably grander—Time's young but perfect offspring—the New Theology—heir of the West—lusty and loving, and wondrous beautiful. For America, and for to-day, just the same as any day, the supreme and final Science is the Science of God—what we call science being only its minister—as Democracy is or shall be also. And a poet of America (I said) must fill himself with such thoughts, and chant his best out of them . . .

You will have observed how intense for Whitman was the despised word (but not by our political institutions) "average"—a word hardly likely to be found bearing this exalted stress in Pound or Eliot or Auden. It is clear that Whitman envisages a post-Christianity (and post-Buddhism, post-Hinduism) which will serve science and, *eventually* (a dramatic qualification, showing how little Whitman was taken in by American pretensions), egalitarianism.

Third: as of what I am calling metaphysics, a very short remark: "To the true and full estimate of the Present both the Past and the Future are main considerations." It is the second part of this that is startling, and calls in question the nature of *time;* I suppose being is either associated with, or precisely dissociated from, time, or is both; this is why I call the present intention metaphysical. We see that the optimism emotionally visible in the national and religious intentions is here intellectually asserted. But since we have come thus so close to what has really to be called doctrine, Whitman's statement having indeed a dogmatic air, it is time to point out his massive insistence upon the word "suggestiveness" in all these connections. "I round and finish little, if anything; and could not, consistently with my scheme." Again: "I think I have at least enough philosophy not to be too absolutely certain of anything, or any results." Again: "A great poem is no finish to a man or woman but rather a beginning."

It is this last quotation that brings him into conflict with current aesthetics, that of the artwork made, finished, autonomous. (Let us concede at once that *The Waste Land* winds up with various bogus instructions, and so might be thought to aim at a beginning; but except for the lines about "the awful daring of a moment's surrender," all this end of that poem is its weakest, most uneasy, crudest, least inventive, most willed part.) The conflict is absolute equally in Whitman's formulation of the fourth or *personal* intention. " 'Leaves of Grass' . . ." he says, "has mainly been the outcroppings of my own emotional and personal nature—an attempt, from first to last, to put *a Person*, a human being (myself, in the latter part of the Nineteenth Century, in America,) freely, fully and truly on record." I call your attention to an incongruity of this formulation with Eliot's amusing theory of the impersonality of the artist, and a contrast between the mere *putting-on-record* and the well-nigh universal current notion of *creation*, or making things up. You will see that, as Whitman looks more arrogant than Eliot in the Personality, he looks less pretentious in the recording—the mere recording—poet not as *maker* but as spiritual historian—only the history must be, as we'll see in a moment, of the Present—and inquirer (characteristically; Eliot's word in the *Quartets*, "explorer," is more ambitious and charged than "inquirer"). Small wonder—I finish with the arbiters—if they resent Whitman: he has sold the profession short. The poet as creator plays no part in Whitman's scheme at all.

For Whitman the poet is a *voice*. Not solely his own—let us settle this problem quickly: a poet's first personal pronoun is nearly always ambiguous, but we have the plain declaration from Whitman that "the trunk and centre whence the answer was to radiate . . . must be an identical soul and body, a personality—which personality, after many considerings and ponderings I deliberately settled should be myself—indeed could not be any other." I would sorrow over the credulity of anyone who took this account-of-the-decision-as-conscious to be historical; but I am convinced of the reality of the decision. A voice, then, for himself and others; for others *as himself*—this is the intention clearly (an underlying exhibitionism and narcissism we take for granted). What others?—Americans, man. A voice—that is, expressing (not creating)—expressing things already in existence. But what is a voice from?—a *body*. And where?—in America, but this is going to be difficult. And when?—but this is going to be more difficult. And what is in existence? (If anyone doubts that Whitman saw the thing—his intention, his subject—in these apparently abstract but in fact quite literal terms, let him consider these expressions: in Section 23 at the center of *Song of Myself*,

"I accept Time, absolutely" and "I accept Reality, and dare not question it"; and as the initial phrase of Section 33, "Space and Time!"—all these capitalized.)

I am going to be most interested in time and existence, but first another word about voice. Other voices in Whitman are regularly metaphors for the human voice, and the voice of the *soul* in Section 5—it must be understood that the "I" in *Song of Myself* often refers only to the body—is metaphorical also, in the exquisite line:

> Only the lull I like, the hum of your valvèd voice.

In the light of "lull," the kind of valve here imagined must be a safety valve (compare "loose the stop from your throat" just above): the soul being that which lets the body free a little and then controls it. In the lines immediately following, incest with the soul is dramatized (*by* the body); and that this is not enough we learn from the lines straight after these,

> Swiftly arose and spread around me the peace and
> knowledge that pass all the argument of the earth,
> And I know that the hand of God is the promise of
> my own . . .

After the New Testament air of the first of these lines, it is clear that "the promise" is a theological allusion, brought over into the New Theology; and suddenly it is also clear that the Johannine *Logos* (God's self-revelation, in Christ—whose name is Word, as His Father's is I AM or Being) influenced Whitman's thought even more than his passion for grand opera, which dominates Section 26:

> The orbic flex of his mouth is pouring and filling me full.

And *when* he is full enough . . . a valve will open. This valve notion, sense of outlet, is crucial to the poem, not only in the fine line discarded in draft (it turned up revised in Section 47)—

> I am your voice— It was tied in you— In me it begins to talk

—but in the marvellous passage in Section 24:

> Through me many long dumb voices
> Voices of the interminable generations of prisoners & slaves,
> Voices of the diseas'd and despairing and of thieves & dwarfs,
> Voices of cycles of preparation & accretion,
> And of the threads that connect the stars, and of
> wombs and of the father-stuff,

And of the rights of them the others are down upon,
Of the deform'd, trivial, flat, foolish, despised,
Fog in the air, beetles rolling balls of dung.

The poet—one would say, a mere channel, but with its own ferocious difficulties—fills with experiences, a valve opens; he speaks them. I am obliged to remark that I prefer this theory of poetry to those that have ruled the critical quarterlies since I was an undergraduate twenty-five years ago. It is as humble as, and identical with, Keats's view of the poet as having no existence, but being "forever in, for, and filling" other things.

Several things have to be said about this passionate sense of identification. In the first place, it supplies the method by which the "I" of the poem is gradually expanded, characterized, and filled with meaning; not until near the end of the poem is the "I" complete—and then it flees. In the second place, the identification is not of course a device adopted for the purposes of the poem; Whitman actually felt thus. Most newspapermen learn to despise the public; but Whitman wrote in the Brooklyn *Eagle*, shortly after he became its editor, "There is a curious kind of sympathy (haven't you ever thought of it before?) that arises in the mind of a newspaper conductor with the public he serves. He gets to *love* them." These italics are his, and I take this declaration literally and observe that one always wishes to identify oneself with the loved object. At the same time we recognize as of psychological origin the profound dissatisfaction (no doubt sexual in character) that aims at *loss of identity*, in the poem, in two ways, through these identifications and through death—this is why death is a major subject. But in the third place, I would deny that this is mystical—indeed, it is the opposite, as a writer in *PMLA* confessed (in 1955) while producing and maintaining the monstrous term "inverted mystical." I object to the word "mystical" in relation to Whitman altogether, as a mere grab-bag term, like "instinct," for whatever we don't happen to understand, unless it refers to the perfectly well-known phenomena described in the *Philokalia*, say, and the works of the English and Spanish mystics. I see no need for a single word to apply to the complicated phenomenon we are now studying, since none exists. In the fourth place, this process of identification has limits; it does not include God. God is envisaged as our lover, first, not very different from ourselves, except that, second, he provides for us. These roles are important, certainly, but still leave man very much on his own—though, Whitman insists, incurious and at peace with this idea. Identification is limited also within humanity: as against "myself and my neighbors, refreshing, wicked, real," in Section 42 there are people so despicable, so unreal, that the poet denies them even personal pronouns, suddenly saying:

> Here and there with dimes on the eyes walking,
> To feed the greed of the belly the brain liberally spooning,
> Tickets buying, taking, selling, but in to the feast
>   never once going,
> Many sweating, ploughing, thrashing, and then the chaff
>   for payment receiving,
> A few idly owning, and they the wheat continually
>   claiming.

It is clear that the allusion to the parable of the Wedding Feast in the third line has called up the participles in the next line corresponding to "wailing and gnashing of teeth," and that what the poet is thinking about is the punishment of the *self*-excluded: the living dead, the sullen, the greedy, the extortionate. These excepted, all are invited to the identification—the New Kingdom.

So much, with various questions still unanswered, by way of pre-amble. I think it will be easiest to speak to these questions—*how* the poem is to favour spiritual and heroic growth, what the *content* of the religious sense is, what are the natures of Time and Being in the poem—by way of a commentary on the progressive unfolding of the work. But I must say first that its form is perhaps misleading, like the form of the Hebrew poem of Job. That mysterious work—never mind the prose folktale in which we find it imbedded—has at any rate the form of a theodicy; but that form is ironic, for God's justice is never vindicated at all, solely his power is demonstrated; so that we have to call the poem a theodicy of power—that is, no theodicy at all. Now Whitman's poem has the form of a paean or exultation—"I celebrate myself"—unconditional, closed, reflexive. But this is misleading, for we do not yet know what "I" is—though in the fourth line we learn at least that it does not include the soul ("I loafe and invite my soul"), which is thus the first guest to be invited. I take the work in fact to be one of Welcome, self-*wrestling*, inquiry, and wonder—conditional, open, and astonished (not exulting as over an accomplished victory, but gradually revealing, puzzling, discovering).

The first five sections I see as the poem's first movement—let's use the musical term, since the poem is as deeply influenced by music as Eliot's poems are. It consists of a double invitation, from "I," or the human body, to the human soul and from "I," or the poet, to the reader. Each invitation is from equal to equal, and from what is already related to what it is already related to—he invents the word "entretied" and later "intertinged." The passionate hatred for hierarchy and dissociation is one of the poem's foremost motives, accounting for the ferocious lines in Section 3, first

> Showing the best and dividing it from the worst age vexes age,

and then the rest of the sentence about God: As God sleeps by me and withdraws, leaving me baskets,

> Shall I postpone my acceptation and realization and scream at
> my eyes,
> That they turn from gazing after and down the road,
> And forthwith cipher and show me to a cent,
> Exactly the value of one and exactly the value of two,
> and which is ahead?

These passages come too early in the work to be successfully entered into by the reader, but I am discussing intention and substance. What the second section is about is air, used as a prime symbol for equality and ubiquity—the earth's air and human air (symbol for life as well as singing, speech, the poem itself) coming together:

> The smoke of my own breath,
> Echoes, ripples, buzz'd whispers . . .
> The sound of the belch'd words of my voice loos'd to
> the eddies of the wind . . .

Since the second invitation, to the reader, may be rejected, the poet proves his equality by attacking poems himself and by standing indifferent,

> . . . amused, complacent, compassionating, idle, unitary . . .

The first invitation, to the soul, is accepted, and results in what I shall call the incest passage of Section 5 ("I mind how once we lay such a transparent summer morning") which, bringing soul and body for the first time together—I cannot avoid remarking what a deeply divided personality created this work—produces the "peace and knowledge" in two lines that I quoted earlier,

> And that a kelson of the creation is love . . .

Meanwhile, the attack upon time that characterizes all great poets has begun in Section 3:

234

> There was never any more inception than there is now.
> Nor any more youth or age than there is now,
> And will never be any more perfection than there is now,
> Nor any more heaven or hell than there is now.

This notion of a continuous present, which is Eastern, he may have derived from "the ancient Hindoo poems" to which he refers, or he may have invented it. How schematic it was will be clear from his statement in the 1855 preface that the poet "is to compete with the laws that pursue and follow time." What it does for Whitman—very briefly—is to enable him to disparage the past, and to contain the future (accessible, equal), and to head in the direction of the line in Section 46,

> You must habit yourself to the dazzle of the light and of
> every moment of your life.

—which takes us far into the heart of the poem's "favoring." The Kingdom will be here, and now, forever.

I pause to notice certain elements of the exquisite transition from the First Movement into the great Section 6, which begins, I think, the Second Movement. After the air (2), that which is like it, being everywhere, uniform, the grass. After the love wrestling of Body and Soul, a child speaks. After all the "knowledge" then claimed, a true instruction: the child's question, and the poet's ignorance and guessings. After the "peace" achieved—and owing to the strength of the union (between soul and body) effected—the question of their sundering, of death. With this question, and the enigmatic, magisterial consolation the poet gives, his work really begins. I want to quote this, wishing to emphasize in particular his extraordinary passage from helplessness through four stages of the jaunty to solemnity and darkest, most grievous mystery, *back* to a sort of helplessness which yet proves consonant with the most exalted and persuasive confidence.

> A child said What is the grass? fetching it to me with full hands,
> How could I answer the child? I do not know what it is any more
> than he.

> I guess it must be the flag of my disposition, out of hopeful
> green stuff woven.

Or I guess it is the handkerchief of the Lord,
A scented gift and remembrancer designedly dropt,
Bearing the owner's name someway in the corners, that we may see
    and remark, and say Whose?

Or I guess the grass is itself a child, the produced babe of
    the vegetation.

Or I guess it is a uniform hieroglyphic,
And it means, Sprouting alike in broad zones and narrow zones,
Growing among black folks as among white,
Kanuck, Tuckahoe, Congressman, Cuff, I give them the same, I
    receive them the same.

And now it seems to me the beautiful uncut hair of graves.

Tenderly will I use you curling grass,
It may be you transpire from the breasts of young men,
It may be if I had known them I would have loved them,
It may be you are from old people, or from offspring taken
    soon out of their mothers' laps,
And here you are the mothers' laps.

This grass is very dark to be from the white heads of old
    mothers,
Darker than the colorless beards of old men,
Dark to come from under the faint red roofs of mouths.

O I perceive after all so many uttering tongues,
And I perceive they do not come from the roofs of mouths for
    nothing.

I wish I could translate the hints about the dead young men
    and women,
And the hints about old men and mothers, and the offspring taken
    soon out of their laps.

What do you think has become of the young and old men?
And what do you think has become of the women and children?

They are alive and well somewhere,
The smallest sprout shows there is really no death,
And if ever there was it led forward life, and does not wait at
    the end to arrest it,
And ceas'd the moment life appear'd.

Song of Myself: *Intention and Substance*

> All goes onward and outward, nothing collapses,
> And to die is different from what any one supposed, and luckier.

I take the last line—which sounds surprisingly, not only in assertion but in tone, like another great poet of death, Rilke—to be anti-existential and to be *literally* true, in the following sense: the death a man considers is his own *now*, not his own *then*, when it will actually take place, to himself another man; therefore he can form no just conception of it; and besides—as of the second part of the line—always considers it as the ultimate disaster, whereas in practice for a great part of mankind it comes as the final mercy. Doctors in numbers are on record to this point: most terminal patients *want* to die.

The Second Movement of the poem runs, I should say, through Section 19 and is concerned, after this prelude of the grass and death, with the "I's" identifications *outward*, beginning

> I am the mate and companion of people, all just as immoral
> and fathomless as myself.

The movement ends as quietly as possible, foreshadowing indeed the tone of the conclusion of the whole work:

> This hour I tell things in confidence,
> I might not tell everybody, but I will tell you.

Few poets have ever been able to sound like this, so simple and intimate; though Robert Frost has.

The Third Movement has for its theme Being—"What is a man anyhow?"—and runs from the beginning of Section 20 nearly to the end of Section 38 and contains most of what is supreme in the poem except for Section 6 and the final sections. I can't hope to do any sort of justice to the triumphant explorations of experience in this movement, but I want to distinguish two series of answers (if we can call them that) given by Whitman to the question that he has asked, what a man is: first, answers that are given as of the *Self;* second, answers that are given as *not* of the Self. Most of the famous passages occur in the first series, but the most intense reality, as a matter of fact, is experienced by him in the second series. *Both* series *become* intolerable, and have to be abandoned (he has been trying, as it were, a series of experiments on himself—two series—to see what he is). I attach importance, in connection with these failures, to his envisaging between them, with obvious envy, an entirely different kind of being, in the animals of Section 32.

The first real answer given then is that man is: a lover. This being so, and in the light of the fact that most men do not appear to know it but think of themselves as intelligences or whatever, an impulse of revolt against accepted ideas gathers head for some time, until he names himself as a "kosmos" and cries out, wonderfully,

> Unscrew the locks from the doors!
> Unscrew the doors themselves from the jambs!

Let no access be barred, that is: let's rip things up and get at the truth (*and* he is alluding to Paul's "Knock, and it shall be opened unto you," for in the lines following he speaks in the person of Christ— that is, a new Revelation is coming). Then we hear the staggering apostrophe to his body—". . . it shall be you! . . . it shall be you!"— wherein even the winds have genitals—written in the same year or so as "Un Voyage à Cythère," such is the inscrutable variety of man's love of himself—and summed up in the ravishing line,

> I dote on myself, there is that lot of me and all so luscious . . .

But at once in the next section (25) we hear:

> Dazzling and tremendous how quick the sun-rise would kill me,
> If I could not now and always send sun-rise out of me,

which if heard aright is thoroughly ominous; and when in 26 he settles down to listen to music,

> It sails me, I dab with bare feet, they are lick'd by the
>   indolent waves,
> I am cut by bitter and angry hail, I lose my breath,
> Steep'd amid honey'd morphine, my windpipe throttled in
>   fakes of death,

the pleasure is rendered as pure pain. Section 28—a wild one—is about his senses as sentries who become *traitors*, and it takes 29, a sort of coda to all this, to stabilize the tone of the poem. So far for the reality of the Self, the core of which is absolutely *touch*.

Then, after a rapid passage demonstrating the incapacity of Time and Space to delimit his incorporations and followings, the magical interlude of the animals:

> I think I could turn and live with animals, they are so placid
>   and self-contain'd,
> I stand and look at them long and long.
> They do not sweat and whine about their condition,

> They do not lie awake in the dark and weep for their sins,
> They do not make me sick discussing their duty to God,
> Not one is dissatisfied, not one is demented with the mania
>   of owning things,
> Not one kneels to another, nor to his kind that lived thousands
>   of years ago,
> Not one is respectable or unhappy over the whole earth.

(We see here, by the way, where one large aspect of Pound's tone in poetry comes from.) But what I am interested in is how little is said about the animals that is not negative—only "placid and self-contain'd," which withdraws from and criticizes the series of violent, out-tending experience just finished, and also the one to come; and "Not . . . unhappy" which comes to an affirmation. At radical points in the poem (in Sections 25 and 50), the word "happiness" is used to characterize the ultimate human reality, the goal of the New Theology, or indeed its permanent condition. Visible to us in creatures nearest to us in the natural scale, this is here the doctrinal point; and because it does not *sound* doctrinal, as in the other passages, it succeeds. I notice that Rilke also was hypnotized by animals—envy of whom expresses again, like death, a longing for escape from the human condition.

The second series begins with an exultation over Time and Space at his command, ". . . I am afoot with my vision"—here, there, then, now—"I fly those flights of a fluid and swallowing soul" (we see the perfect double sense of "swallowing," either of which would be artificial alone, but together instead of being worse seem natural and indeed pass almost unnoticed)—but increasingly in pain—

> All this I swallow, it tastes good, I like it well,
>   it becomes mine,
> I am the man, I suffer'd, I was there.

This superb last line probably includes an allusion to "Ecce homo" and so another Christ-identification, but this is incidental to its compendious report of what an artist is up to. The Self, of course, has disappeared, been put aside; the "I" is now Soul only, the imagination. As if in passing, in its perpetual present, itself assumes the functions of Time:

> Distant and dead resuscitate,
> They show as the dial or move as the hands of me,
>   I am the clock myself.

239

Then comes the land fight ("the murder of the four hundred and twelve young men," telling the poet's time), the admirable narrative of the fight at sea and its magnificent, dreadful aftermath—the poet, out of sight, coming closer and closer into the experience, which is his—I quote only the close of the brilliant sentence that is Section 36:

> Cut of cordage, dangle of rigging, slight shock of the
>   soothe of waves,
> Black and impassive guns, litter of powder-parcels,
>   strong scent,
> A few large stars overhead, silent & mournful shining,
> Delicate sniffs of sea-breeze, smells of sedgy grass
>   and fields by the shore, death-messages given in
>   charge to survivors,
> The hiss of the surgeon's knife, the gnawing teeth of
>   his saw,
> Wheeze, cluck, swash of falling blood, short wild scream
>   and long, dull, tapering moan,
> These so, these irretrievable.

"Irretrievable" mediates between two facts for the poet: that they *are* retrievable (he retrieves them) and that they are *intolerable*. So we get the lines next, opening 37:

> You laggards there on guard! look to your arms!
> In at the conquer'd doors they crowd; I am possess'd!

Yet still the presences that he must be come, throng, then more and more quiet, isolating, not less but more harrowing, down to

> Not a cholera patient lies at the last gasp but I
>   also lie at the last gasp,
> My face is ash-color'd, my sinews gnarl, away from
>   me people retreat.
>
> Askers embody themselves in me and I am embodied in them,
> I project my hat, sit shame-faced, then, and beg.

This terrible, almost funny, deeply actual, final humiliation to the poet's dignity and independence brings on

> Enough! enough! enough!
> Somehow I have been stunn'd. Stand back!
> Give me a little time beyond my cuff'd head,
>   slumbers, dreams, gaping,
> I discover myself on the verge of a usual mistake.

> . . . I remember now
> I resume the overstaied fraction . . .

He becomes, in self-defense, a Self again—he resumes his (too long in coming back, "overstaied") Body, which, like most men ("a usual mistake") he had forgotten; the Body that anchors us among the swallowings of the Soul, the predicaments of the imagination, the Body which is *also* part of his subject, a fraction of Man.

The Fourth Movement is addressed to his "Eleves"—disciples— "lovers of me, bafflers of graves." Not all, as we have seen, but all who will. The form used is a setting out, there are instructions, recapitulations, but

> Not I, not anyone else can travel that road for you,
> You must travel it for yourself.

Therefore, the poet gradually withdraws. Part of this might be taken as coda, but I prefer at present to see the Fourth Movement as including everything from the salute near the end of Section 38 through 52, the final section. Little, until toward the close, is impressive in itself, but much, when read in the poem and especially the close, affects me like some of the late, great songs in *Winterreise* and above all "Leiermann." I take some lines from 49, the little, pleading Section 50, and 52, which truly sounds like the speech-back-to-us of a being already elsewhere, *in* Happiness as a place. One might be surprised that he troubles to speak back, but this is his nature.

We listen to these final sections, I think, with a peculiar intimacy of involvement—the reason being that we have been with him now so long in a personal way, unlike what happens in Lucretius, and without any intervening narrative distance such as one experiences in most long poems—an intimacy such, I say, as to make one friendly to his resistance to his work's being taken as literary; one feels what he means, and sympathizes; although it is of course a literary work—too idiosyncratic, like *Paradise Lost,* to rank with the very first poems (I am thinking of the *Iliad,* the poem of Job, the *Oedipus Tyrannus,* the *Mahābhārata,* the *Commedia, King Lear*), but one that will do good to us so long as our language persists and the human race remains capable of interest in such things.

1957

Hardy and His Thrush

HARDY'S REPUTATION HAS ALWAYS BEEN FURIOUSLY UN-
stable. So was his practice. I think we all loved when young three
novels, *The Mayor of Casterbridge, Tess of the D'Urbervilles*, and *Jude
the Obscure*, but it was with *The Return of the Native* that we were
tortured in school. Moreover, not only were the three important
novels attacked but they were attacked by people like Henry James,
with some justice, since they are unrereadable. As for his poetry,
opinions also strangely differ. We have violent comments on both
sides. T. S. Eliot pronounced him a minor poet, whereas Robert Lowell
thinks that along with Rilke he is one of the greatest poets of the century. Surely both are wrong. The author of "An Ancient to Ancients,"
"The Oxen," and "The Darkling Thrush" cannot in my mind bear to
be regarded as minor, and yet there is the true fact that Hardy was
quite unambitious: he once said that all he wanted was to place one or
two poems in a good anthology like *The Golden Treasury*. Now,
ladies and gentlemen, ambition along with luck and health is a serious
factor in artistic accomplishment. One has to *love* Hardy—W. H.
Auden once remarked in print that he loved him, but that is a very
different matter from critical judgment—but just because he was so
modest does not mean he was great. I love Hardy, too, but for his
poetry. He took areas of dying rural England and made them permanent for us. He worked in three main modes as a poet. He was a lyric
poet of genuine distinction. He also wrote meditative poems of great
power, like "The Darkling Thrush." And then he wrote, too, occasional poems like "The Convergence of the Twain" and "The Darkling
Thrush," with which at the new year in 1900 in *The (London) Times*
he greeted the new century.

We have an isolated bird. As in Walt Whitman the term "aliena-
tion" would not be excessive. But the bird is very different from
Whitman's; the bird is happy, and throughout the poem it *sounds* as

if the poet were identifying with the bird as in Whitman, but actually this is not so. The poet is in despair while the bird feels fine.

Hardy kept proclaiming himself a meliorist—he refused the label pessimism; but actually, when you begin to dig into his work anywhere, repeat anywhere, the mind involved is dark. Therefore, let us suppose that the bird, the thrush, at dark represents a dream of Hardy's, not an author-figure. Does the dream succeed? Is the question worth asking? Men should be allowed their secrets. If we had this wonderful person on the telephone, would or could he tell us?

The truth of the matter is a presentment out of the imagination, the author's opinions being irrelevant.

The nineteenth century, with its fatal heritage to us, comes on an end in this poem—the bird thinks; the poet knows better. He sees that the insane nationalism and dreads of the nineteenth century will also dominate the twentieth. But he does not insist on this. It turns up almost by accident in the final line. So how shall we put the matter of emphasis—do we have one poem or two? Surely two. One called "The Darkling Thrush," the other called Thomas Hardy explicat. It's true that the second poem only contains one line, but it dominates the little masterpiece.

I have used the word "little" and I have quoted Eliot's word "minor" and I've seemed to be friendlier to these judgments than to Lowell's and John Crowe Ransom's. It is too soon to form an opinion about Hardy's ultimate place in our international English-speaking literature. He wrote one thousand pages of the worst short stories that the world has ever seen. He wrote some ridiculous novels. *The Dynasts* is a dud, fit only for graduate study. He wrote many atrocious poems also, but the main novels will always be available for young people. As for the rest of us—I now change my position entirely and line up with Ransom—we are happy with a handful of magnificent devoted poems which that formidable little man happened to leave to us as a legacy.

Hardy's most formidable disciple was W. H. Auden. Tell you a story. Ransom, who practically calls Hardy "Mr Hardy," once came and gave a chat to my little students. At one point he said, "In one of his poems ["Afterwards"] Hardy is considering the thing as it will be after his death. One can imagine what Tennyson or Browning would have made of this theme; but all Hardy says is, After I'm gone, will there be someone who looking at a sunset will think, Well, he was the kind of man who liked sunsets? Seems a pretty small thing to ask."

For detailed analysis: it's an old man's poem—Hardy in fact

was sixty when he sat down to it—even the thrush is aged. Hence "leant," "spectre-grey," "dregs," "desolate," "weakening," "broken," "haunted," "outleant," "crypt," "death lament." I do not like the second stanza, especially the end of it. May we inquire how it is that Hardy knew that "every spirit on earth seemed fervorless as I." We may inquire in vain. This radar romanticism is incredibly boring. I thought it went out with Shelley, who is Hardy's actual master, different as they appear. Now for the sad old thrush who occupies the title and the last two stanzas, that is to say, half the poem. I will only say that out of such personal misery to bring such brilliant joy is, friends, not easily done.

One final point. The poem occurs in the volume called *Poems of the Past and the Present,* along with other bird songs, one of the closest being a villanelle called "The Caged Thrush, Freed and Home Again." Subject of the first line, "Men know but little more than we," is an inversion of the "The Darkling Thrush" theme, where the bird knows more. Now, until a writer begins to bore us, it is a matter of supreme importance that he handle characteristic materials characteristically. Hardy does this, therefore we love him, and I am able almost without reservation to recommend to you one of his masterpieces, "The Darkling Thrush."

Of course, at a deeper level, the bird and the man are one. The bird, "aged," half ruined, is *still* singing. So is the poet. Most poets at sixty, as Hardy then was, have quit. Their messages differ, but here is the true motive of this matchless song. Hardy's great lyric "He Resolves to Say No More" was published posthumously in what would have been his eighty-eighth year.

1966

The Ritual of W. B. Yeats

THE TWENTY-ONE PLAYS IN YEATS'S MOST RECENT COL-
lection* represent the work of forty-two years, from *The Countess
Cathleen* in 1892 to *The Words upon the Window-pane* in 1934; and
a chronological reading of them suggests many problems. I intend to
consider in some detail the six dance plays, but since his dramatic writings have been generally neglected by American critics, a few general
remarks should be made and some of the major approaches indicated.

Enough has been written about Yeats's great part in the founding
of modern Irish literature; our present concern is directly literary,
not historical. The striking fact about this body of work, then, is its
triviality, considered in the tradition of English dramatic literature.
The volume is apparently arranged to culminate in the two "modern
versions" of Sophocles' *Oedipus the King* and *Oedipus at Colonus*,
and these are unquestionably the most full-bodied, the most satisfactory plays Yeats has written. With four exceptions, the others are all
brief and relatively thin, if interesting and even excellent in special
ways. In only one, *The Hour-Glass*, is anything like dramatic tension
achieved; the rest relate delightfully and inconsequentially the
legends of the Irish heroic age, of Cuchulain and Emer of Conchubar,
of Deirdre, of angels and demons, the cats and the Shape-Changers,
beggars and fools and kings.

It is clear that Yeats has not been concerned, as Shakespeare (we
assume) was concerned, with the creation of recognizable and individual character. The people in his plays are typical or symbolic or
mythical (and, as such, acceptable), or they are necessary figures to
speak his lines in the interests of presentation and description. No one
of them can be discussed apart from his immediate context and said to
exist in his own right. They are, in fact, simple as a morality mask is
simple; such inconsistencies as we note are the product of typical

* *The Collected Plays of William Butler Yeats*, 1936.

change or dramatic indirection—verbal ambiguity with a plastic end in view. Nor has Yeats been interested, clearly, in representation of the natural world, except in *The Words upon the Window-pane*, where realistic conversational prose serves to lend verisimilitude to his revelation of Swift's spirit through a medium. What then was Yeats doing in these plays?

The answer is threefold, insofar as we can discover it. He wanted, first, to hear his poetry spoken, and spoken under the most emphatic conditions obtainable—those of the theatre; probably he knew also that the discipline of dramatic verse would be good for his early luxuriance and imprecision, as indeed it was. He wanted to re-create the body of Irish legend and myth, seeing this re-creation as a necessary step in the nationalist movement of the early nineteen hundreds and believing that the theatre was the most popular and thus the most adequate means. And he wanted, particularly in his later plays, but to a degree in all, to dramatize his beliefs and doubts and preoccupations. These intentions, if I have stated them correctly, will describe the limits within which he has worked. His failure to achieve perfection within these limits must be ascribed to something else: Yeats's habit of mind is not dramatic but meditative. He speaks naturally, in other words, in reflection, not (as Congreve and Molière and O'Neill undeniably do) in terms of situation and action. Thus only is it possible to account for the fact that Yeats, who is probably the greatest living poet and who has worked in the theatre for forty-five years with all his intelligence and energies, has not written great plays or anything like great plays.

The four longer plays mentioned above, and one other, ought to be discussed briefly. In *The Countess Cathleen* a single atmosphere, of ominous and imminent disaster, is established and maintained more effectively than in any other play here of similar length; the incongruous salvation of Cathleen, which Yeats himself has recently deplored, is unfortunate, but it does not destroy the mood. Emphasis by contrast Yeats has secured in only one case, the brief *On Baile's Strand*. The heroic strife between the great king Conchubar and Cuchulain, who speak in blank verse, is enclosed in the framework of the Fool and the Blind Man, who begin and end the play, speaking a nervous and idiosyncratic prose; the device is not wholly successful, but it is notable, for it represents Yeats's only effort to attain this kind of complexity; actually it is only a rudimentary step in the direction of the highly individual, unmistakable accent of Shallow and Hamlet, Lear's Fool, and the Bastard Faulconbridge.

The Unicorn from the Stars and *The Player-Queen* are more recognizably dramatic pieces than any other original plays Yeats has written, particularly the latter, which is a very charming fantastic comedy in two long scenes, with little supernatural and legendary reference. The other play is allegorical, probably with a basis in legend; standing alone, it is too confused to admit of a single interpretation. Martin, the young dreamer who is led from his work by visions of great white unicorns trampling vineyards, remains an inexplicable shadow, and even his death is ambiguous.

Owing to Yeats's constant revision of all his plays, we find a remarkable uniformity of style here. As in his poetry, we see his vocabulary becoming more concrete, dependent on nouns rather than on adjectives, the unit of sound within the line briefer; and the later plays are written in a prose which differs in a similar way from the prose of *Cathleen Ni Houlihan* (1904). But the change in the verse of the plays is as nothing to the complete remodelling of his style in his later poems.

It is in the songs that we find development, a basic and strong melody that is lacking in the early songs, no matter how delightful. Compare

> Impetuous heart be still, be still,
> Your sorrowful love can never be told,
> Cover it up with a lonely tune.
> He who could bend all things to His will
> Has covered the door of the infinite fold
> With the pale stars and the wandering moon.
>
> [1892]

with

> The Babylonian starlight brought
> A fabulous, formless darkness in;
> Odour of blood when Christ was slain
> Made all Platonic tolerance vain
> And vain all Doric discipline.
> Everything that man esteems
> Endures a moment or a day:
> Love's pleasure drives his love away,
> The painter's brush consumes his dreams;
> The herald's cry, the soldier's tread
> Exhaust his glory and his might:
> Whatever flames upon the night
> Man's own resinous heart has fed.
>
> [1933]

The talented young man who wrote the first lyric has become a major poet in the last; but the forty years that have intervened have wrought no such transformation in his dramatic verse. Yeats may have realized this: the six plays since 1920 have been entirely in prose, except for songs and choruses.

Yeats wrote the first of what he calls his "dance plays" in 1917, and he has used the form five times since (or six, if we include *The King of the Great Clock-Tower*, 1935, which is not included in this volume and is hardly worth independent comment, despite three beautiful lyrics, for it resembles the others closely). The term is hardly appropriate, for although dances do occur in two of them, gesture and action are almost completely subordinated to speech; the nature of the form can be shown best by quotation from the stage direction of *At the Hawk's Well*, the first of these plays:

> The stage is any bare place before a wall against which stands a patterned screen. A drum and a gong and a zither have been laid close to the screen before the play begins (or) they can be carried in, after the audience is seated, by the First Musician . . . the most effective lighting is the lighting we are most accustomed to in our rooms. These masked players seem stranger when there is no mechanical means of separating them from us. The First Musician carries with him a folded black cloth and goes to the centre of the stage towards the front and stands motionless . . . the two other Musicians enter and go towards him and slowly unfold the cloth, singing. [They] make a triangle with the First Musician at the apex, supporting the centre of the cloth . . . then slowly fold up the cloth again, singing (and disclosing the player or players).

Such action as there is takes place within this limited space; at the end the Musicians unfold and fold the cloth as before, singing, in order to allow the players to leave the scene unobserved.

This narrow and almost private form is clearly very different from the dance dramas of Egypt and medieval Europe, but the at-once-implied classification of "ritual" is very useful; it may help us to understand the function and the real value of Yeats's work in these plays. Let us take "ritual" to signify a code or form of ceremonies, the formal character imposed on any experience as it is given objective existence by the imagination working in craft; the experience attains independent aesthetic vitality precisely through and by its limitation. Coming nearer to Yeats, we can say that this effective form will be meditative and single, that the experience will be largely from the body of myth and personal belief, and that the vitality will be dependent not at all on reference but on the skill and accuracy of insight as it is objectified.

It was appropriate and even inevitable that Yeats, a self-conscious and deliberate artist, should evolve some such form as this, as his most satisfactory means of expression, apart from the personal lyric. In agreeing to work within the narrowest possible "dramatic" limits, he at once lessened the probability of failure by obviating the necessity of using techniques not natural to him, and emphasized his accustomed talent by letting it work alone to the fullest advantage and with an appropriate subject matter.

His most important device, which allows him to establish and control almost in his own person the mood or system of reference of a given play, is the singing as the cloth is unfolded and folded before and after the action. Thus, in *Calvary* these songs are so important that the play might be incomprehensible without them. Christ is discovered leaning on his cross, and the atmosphere of doubt and mockery is set by the words of the First Musician, who acts as a chorus. Lazarus enters and curses Christ for having raised him:

> I had been dead and I was lying still
> In an old comfortable mountain cavern
> When you came climbing there with a great crowd
> And dragged me to the light . . .

Then Judas comes; he knew the God and betrayed Him that he might be the stronger; he tells Christ:

> When I planned it
> There was no live thing near me but a heron
> So full of itself that it seemed terrified.
> I did it,
> I, Judas, and no other man, and now
> You cannot even save me.

Christ says, "Begone from me." And after the soldiers have mocked Him, His last words are "My father, why hast Thou forsaken me?"

The theme is probably clear: it is Christ's failure to reconcile His divine and His human natures. But in the songs Yeats picks the most emphatic aspect of the theme, and the presence of the heron becomes almost the subject of the play; the first song begins:

Motionless under the moon-beam,
Up to his feathers in the stream;
Although fish leap, the white heron
Shivers in a dumbfounded dream.
God has not died for the white heron.

And the final song ends:

But where have last year's cygnets gone?
The lake is empty; why do they fling
White wing out beside white wing?
What can a swan need but a swan?
God has not appeared to the birds.

The songs serve as a frame, an intelligible and coherent structure on which the action depends, as brickwork on girders.

Another important feature of the ritual is the use of masks; they figure more or less significantly in all six of the dance plays, but particularly in *The Only Jealousy of Emer*, which is impossible to conceive in anything like its present form without masks. The body of the renowned Cuchulain, "that amorous, violent man," has been washed ashore, and Emer, his wife, watches beside it; she sends for his mistress, Eithne Inguba, the woman he loved last, for Cuchulain is not dead: Bricriu of the Sidhe, the company of evil powers, has entered into him and dispossessed his spirit. All the players are masked, and the masked Ghost of Cuchulain crouches near the bed. Bricriu calls up a Woman of the Sidhe to take Cuchulain away, unless Emer will renounce forever his love; the Ghost and the Woman go out, but under the hypnotic urging of Bricriu in the Figure of Cuchulain, Emer gives up her claim and the Figure sinks back, to be awakened as the living Cuchulain by Eithne Inguba. Heroic and distorted masks are in large part responsible for the strange power of the play when it is read; in performance the effect of their rigid impersonality while passionate speech comes from their lips must be startling. More broadly, the stylized terms in which Emer's sacrifice is enacted are not merely the conductor but the cause of the play's strength and beauty.

The Dreaming of the Bones is the only dance play with a contemporary setting. A young Irish patriot, escaping through the hills after the fighting in Dublin in 1916, meets two strangers with heroic masks, a man and a young girl; they take him to the ruined Abbey of Corcomroe, where the dreaming bones of the dead wander in torment, and tell him the story of Dermot and Dervorgilla, who brought the Norman into Ireland to fight for them and who must wander until one of their race says, "I have forgiven them." Unknowing, the young man curses that pair, and when he learns, as they dance, their identity, he is yet stern:

> They have dropped their eyes,
> They have covered up their eyes as though their hearts
> Had suddenly been broken—never, never
> Shall Dermot and Dervorgilla be forgiven.

This is perhaps the simplest and most compact of all the plays; great emotional intensity is secured through a curious and eerie relaxation of the verse: the players dream rather than speak, except when the young man's angry hatred lashes out against a seven-hundred-year-old treachery. A very interesting device, which illustrates the freedom that can be obtained through strict adherence to ritual, is used here and again in *The Cat and the Moon:* symbolic progress, action represented by the direction, "They go round stage once. The Musicians play." Any mode of writing, however narrow when it was adopted, is constantly available to intelligence for development in subtlety and scope; and, frequently, the more restricted the imagination, the more splendid its activity.

At the *Hawk's Well* and *The Cat and the Moon* are slight in effectiveness as well as in range. In the first, Yeats fails to make his play independent of the legend it relates, that of the Irish well which deludes men with its promise of immortality, and of its fierce Guardian; success and even understanding are provisional, dependent on external knowledge; the action between the frame songs has reference still to the insight which preceded expression. *The Cat and the Moon* is a brief allegory of practical faith and spiritual faith; here again the system of symbolic reference within the play is not explained, and a dozen interpretations, all tentative, are possible.

The Resurrection deals explicitly with a problem of personal faith; it is more flexible than the other dance plays, having been written first for an ordinary stage, but it is still doubtful whether Yeats could have succeeded without the conventional restrictions of this form. After the Crucifixion the eleven are a confused and tormented group and have gathered apart in the room where the Last Supper was held; in a guardroom, which is the scene, a Greek and a Hebrew converse, maintaining their individual heresies: the Greek says that Christ was pure spirit, He "only seemed to be born, only seemed to eat, seemed to sleep, seemed to walk, seemed to die"; the Hebrew says that Christ was merely the best man who ever lived and that he came to believe himself the Messiah. What we are in the habit of considering the characteristic tempers of the Greek and the Hebrew minds are admirably given. But a Syrian appears with the news that Christ had risen, has spoken with the women, and will come; He comes, and the Greek shrieks, "The heart of a phantom is beating! The heart of a phantom is beating!" A procession of worshippers of Dionysius having passed and sung in the street below the room, the theme is clear; Yeats is not saying simply that religions are continuous and one and impure, he is dismayed at the destruction of the classic temper. The last words of the play, spoken by the Greek, are:

O Athens, Alexandria, Rome, something has come to destroy you. The heart of a phantom is beating. Man has begun to die. Your words are clear at last, O Heraclitus. God and man die each other's life, live each other's death.

Only through the elastic freedom achieved by the bondage of ritual is such statement possible in anything like dramatic terms.

1936

The Poetry of Ezra Pound

Since Pound has been for several generations now one of the most famous of living poets, it may occasion surprise that an *introduction* to his poetry (such as I was lately invited to make for New Directions) should be thought necessary at all. It may, but I doubt that it will. Not much candour is wanted for the observation that, though he is famous and his poetry is famous, his poetry is not familiar, that serious readers as a class have relinquished even the imperfect hold they had upon it fifteen years ago and regard it at present either with hostility or with indifference. The situation is awkward for the critic. Commonly, when the object of criticism is at once celebrated, unfamiliar, and odious, it is also remote in time; the inquiry touches no current or recent passion. Our case is as different as possible from this enviable condition.

> In a few years no one will remember the *buffo*,
> No one will remember the trivial parts of me,
> The comic detail will be absent.

After thirty-five years neither comic nor tragic detail is absent. Whatever the critic may wish to say of the poetry runs the risk of being misunderstood as of the poet; one encounters *eager* preconceptions; and no disclaimer is likely to have effect. I make, however, no disclaimer just yet. Let us only proceed slowly—remembering that it is the business of criticism to offer explanations—toward the matter of hostility, beginning with the matter of indifference.

It *is* very surprising, perhaps, that readers of poetry should remain indifferent to the verse of a poet so influential as Pound has been. As one of the dominant, seminal poetries of the age, one would expect readers to want to become acquainted with it as a matter of course. That many do not want to suggests that they do not in fact so regard it, or regard it as only in some special sense an influence; and I think this is the case. They regard *Pound* as a dominant influence.

253

They are quite right, of course. But even this is often disputed or ignored, so we cannot avoid some discussion. It is necessary to see Pound under two aspects: as he worked upon poetry and as he worked upon the public. The notion of him as publicist for Joyce, Eliot, Frost, a hundred others, being still current, I feel free to select instances displaying rather the first aspect, and take his relations with W. B. Yeats, with Imagism, and with *The Waste Land*—with the major poet, that is, the major movement, and the major poem, of the century so far.

Pound went to London in 1908, at twenty-three, to learn from Yeats how to write poetry, in the belief that no one then living knew more about it. Swinburne was just alive (when he died the following April, "I am the King of the Cats," said Yeats to one of his sisters meeting her in the street), inaccessible behind Watts-Dunton.

> Swinburne my only miss
> and I didn't know he'd been to see Landor
>   *and* they told me this that an' tother
> and when old Mathews went he saw the three teacups
>   two for Watts Dunton who liked to let his tea cool
> So old Elkin had only one glory
>   He did carry Algernon's suit *once*
> when he, Elkin, first came to London.
>   But given what I know now I'd have
>   got thru it somehow . . . Dirce's shade
>   or a black jack.   (Canto LXXXII)

Pound was a most odd disciple; he regarded himself as the heir of Browning, he was stirring free of Fitzgerald and the nineties, he had already begun the war on the iamb and the English heroic line that would never end (consider the two opening dactyls here and then the spondee-two-dactyls-and-trochee of the beautiful sixth line), he was full of the Troubadours, and he was becoming obsessed with the concept of verse-as-*speech*. He had as much energy as Yeats. The older poet has recorded his debt to the younger for advice against abstractions, underlinings of them, help in revision, and so on. But the change that began to move in Yeats's verse about this time was toward speech, the beginning of his famous development, and like one or two others I have always supposed Pound the motor. What seems to have happened was this: Pound was going in the afternoons to see Ford Madox Hueffer (Ford), and in the evenings to see Yeats; the older men did not get on. Of four "honourable debts" he acknowledged later, the chief was Hueffer, who "believes one should write in a contemporary spoken or at least speakable language"—not the same thing, it will be observed, as Pound's famous earlier formulation of "Mr. Hueffer's realization that poetry should be written at least as well as prose."

> So old Ezra had only one glory

here, that he passed on without source in the evening what he had heard in the afternoon.

Then Imagism. There were two "Imagist" movements (besides a dilution of the second, conducted by Amy Lowell, which reached the public), both in London. The first was started in March 1909 by T. E. Hulme, who was insisting on "absolutely accurate presentation and no verbiage," F. S. Flint, who had been advocating "vers libre," Edward Storer, who was interested in "the Image," and others, all strongly under the influence of French Symbolist poetry. Pound joined the group on 22 April—Elkin Mathews had published the week before a third collection of poems, *Personae*, his first book proper, which would establish him. Pound read out to the startled Soho café a new poem, "Sestina: Altaforte." *Exultations*, issued later that year, and *Canzoni* (1911), continuing his Provençal investigations, display no Imagist affiliation; *Ripostes* (1912) does, and at the end of it he printed Hulme's five poems and named the movement, which had passed away meanwhile, perhaps because none of its other members could write poetry. Through Pound personally, the first movement reached the second. The second consisted of H.D. and Richard Aldington, who were inspired not by French but by Greek verse, in 1912; Pound got their work printed, wrote the movement's essential documents (in *Poetry* for March 1913, "A Few Don'ts" and an interview with him signed by Flint), and edited *Des Imagistes*, which appeared in March of 1914. By the time Miss Lowell arrived with her retinue that summer, Pound, joined now with Wyndham Lewis and the sculptor Gaudier-Brzeska, had launched Vorticism, in the opening *Blast*. The importance of literary movements is readily exaggerated; conceivably in the end Imagism will seem valuable above all as it affected Pound's verse. Still, with a doubtful exception for the unnamed movement of the Auden group about 1930, it is the migration to a new position, for our time, that retains most interest, and is a fair sample of Pound's activity.

His now celebrated operation some years later upon *The Waste*

Land, disengaging that work as we know it from what its author describes as a sprawling, chaotic poem twice as long, is another. Keeping our wits and facts in order, we need not follow a critic sometimes so penetrating as Yvor Winters in seeing Pound as the "primal spirit" behind every gesture, every deplorable gesture, of the deplorable Eliot. "The principal influence" upon Eliot's verse, Winters writes, "is probably that of Laforgue, whose poetry Pound had begun to champion at least as early as 1917." This is very early indeed, only seven years after Eliot's "Humouresque, After J. Laforgue" in the *Harvard Advocate.* No, Eliot started alone. The two poets met first, and Pound persuaded *Poetry* to print "The Love Song of J. Alfred Prufrock" in 1915, by which date Eliot was nearly through with Laforgue. Winters's remark neglects also the serial character of the influences on Eliot's poetry, which include Laforgue, Webster, James, Baudelaire, Pound, Gautier, Joyce, Apollinaire, Dante. It is emphatically not a mistake, however, to regard Pound's personal influence as great from 1915 on; and great on the period as a whole.

The reader who is not a student of poetry has another ground for indifference. Pound, he has always heard, has no "*matter.*" Granting the "importance" of his verse, granting the possibility that having been for poets fertile it might prove on acquaintance agreeable or beautiful, what has he to do with this sport, a matterless poetry? This is a much more sophisticated dissatisfaction, and can claim the highest critical support. "I confess," Eliot once wrote, "that I am seldom interested in what he is saying, but only in the way he says it"; and R. P. Blackmur, "He is all surface and articulation." We notice Eliot's qualification ("seldom") and we are puzzled by an ambiguity in Blackmur's "articulation" (is this jointing or merely uttering?); but on the whole they put authoritatively the established view. Now there can be no question of traversing such authorities directly. But it is a violent and remarkable charge; I think we are bound to look into it a little.

If his critics are right, Pound himself misconceived his work from the beginning and has continued to do so. This is of course not impossible; in fact, I shall be arguing presently, in another sense, that it is just what he has done. But let us hear what he has said. In a very early poem, "Revolt, Against the crepuscular spirit in modern poetry," he says:

> I would shake off the lethargy of this our time, and give
> For shadows—shapes of power
> For dreams—men.

If the poem is bad, the programme is distinct. Then one of his debts, he records later, "may be considered as the example of or hint from Thomas Hardy, who, despite the aesthetic era, has remained interested in his subject, i.e., in distinction to being interested in 'treatment.'" Among other passages to the same effect, I give one more, later still, which readers must have come on with surprise. Speaking of Eliot and Miss Moore, Pound remarks, "Neither they nor anyone else is likely to claim that they have as much interest in life as I have, or that I have their patience in reading."

The "literary" or "aesthetic" view taken of Pound now for many years will not be much disturbed by such assertions, until we observe how oddly they are confirmed by the opinions expressed in 1909 about *Personae*. These opinions are worth attention, because Pound's literary personality became known as a leader's thereafter, and most reviews his books have received since show the impress of this knowledge; they are impure. It is hardly too much to say that the first *Personae* was the last volume of Pound's that was widely judged on its merits. What did the old reviewers say? "He writes out of an exuberance of incontinently struggling ideas and passionate convictions . . . He plunges straight into the heart of his theme, and suggests virility in action combined with fierceness, eagerness, and tenderness"—so R. A. Scott-James, whose excitement, by the way, about "the brute force of Mr. Pound's imagination" did not prevent his noticing the unusual spondee-dactyl use, which he exemplified with a lovely line from "Cino":

Éyes, dréams, / líps, and the / níght góes.

It is absolutely unnecessary, and appears to a scholar probably very ridiculous, to patronize the reviewers of an earlier age. "The beauty of ["In Praise of Ysolt"] is the beauty of passion, sincerity and intensity," wrote Edward Thomas, "not of beautiful words and images and suggestions . . . the thought dominates the words and is greater than they are." One hardly recognizes here the "superficial" or "mindless" Pound whom critics have held up to us since. Faced with a welter of Provençal and Browning and early Yeats, not to mention Villon, the reviewers nevertheless insisted upon the poet's strong individuality: "All his poems are like this, from beginning to end, and in every way, his own, and in a world of his own." Faced with this learning (the notes quote Richard of St. Victor, etc.), they admired "his fearlessness and lack of self-consciousness," the "breath of the open air." "He cannot be usefully compared," Thomas went on, "with any living writers . . . full of personality and with such power to express it, that," and so on. The Oxford *Isis* agreed that "physically and intellectually the verse seems to reproduce the personality with a brief fullness and adequacy." Instead of pursuing the engaging themes thrown up by this medley of exaggeration and justice, culled mostly from the back leaves of *Exultations*, let me pass to a third, more serious difficulty with the view that Pound has no "matter."

Pound's poetry treats of Provence, China, Rome, London, medieval living, modern living, human relationships, authors, young women, animals, money, games, government, war, poetry, love, and other things. This can be verified. What the critics must mean, then, is that they are aware of a *defect*, or defects, in the substance of the poetry. About one defect they have been explicit: the want of originality of substance. Pound has no matter *of his own*. Pound—who is even in the most surprising quarters conceded to be a "great" translator—is best as a translator. "The *Propertius* is a sturdier, more sustained, and more independent poem than *Mauberley*," writes Blackmur. "Craftsmanship may be equally found in both poems; but Mr. Pound has contributed more of his own individual sensibility, more genuine personal voice, in the *Propertius* where he had something to proceed from, than in *Mauberley* where he was on his own . . . This fact, which perhaps cannot be demonstrated but which can be felt when the reader is familiar enough with the poems, is the key-fact of serious judgment upon Mr. Pound." I do not feel sure that time is bearing out the first part of this careful judgment; the finest sections of Pound's postwar farewell to London, where the grotesquerie of Tristan Corbière is a new element in the complex style, naïve and wily, in which he celebrates the modern poet's difficulties and nostalgia, seem to me somewhat more brilliant, solid, and independent than the finest sections of the Roman poem. But my objections to the point of view begin well behind any value judgment. *All* the ambitious poetry of the last six hundred years is much less "original" than any but a few of its readers ever realize. A staggering quantity of it has direct sources, even verbal sources, in other poetry, history, philosophy, theology, prose of all kinds. Even the word "original" in this sense we find first in Dryden, and the sense was not normalized till the midcentury following. A few hours, or days, with several annotated editions of *Lycidas* will transform the reader's view of this matter, especially if he will bear in mind the likelihood that the serious modern poet's strategy resembles Milton's—exceptional as Milton was—far more closely than his (the reader's) attitude and knowledge resemble Milton's contemporary reader's attitude and knowledge. Poetry is a palimpsest. "The old playwrights took old subjects," remarks a poet who has not been accused of want of originality, "did not even arrange the subject in a new way. They were absorbed in expression, that is to say in what is most near and delicate." So Yeats; but our literary criticism, if at its best it knows all this well enough, even at its best is inclined to forget it and to act as if originality were not regularly a matter of *degree* in works where it is worth assessing at all. A difficulty is that modern critics spend much of their time in the perusal of writing that really is more or less original, and negligible. This African originality is very confusing. One of the writer's favourite poems is perfect Thomson in manner as well as perfect Wordsworth, the substance is all but purely Wordsworth's, and how are we accustomed to deal with this? The answer is that we are not. It clearly troubles Eliot that the two first sections of "Near Perigord" resemble Browning, Pound's master, though the poem seems to him (as to me) beautiful and profound; this poem is extremely original in substantial development. Now, though Blackmur is preferring derivation and Eliot is deprecating it, they appear to illustrate an identical disorder of procedure, that of a criticism which is content to consider in isolation originality of either matter *or* manner, without regard to the other, and with small regard to degree. I term this a disorder rather than a defect, because with regard to a poetry as singular as Pound's, and with such diverse claims upon our attention, it is all but fatal to criticism. The critics were writing, one fifteen years ago, the other twenty, but I do not know that our situation has much improved, and it goes without saying that the best criticism of the period has addressed itself almost exclusively to manner, except for the proliferation in the last decade of an exegetical criticism similarly limited and comparatively abject. Until we get a criticism able to consider both originalities, in degree, Pound's achievement as a poet cannot be finally extricated from the body of his verse; and prepossessions should be avoided. That he has translated so much has no doubt cost him many readers, who (despite Dryden and Pope) cannot imagine that a "real poet" would be content to translate so much; but criticism should be wiser.

Why *has* Pound translated so much? The question is an important one, and the answers usually given ignore the abyss of difference between his just-translations, like the Cavalcanti (the Canzone aside, of which his final version opens Canto XXXVI), such as might have been made by another poet of superlative skill, and renderings like those in *Cathay* and *Propertius*, which are part of Pound's own life-poetry. The first class may be considered as exercise, propaganda, critical activity, taken in conjunction with his incoherent and powerful literary criticism. The second class requires a word about Pound's notion of *personae* or masks, which issued successively in the masks of Cino, Bertran de Born, various Chinese poets, Propertius, Mauberley, fifty others. They differ both from Yeats's masks and from the dramatizations, such as Prufrock and Auden's "airman," that other poets find necessary in a period inimical to poetry, gregarious, and impatient of dignity.

We hear of the notion in two of his earliest poems, a sonnet "Masks" about

> souls that found themselves among
> Unwonted folk that spake a hostile tongue,
> Some souls from all the rest who'd not forgot
> The star-span acres of a former lot
> Where boundless mid the clouds his course he swung,
> Or carnate with his elder brothers sung
> E'er ballad makers lisped of Camelot . . .

and *In Durance:*

> But for all that, I am homesick after mine own kind
> And would meet kindred even as I am,
> Flesh-shrouded bearing the secret.

The question is, what the masks are *for*.

Does any reader who is familiar with Pound's poetry really not see that its subject is the life of the modern poet?

It is in *"Famam Librosque Cano"* and *"Scriptor Ignotus"* of *Personae—*

> And I see my greater soul-self bending
> Sibylwise with that great forty-year epic
> That you know of, yet unwrit
> But as some child's toy 'tween my fingers . . .
>
> If my power be lesser
> Shall my striving be less keen? . . .

It is in "Histrion" of *Exultations—*

> 'Tis as in midmost us there glows a sphere
> Translucent, molten gold, that is the "I"
> And into this some form projects itself . . .
>
> And these, the Masters of the Soul, live on.

It is in one of the few good lines of *Canzoni*—

> Who calls me idle? I have thought of her.

It is in "N.Y." of *Ripostes* (1912), the volume in which Pound established his manner and the volume with which modern poetry in English may be felt to have begun—

> My City, my beloved, my white! Ah, slender . . .

> Delicately upon the reed, attend me!

> Now do I know that I am mad,
> For here are a million people surly with traffic:
> This is no maid.
> Neither could I play upon any reed if I had one.

It is everywhere (as well as in the Chinese work) in the more "original" poems and epigrams of *Lustra*, written 1913–16. (A lustrum is "an offering for the sins of the whole people, made by the censors at the expiration of their five years of office." It has not perhaps been sufficiently observed that Pound is one of the wittiest poets who ever wrote. Yet he is serious enough in this title. In certain attitudes—his medieval nostalgia, literary anti-Semitism, others—he a good deal resembles Henry Adams; each spent his life, as it were, seeking an official post where he could be used, and their failure to find one produced both the freedom and the inconsequence that charm and annoy us in these authors.) It is in the elaborate foreign personae that followed, *Cathay* (1915)—

> And I have moped in the Emperor's garden, awaiting
>   an order-to-write!

and *Propertius* (1917)—

> I who come first from the clear font
> Bringing the Grecian orgies into Italy
>   and the dance into Italy.

It is in *Mauberley*, of course—

> Dowson found harlots cheaper than hotels;
> So spoke the author of "The Dorian Mood,"

> M. Verog, out of step with the decade,
> Detached from his contemporaries
> Neglected by the young,
> Because of these reveries.

Meanwhile, Pound's concept of method had been strongly affected by Ernest Fenollosa's essay *The Chinese Written Character as a Medium for Poetry* ("Metaphor, the revealer of nature, is the very substance of poetry . . . Chinese poetry gets back near to the processes of nature by means of its vivid figure . . . If we attempt to follow it in English we must use words highly charged, words whose vital suggestion shall interplay as nature interplays. Sentences must be like the mingling of the fringes of feathered banners, or as the colors of many flowers blended into the single sheen of a meadow . . . a thousand tints of verb") and for years he had been trying to work out a form whereby he could get his subject all together; by the time of *Mauberley* he had succeeded, in the final version of the opening *Cantos*. And it is, as we shall see, in the *Cantos* also.

Above all, certain themes in the life of the modern poet: indecision-decision and infidelity-fidelity. Pound has written much more love poetry than is generally realized, and when fidelity and decision lock in his imagination, we hear extraordinary effects, passionate, solemn. A lady is served her singer-lover's heart, eats, and her husband tells her whose:

> "It is Cabestan's heart in the dish."
> "It is Cabestan's heart in the dish?
> "No other taste shall change this."   (Canto IV)

She hurtles from the window.

> And in south province Tchin Tiaouen had risen
> and took the city of Tchang tcheou
> offered marriage to Ouang Chi,
> who said: It is an honour.
> I must first bury Kanouen. His body is heavy.
> His ashes were light to carry
> Bright was the flame for Kanouen
>   Ouang Chi cast herself into it, Faithful forever
>   High the hall TIMOUR made her.   (Canto LVI)

"His body is heavy." The theme produces also the dazzle and terror of the end of "Near Perigord," where we finally reach Bertran *through* *Maent*, whom we'd despaired of. If there are a passion and solemnity beyond this in poetry—

> Soul awful! if the earth has ever lodg'd
> An awful soul—

we have to go far to find them. If Pound is neither the poet apostrophized here nor the poet apostrophizing, not Milton or Wordsworth, his place will be high enough. These themes of decision and fidelity bear on much besides love in his poetry, and even—as one would expect with a subject of the poet-in-exile (Ovid, Dante, Villon, Browning, Henry James, Joyce, Pound, Eliot, as Mann, Brecht, Auden) whose allegiance is to an ideal state—upon politics:

> homage, fealty are to the person
> can not be to body politic . . .   (Canto LXVII)*

Of course there are other themes, strong and weak, and a multiplicity of topics, analogies to the life of the modern poet, with or without metaphor the *interests* of the poet. But this would appear to characterize any poet's work. I mean more definitely "Life and Contacts," as the subtitle of *Hugh Selwyn Mauberley* has it.

It is not quite Ezra Pound himself. Yeats, another Romantic, was also the subject of his own poetry, himself-as-himself. Pound is his own subject *qua* modern poet; it is the experience and fate of this writer "born / In a half savage country, out of date," a voluntary exile for over thirty years, that concern him. Another distinction is necessary. Wallace Stevens has presented us in recent years with a series of strange prose documents about "imagination" and "reality." If Stevens's poetry has for substance imagination, in this dichotomy, Pound's has for substance reality. A poem like "Villanelle: the Psychological Hour" or the passage I have quoted about Swinburne could have been made only by Pound, and the habit of mind involved has given us much truth that we could not otherwise have had. Two young friends did not come to see the poet! The poet missed a master! This is really in part what life consists of, though reading most poetry one would never guess it.

> And we say good-bye to you also,
> For you seem never to have discovered
> That your relationship is wholly parasitic;
> Yet to our feasts you bring neither
> Wit, nor good spirits, nor the pleasing attitudes
> Of discipleship.

* Without allusion to the poet's personal situation (in 1949), which is rather a matter for courts, which have reached no verdict, and psychiatrists, who have declared the poet insane, than for literary criticism, it will be recalled as a gloss for these lines that when the Irish patriot Sir Roger Casement was tried for treason a war ago, he had to be tried under a statute centuries old, the charge being based upon a conventional oath of *personal* loyalty to the King made when Casement was knighted for services "to the Crown" as a civil servant investigating atrocities in the Putomayo.

It is personal, but it is not very personal. The "distance" everywhere felt in the finest verse that treats his subject directly has, I think, two powerful sources, apart from the usual ones (versification and so on). First, there is the peculiar detachment of interest with which Pound seems to regard himself; no writer could be less revelatory of his passional life, and his friends have recorded—Dr Williams with annoyance—the same lifelong reticence in private. Second, his unfaltering, encyclopedic mastery of tone—a mastery that compensates for a comparative weakness of syntax. (By instinct, I parenthesize, Pound has always minimized the importance of syntax, and this instinct perhaps accounts for his inveterate dislike for Milton, a dislike that has had broad consequences for three decades of the twentieth century; not only did Milton seem to him, perhaps, anti-romantic *and* anti-realistic, undetailed, and anti-conversational, but Milton is the supreme English master of syntax.) Behind this mastery lies his ear. I scarcely know what to say of Pound's ear. Fifteen years of listening have not taught me that it is inferior to the ear of the author of *Twelfth Night*. The reader who heard the damage done, in my variation, to Pound's line—*So old Elkin had only one glory*—will be able to form his own opinion.

We write verse—was it Lautrec, "I paint with my penis"—we write verse with our ears; so this is important. Forming, animating, quelling his material, that ear is one of the main, weird facts of modern verse. It imposes upon the piteous stuff of the *Pisan Cantos* a "distance" as absolute as upon the dismissal of the epigram just cited. The poet has listened to his life, so to speak, and he tells us that which he hears.

Both the personality-as-subject and the expressive personality are nearly uniform, I think, once they have developed. In Yeats, in Eliot, we attend to re-formations of personality. Not really in Pound; he is unregenerate. "*Toutes mes pièces datent de. quinze ans,*" he quoted once with approval from a friend, and the contrast he draws between the life of the poet as it ought to be (or has been) and as it is, this contrast is perennial. But if this account of the poet's subject is correct, what can have concealed it from most even sympathetic and perceptive critics and readers? With regard to critics, two things, I believe. All the best critics of Pound's work themselves write verse, most of them verse indebted to Pound's, much of it heavily; they have been interested in craft, not personality and subject. Also, they have been blinded, perhaps, by the notion of the "impersonality" of the poet. This perverse and valuable doctrine, associated in our time with Eliot's name, was toyed with by Goethe and gets expression in

Keats's insistence that the poet "has no identity—he is continually in, for, and filling some other body." For poetry of a certain mode (the dramatic), this is a piercing notion; for most other poetry, including Pound's, it is somewhat paradoxical, and may disfigure more than it enlightens. It hides motive, which persists. It fails to enable us to see, for instance, that the dominant source of inspiration in Keats's sonnet on Chapman's Homer is *antagonism*, his contempt for Pope and Pope's Homer. (This view, which I offer with due hesitation, is a development from an industrious and thoughtful biography of the sonnet by a British scholar in *Essays and Studies* for 1931.)

The reader is in one way more nearly right than the majority of critics. He is baffled by a heterogeneity of matter, as to which I shall have more to say in a moment, but he hears a personality in Pound's poetry. In fact, his hostility—we reach it at last—is based upon this. The trouble is that he hears the personality he expected to hear, rather than the one that is essentially there. He hears Pound's well-known prose personality, bellicose, programmatic, positive, and he resents it. Pound is partly responsible. This personality does exist in him, it is what he has lived with, and he can even write poetry with it, as we see in "Sestina: Altaforte" and elsewhere early and late. A follower of Browning, he takes a keenly *active* view of poetry, and has, conceivably, a most imperfect idea both of just what his subject is and of what his expressive personality is like.

This personality is feline, supra-delicate, absorbed. If Browning made the fastest verse in English, Pound makes the slowest, the most discrete and suave. He once said of a story in *Dubliners* that it was something better than a story, it was "a vivid waiting," and the phrase yields much of his own quality. There is restlessness; but the art of the poet places itself, above all, immediately and mysteriously at the service of the passive and elegiac, the nostalgic. The true ascendancy of this personality over the other is suggested by a singular fact: the degree in which the mantic character is absent from his poetry. He looks ahead indeed, looks ahead eagerly, but he does not *feel* ahead; he feels back. (Since writing the sentence, I come on the phrase in Fenollosa, an impressive remark, "The chief work of literary men in dealing with language, and of poets especially, lies in feeling back along the ancient lines of advance.") It is the poetry of a late craftsman; of an expatriate—

> Moaneth alway my mind's lust
> That I fare forth, that I afar hence
> Seek out a foreign fastness.   (*"The Seafarer"*)

Here we are, picking the first fern-shoots
And saying: When shall we get back to our country? . . .

Our sorrow is bitter, but we would not return to our
    country.   (*Cathay*'s first lines)

—of a failing culture. The personality is full already in "The Return" from *Ripostes*—return of the hunters, or literary men, for like others of Pound's poems this is a metaphor: those who in an earlier poem had cried

"Tis the white stag, Fame, we're ahunting,"

now come back illusionless.

The *Cantos* seem to be a metaphor also. This immense poem, as yet untitled and unfinished, is seriously unfinished: two cantos are missing and sixteen are to come, if the poet recovers sufficiently to be able to write verse again. Since Canto LXXIV alone is twenty-five pages long, it is clear that the last sixteen of the hundred may alter radically views we have formed of the work as a whole from the part we know; and we want to avoid the error (if it was one) of Pound when he hazarded in 1933, of the still untitled and unfinished *Finnegans Wake*, "It can hardly be claimed . . . that the main design emerges above the detail." Nevertheless, I must say something of the subject and form of this epic. I believe the critical view is that it is a "rag-bag" of the poet's interests, "a catalogue, his jewels of conversation." It can be read with delight and endless profit thus, if at any rate one understands that it is a work of versification, that is, a poem. The basal rhythm I hear is dactylic, as in the Swinburne and Ouang Chi passages and in the opening line, "And then went down to the ship,"—in this line we see the familiar tendency of English dactyls to resolve themselves into anapests with anacrusis, but the ambiguity seems to me to be progressively avoided as the poem advances. But the rag-bag view depends for support upon lines that Pound cut out of the primitive printed versions of the earliest cantos; the form greatly developed, the form *for the subject*. For a rag-bag, the poem sets out very oddly. I will describe the first three cantos.

    1. The Poet's, the Hero's, physical and mental travel: what can "I" expect? Persona, Odysseus-in-exile; antagonist, Poseidon (the "godly sea"—an ironic pun). Material: escape-from-transformation, sacrifice, descent to Hell, recognition of and obligation to the Dead (parents, masters), prediction of return *alone* over the seas, "Lose all companions." (This is exactly, thirty years later, what happened to the poet.) Form: a depth-introduction, heroic Greek (*Odyssey*, xi)

through Renaissance Latin (Divus) in old-heroic-English style as modified by modern style. So the first canto, about sacrifice to the enemy, acknowledgment of indebtedness, and outset.

2. The orchestra begins, the poet's nineteenth-century English master to Provençal to Chinese to ancient British to modern Spanish (another exile) to ancient Greek, very rapidly; then the Poet's theme and temptation, Beauty, a faithless woman (Helen); then an exquisite, involved color and sense lyric (the first of dozens) in honor of Poseidon's beloved; then the canto proper, about *betrayal*, the metamorphoses into "Sniff and pad-foot of beasts" of all those who do not recognize and wish to *sell* (sell out) the God—Dionysus and Poseidon are linked as having power each over the sea, and those false to them are the "betrayers of language" of Canto XIV, Mr Nixon of *Mauberley*—"I" (Acoethes, the persona) alone have not. Exilic Ovid is the fable's source.

3. Three themes: (1) A stronger sea ceremony than sacrifice, *embracing* of difficulties, the Venetian *"sponzalizio del mar"* ("to wed the sea as a wife," Canto XXVI), *"voce tinnula"* below being Catullus' "with ringing voice" for nuptial songs; (2) enmities and poverty that beset the Poet or Hero (persona, the Cid), *proscription;* (3) artistic mortality, a Mantegna fresco flaking, and just before, an opposite example, Ignez da Castro stabbed by her lover's order (Pedro I of Portugal) in 1355, then avenged by her son, exhumed and *crowned* ("here made to stand")—

> Time is the evil. Evil.
>
>   A day, and a day
> Walked the young Pedro baffled,
>   a day, and a day
> After Ignez was murdered.
> Came the Lords in Lisboa
>   a day, and a day
> In homage. Seated there
>   dead eyes,
> Dead hair under the crown,
> The King still young there beside her.   (Canto XXX)

This kind of interpenetration of life and art, in metaphor, is one of the poem's triumphs, a Coleridgean "fusing."

Such, according to the notes I once made in my margin, is the beginning of this famous "formless" work, which is, according to one critic of distinction, "not about anything." Reviewers of the *Pisan Cantos* have showed surprise that they were so "personal," and yet very fine,—it is the most brilliant sequence indeed since the original thirty. The *Cantos* have always been personal; only the persona increasingly adopted, as the Poet's fate clarifies, is Pound himself. The heterogeneity of material, every reader remarks, seems to have three causes. The illusion of Pound's romanticism ("—if romanticism indeed be an illusion!" he exclaims in *Indiscretions*) has given him an inordinate passion for ages and places where the Poet's situation appears attractive, as in the Malatesta cantos, where Sigismondo is patron as much as ruler and lover (VIII–XI), and the Chinese cantos (XIII, XLIX, LII–LXI); here he is sometimes wonderful but sometimes ungovernable. Then he is anxious to find out *what has gone wrong*, with money and government, that has produced our situation for the Poet; several of the money cantos, XLV and LI, are brilliant, but most of the American historical cantos (XXXI–IV, XXXVII–VIII, LXII–LXXI) are willed, numb, angry—the personae Jefferson and John Adams are not felt and so the material is uncontrolled. The rest of his heterogeneity is due to an immoderate desire, strong in some other modern artists also, for mere conservation—

> And lest it pass with the day's news
> Thrown out with the daily paper.   (Canto XXVIII)

Once the form, and these qualifications, are understood, Pound's work presents less difficulty than we are used to in ambitious modern poetry. Pieces like "A Song for the Degrees" (an anti-Psalm) and "Papyrus" (a joke, for that matter, a clear and good one) are rare. Occasionally you have to look things up if you don't wish to be puzzled; and it does no harm to use the index volume of Britannica 11th, and various dictionaries, and to be familiar with Pound's prose, when you read the *Cantos;* the labour is similar to that necessary for a serious understanding of *Ulysses,* and meditation is the core of it. To find out what a modern poet has done, we have often to ask *why* he did it.

The poet's own statements must be accepted with a certain reserve, which neither his admirers nor his detractors have always exercised. Thus the *Cantos* are said to be written in an equivalent for ideogram. We have recognized their relation to parts of Fenollosa. But Fenollosa's technical center is an attack on the copula; I observe that four of the lines about Ouang Chi successively employ the copula without loss to characteristic beauty, and I reason that we must inquire into these things for ourselves. More interesting, far, are the equivalents for musical form, and the versification. So with Pound's remark that the *Cantos* are "the tale of the tribe"; they seem to be only apparently a historical or philosophical epic, actually a personal epic—as he seems to understand himself elsewhere in *Culture* when he suggests that the work may show, like Beethoven's music, the "defects inherent in a record of struggle." Pound, too, may really, like his critics, regard the work as nearly plotless and heroless. Writing of Dr Williams, he says, "I would almost move . . . to the generalization that plot, major form, or outline should be left to authors who feel some inner need for the same; even let us say a very strong, unusual, unescapable need for these things; and to books where the said form, plot, etc., springs naturally from the matter treated." "Almost," and he is not speaking of the *Cantos* directly, but the passage is a very striking and heretical one. I put in evidence against it his long labours on the opening cantos, and the cantos themselves in my simple analysis, where the arraying of themes is quite different from casualty. The Hell allusions in the first half of the work, with the allusions to Heaven in recent cantos, also strongly imply a major form. But all present discussion must be tentative. I have the impression that Pound allowed, in whatever his plan exactly is (if it exactly is, and if it is one plan), for the drift-of-life, the interference of fate, inevitable in a period of violent change; that this may give us something wholly unpredictable in the cantos to come, as it has given us already the marvellous pages of the *Pisan Cantos*. Here we feel the poet as he felt D'Annunzio in 1922: D'Annunzio, he wrote from Paris to *The Dial*, "lies with a bandaged eye in a bombarded Venice, foaming with his own sensations, memories, speculations as to what Dante might or might not have done had he been acquainted with Aeschylus." Foaming, yet always with the limpidity, *clarté*, the love against rhetoric, for which his poetry is our model in this century. It would be interesting, if the *Cantos* were complete, to compare the work with another poem, not more original in conception, exhibiting, if a smaller range of material and technical variety, greater steadiness, a similar substance, and a similar comprehensive mastery of expression, *The Prelude;* but the argument of my very limited essay is ended. Let us listen to this music.

1949

Prufrock's Dilemma

To BEGIN WITH ELIOT'S TITLE, "THE LOVE SONG OF J. Alfred Prufrock," is the second half quite what the first led us to expect? A man named J. Alfred Prufrock could hardly be expected to sing a love song; he sounds too well dressed. His name takes something away from the notion of a love song; the form of the title, that is to say, is reductive. How does he begin singing?

> Let us go then, you and I,
> When the evening is spread out against the sky . . .

That sounds very pretty—lyrical—he does seem, after all, in spite of his name, to be inviting her for an evening; there is a nice rhyme—it sounds like other dim romantic verse. Then comes the third line:

> Like a patient etherised upon a table . . .

With this line, modern poetry begins.

In the first place, the third line proves that the author of the first two lines did not mean them. They were a come-on, designed merely to get the reader off guard, so that he could be knocked down. The form, again, is reductive; an expectation has been created only to be diminished or destroyed. (Presently it will prove that "you" is not the woman at all, since "you" is invited to make a visit with "I" *to* her; we can hardly say yet who "you" is; an assumption has been destroyed.) And the word "then"—"Let us go *then*"—is really very unpromising; if he had only said, "Let us go," it would have sounded much more as if they were going to go; "Let us go then" sounds as if he had been giving it thought, and thought suggests hesitation. Of course he never goes at all: *the* visit, involving the "overwhelming question," the proposal of marriage, is never made. Here again we come on a reduction.

Also, the simile is not visual: it only pretends to be. No reader could possibly be assisted in seeing the evening spread out against the sky by having his attention suddenly and violently called to a patient laid out on an operating table. The device of simile is being put to a novel use, violating the ordinary logic of verse, just as the abrupt vision of a hospital violates the lyrical notion of an evening stroll.

What does the line mean? We are obliged to resort to suggestion, not to logic. The situation of a patient under ether is unenviable, risky: he is about to be cut into, soon he may be dead. This fear is basic to the poem: Prufrock finally says, in fact, "I was afraid." On the other hand, the situation of the patient can be regarded as desirable in that he *has* made a decision and now the result is out of his hands, he has no further responsibility, it is up to the surgeon to save him or not. This desire—to *have made* the proposal, and to have his fate left up to the woman—is also basic to the poem. We may think of that as quite a lot of work to get done in one line. Of course, the suggestion that Prufrock sees himself as *ill* is important also, and we will return to this.

Between the title, with its slight effect of double-take, and these opening lines, with their full effect of double-take, the poet has inserted an epigraph in Italian, six lines of it. A knowledge of Italian is of very little help. All the lines say is, "If I thought what I am going to tell you would ever get back to the world, you would hear nothing from me. But as it is," and so on. One has to know *who* is speaking in Dante's *Divine Comedy*. This is a lost soul, in Hell, damned in particular because he tried to purchase absolution *before* committing a crime. We are obliged to consider, that is, as of Prufrock with his dilemma of whether or not to propose marriage, whether the fundamental reason he does not do so—his sin—is his refusal to take the ordinary, inevitable human risks: he wants to know beforehand whether he will be accepted or not—in fact, he does *think* he knows already what will happen—but this belongs later for us.

Everything we have been saying paints a picture as different as possible from that of a writer sitting down to entertain, beguile, charm, and lull a reader or readers. Obstacles and surprise, of no pleasant kind, are this poet's stock-in-trade. The reader's expectation that *one* thing will happen is the first to be attacked. Several things are going to be happening simultaneously. One feels, even, a certain hostility on the part of the poet. The modern poet, characteristically, has *lost confidence* in his readers (this is not altogether surprising, considering the quality of most contemporary education); but so far from causing him to reduce his demands therefore, this loss of confidence has led to an *increase* in his demands. Good poetry has never been easy to read with any advanced understanding, but it has seldom been made so deliberately difficult.

Shall we connect this deliberate difficulty with the reductive devices studied earlier and suggest that the poet's impatience is based on the fact that the reader's mind is full of vague and grandiose assumptions which seem to the poet contemptible? The poet sees himself as a warning voice, like a Hebrew prophet calling on the people to repent, to understand better themselves and the world. Of course, this *is* a reduced world. In one celebrated view, we have undergone three crucial scientific revolutions. The first was the astronomical, in the sixteenth century, which taught man that so far from occupying a splendid position at the heart of the universe, he lived in a suburb, and one of no importance. He digested this unwelcome information very slowly. Then he was informed, by Darwin and others, a hundred years ago, that he was not unique but continuous with the animals whom he had always patronized. Our periods of time are getting much shorter. He had barely fifty years in which to learn to accept this biological insult, when the psychological revolution associated with the name of Freud informed man that he was not even king inside but stood at the mercy of gigantic unconscious forces within himself. All this ought to have rendered him distinctly uneasy, let us say, and has done so, depending on his degree of self-awareness; but hardly to a degree acceptable to the exceptional self-awareness of the poet. Eliot had pretty certainly not read Freud when he wrote this poem. In some ways, however, their thought is parallel, for the "you" whom Prufrock invites to go with him for the visit must be another part of his own personality, whom he vainly invites to join him in the great task before them—the instinctual part of man (as against the façade that knows itself, the I, the ego), for which Freud was to borrow the word "id" from Groddeck.

But the "you" is perhaps also the reader, addressed thus surprisingly in this dramatic monologue; and this device is French, part of the general air of elaborate sophistication adopted by Eliot in this poem. This tone is not original; it is borrowed from the French symbolist poet Jules Laforgue (1860–87), under whose influence Eliot first found his own voice. Some of the characteristic properties in "Prufrock" are Laforgue's, allusions to Hamlet and the sirens. But there is influence also from Elizabethan drama, in the speech rhythms (the poem is written in what is called "free verse," which only means that the laws it obeys are different from those of traditional stanza or blank verse); and there is influence from prose works, especially the expatriate American novelist Henry James's. In any event, Laforgue could never have conceived or written the poem. He only supplied the *manner*, and anyway his music—very beautiful sometimes—is hardly Eliot's.

Eliot's manner is highly sophisticated, but perhaps we ought not to call the poem sophisticated. Let us call it primitive. The poem pretends to be a love song. It is something much more practical. It is a study—a debate by Prufrock with himself—over the *business* of proposing marriage, agreeing to lay your fate in someone else's hands, undertaking to spend your life with her, to beget and rear children, and so on. He never makes it. The first half of the poem looks forward to the proposal, the second half looks back on how it *would* have gone if it had gone at all. The poem is intensely anti-romantic, and its extremely serious subject, in a so-called Love Song, is another rebuke to the (probably romantic) reader. Primitive societies take a dim view of not marrying. Hawaiian mythology, for instance, describes a god called Nanggananaag, whose job it is to stand with an immense club on the Road to Paradise and smash off it, into nothingness, any unmarried male who, having died, tries to get by. This way of thinking is precisely Eliot's. Late in the poem Prufrock looks forward with dismay (and a certain jaunty pathos) to his endless bachelorhood—the sameness and triviality that are the lot of one who never succeeded in adopting his human responsibilities at all. It is clear that the poet sympathizes with Prufrock. It is also clear that the poet damns Prufrock. Some of the basic emotions of the poem are primitive also—fear, malice—but lust is absent, and the prevailing surface tone is one of civilized, overcivilized anxiety. Prufrock's feelings are rather abstract; he never makes the woman real at all, except in one terrible respect, which let us reserve a little. He is concerned with himself. He is mentally ill, neurotic, incapable of love. But the problem that he faces is a primitive problem.

Eliot brings to bear on Prufrock's dilemma four figures out of the spiritual history of man: Michelangelo, John the Baptist, Lazarus, and Hamlet. Prufrock identifies himself, in his imagination, with Lazarus; he says that he is *not* the Baptist or Hamlet. About the first all he says is:

> In the room the women come and go
> Talking of Michelangelo.

What are we to make of this? There is a twittering of women's voices. Their subject? A type of volcanic masculine energy—sculptor, architect, as well as painter—at the height of one of the supreme periods of human energy, the Italian Renaissance. Chit-chat. *Reduc-*

tion, we may say. Michelangelo, everything that mattered about him forgotten or not understood, has become a topic for women's voices —destructive, without even realizing it. Then Prufrock says,

> Though I have seen my head (grown slightly bald)
>> brought in upon a platter,
> I am no prophet—

The situation is a visit, or the imagination of a visit, to the woman; it was *women* who got the Baptist beheaded. We might phrase the meaning as: I announce no significant time to come, I am the fore-runner of (not children, not a Saviour) nothing. Then Prufrock is speculating about how it *would* have been, IF he had

>> squeezed the universe into a ball
> To roll it toward some overwhelming question,
> To say: "I am Lazarus, come from the dead,
> Come back to tell you all, I shall tell you all"—

We have seen Prufrock already imagined as dead, the suggestion of the epigraph, and at the end of the poem he drowns. Here he thinks of himself as *come back*. Lazarus, perhaps, is the person whom one would most like to interview—another character from sacred history, not Christ's forerunner but the subject of the supreme miracles (re-ported, unfortunately, only in the Fourth Gospel)—the one man who would tell us . . . what it is like. Prufrock has a message for the woman that is or ought to be of similar importance: here I am, out of my loneliness, at your feet; I am this man full of love, trust, hope; decide my fate.

Now—postponing Hamlet for a second—what Prufrock imag-ines the woman as saying in return for his Lazarus-communication explains his despair:

> If one, settling a pillow by her head,
>> Should say: "That is not what I meant at all.
> That is not it, at all."

Here the reason for his inability to propose becomes clear. He is convinced that she will (or would) respond with the most insulting and unmanning of all attitudes: Let's be *friends;* I never thought of you as a lover or husband, only a friend. What the women's voices did to Michelangelo, her voice is here imagined as doing to him, unmanning him; the sirens' voices at the end of the poem are yet to come. This is the central image of Prufrock's fear: what he cannot face. We see better now why the image of an *operation* turned up so early in the poem, and the paranoid passages swing into focus:

> when I am formulated, sprawling on a pin,
> When I am pinned and wriggling on the wall . . .

and:

> But as if a magic lantern threw the nerves in patterns
> on a screen . . .

A reasonable study of these fears of exposure would take us not only into our well-known Anglo-Saxon fear of ridicule but into folklore and psychoanalysis.

As for Hamlet, Prufrock says he is "not Prince Hamlet." He is not even the hero, that is to say, of his own tragedy; let us have in mind again the scientific revolutions and also the hero of one of Franz Kafka's novels, *The Trial*, who suddenly says, when recounting his arrest afterward, "Oh, I've forgotten the most important person of all, myself." Prufrock is merely, he says, an extra courtier, an adviser (to himself a very bad adviser—the name "Alfred" means, ironically, good counselor, and the character in Dante who supplies the epigraph was an evil counselor). But of course he *is* Hamlet—in one view of Shakespeare's character: a man rather of reflection than of action, on whom has been laid an intolerable burden (of revenge, by the way), and who suffers from sexual nausea (owing to his mother's incest) and deserts the woman he loves.

The resort to these four analogues from artistic and sacred history suggests a man—desperate, in his ordeal—ransacking the past for help in the present, and *not finding it*—finding only ironic parallels, or real examples, of his predicament. The available tradition, the poet seems to be saying, is of no use to us. It supplies only analogies and metaphors for our pain. Needless to say, the author of this poem was not a Christian; he became one years later.

Prufrock cannot act. He can, however, reflect and feel and imagine. Here we might think of W. B. Yeats's lines in a celebrated poem called "The Second Coming":

> The best lack all conviction, while the worst
> Are full of passionate intensity.

Prufrock would be among Yeats's "best" only for sensitivity and intelligence, it is true, his human failure being otherwise complete. Let us explore a little, however, his *positive* courses of imagination;

and Hamlet's desertion of Ophelia, and his "intolerable burden," as we called it, point our way.

Prufrock's not proposing to the lady (there is no suggestion that anyone else will) might be thought of as aggressive: at whatever cost to himself, he deprives her of a mate, a normal married life. For such fear and humiliation as he suffers, we should expect some sort of revenge taken. But Prufrock suffers from the inhibitions that we might imagine as accompanying a man of such crucial indecision. He has difficulty in expressing himself, for instance, and this difficulty is brought prominently into the poem. Notice particularly the lines

> And how should I begin?
> It is impossible to say just what I mean!

His incoherence is a token of his struggle, and it is hardly surprising that his resentment against the woman in the poem emerges only in malicious detail ("catty" we would call this) as—of her arms—

> in the lamplight, downed with light brown hair!

What does come forward openly is his imagination of escape from the dilemma altogether.

Prufrock's burden is that of proposing marriage when he does not know whether or not he may be ridiculed. His desire, from the outset, to have the whole thing over with, no matter how, we have seen already in the line about the "patient etherised upon a table." At the very end of the poem, in an excited and brilliant passage which might be characterized as one of negative exaltation, he imagines—like Hamlet—his death, as an escape at any rate from the dread anxiety of his ordeal. These are mermaids, sirens, the women of the poem come into the open as killers:

> I have seen them riding seaward on the waves
> Combing the white hair of the waves blown back
> When the wind blows the water white and black.
>
> We have lingered in the chambers of the sea
> By sea-girls wreathed with seaweed red and brown
> Till human voices wake us, and we drown.

This death is *desired*—like the hospital situation—as well as feared. But the basic image of escape occurs in the dead center of the poem, in a couplet, without much relation to anything apparently, *lacking* which this would be a much less impressive poem than it is. These are the lines:

> I should have been a pair of ragged claws
> Scuttling across the floors of silent seas.

You notice, first, that this is not much of a couplet, though it *is* a heroic couplet; the off-rhyme speaks of incongruity. As abruptly, second, as we were transferred from the prospect of a romantic evening to a hospital, are we here plunged, away from modern social life ("I have measured out my life with coffee spoons") into—into what? Man's biological past, continuous with him, but unimaginably remote, long before he emerged into the tidal areas: Prufrock sees himself, in his desire, as his own ancestor, *before this ordeal came up*, when he was sufficient unto himself, a "pair," not needing a mate. Now the whole crustacean is not imagined—only the fighting part, which is taken for the whole—the claws. But these do not seem to be in very good condition ("ragged"), and unquestionably we must take them also to be full of fear ("scuttling"), like Prufrock now. But the seas are *silent:* no woman speaks. Therefore, the situation is desirable, protected. We really need to resort to the later formulations of Freud to understand this. When a human being encounters a problem beyond his capacity to meet, Freud thought, *regression* occurs: the whole organization of the emotional and instinctual person escapes from the intolerable reality by reverting to an earlier, or ancient, stage of his individual development—paying the price of symptoms but securing partial oblivion. The antagonism toward civilization in Eliot's couplet is unmistakable. It contains, indeed, a sort of list of the penalties that civilization has exacted from man's instinctual life—having cost him: open expression of hatred, fear, remorse, intolerable responsibilities.

"I am no prophet," Prufrock says. It must be obvious, however, that this extraordinarily ambitious poem, including as it does acrid sketches not only of man's spiritual but of his biological history, is not designed as entertainment, whatever the author may say to us (Eliot has defined poetry as "a superior amusement"), and whatever his mask *inside* the poem: the sophisticate, the disillusioned, the dandy with his particular social problem in Boston, as Baudelaire had had his in Paris and Belgium and Laforgue his in Berlin. The poet has adopted the guise of light verse, but he writes as a prophet, without any trace of conciliation toward any possible audience. He does not write *directly*. He uses the mask of Prufrock—whose fate is like that of what are called the Vigliacchi in Dante. These sinners did neither good nor evil, and so they cannot be admitted even to Hell, lest the damned feel a certain superiority to them; they suffer eternally in what is called the vestibule of Hell. It is better, as Eliot says in one of his critical essays, to do evil than to do nothing. At least one exists in a relation to the moral world. Under this mask he sets up a ruinous antithesis to Victorian hope—in particular, to what must have seemed to him the vacuous optimism of the most recent master of dramatic monologue in English before him, Browning. Civilization is not condemned. The *results* of civilization are dramatized, that is all; above all, the destruction of the ability to love, and—in the well-meaning man—to be decisive. The poet speaks, in this poem, of a society sterile and suicidal.

1960

The Sorrows of Captain Carpenter

"CAPTAIN CARPENTER" IS A HIGH-SPIRITED DESOLATE BAL-
lad about a reformer, a redresser of wrongs, primitive in its physical
arrangements but so cunning in its moral and symbolic arrangements
that what one says when talking about one aspect of John Crowe Ransom's poem one is tempted to contradict when talking about another.
Maybe that's not a mistake. I have been told that Ransom frowns on,
or at least is inclined to look askance at, a view which would see the
captain as a Christ-figure. I can't care much about this, even if the
rumour is true; I used to take more seriously than I do now the denials
and asseverations, including my own, of poets about their work. For
one thing, one honestly forgets, when considering poems written long
before; for a second, a certain sly desire to baffle the onrushing critic
is nearly standard in poetic temperament; finally, one gets bored with
one's own old work—a condition that extends to the reading of it.
More than twenty years ago I heard Ransom read "Captain Carpenter"
at Harvard in a way that proved he couldn't have written it—insensitive
and perfunctory; whereas there is at the Library of Congress a reading
by him of another early poem, "Philomela," as airy and fresh as if he
were making it up as he went along. Maybe not a Christ-figure, then,
but maybe something of one, given Christ's traditional occupation, his
pity, his desire to change the world, his leadership (though the captain seems to have no followers—a matter we'll come back to), and his
failure. None of these items, taken singly, is impressive, but together
they are.

More impressive: a figure of chivalry, extremely active, extremely ineffective, a comic and suffering man of war, given to lust
(as the Don is in Chapter 16), continually defeated both in detail and
in the end: in short, Don Quixote.

Don Quixote, though, of course, transposed. The Don was old-
fashioned, out of date (his creator was *not:* Cervantes, particularly in
Part II, was as avant-garde as his only living peer writing in Eng-

land), driven mad by romances, but the novelist's attitude toward both him and his ideals is ambivalent, a complex of scorn, nostalgia, and love. In a moment I wish to suggest that precisely this ambivalence characterizes Ransom's feelings for his captain. But first it must be emphasized that this supreme masterpiece of the Counter Reformation was a product of a Spain in full, rapid, and final decline. Cervantes's loyalty and faith were complete, but so was his vision clear and agonized. Long associated with Spanish imperial military power, he composed Part I of *Don Quixote* (published 1605) in the wake of the destruction of the Armada.

Now it would be uncivil, or grotesque, to attempt to compare with the greatest novel ever written Ransom's vivid little poem, but we are not doing that: we are investigating correspondences in genesis, ambience, intention. Whatever else Christ may have been, he was not a picaresque figure, a man of adventures as the Don and the captain are. The adventures are almost regularly hopeless, and show forth indeed traditions hopelessly defeated. Ransom is the most intransigently Southern of our authors except Faulkner, and neither the slightness of his mode (he has never attempted a long poem and, instead of developing after his early work, fell silent) nor the elegance of his irony ought to conceal from us this basic fact. The Civil War may seem a long way back from the 1920's—when Ransom's important work was done—except to a Southerner; and, as the reader will no doubt know, Ransom was a leading figure in the literary-agrarian movement now called the Fugitives, whose chief social manifesto was *I Take My Stand* (1931). The antebellum air of the properties in "Captain Carpenter" gives this purely modern poem a second dimension, and I cannot but remark here that Ransom came slowly (largely under the influence, I believe, of his junior Allen Tate) to what used to be called "modernism": he hated, in print, *The Waste Land* when it appeared. As in *Don Quixote*, then, we attend with the Captain to ambiguous attitudes, failed and even ridiculous ideals, an irretrievable grandeur of senseless aspiration, the persistence into modern life (1605, 1930) of the discredited. Stylistically this double feeling comes clear in the wry, affectionate use of the old-fashioned "well-nigh" and "rout" (Old South for a party, a ball) in a poem from which he deleted the punctuation. It is from one great mansion of the past to another that the spry, twentieth-century Captain (not a Colonel—that would have been one inch too far) wanders on his doomed quest.

One further analogy, which I will advance as decisive for the view I am here adopting, and we are done with Cervantes, or almost done.

Casual rememberers, I think, among the very few non-Spaniards who have troubled to read *Don Quixote* to the end, feel that the Don has died. But this is not quite so: he has both died and not died; one is shaken with an ambiguity only less mysterious than the corresponding event in *Oedipus at Colonus*. Hesitant in allusion to these unsurpassable works, I suggest all the same that casual rememberers of "Captain Carpenter" see him as totally dismembered. But that is not so, and the meaning of the fact that that is not so will emerge only from some rehearsal of the events of the poem.

Do they need rehearsing? He appears to lose *everything*. Only no: in the brilliant peroration is stealthily concealed the fact that along with his heart is *not* taken his tongue, so presumably he (the tradition, both of chivalry and Art) talks on, like Faulkner's Man in the Nobel Prize address.

Two points: there may be some anti-Romanism, as in "Lycidas." There may be, in the final line, some assimilation of the feminine-betrayal motif in "The Twa Corbies." As to the "rogue in scarlet and grey," I confess my imbecility; teasing colours, almost those of my prep school.

The poem is a fantasia on bruised Southern gentility and the prototype of bruised Christian chivalry, Don Quixote. Just who the female enemy is is not clear. Suggestions might be in order. Not wanting to bother Ransom, I once put the matter to our old, close, and intelligent friend Allen Tate, who said offhand: "Perhaps it's the *World*." I can't do better than that.

1966

Dylan Thomas:

The Loud Hill of Wales

THE UNMISTAKABLE SIGNATURE OF DYLAN THOMAS'S poetry, so far as we have it in his three English volumes or in the forty poems here* selected from them, is certainly its diction. Here are some of the key words: blood, sea, dry, ghost, grave, straw, worm, double, crooked, salt, cancer, tower, shape, fork, marrow; and the more usual death, light, time, sun, night, wind, love, grief. Each of these appears many times and has regularly one or several symbolic values. The verse abounds in unusual epithets (the grave, for example, is called, at various points in seven poems, moon-drawn, stallion, corkscrew, running, savage, outspoken, country-handed, climbing, gallow), compounds (firewind, marrowroot, fly-lord, manstring, manseed, man-iron, man-shape, manwax), old, new, obsolete, coined, and colloquial words (scut, fibs, hank, boxy, morsing, brawned, cockshut, mitching, no-wheres, pickthank, macadam, scrams, etna, rooking, hyleg, arc-lamped, contages, natron, herods, two-gunned, pickbrain). Colours are frequent, especially green, which occurs twenty-eight times and connotes origin, innocence (green Adam, green genesis, green of beginning); red is for experience, violence. The notions of halving, doubling, quartering, dichotomy, multiplicity of function, appear often, affecting the precise look of the diction; the concept of number and division organizes several poems. Some of the language is Biblical. But the principal sources of imagery are the sea and sex. In ten poems the dominant imagery is marine, and marine imagery occurs incidentally in twenty-four others. A host of terms show the sexual emphasis, sucking, kiss, loin, naked, rub, tickle, unsex, nippled, virgin, thigh, cuddled, sea-hymen; metaphors extend the reach and importance of this area. All these words, and stranger others, meet violently to form a texture impressive and exciting. One has the sense of words set at an angle, language seen freshly, a new language.

The themes upon which this wealth of diction is employed are

* *The World I Breathe*, 1940.

simple, but not, I think, so unimportant as Julian Symons calls them in a very bad article once published in *The Kenyon Review*. I have not time to notice any considerable part of Symons's nonsense; one quotation must serve. "What is said in Mr. Thomas's poems is that the seasons change; that we decrease in vigour as we grow older; that life has no obvious meaning; that love dies. His poems mean no more than that. They mean too little." Evidently it is necessary to point out to Symons what is elementary, that a poem means more than the abstract, banal statement of its theme: it means its imagery, the disparate parts and relations of it, its ambiguities, by extension the techniques which produced it and the emotions it legitimately produces. A poem is an accretion of knowledge, of which only the flimsiest portion can be translated into bromide. A poem that works well demonstrates an insight, and the insight may consist, not in the theme, but in the image relations or the structure relations; this is a value and a meaning which cannot appear in Symons's catalogue. Even the single lines mean more than their prose doubles:

> The fruit of man unwrinkles in the stars.

> Glory cracked like a flea.

> Sigh long, clay cold, lie shorn.

> The terrible world my brother bares his skin.

Each of these presents a perception and an attitude, even a process of sensibility. I do not find them in Symons's catalogue. Here is the short final poem:

> Twenty-four years remind the tears of my eyes.
> (Bury the dead for fear that they walk to the grave in labour.)
> In the groin of the natural doorway I crouched like a tailor
> Sewing a shroud for a journey
> By the light of the meat-eating sun.
> Dressed to die, the sensual strut begun,
> With my red veins full of money,
> In the final direction of the elementary town
> I advance for as long as forever is.

The figures and their interaction cannot be expressed as "life has no obvious meaning": where is the body seen as a shroud worn on the way to the *elementary* town? where is the hovering "dressed to kill"? What Symons misses is the value of presentation, the dramatic truth of metaphor. A good poem is not, as he says, restatement but statement. His catalogue, moreover, on a simpler level is seriously incomplete. Several of the poems are religious in substance and address; two poems deal mainly, and others deal in part, with the poet's gift of speech; other examples of exceptions could be adduced. It is worth emphasizing, however, that few poems describe what may be called a human situation, a recognizable particular scene. There is a subject matter, but it is general, as indeed the diction would lead one to expect. The treatment is concrete, in the language, but the conception is abstract.

Much of Thomas's inventive energy, then, goes into technique; he faces in a lesser degree than most poets the problems of a given subject. Alliteration, internal rhyme, refrain and repetition, puns, continuous and complicated tropes, are some of the devices. He works usually in rigid stanzas, six-line in the earlier poems, the lines of equal length; recently he has used very elaborate stanzas and varied the line lengths. The metrical development is from iambics to manipulation, spondees, anapests; in the short-line poems especially, the movement is expert. Certain technical derivations there are, despite one's impression of originality: from Blake (the *Songs of Experience* and *Thel*), Hopkins, Yeats (the middle and later poetry), Auden (the 1930 *Poems*); I think it likely also that he and Auden learned, independently, something in tone, consonance, extra syllables, and feminine rhymes, from Ransom. Possibly the verse has roots in Welsh poetry, folk or professional, with which I am not familiar. Hart Crane offers a parallel development, in part similar but not influential. This brings us to the question of obscurity.

That a good many of these poems are difficult cannot be denied. The difficulty has various causes, some of them being distortion or inadequacy of syntax (sometimes the pointing is responsible), compounding of negatives, mixing of figures, the occasionally continuous novelty of expression and relation, employment of a high-pitched rhetoric as in poem 29, and the use as subjects of nightmare, fantasy, as in poem 2. Personification is so frequent and is accomplished with so little ceremony that the reference of personal pronouns is now and then erratic; in general, the practice with pronouns and antecedents is careless. In many passages, insufficient control is exerted by the context on a given verbal ambiguity; the ambiguity, indeed, may be made the basis for a further, and absolutely puzzling, extension of metaphor. Development in the poem, when it exists, may be sidewise, will probably be interrupted, may be abandoned; in the difficult poems it is never straightforward. All this is unfortunate when it interferes with communication, and the trouble is found not only in the weakest poems (21, 29) but also in some of the best (11, 28, 38). But the whole matter can be, and by most of Thomas's critics has been, exaggerated. At least fifteen poems, more than one third of those in the book, present no substantial difficulty to a conscientious reader; some present no difficulty at all. Of the rest, perhaps eight are largely insoluble or only provisionally soluble. This is not a large number, and it is simply the price one pays for what is valuable and cannot be got elsewhere. One would have more reason to complain, were not much of the finest twentieth-century work difficult; Yeats, Lorca, Eliot, Stevens are sufficient reminder. Thomas's obscurity is not greater than Crane's, and their values are comparable.

This verse cannot be called "promising," however, in the ordinary way, although its author is a young man. Poets progress usually by moving to a new substance or by extending their technique to handle a new part of an old substance. But Thomas's work is so special, and his substance so restricted, that neither of these paths, if I am correct, is really open to him. This is not to say that no development can be seen in the poems. They are arranged in order roughly chronological, and the latest poems are harsher, more closely worked; some technical changes have been noted; the subjects are more often violent. The diction has partly altered; for instance, blood or a derivative occurs twenty-four times in the first twenty poems, only nine times in the second twenty, and where the concept remains, it may be transformed: "my red veins full of money." But Thomas's verse does not show the major signs, such as a powerful dramatic sense, wide interests, a flexible and appropriate diction, skill over a broad range of subjects, that are clear in the work of his American contemporary Delmore Schwartz, and point confidently to the future. Any large development is probably not to be expected. This circumstance, of course, cannot affect the present achievement, which is formidable. All the poems should be read with attention by anyone who is interested in poetry. In a dozen of these pieces, some of them imperfect, all brilliant—"A saint about to fall," "Especially when the October wind," "Then was my neophyte," and "Light breaks where no sun shines" may be mentioned in their four kinds— Thomas has extended the language and to a lesser degree the methods of lyric poetry.

1940

Robert Lowell and Others

IN SOME VERY SERIOUS SENSE THERE IS NO COMPETITION either on Parnassus or on the hard way up there. Darley, that is, with *Nepenthe* and a lyric or so, is as good as Keats. Ransom was probably wrong both in theory and practice when he concluded an unfriendly study of *The Waste Land*, many years ago, with the remark that there was not room in the pantheon for both Wordsworth and Eliot, and he thought the prior occupant of the seat would dispute it stoutly; a position, no doubt abandoned since, which I recall to illustrate what can never receive illustration enough, namely, the difficulty and uncertainty of contemporary judgment. But there is another sense in which it is sometimes worth saying that work like Keats's demonstrates that work like Darley's doesn't even exist. You can find in Keats everything you can find in Darley, and you find it with transfigured power, and you find many other things as well. Whatever the devotion of a lesser poet, it may be put as the difference between the *occasional* and the *thematic*, between the making of a few fine poems and the conversion of a whole body of material. If the first is impressive, the second is oppressive as well, troubling, overwhelming. Now Robert Lowell seems to me not only the most powerful poet who has appeared* in England or America for some years, master of a freedom in the Catholic subject without peer since Hopkins, but also, in the terms of this distinction, a thematic poet. His work displays, in high degrees, passion, vista, burden. He looks

> Beyond Charles River to the Acheron
> Where the wide waters and their voyager are one

and when he addresses his Maker there is no device, the verse wheels and enlarges, the man really sounds like a prophet,

* *Lord Weary's Castle*, 1947.

Lord, from the lust and dust thy will destroys
Raise an unblemished Adam, who will see
The limbs of the tormented chestnut tree
Tingle, and hear the March-winds lift and cry:
"The Lord of Hosts will overshadow us."

Without first-rate qualities, ambition is nothing, a personal disease; but given these qualities, the difference is partly one of ambition. Hardy, for instance, had little and notwithstanding a long and reverent love for Hardy, I think Eliot was right when he observed on the occasion of Yeats's seventieth birthday that Hardy now appeared, what he always was, a minor poet. There is much human development over the sixty years between "Hap" and "He Resolves to Say No More," but little poetic development, nothing comparable to what Lowell has achieved in the two years between his first book and *Lord Weary's Castle*. I should say from the poems that this author's ambition is limitless. Whether he has yet written poems as good as Hardy's best this is no moment for judging, though I think the question will one day come up. What is clear just now is that we have before us a genuine, formidable, various, and active poet; as to which character I put in evidence "The Drunken Fisherman," "The Quaker Graveyard in Nantucket," "The Exile's Return," "At the Indian Killer's Grave," "After the Surprising Conversions," and parts of a dozen other poems.

Readers of the new book will find it very different from *Land of Unlikeness*, though it brings over ten poems from that book, heavily rewritten as a rule. The earlier poems writhed crunched spat against Satan, war, modern Boston, the Redcoats, Babel, Leviathan, Babylon, Sodom. The style was bold, coarse, surexcited, so close in some respects to its models—the Jacobean lyrists, early Milton (as Jarrell pointed out in a perceptive review), Allen Tate as a Roman and polemic writer, Yeats as a dynastic—that it was surprising that one had nevertheless a stormed impression of originality. Lowell avoided by instinct the chief religious influences that might have crushed him, Hopkins, and Eliot, as well as the influence (Auden) that has straitjacketed much talent among men just older than himself; but he began like Eliot and Auden with satire—as most ambitious writers in a society like ours apparently must do. Despite some continuing violence of style, however, and the persistence of sardonic detail, the general effect of *Lord Weary's Castle* is not satirical. It is dramatic, moral, elegiac; and the escape from satire represents a triumph for a talent not essentially satirical. Not only is there nothing here like the tosspot "Christ for Sale," but the whole uncontrolled ferocity of poems like it has disappeared. The best new poems, insofar as they reflect the same interests, develop less from that tone than from the trumpet and the sigh simultaneous in the extraordinary distich quoted in *Partisan Review* by Jarrell:

> When the ruined farmer knocked out Abel's brains,
> Our Father laid great cities on his soul . . .

I give the lines again because, though the poem they began has been discerningly scrapped, they announce a major theme. Such a writer's symbols are worth examination. I propose that we take seriously both the title and the illustration on the title page, of Cain's second crime (the murder and flight), and see what they come to. The precise cause of Cain's ruin has been lost, but the cause of Lord Weary's—the title comes from the ballad of *Lamkin*—is known: when his castle was finished he refused payment to his mason Lamkin and sailed away, whereupon Lamkin, helped by the false nurse, broke into the castle and destroyed his wife and babe. Lord Weary's castle is a house of ingratitude, failure of obligation, crime and punishment. Possibly Cain did not bring *enough* of his first fruits, or brought them grudgingly: "I canna pay you, Lamkin, / Unless I sell my land," which he will not do. Later, as the stabbed babe cries in death, Lamkin calls up to its mother, "He winna still, lady, / For a' his father's land"; and the wandering blood of Cain cannot repent. Besides frequent references to Cain, the stories may be deliberately juxtaposed in a sonnet based on Rilke's *Letzter Abend* ("Wearily by the broken altar, Abel," etc.; though *wearily* is taken from MacIntyre's translation, which other details of the poem repeat, it must have been retained for a reason). But of course the myths are suggestive not symmetrical. Thus, Cain's guilt rings through the war poems; the nurse is Eve, who, letting in the Devil, brought vengeance on Adam; but Lamkin, sometimes the Serpent who murdered innocence (at the ballad's end he and the nurse are executed), mainly is the Lord, who enters with sharp sword the faithless house He built.

Therefore, most of the thematic poems occur in Hell or ante-Hell, the world "that spreads in pain," the rich house we use without paying for; which the defrauded One will enter suddenly. Already with the capitalist of an early poem, here revised into "Christmas Eve under Hooker's Statue," Lowell had begun to imagine characters moving about in it, but for the most part in the first book he simply abused it. By a shift toward the dramatic which is one of the large features of his development, he is now peopling it. (It is to be noted that Lowell is an *objective* poet; except as a Christian or a descendant he scarcely appears in his poems.) The most elaborate example is a dramatic sequence "Between the Porch and the Altar," at the end of which, with astonishing style, he damns the mother-fixed adulterous drunken protagonist,

> the Day
> Breaks with its lightning on the man of clay,
> *Dies amara valde*. Here the Lord
> Is Lucifer in harness: hand on sword,
> He watches me for Mother, and will turn
> The bier and baby-carriage where I burn.

The Lord has often this aspect in these poems. If reproached with it, the poet might reply in the words of the Katherine of this poem: "The winter sun is pleasant, and it warms / My heart with love for others, but the swarms / Of penitents have dwindled"; or say that he had taken John Davidson's impressive advice, "Enlarge your Hell; preserve it in repair; / Only a splendid Hell keeps Heaven fair." Still one wonders whether he would have allowed the piercing, non-formulary salvation imagined by the Balzac of *Christ in Flanders*, and one is surprised that, with two poems based on writings by the prodigious Edwards, he passed over "Sinners in the Hands of an Angry God."

But the poems are rich with nonformulary life, and Lowell has other religious tones also.

> John, Matthew, Luke and Mark,
> Gospel me to the Garden, let me come
> Where Mary twists the warlock with her flowers—
> Her soul a bridal chamber fresh with flowers
> And her whole body an ecstatic womb
> As through the trellis peers the sudden Bridegroom.

He is weakest on the whole when near a substance-model, he seems to rely on the model as well as on himself, and his evergreen ingenuity gets too-free play; yet even the poems with immediate sources show, together with their defects, qualities thoroughly rare and valuable. (About a third of the new poems have direct literary or historical sources, transformed under his imagination.) His "Ghost," based on a beautiful elegy of Propertius (iv. 7) not touched by Pound, is not by some distance as fresh delicate firm as Pound's "Homage," but it will stand the comparison without looking idiotic—a sufficient compliment. Lowell is as individual; less energetic with more appearance of energy (that is, higher keyed—*beat*, to take an amusing detail, rendering equally *effugit* and *pelle*); more original in the respect that he is indifferent where Propertius is magnificent, best where nothing remarkable is happening in the Latin or he is inventing; more faithful, only transposing lines 49 ff. and 73 ff.; less flexible; much less witty; as capable as Pound of a dense memorable detail, "At cock-crow Charon checks us in his log." Some of these poems are "imitations" in the eighteenth-century sense, and despite their heightened tone should perhaps be judged by a special standard. More independent is the second Edwards piece, "After the Surprising Conversions," which is written in that phoenix metre, heroic couplet, the best run-on couplets I have seen in a long time:

> In the latter part of May
> He cut his throat. And though the coroner
> Judged him delirious, soon a noisome stir
> Palsied the village. At Jehovah's nod
> Satan seemed more let loose amongst us: God
> Abandoned us to Satan . . . / We were undone.
> The breath of God had carried out a planned
> And sensible withdrawal from this land.

Set the simplicity and manliness of this poem beside the mysterious frenzy of "The Drunken Fisherman" or the drenched magnificence of "The Quaker Graveyard" and you will observe a talent whose ceiling is invisible.

But I don't wish to make a noise about Lowell, reviewers in other channels being equipped for this, and popularity in the modern American culture having proved for other authors not yet physically dead a blessing decidedly sinister. One certainly wants to see fine poems honoured and read; and "I say it deliberately and before God," Hopkins wrote to Bridges, "that fame, the being known, though in itself one of the most dangerous things to man, is nevertheless the true and appointed air, element, and setting of genius and its works." The secular dangers are to candour and development, perhaps to fellow feeling, considering the kind of honour a comics culture can confer; self-consciousness is the general reef. Luckily Lowell is so intense tough unreasonable that he will probably be safe. I will only make a historical remark. The author of a very interesting leading article recently in *The Times Literary Supplement*, taking *The Orators* as the key book of the thirties, mentions in his conclusion the fact that writers of the period, young and old, "preferred to precision of design and execution an approximate; a general feeling arose that careful finish was in some way base . . . the brilliant improvisation became a standard instead of an adventure." This is so just as scarcely to need illustration; you can see it best, after Audèn's early books, in the beautiful work done by Delmore Schwartz at the decade's end in America—to name one line of corroboration, Blackmur hung his review of *In Dreams Begin Responsibilities* on the word "improvised." Of course Auden himself reacted at once (even in *Look, Stranger* regular forms predominate), as Eliot's 1920 volume, under the influence of Gautier, reacted against "Prufrock"; and there have not been wanting other signs. But Lowell's poetry is the most decisive testimony we have had, I think, of a new period, returning to the deliberate and the formal. In other respects, it is true, the break is incomplete. Our best work is still difficult, allusive, and more or less didactic in intention.

A few technical notes. Lowell uses very heavy rime, and thud metre, spondaic substitution being much commoner than any other; these characteristics alone permit him to indulge frequently and not cripplingly in the hard short runover that generally marks bad poets. He stops as a rule after the first, the seventh, or the ninth syllable. For instance, *each but one* of the nine lines quoted above from "Between the Porch and the Altar" shows caesura after the seventh syllable (the first begins, "and the day"). Perhaps only a master could keep in so narrow an area and make it interesting, but the mastery is as yet certainly very limited. Poets half his size are much more resourceful by way of movement. His ear is not infallible, and this may have something to do with refrain weakness; though repetition, a considerable element in his designs, he handles admirably (see a fine passage on p. 10). What we might call simultaneous repetition-with-variation, or the serious pun, he abounds in, and the examples sometimes sound better than they are. Thus search guns "nick the slate roofs on the Holsterwall / Where torn-up tilestones crown the victor"; here *crown* is effective, if it is, against the implausibility of one meaning (invest, reward) and the infrequency of the other (fall on, finish off): one leg ought to be firmer. The same wish to crowd meaning is responsible for a good many of the slurred references of which Jarrell complained in the earlier poems, and these continue, now and then confusingly. Direct echoes are rare; "Fear with its fingered stopwatch" remembers Auden's "Fear gave his watch no look"—a later "Fear, / The yellow chirper, beaks its cage" is original and good. Considering the complication of his tradition, the book is notably fresh and consistent. Sonnets, for whatever reasons, tend to be inferior to other forms. The chief danger for a writer so dense is obviously turgidity, and in the sonnets it is least successfully avoided. Whether Lowell owes anything to a poet similarly "packed," Dylan Thomas, it is not easy to say, and so he cannot owe much; there is some common ground in diction for movement (lurch, blunder, lumber, sidle, heave, etc.) and an illimitable barrier in religious attitudes; like Thomas's early similarities to Hart Crane, whom he had not read, I set down to temperament and tradition such resemblance as there is. Finally, despite a good deal of international reference, perhaps inevitable now in the work of a sophisticated poet, and despite some objection I feel to the very obscure word "American," used chiefly as it is by canters and radio announcers, nevertheless it seems worthwhile saying that Lowell's poetry is deeply a local product.

The demand for anthologies is so ferocious at present, or publishers think it is—the truth is that we are passing through a deadly and vacant period, with an absence of good new manuscripts to print —that when no general anthology is available for the presses, they anthologize a single man. Dylan Thomas's new book* is a selection by the publisher: a few poems from his first two English books (weirdly omitting "Light breaks where no sun shines," "The hand that signed the paper felled a city," "I have longed to move away," etc.), many from *The Map of Love* and the new *Deaths and Entrances*, some prose; it overlaps both his earlier New Directions books and, like all the volumes reviewed here, costs too much. But Thomas is one of the three best poets writing in England and anyone who pretends interest in these matters will need both his book and Lowell's. I tried to describe his verse some years ago (1940) and want at present to make only one or two points.

About his development. Any poet *may* turn out an opsimath like Yeats, it happens at least once a century, but in general it should be possible for a critic to say with confidence from a poet's first good book what sort of development, if any, is to be expected thereafter. By development we mean a movement from one kind of thing to another (getting better at the same thing is called improvement). The law is this: poets, even fine ones, do not develop. Then you have the exceptions. Thomas began very young at a high level. What made it improbable that he would move from the kind of poem he was writing to another kind is that he was incapable of handling a subject without dissolving it into his own obsessions and imagery until the

* *The Selected Writings of Dylan Thomas.* Preface by John L. Sweeney, 1947.

subject disappeared. He is still more or less incapable of this. Instead of comparing him to Shakespeare and cooing over his development, his English admirers should thank heaven and his character that he has continued to write *extremely well*, without undue self-imitation, and with a mildly expanding range of subject. Some of his finest poems are recent, for example "Holy Spring." A poem like "Among Those Killed in the Dawn Raid Was a Man Aged One Hundred," cited as an instance of his new particularity, becomes at once, in fact, a Thomas dream.

This poem is full of locks and keys. John L. Sweeney, in his interesting preface, speaks of "regeneration." The concept is not clear to me, but something similar is clear: that Thomas's poems are about *breaking loose*. There is a *lock* (and a congeries of related symbols for repression). Infrequently a *key* is available, but on the whole one has to *break* the lock (congeries of expressions for these also). This action takes place at dawn, the poems are full of *waking*. Difficulty after difficulty disappears once this theme is grasped. A spiritual movement forward, sometimes represented as flight, toward *light* or freedom. The intensity and freshness of Thomas's variations on the theme are a continuing source of delight.

Thomas has been called, not plausibly, a surrealist, and surrealism has affected the detail of some of Carrera Andrade's poems. But André Breton is an exclusive and dogmatic surrealist, that is, an *idiot*. I intend nothing invidious, merely that on principle he still sends his mind next door whenever he sits down to work. His new book,* according to the irresistible jacket, is in "the classic tradition of the Surrealists . . . morally steadfast," and shows I think his usual modesty and resource:

> My wife with the sex of a mining-placer and of a platypus
> My wife with a sex of seaweed and ancient sweetmeat

It is true that the glory of the French is lacking in this translation I quote (and *chacun à son fout*); but, French or English, this helplessly recalls the worst poet not contemporary I ever read, poor Thomas Purney, Newgate's chaplain, the baby-talk pastoralist, whom a heartless scholar once tried to revive:

> Why may'nt we Men, yquoth the youngling *mey*,
> And why may'nt we grasp them? Us graspen they!

or

* *Young Cherry Trees Secured against Hares*, 1947.

> The dabling *dew* fell all emong;
> Her buding Breasts so fair and young;
> Her buding Breasts, that bloomie grew,
> Soft shrinked at the dabling *dew*.

(These are real quotations from the actual printed books.)

M. Breton has more ability than Purney—the *momie d'ibis* section of *Fata Morgana* is the best thing in his book—but I doubt if he will last two centuries as Purney at least nominally has done. They have more than tastelessness in common.

The worst contribution of literary surrealism, the senseless iteration, Señor Carrera Andrade easily avoids because he has always a subject in hand and can't waste time like a true surrealist. His quiet, graceful, affecting poems were among the most impressive in H. R. Hays's *Twelve Spanish-American Poets,* and the larger selection now published* deserves better attention than my semi-Spanish can give it. He is said to be Ecuador's leading poet, and is as good as the late John Peale Bishop's excellent introduction says he is. This book and Breton's are printed in the way foreign poetry should be, original and close translation facing. I wish some well-fed or even hungry publisher would do the same for Corbière, a large and acute selection of Goethe's poems, and other works; Michael Hamburger's Hölderlin (1943) should be reprinted in this country.

H.D.'s *The Flowering of the Rod* (1947) is the conclusion of a three-volume poem or poems written in London during the war. Three volumes, but H.D. has always been strong on white space, and she uses here the distich stanza (a form, rarely handled well, except by Wallace Stevens, in which you get the most attention for the least effort), so that there is not much of it. There is not much to it, either, unless I am greatly mistaken. The reference is Egyptian and vaguely Christian, instead of Greek; there is said to be a story; "it explains symbols of the past / in to-day's imagery," she wrote in the first part, but I doubt if it does. In a poem sequence even 2,500 lines long, one feels, a good deal ought to happen. I preferred the second part (*Tribute to the Angels*) to the others. (The English price, printed on the back of my copy, is instructive: 3/6 or seventy cents, against two dollars American.)

The collection of Janet Lewis's poems† is more rewarding, though it will disappoint readers who remember *Twelve Poets of the Pacific.* A new tone is tried only in "Country Burial," unsuccessfully.

---

* *Secret Country.* Introduction by John Peale Bishop, 1947.
† *The Earth-Bound,* 1947.

Her best work is still small and elegiac. It is more real and more skillful than some better-known women's, and not devoid (as some critics think Winters's theories produce poetry devoid) of emotion—

> O gone forever, while joy mounts my stair
> With staggering feet and high uncertain voice,
> I remember your death.

But it is so slight that I wonder whether even a stanza as handsome as this one will keep it in memory:

> She climbed a farther hill
> More fair than show
> The meadows here
> Into an air more clear,
> A light more still.

It might. Poets capable of the hesitation on *show*, as if it were a substantive (and how beautiful the hovering meaning), are not very numerous.

Omnibus reviews lead sometimes, as here, to juxtapositions inexpressibly violent. Kenneth Patchen undoubtedly has, or has had, some talent, and only a man in his right senses would deny that his work* is interesting.

> The land is darker than the sea, but God
> Is darker than the land.
> Move your left breast nearer.
>
> When the soldier scrammed
> I heard a blond girl weeping her guts out,
> Which is more than you did. Or you.
>
> Holy as stars and flowers,
> Sadder than Mary, filthy as human war,
> I endure the afflictions of the birds.

I think this piece is characteristic in its air (God, sex, weeping, war, the Virgin), its intimacy ("Come here, reader, look in my pocket"), and its vices (incoherence, blasphemy, cant, vagueness, sentimentality, the un-subject and un-form). Yet it moved me deeply as I made it up two minutes ago, and I believe the only things I neglected to put in were Patchen's apocalypticism, his righteous wrath, snow, and his "Brothers." Writing like Patchen's is usually called self-expression,

---

* *Selected Poems*, 1947.

but I am convinced that this is a mistake. On the contrary: you take your eye off your self (also off the subject, if any, the English language, the forms of poetry, the world, and the spirit) in order to fix it solely and ardently upon your reader. Anything goes. It is very easy, frankly, to write this way; all you want is to convince the reader that you are real, the means, of course, being rhetoric. "There are two ways of falsifying," says Valéry: "one by the work of *embellishment*, the other by the effort to *make true*. The latter case is perhaps that which reveals the more acute affectation. It also marks a certain despair of arousing general interest by purely literary means." This applies, I feel, perfectly to Patchen; though the great critic now dead probably did not anticipate a writer who would illustrate with equal force and at once both kinds of falsification.

The poems of Byron Vazakas* are exactly the honest, not very interesting sort of work that one would expect to see introduced by William Carlos Williams, whose hospitality is a credit to the country. He says that they are better collected than single, but I confess that, rereading them all before I looked at the introduction, my feeling was just the opposite. Together they show as clumsy, derivative, and rather flaccid; the similes are vague, the diction is nothing. I liked better than any of them a poem in *Accent* last year, "Liebestod," which Vazakas has not reprinted. There is a possibility of something's happening, however, and some life around, which distinguish the book from the other "first books" the editors sent me. These I couldn't welcome and see small point in damning, so I am not printing my notes on them. Not the worst was a Scot, very up to date, who now and then gave the show away with a line like

oh, I am lost in vast immensities—

as distinguished from the small immensities or just immensities, or just dull vague period style in which the others are lost.

1947

* *Transfigured Night.* Preface by William Carlos Williams, 1947.

Poetry Chronicle, 1948:

Waiting for the End, Boys

TEN OR TWELVE YEARS AGO THERE WAS STILL MUCH ELAB-
orate talk about "modern poetry." At one level, the exciting first
volumes of *The Southern Review* were full of studies and exhortations
defining it, analyzing it, telling how to achieve it. At another level, a
foolish book appeared, *This Modern Poetry*, serving much the same
purpose for the unenlightened that an ineffable recent "history" does.
The word "modern" now seems less important. It is not easy now to
imagine a poet attempting to be modern. In fact, one sensitive and
experienced critic—Randall Jarrell—has described Lowell's poetry as
"post-modernist"; and one certainly has a sense that some period is
drawing to a close. I want here to document this sense, explaining why
it seems to me a very good thing that the period is closing, and to study
a little England's new poet, Henry Reed; but first a word or so on the
period's characteristic marks: the imprint it sets upon young work.

By 1935—referring only, for the moment, to this country—the
Auden climate had set in strongly. Poetry became ominous, flat, and
social; elliptical and indistinctly allusive; casual in tone and form,
frightening in import. So far as I know, the only large challenge to
this climate, as yet, has issued from rather an unexpected quarter, the
work of Wallace Stevens. There have, of course, been writers who
stood outside, and our whole tradition is by now one of great complexity. As an example I take the jacket statement of a young California poet: "I owe much in the development of my poetics to the
work of Wyatt and Surrey, to *The Temple* of George Herbert, to
the work of such moderns as Wallace Stevens, D. H. Lawrence, the
Spender translation of Rilke's *Duino Elegies*, and Edith Sitwell's
Street Songs. In my psychological concept I am indebted to Sigmund
Freud, Karl Barth, and particularly to *Dark Night of the Soul* by the
16th century St. John of the Cross." I find this charming, especially
the frank admission that, like tens of millions of his contemporaries,

he is indebted to Freud; to Wyatt and Surrey he owes, in fact, nothing beyond what every poet who uses English owes them, except the spellings shadowd, begd, etc.; and the whole statement is evidently rhetorical ("Heavens," you cry remorsefully to a friend, "why don't I return that book *Gide* lent me"). But it will repay our analysis. "Barth" stands for Auden, who is scarcely ever named on these occasions, just as "St. John of the Cross" stands for Eliot, and the substitutions are a sign—not that we needed one—of how influential American *criticism* has been on the poetry of the period. The grateful allusions to the early English poets, together with the failure of profit from their influence in Duncan's book ("My life may come to rest in me / where I shall restless in the future be"), may remind us of how wasteful of opportunity and ignorant our poetry is; thus one might learn much from Wyatt (and from the best discussion so far of the difficult problem of his versification, in *Scrutiny* for December 1946), and Lowell has learned much from Herbert. The mention of Rilke—that it is a translation notices our ignorance again—reminds us of how few foreign-language poets have been operative in the period: Rimbaud, Rilke, Valéry, Lorca. The mention of Lawrence suggests that we are in dark and mindless California, but suggests also how little things generally have changed in the dozen years since Day Lewis's influential *A Hope for Poetry* named Hopkins, Lawrence, and Owen as the ancestors of Auden Ltd. (Inc., I should perhaps say). With the mention of Miss Sitwell, however, we enter the anglophilism of California and leave the American scene proper. Let us return momentarily to see how it is that the Auden climate and the Stevens ascendant, though suffering much static of this nature, have held their sway here.

There is no mystery in it. The poets who fill the magazines, who publish book after book, are Auden and Stevens. With much more competition, so to speak, than they have had, they would have reigned still. But they have not had much. Eliot's perennial influence is by this time so diffused that poets usually work through it before they reach print; and then he has published nothing but the *Quartets*, which though profoundly admired have exerted less influence than one would have expected—with a notable exception to be described in due course. The other senior poets have continued to publish, but Pound's influence is intermittent, and nobody of interest imitates Frost or Williams much; Ransom has written almost nothing; Aiken and Jeffers have lost heavily; perhaps Miss Moore's work has been most fruitful, especially in the best women poets who have appeared for a long time, Elizabeth Bishop and now Jean Garrigue. As for the middle generation, it has gone to pieces. Tate has published one booklet in a decade, Crane died, MacLeish evaporated. Léonie Adams and Putnam fell silent, Louise Bogan nearly so, Van Doren and Warren developed no following; only Cummings, to one's pleased surprise, kept on and improved, and his influence has regularly been atrocious. The other most active members of the generation have been Winters and Blackmur as critics. The young poets lately, in short, have had not fathers but grandfathers. Not much generative time is needed, however, for Auden himself is a grandfather: a writer like Hugh Chisholm, though unable to summon the flow and glitter of Prokosch, being more properly his son than Auden's; and other young writers being Delmorean or Shapiro-like or even Barkerish. So William Jay Smith's poem "Cupidon" (which seems to Marianne Moore "a permanence," and to me a predictable harmless farce piece like the rest of his quasi-religious, quasi-satirical, agreeable, and empty lyrics) is founded not on Yeats but on Theodore Spencer. The failure of Yeats's influence to take stronger direct hold during the period requires some explanation. First, it is puzzling and remarkable, but true, that young poets are frequent who have simply not read his later poetry. In the second place, Yeats's personality is so distinct and powerful that few writers have cared to submit to it in the hope of coming out themselves. His craft had a generalized influence on two important books published ten years ago, *Look, Stranger* and *In Dreams Begin Responsibilities,* and on the whole concept of stanza formation since then, but poets with less safeguards than Auden and Schwartz have tried to keep away: Auden being fully developed (like Spender and Tate when in turn they took up Yeats), Schwartz drenching Yeats with Eliot, Stevens, and Rilke, to say nothing of a philosophical discipline and a radically different subject matter.

The period in England presents a greater appearance of activity, owing partly to the fact that a poet who might never achieve a volume here at all can there go through three or four volumes and even acquire a reputation; but it has been undoubtedly, on the whole, much less interesting. Stevens, and a number of other first-rate American poets down to Schwartz and Lowell, are absent from the picture because unavailable there; in 1935 MacLeish's collected poems appeared in London—and then the tiny *Twentieth Century Verse* devoted a few pages to Stevens; whether his books have yet been published there I don't know. Auden's blanket was spread earlier at home, and stifled more, at the same time that it warmed more into issueless activity. Dylan Thomas was closer and had an influence much greater than he has ever had here—again, there was a transatlantic lag in publication. Then Auden was withdrawn. This is the first of three circumstances that seem to me to account for what can only strike one as the general unreality of the British impression of their poetic scene. Their pride in Eliot imperfect, because he is by birth an American, they felt denuded after Auden left; so that to clothe themselves they inflated almost to absurdity the reputations available to them, Edith Sitwell's, Herbert Read's, Spender's; and praised their young poets beyond recognition. Second, all this was possible because along with a public interest in poetry—much more intense and widespread than public interest in poetry in America—goes inevitably a degree of gullibility; and it was possible, third, because literary criticism was feeble. Thus, *The New English Weekly* all during the war devoted far more space to reviews of verse (and indeed to poems) than any comparable American magazine, but the reviewing was for the most part extremely bad, having no responsible contemporary criticism to rely on. The situation is extraordinary. Julian Symons, in an article in *The Critic* last spring on "Some American Critics," while recognizing the British weakness (". . . if we are ever lucky enough to get a general body of serious literary criticism") and correctly isolating *Primitivism and Decadence* as "the most extreme and in some ways the most valuable work of these writers," himself showed how imperfect is the present British sense of these matters by relying on the old Marxists-Formalists grouping in Kazin's *On Native Grounds*, and by remarking, in a footnote to a paragraph that recommends *The New Criticism* and *An Anatomy of Nonsense*, as if he had read them, that "Mr. Winters, certainly, *would* find many points of difference between himself and Mr. John Crowe Ransom." The laxity of criticism in England has had one very striking negative result, which I must take up later. But it has helped the inflation of Miss Sitwell (who is, no doubt, unduly neglected in this country) and of Spender, giving recent British poetry a romantic cast and a fluid style or unstyle uncommon here. Since what is eccentric is imitated from Thomas more often than what is normal and profound, he has had a contributory effect. Lacking a dominant tradition, the neo-Romantics have split into various groups, vying with each other not only in wretchedness of execution; and the influence of poets like Graves, Muir, MacNeice, and Empson appears not to have been strong.

I have spoken of the transatlantic lag. Empson is the outstanding English victim of it, or we are its victims: his poems, rumoured often enough, have still not appeared. Even so, his spry, compact, and brainy verse has had some effect (Howard Nemerov's "Two Sides . . . Meditation from Empson" achieves his tone only in three lines, the fourteenth, seventeenth, twenty-third; but another poem, "To the Memory of John Wheelwright," is more successful with it; and see William Jay Smith's "Villanelle") and would have effects better still if it were collected here. We are more willing perhaps than the British to trouble to secure non-domestic books, but it is not enough. Englishmen are published here occasionally. There have been Treece and Manifold and Keyes and others, while for some reason there have not been Roy Fuller or Vernon Watkins. One of the latest is Laurie Lee, who will represent the situation well enough. His stylistic affiliation is announced in his second line with "morning slender sun," echoing Spender's "morning simple light," and the poems are very "lyrical." Generally in unrhymed stanzas, and he takes it easy metrically, obeying his impulses: in short, he has only diction and images as tools, and what he can learn or impart is rather limited. Stanzas, I am bound to report, could be shifted from poem to poem without notice or disturbance if one did it cunningly. His mind is lazy or medieval: "the iron sleep our senses wear." But his feeling for nature is real and might make a very interesting hole if it were not digging with its fingers. He is best in a simple piece like "Landscape" where his love-and-nature identifications are not sweating for Lorca's passion but gently reminiscing. This theme is genuine: "I hear the forest open her dress," "as the hills draw up their knees," "O the wild trees of home / with their sounding dresses," "the bank of your breasts / with their hill-cold springs," "a womb of leaves,"—small and not indispensable, but genuine. And now Henry Reed has been published here. But I must say more of the situation into which he has been published.

One has the impression here and there, reading through John Ciardi's book *Other Skies*, his second, that the Auden Climate has now made it possible for a hat rack to write a perfectly presentable poem on any standard subject (beaches, teaching, flying, birthdays, oiling a machine gun, death, Saipan, pin-ups, drugstores, hospitals, photographs), and I think there is truth in the impression. On the other hand, one has the impression here and there in reading through Nemerov's *The Image and the Law* that the Auden Climate has driven technical accomplishment straight to zero, besides encouraging the Flat to take us over altogether; for instance, the third of five Nemerov stanzas weirdly crawls as follows:

The citizen reads the Sunday papers.
He thanks his God he is not
In Posnan or Allenstein or Belgrade.
He is, for example, in Chicago.
The world situation is terrible,
The famine a terrible thing.

(What matters is not that the poet has done this badly but that he supposes it the thing to do at all.) And I think there is truth in this impression also. Well? Are we to say merely that Ciardi is more experienced than Nemerov? He is; but this is hardly more relevant to the dilemma (if a hat rack can write so well, why not Nemerov?) than is the fact that Auden is himself a virtuoso (since for years he concealed his virtuosity from the rank and file of his followers). The explanation is that Ciardi has barely a tithe of Nemerov's talent. That is, the Climate at this date resembles somewhat the current musical scene, which is good for union members but bad for artists.

I had better prove at once that Nemerov is an artist.

For W. Who Commanded Well

You try to fix your mind upon his death,
Which seemed it might, somehow, be relevant
To something you once thought, or did, or might
Imagine yourself thinking, doing. When?

It was, once, the most possible of dreams:
The hero acted it, philosophers
Could safely recommend it to the young;
It was acceptable, a theme for song.

And it was wrong? Daily the press commends
A rationed greed, the radio denies
That war is right, or wrong, or serious:
And money is being made, and the wheels go round,
And death is paying for itself: and so
It does not seem that anything was lost.

It would be hard to claim that this unemphatic and thoughtful poem is expertly written, but it is impossible to deny that the talent and feeling are real. What happened to them is that the author inherited from both Auden and Stevens a tradition of improvisation. We may write a sonnet, say, but for God's sake, let it be as little like a sonnet as possible: appear to take it easy. Tate's frightful wrenchings in his early sonnets, producing sometimes similar effects, proceeded from an exactly opposite desire: *not to take it easy*. Either program, it goes without saying, could be fruitful or sterile; I am not preferring one to the other. Well, as Tate's restless dead-seriousness has prevented his ever steadying down in an acquired technique sufficiently to produce a consistent and considerable body of work, so the Climate's hell-with-it has kept Nemerov from acquiring a craft commensurate with what (considering "The Place of Value," "Portrait of Three Conspirators," "Lot's Wife") one takes to be his native ability. The rhyme-dim "sonnet" I have quoted is simply a masterpiece compared with his normal sonnets, and he is the author of the two worst-conceived and worst-executed sestinas (I hope) in the English language. These sestinas show an incomprehension of the whole nature of a sestina so startling that after recovering from them I looked up and reread all my favorite sestinas from Arnaut to Jarrell to see whether I had lost my mind. It can only mean, in a young writer otherwise knowing enough, an *acquired insensitivity* to form. His intensely literary book includes too much apprentice work (especially in Sections II and III), chewing over many influences besides Auden's and Stevens's; occasionally he writes poems in what is best called short-line prose; but the maturer work displays very clearly the languors and rigours suffered by talent under the Climate.

Direct a light upon the work at present done for union members by the Climate, and their own contributions dwindle to their own contributions. We see that Howard Griffin, for all the properties lent him (Chardin, krakens, Trinc, neon, assoil, Persephone, the Mills Hotel, the sad iambic sea, chatoyances of air), is not a poet at all, since he can't contrive to do the elementary thing required, which is to *sound as if he meant it*. He was in the Signal Corps, and here are the beginning, middle, end of a poem from his book, *Cry Cadence:*

> This hand that shields my heart when darts are near . . .
>
> has killed.
>> And now forever let my flesh be cursed,—
> this pervious parchment, this farce-like frame
> let it decay . . .
>
> Curse my right hand. That both were lefts
> or honest claws—

We see that Selden Rodman is unrewarding and sometimes intolerable as a poet because he has no *tone*. His new book, *The Amazing Year*, designed as a marvel of virtuosity (50 Beautiful Forms 50), is vaguely and unhappily characterless; only fashionable and busy. What he can do is a serious-gag poem like "Pearl Harbor"; the rest is manufactured chaos, and the better the subject (like Esmond Romilly), the more inadequate the treatment, the grimmer the Flat, the more helpful the Climate. This is a union member in good standing.

We see that Ciardi, who is as sharply superior to these writers as Miss Garrigue is superior to him, ought not to be content with the Climate which can sing him a mild and simple poem like "Sea Burial," but can do nothing for him when he is up against it at the end of "First Summer After a War," with a twelve-clause sentence in three quatrains, only one clause being independent; again, at the end of "I Meet the Motion," he has an eleven-clause sentence in four quatrains, only one clause being independent; and the rhetorical skill necessary to deal with this is hardly to be found since the Renaissance. I don't say that endless falsification of the substance is not involved in *trying* to do it this way; but what can the chop-chop-chop syntax of the Climate do with it? For the simplest periodicity one must cast about.

Jean Garrigue has cast about and about. If the record of her inquiries is too full, it is also more active and honourable than any woman's for years except Miss Bishop's. In *The Ego and the Centaur*, she is interesting on all the ranges from "Banquet of the Utilitarian" up through "Iowa City Zoo" and "Oration against the Orator's Oration" to the elaborate poems she has placed first and last in her book. But her air of freshness and seriousness, probably, is more important so far than her finished poems. Does she finger them enough?

> They kick him in the head, jammed there.
> They are kicking a man in the head to death.

I see no loss, some gain, in an order altered to "kicking in the head a man"; and another passage, "that old man / Sourly drags the broom through vestibules," might gain from the obvious change. Or it might not, or it would change the style. But looking again at the high-keyed poems, "Poem" and "The Circle," I again feel inclined to be quiet and see what she does or her poems do. She is not quite in the Climate. Stevens is strong (as "The Mask and Knife"), Miss Moore is ("False Country of the Zoo"), Thomas is ("In Praise of that Epic Dream"); she has often a metaphysical surface (as "Theme and Variations") and is fond of paradoxes like "rain fell black / Muddy-eyed from the eye of night" and "the junket of word-mouthed words"; but experiencing a style is above all a question of *hearing*—time, as a rule, is important in it (the poem I hear best is "The

Stranger," simply because I have known it longest)—and in short I feel at present more that Miss Garrigue *has* a style than that I can hear it precisely or say what it is. The poems seem much more impressive collected than they did when they first appeared, a few at a time, in separate publications. Since just the opposite is true of most poets—those who have interest at all, I mean—this fact is more of a commendation than it may appear. And Miss Garrigue is, finally, the rare contemporary who writes love poems, actual and surprising and sometimes moving love poems.

The revolutions by which a poetry is diverted from its course to a new course are as dramatic as anything in literary history. One occurred about 1600 when the boy Donne jammed a speaking voice, jammed hesitation and thought and passion, into Elizabethan song. Another—more interesting to us, I think, just now—occurred at the mid-century following: when Edmund Waller, according to Dryden, reformed English versification, giving it sweetness and regular pause and elegance. Modern critics incline to minimize Dryden's view and Waller's achievement, and I incline to minimize the critics. Waller not merely for everyone gathered verse again into forms, like the couplet, but so controlled the forms in his best poems as to produce an expectation differing wholly from previous expectations, and then by violating the expectation got his effects. These effects are quiet, and amazing. In a period as licentious as our own, it is very difficult to hear them. But it is very important to hear them, because if our license is not to continue, we will one day be asked to hear effects analogous to them from one of our contemporaries. They are the sound of the change of a national mind. "Of English Verse" contains one, perhaps the greatest. The theme of this poem, written not many years after Bacon had wasted his age translating his English works into Latin, is the futility of writing in English, because the language daily changes. For seven quatrains, divided severely into couplets, the poet argues; and then there is a final quatrain. If the main theme should seem to anyone outdated, I trust that the substance of the last two quatrains (as quoted now in an age when for many attentive to the developments of science the future has ceased to exist) will not:

> This was the generous Poets scope
> And all an English Pen can hope:
> To make the fair approve his Flame
> That can so far extend their Fame.

> Verse thus design'd has no ill fate
> If it arrive but at the Date
> Of fading Beauty, if it prove
> But as long liv'd as present love.

The final quatrain's exquisite runover can be heard justly, of course, only at the end of the whole poem; but even as mangled here it may convey some of its mastery.

Now I am far from wishing to produce Henry Reed as Waller. But if Reed can be listened to with the general present situation in mind as I have described it (subject to correction by critics who know it better), understanding may be quickened. His first book, *A Map of Verona and other Poems*, published recently in England and more recently here, contains a poem called "Lessons of the War" or a suite, so called, composed of distinct poems, three of them; the first, entitled "Naming of Parts," begins as follows:

> Today we have naming of parts. Yesterday,
> We had daily cleaning. And tomorrow morning,
> We shall have what to do after firing. But today,
> Today we have naming of parts. Japonica
> Glistens like coral in all of the neighboring gardens,
>   And today we have naming of parts.
>
> This is the lower sling swivel. And this
> Is the upper sling swivel, whose use you will see,
> When you are given your slings. And this is the piling swivel,
> Which in your case you have not got. The branches
> Hold in the gardens their silent, eloquent gestures,
>   Which in our case we have not got.

In these stanzas, it seems to me, we actually hear a style creating itself. It is as if the poet said to himself: "All these other poets. They are Flat? I will outflat them. Whom can I learn from? Eliot, Eliot's *Quartet* style, and Auden, a little, who holds unrhymed stanzas together with a short final line—and other things—and I will make them *recognizable* before I kick them over. All in the open, because Flattest—no sleight-of-hand; only here and there, just for a moment, I will be richer than anyone. What is simplest? In the first stanza, iteration: 'Today' against Auden's fat 'Tomorrow' (in 'Spain') if anyone cares, with Eliot flickering in the middle lines; then claim the stanza—not too hard—in the short line. In the second, pointing: just like and just against Eliot's faked magic in 'The Waste Land' cards, if

306

anyone cares. Then wipe them out and, in the second short line, claim everything. *Speech* everywhere. *Loosen* everything. What do poets do? They do things *again*. I will *do things again*, as they have never been done before." And the marvellous poem continues on its way:

> This is the safety-catch, which is always released
> With an easy flick of the thumb. And please do not let me
> See anyone using his finger. You can do it quite easy
> If you have any strength in your thumb. The blossoms
> Are fragile and motionless, never letting anyone see
>   Any of them using their finger.
>
> And this you can see is the bolt. The purpose of this
> Is to open the breech, as you see. We can slide it
> Rapidly backwards and forwards: we call this
> Easing the spring. And rapidly backwards and forwards
> The early bees are assaulting and fumbling the flowers:
>   They call it easing the Spring.
>
> They call it easing the Spring: it is perfectly easy
> If you have any strength in your thumb: like the bolt,
> And the breech, and the cocking-piece, and the point of balance,
> Which in our case we have not got; and the almond-blossom
> Silent in all of the gardens and the bees going backwards and forwards,
>   For today we have naming of parts.

It is all done without effort, or appears to be done so. Then suddenly you feel like weeping. This is a poet whose slightest shift can contrive excitement. His poems accumulate, perfectly flat and then perfectly suggestive, so naturally that at the second reading one of them is familiar as if one had known it for weeks or months. He mixes strange emotions. This warm familiarity is one; he says more completely than you expect *what* you expect. Another, which poets are more often said to have than have, is humour. The second and third "Lessons of the War" are more openly grievous than the first by the time they end, yet somewhere under them plays this real humour; I laughed. He has irony when he likes, and he can shut it off. He can frighten. But one's strongest sense is of an *accepting* poetry, and two of the most wonderful passages in his book are the ante-penultimate and last paragraphs of "Tristram," which dramatize resignation. These are not detachable; they take place, like almost everything else in Reed, in a progression *in* the poem—just as each poem when you read it seems to have a place *in* the progression of his poetry. Very little is detachable: a blazing detail across the page from "Tristram":

> In the golden collapse of the summer, or the tearing days
> Before the beginning of spring . . .

In these lines what used to be called the quality of high imagination is plain as the sun. Read the whole book.

I never read a line of Reed's poetry till day before yesterday, and never heard him mentioned but once several months ago along with four other young English poets; I am glad I do not have to appoint his eternal place. But we have Eliot's word for it that genuineness will do, and genuineness is what I affirm. It will trouble some readers that Reed's work is so close to its main stylistic source, the *Four Quartets*. So it is, very; some even of the properties in "Triptych" are the same as Eliot's. What then? The awkward truth is that Reed is an alchemist. He could rewrite "Resolution and Independence" in his own style and fascinate you. The same readers may be troubled by his passages of open emotion; and to these I think we must adjust ourselves.

Strategies and strategies. Confronted equally with difficult situations, Reed *relaxed* beyond relaxation and Lowell *tightened* beyond tightening. Reed breaks metre into anapests, feminine endings, extra-syllabled lines of all sorts, Lowell into spondees and humped smash. Lowell's work is "difficult," Reed's on the whole "plain," in extreme degrees. *Lord Weary's Castle* is the natural product of an elaborate, scrupulous, and respected literary criticism. It could hardly have been produced in England, where there is nothing to prepare for it or to receive it (Empson's less formidable first book was dismissed, for instance, by MacNeice as not the sort of thing needed just then—indeed it wasn't, or it still is). On the other hand, *A Map of Verona* could hardly have been produced in the United States, under our distrust of the shapely and gentle and easy—just in Reed's poems: the poet would have been haggard with self-consciousness before he began. The indifferent state of criticism in England was exactly what Reed needed. He and Lowell exist, in short, at the poles of the visible scene. But they have something in common besides excellence and responsibility. Both are out of the Climate: moving both toward the legendary, Reed with the Greek and Ahab poems, Lowell with the David and Bathsheba poems. I am not sure whether either is Waller, and if so which one, or whether both are Waller, or whether they prepare the way for Waller, or whether they make Waller unnecessary, but the questions seemed to come up with such agreeable urgency that I took my title from the refrain of Empson's "Just a Smack at Auden" (the best parody of the sort I know, unless Reed's "Chard Whitlow" about Eliot is) and hoped for the best.

1948

From the Middle

and Senior Generations

JUSTICE WILL NOT BE EXPECTED, IN A SHORT ARTICLE, TO four of the salient careers of the age in American poetry; but even for a short article a point of view, or points of view, is necessary. One we may elicit from our title. Another will associate itself with the notion of self-reformation. A third might be sought in the contrast between the methods of the two men, Robert Lowell and Theodore Roethke,* whom I take to possess the most powerful and original talents that have emerged during the last fifteen years. The contrast is so deep that one would almost be justified in adopting the terms "Eastern" and "Western" style, without much reference to the fact that Lowell is from Boston and lives there, Roethke from Michigan, living in Seattle. Lowell's work is Latinate, formal, rhetorical, massive, historical, religious, impersonal; Roethke's Teutonic, irregular, colloquial, delicate, botanical, and psychological, irreligious, personal. It is hardly an exaggeration to say that Lowell is a poet of completed states, Roethke a poet of process. Both are witty, savage, and willing to astonish, but the fundamental unlikeness is great. If both are authoritative, the nature of their authorities differs, Lowell's being a traditional authority, Roethke's an experiential one. Lowell is formidable, Roethke endearing. One gets an impression, in their work, of the American spirit advancing on different fronts rather than on different parts of the same front; and I will come back to this.

Lowell, the younger by some nine years, found his main style earlier and held to it longer. After a merely promising beginning, it was not until 1948 that Roethke published a group of poems proving that all previous poets' attention to plants had been casual. Flowers and weeds alike writhed and lived on the page as they never had before. One hesitates even to regard these poems as symbolic, although of course they are. Instead of making a career out of this, the poet deepened botany into biology, took on the full influence of Whitman, made his rhythms jump, and produced the extraordinary

* *Words for the Wind: The Collected Verse of Theodore Roethke,* 1959.

310

sequence of longish poems in *Praise to the End* (1951), which is his largest achievement and one of the fixed objects, I should think, in our poetry. Childhood, money, eating, love, lostness and foundness in natural process, fear, consolation (Roethke is one of the few tender American poets) are the interlocking, joking, dissolving subjects. Since 1951 his jokes have become less sinister and desolate; and although he has written delightful poems, one has a sense of a marking of time in relation to the giant steps earlier. Surprisingly, much of his work has become "literary"; he has submitted gleefully to the influences—mostly disastrous—of Yeats, even Eliot, and others. One does not need the persistence of delicious detail—

> I am my father's son, I am John Donne
> Whenever I see her with nothing on

—to see that his talent, or genius, is still fully alive. But I think few critical readers will feel that his new self-reformation is as yet either at all complete or satisfying. The channel is unclear. One can only express gratitude and wish luck.

Can we regard Roethke and Lowell as members of one poetic generation? Considering the figure of Karl Shapiro, whose age divides theirs and who, as we will see in a moment, certainly ought to be able to be regarded as a member of a generation, it would seem that they can. But I wonder whether the question has meaning in a society where the attention paid to poetry is so very slight. A "generation" in this sense, apart from the private sense of co-working that an artist may have, is a public conception—one that still exists in England and France. But probably the American conception of a poet is of a man dead, or in his eighties (Frost, Sandburg), or a European (*Time*, a fair barometer, reviews European poets with noticeably more enthusiasm than Americans, when it reviews poets at all). No sense of a generation of poets will flow from this conception; one thinks instead of isolated pockets of spiritual activity. Of course Americans do not read anything. Some poll lately suggested that only one college graduate in four had read a book—any book—during the past year; the populace at large, as one would expect, reads a little more, but not much. Poetry is only read *less* than other sorts of writing. "The poet is like one who enters and mounts a platform to give an address as announced. He opens his page, looks around, and finds the hall— *empty*." If this could be written forty years ago in England, what shall we say now of America? It is customary to blame the poets for the situation. But it is hard to feel that Thomas Hardy, or Lowell or Roethke, is not doing his job.

I am putting a case, in terms of the poet's presumable feeling, that will affect his work and so matters to us. It is worth notice, then, that the American poet has come to enjoy almost no immediate audience at a time, exactly, when the notion of a posterity is obscured (and when serious music, largely by dead men, and modern painting have, against expectation, developed very large paying audiences—perhaps rather as spectator sports than as involving much of the participation essential to poetry's effect). Is this matter for discouragement? It is a matter for despair, perhaps, if unduly attended to, or for indifference, in a busy man, but I hope not discouragement. The motives for making poetry have regularly been complex beyond analysis: love of the stuff and of rhythm, the need to invent, a passion for getting things right, the wish to leave one's language in better shape than one found it, a jealousy for the national honour, love for a person or for God, attachment to human possibility, pity, outletting agony or disappointment, exasperation, malice, hatred. Desire for fame and entertaining an audience are only two other motives, forgoable, particularly in the consciousness of a final two, which may be more central than any yet mentioned. Poetry is a terminal activity, taking place out near the end of things, where the poet's soul addresses one other soul only, never mind when. And it aims—never mind *either* communication or expression—at the reformation of the poet, as prayer does. In the grand cases—as in our century, Yeats and Eliot—it enables the poet gradually, again and again, to become almost another man; but something of the sort happens, on a small scale, a freeing, with the creation of every real poem. We may feel sorry for the society, as we do for a man who has never been in love, but hardly for the poet. But let us avoid cant about poetic generations and war poets and other things we care nothing about.

Karl Shapiro is an Easterner who has written for a long time now, with success, in an individual variant of one main period style of the late 1930's and early 1940's. Prosaic, candid, awkwardly careful to be just to the feeling desired, he, more than some poets his superior, evokes constant sympathy. His oddly titled new book, however, *Poems of a Jew* (1959), is not new but a collection of poems from his selected volume, *Poems 1940–1953*, as well as some omitted from it, and a few new ones, gathered with reference to his title—a thing upon which his strange introduction throws, for me, little light. "These poems are not for poets," he begins, ". . . not religious poems . . . they present . . . the states of mind which in my case led to the writing of poems . . . Being a Jew is the consciousness of being a Jew," et cetera. This is not the first time that Shapiro's prose has seemed to me more self-contradictory and obscure than his verse, and I would commend to the reader, instead of his introduction, Isidore Epstein's admirable little Pelican book, *Judaism*. The poems are another matter. Omitting some of Shapiro's tough, vivid early work, this book gives a less satisfactory overall view than the 1953 volume; but there is much pleasure to be had from it, and now and then thematic illumination *is* cast on a familiar piece, such as "Travelogue for Exiles," which I confess I had never thought of as Jewish. The particular poems are regularly better than the general: "The First Time," for instance, is better than "The Synagogue" or "Israel," which should somehow have been better than its last stanza lets it be. Even the "Adam and Eve" suite, as he says himself in a note, is *not* symbolic. This contains his most open, finest work, I think, so far.

> And for the third time, in the third way, Eve:
> "The tree that rises from the middle part
> Of the garden." And almost tenderly, "Thou art
> The garden. *We.*" Then she was overcome,
> And Adam coldly, lest he should succumb
> To pity, standing at the edge of doom,
> Comforted her like one about to leave.

Surely this is remarkable, Dantesque; I have no feeling that his best work is yet written. One different point: the temptation to say beautiful things that may or may not be *true* seems hardly to have been experienced by this poet at all. It is something one would seldom recommend (Wallace Stevens is probably our most distinguished victim since Poe), but in so special and as it were muscle-bound a case . . .

Cummings and Dr Williams are Westerners, of course, versing briskly away in their mid-sixties and mid-seventies to everyone's delight, loaded with merited honors, impenitent, irregular, mannered. Mannerism, curiously, is a greater danger in Western style than it is in Eastern; it sticks out. What Cummings would do without parentheses is not easy to see. He makes use of them in all but seven of his ninety-five new poems,* needs them in most, and some poems could not have been conceived without them: see *19, 20, 23.* They are the more obtrusive because he uses little other pointing—exception made for

s.ti:rst;hiso,nce;ma:n

which says "stirs this once man." What can the obsession with parentheses mean to Cummings? Simultaneity, no doubt, and inextricable

* *95 Poems,* 1959.

relation, and offhandedness, informality. But I wonder whether they do not constitute also a sort of instinctive defense invoked by his talent against one of its worst faults, a hollow rhetoric of which 77 is the most embarrassing example in his new book. Along with his jerky, maze-like little poems has always gone an organlike, Keatsian propensity, which has given him (and us) some of his stunning successes, but which he is quite right to distrust, for when the little poems fail they are only trivial, but when the others fail they are false.

Cummings is extremely sentimental, a fact long partly disguised by his satirical and tough-guy attitudes and still partly disguised by some of his language, but more patent throughout this book than ever before. I am not objecting, just reporting. The eternizing of which he has always been very fond—it is not done in Shakespeare's manner but it is eternizing all the same—is more frequently in evidence, too. Otherwise the new book is as usual: love poems galore, moons, flowers, dreams, thrushes, miracles, vignettes on drunks and floozies, harridans, nice old ladies, businessmen, disquisitions on "why" and time. It is littered with the trademarks of his fine poems of the past, "little" and its allies, "un-," "almost," *x* "by" *y*. It should not be read in large chunks. The most effective poems, I think, are *13, 16, 76,* and *95,* but there are amusing and touching passages in many others. Nothing, unless I am wrong, is up to the standard of his finest work, and the very loud poems are mostly bad. What is truly amazing is the scarcity of allusion to old age: *57, 61,* a few others. It is a pity that one very dark poem, *30,* is not better. Cummings's high spirits are partly an act, naturally, one in which he has been engaged for so long that he must in some degree be taken in by it himself, and so some of his deepest feelings scarcely emerge.

Paterson, Book Five (1959) is a kind of ecstatic addendum to William Carlos Williams's long poem. I wish everyone would read it. The Unicorn (in tapestries, which the old man, "I, Paterson, the King-self," goes to see—question of bus schedules for getting to the Cloisters) and the virgin, other women, satyrs, painters, flowers, letters from old friends (verbatim), the process of age, are the themes and materials—

> (I have told you, this
> is a fiction, pay attention).

Many rhythms remind one of Pound's in the later cantos; well, who has a better right to them than Dr Williams? The gaiety of this old man is adorable. Any reader will find passages for himself. My own favourite is two pages at the beginning of Section 2 (after a translation from Sappho and a page of economic junk that must be Pound) about a woman seen in the street whom he *certainly wishes he had spoken to!*

1959

Despondency and Madness:
On Lowell's "Skunk Hour"

A TITLE OPAQUE AND VIOLENT. SINCE IT THROWS, AT ONCE, little or no light on the poem, we inquire whether the poem throws any light on it, and are underway. Our occasion is the approach of a crisis of mental disorder for the "I" of the poem—presumably one leading to the hospitalization, or hospitalizations, spoken of elsewhere in the volume, *Life Studies*, where it stands last. Lowell's recent poems, many of them, are as personal, autobiographical, as his earlier poems were hieratic; and it is certain that we are not dealing here purely with invention and symbol. One thing critics not themselves writers of poetry occasionally forget is that poetry is composed by actual human beings, and tracts of it are very closely about them. When Shakespeare wrote, "Two loves I have," reader, he was *not kidding*.

Back to the title then. The Hour of the Skunk, I suppose, would be one of the most unprepossessing times of the day, far less livable than the Hour of the Bear, say, or the (Chinese) Month of the Dog. Noon is held a luckless time for Sikhs. Up and down India, when anything goes wrong for a Sikh near midday, all nearby Hindus and Moslems have a ball. Skunk hour: the poet's Sikh noon. The skunk is a small, attractive, black-and-white creature, affectionate and loyal when tamed, I believe, but it suffers (or rather it does *not* suffer, being an animal) from a bad reputation, owing to its capacity for stinking. (The poet, in the identification, knows; and suffers.) Cornered, it makes the cornerer wish he hadn't. Painful, in symbolization, is the fact that its sting, so to speak, can be drawn, its power of defending itself removed—as the poet can be made helpless by what is part of his strength: his strangeness, mental and emotional; the helplessness of a man afraid of going mad is the analogue. The skunk is an outcast; this is the basis of the metaphor, and how a mental patient feels. I hate to call the associations complex, but they are, and with a poet so daring or offhand that he once arranged a masterly elegy around his literal translation of the gambling expression *"Rien ne va plus,"* we must take it. The skunk, its little weakness or weapon apart, is charming; cheer-up. But nobody likes: paranoia. It is not what it seems: the reality belies the benign appearance—as with the statesman Forrestal, who supervises American industry's brawl-for-contracts with scrupulous honour and kills himself, or the poet, brilliant, famous, appearing, who goes off his rocker. We like, in mature professional life, to know who we are; which may be on the point of becoming out of the question for the "I" of the poem.

If the topic seems to anyone theatrical, may I mention suicides: two of the three or four most important early Soviet poets, Essenin and Mayakovsky; while Hart Crane and Vachel Lindsay (and for that matter, Sara Teasdale—writing really well toward the end), who destroyed themselves here, were not our worst poets. Poets in odd ages have killed themselves or gone mad, Poe and Dylan Thomas as clearly as Swift, Chatterton, Smart, Beddoes, and many have written about it from inside and outside, from Cowper's posthumous "The Castaway" to Miss Bishop's wonderful "Visits to St. Elizabeth's" and Rilke's *"Das Lied des Idioten."* It is better not to feel so strongly:

> We poets in our youth begin in gladness,
> But thereof comes in the end despondency and madness.

Wordsworth once said that if he had written what he most deeply felt no reader could have borne it, Coleridge that he gave up original poetical composition (but the fine, bleak "Work without Hope" is late) because he was unable to bear it. One poem does not edge into the terror, but starts there and stays there: Jon Silkin's "Death of a Son." This you will find in the Hall-Simpson paperback anthology of recent verse, and it is as brave, and harrowing, as one might think a piece could be. But Lowell's subject is different from all these others'.

His target is the dreadful aura—in epileptic analogy—the coming-on, handled by Hölderlin in *"Hälfte des Lebens,"* which may be the deepest European poem on this unusual theme. You feel you're going too fast, spinning out of control; or too slow; there appears a rift, which will widen. You feel *too* good, or too bad. Difficult subject. Perhaps there is a quarter inch of mordant humour, by the way, very like this author, in the title: dogs have their day, even the skunk has an hour, characteristic. An inverted celebration. Take the poet's arrangements in three parts, and one critical problem will be to determine how they culminate in the hallucinatory intensity of the seventh stanza. We have the opening stanzas (*praeparatio*), then statement—understatement ("My mind's not right"), then the skunks. One of the poem's desperate points is their *cyclical* approach, each night; as episodes of mental illness are feared to recur. The skunks, too, can we wonder, replace him (they will survive as he goes or is taken off) as well as figure him. But we're getting too far ahead.

Very good poem, incidentally, and gets better, explored. Perhaps one of his absolutely best; early to say. Maybe the Faustus allusion is overdrawn. Who cares to hand grades to a writer who could first *make* the Ovid stanza in "Beyond the Alps" (I believe it appeared in the *Kenyon* version) and then delete it? The reader may not have come on this, so I put it in evidence.

> I thought of Ovid, for in Caesar's eyes,
> That Tomcat had the number of the Beast.
> Where the young Turks are facing the red east
> And the twice-stormed Crimean spit, he cries:
> "Rome asked for poets. At her beck and call,
> Came Lucan, Tacitus and Juvenal,
> The black republicans who tore the teats
> And bowels of the mother wolf to bits.
> Beneath a psychopath's divining rod,
> Deserts interred the Caesar-salvaged bog.
> Imperial Tiber, O my yellow Dog,
> Black earth by the Black Roman Sea, I lie
> With the boy-crazy daughter of the God,
> Il duce Augusto. I shall never die."

Lowell once told the present writer that the stanza took him a hundred hours; it is worth every second of the time, and may be read, despite its author, for as long as things not formular are read.

I hear the first four stanzas of "Skunk Hour" as a unit. Grandiose figures—the senile aristocrat, the summer millionaire—from the past, outworn, gone, or not gone: the theme of the first stanza is survival—but survival how?—doting; anti-gainfully employed (second stanza, and the "eyesores" "let fall" are the first prefigurings of the paranoid aspect of the skunk symbol), living in the past. Relevance?—for re-reading (all poems are built of course for rereading, but this more than most): the poet is afraid of outliving himself, going away, like Hölderlin, Swift, Maupassant. Destructive second stanza, but queerly abstract and arbitrary, anachronistic; as for "privacy," in the modern world (so the underground thought goes) unattainable, hospital life is unspeakably public—one is available without will to doctors, nurses, even (usually) other patients. The sheep have things easy, so to speak, and the radio "bleats" to the untense satisfied lovers in Stanza VI; no human responsibilities, any more than the skunks are to have.

Despondency and Madness: On Lowell's "Skunk Hour"

The poem makes use of the animal-morality tradition without quite belonging to it. "Spartan" I reserve. "Hermit" and "winter" make nearly standard associations with madness.

Note that we have first a true aristocrat, irresponsible ("heiress" —mental illness can be inherited), then a pure money figure; an ominous declension. (L. L. Bean: I haven't seen a catalogue for years, some boys at my school in Connecticut had them; they were beyond Sears Roebuck and even Alex Taylor for fascination—compare Abercrombie & Fitch, if they put out a catalogue.) Somebody rooted, but off; somebody rootless, gone. Blue Hill I take to be Blue Hill, Maine, where I never saw foxes but don't doubt that they flourish. This is the poem's hard line. "A red fox stain covers Blue Hill." Even the syntax is ambiguous—the stain may be red, or it may merely be that red foxes stain with their numbers (a plague to farmers) Blue Hill. Is the sportsman accused of having shot foxes?—but this seems sentimental and improbable; or is the fox population said to have increased since he quit shooting foxes?—but this seems even more implausible. I can't feel the implied narrative is clear. Perhaps there is no implied narrative (but shouldn't there be, tied to the millionaire as the line is?) and we have a straight dream item: for the meaning is certainly to be found in the association backward to "Spartan." This is the boy who stole a fox which, hugged to him in public, ate his vitals, the stain spreading, until stoical he fell dead; clearly a figure for the poet, still unheard of, with his growing hidden wound. At this point "Blue Hill" becomes extra-geographical and macabre: the dying Spartan boy turning blue, the tall poet sad, "blue" (the use of a popular song presently makes this likely).

Now in a succinct modulation from blood (and courage) to pale "orange," appropriate to the "fairy," comes the decorator, to fix things up inside (as psychiatrists will try to do for the poet); miserable, though, things not going well. "Marry" is callous and fraudulent, a last resort. The three figures, on their descending scale, are fruitless. The useful put just to decoration (fishnet), deprived of function, looks on to the poet's fear. One will get, in the poem, no sense of his *doing* anything, only waiting, driving about, skunk-watching, sleepless. (In the opposite conversion, just before, the sporting being put to work, the yawl, I hear as the dominant affect: longing.) This is a late-summer poem, idle, apprehensive.

It's half over. Outworn, gone, queer; analogous figures, tangential all—the first *having been* central, the second having mattered to local revenue. The four stanzas are unemphatic, muted. But their quiet, insistent mustering of the *facts* of an extant world opens toward the danger of its being swept away, into delirium. I have seldom seen stanzas (and by this poet, composer of the Ovid stanza) so un-self-evident. He's holding his fire, let's say. Down-rhyme, casual, unlike earlier Lowell, suggests Miss Bishop's practice; to whom the poem is dedicated; though the heavy, fierce rhyming of "The Quaker Graveyard" will be admitted in the final stanzas. Money-wellness, however misused (compare Eliot's ruined millionaire, Adam, in the *Quartets*—the auctioning off of the boat does not suggest that this one is doing very well), seems important all through the three figures and winds up in a "rich" air, freedom, the poet's to lose. The "fairy," poor, is already sick with perversion.

Since, on the entrance of "I" in Stanza V, he climbs a sort of Golgotha (Place of the Skull), I will observe that there is more Christian detail in the poem than might have been expected. There's the bishop (I see no assimilation here to Chekhov's overwhelming story, which, however, I haven't read for years), the Marlovian hell of Stanza VI ("where we are in hell," as Mephastophilus says at line 554 of Tucker Brooke's criminal edition, and compare other texts in that corrupt play, which even Greg was unsatisfactory with), the Trinitarian Church, and even the interior decorator goes in for suspicious properties: a fishnet (Peter, but Peter was married), cobbling (but Christ is said—on the Synoptic evidence, see Guignebert's *Jesus*, p. 106—to have been a carpenter). The detail is not, I think, systematic, and serves the purpose of a kind of hopeless casting about for aid—unavailable, as in Hemingway's "A Clean, Well-Lighted Place," in *The Trial*, in *Waiting for Godot*, you name it. I should say that Lowell works rather in parable form than in forms of allegory. There is no point-to-point correspondence, the details are free. The (hoped for?) rescue figures are simply sinister and pathetic, the senile old lady who lets houses decay, the unhappy homosexual who would like to fix up their interiors. Who knows where the bishop is?

In Stanza V there is much more than: furtive love, furtive madness. But both come out loud and open in Stanza VI, and the loss of the person, in its last line, leads to the oneiric vision of the skunks.

Their ceremonial line, for (their kind of) nourishment, may belong with the religious traces. They have taken over the world; the poet has a final instant of freedom at the start of the last stanza. "Moonstruck" and "ostrich" (I am lunatic, hidden—hidden?) then take over. We began with one mother (of a bishop) and wind up with another (of a column of little skunks) in a sort of greedy parody of the Eucharist; the ultimate help. Some of Lowell's early poems were savagely Marian. I would not call this poem at all friendly to Christianity, which appears to have failed the shelving (and to be shelved) man. We feed instead on garbage. The "cream" is sour. The last line equals: "I will, I *do* 'scare.'" It is man's right, foreseeing, to be frightened. But the stubbornness of the mother skunk, like that (merely in association) of the Spartan boy, make up a small counterpoise to the poem's terror.

We attend, so, to a sense of having been failed by the biological and mental and emotional (and religious) probabilities: not all, or most, have to feel this way; many can believe. There is a staving-off, with dramatization, of self-pity; an implied (at the end) confession of fear. I have a feeling that the poem may look better fifty years from now, even better. Snatching at war terms irritates one, as of writers; Baudelaire hated "avant-garde"; but it takes moral courage, at least, to write in this poem's direction.

I must pause, briefly, to admire its administration of time. In general for it time narrows: a vista of decades, "The season's ill," *one* night, and so down to the skunk hour. But I notice two substantial exceptions to the method. The second stanza opens a longer vista still than the first, with "century." And the "Hour" is *nightly*, expanding again into a dreaded recurrence. Most real poets work in this way, but Lowell decidedly rather more than most. I will now admit that I cannot like "my ill-spirit sob in each blood cell"; the expression is just what it should not be, rhetorical, exterior, especially with "hear."

For convenience in exposition, with a poem so personal, I have been pretending that "I" is the poet, but of course the speaker can never be the actual writer, who is a person with an address, a Social Security number, debts, tastes, memories, expectations. Shakespeare says, "Two loves I have": he does not say *only* two loves, and indeed he must have loved also his children, various friends, presumably his wife, his parents. The necessity for the artist of selection opens inevitably an abyss between his person and his persona. I only said that much poetry is "very closely about" the person. The persona looks across at the person and then sets about its own work. Lowell's careful avoidance, in "Skunk Hour," of the grand style he was still wielding in the Ovid stanza, for instance, makes the distinction material here. This mysterious "I" that poets deploy can certainly never be defined, but a good recent stab at characterization was Ransom's in an earlier one of these symposia, about Roethke: "The true self or soul or mind of the highly compounded authorial 'I' . . ." I would call it virtually certain that Lowell had in mind and at heart during this poem not only his own difficulties, whatever they may be or have been, but the personal disorders to which other poets of his age and place have been furiously subject.

Another question raised with acuteness by the poem is how far it is fair to take associations. A characteristic vice of modern criticism is taking them too far. One of Randall Jarrell's remarks sticks in my head: "As people ought to know, very complicated organizations are excessively rare in poetry." I am in ringing agreement. Hurrah. But whether the dictum applies to Lowell's poems, or to an onslaught against the Old Testament and the New Testament like Thomas's "A Refusal to Mourn . . ." seems to me very doubtful; as I think Jarrell concedes in his handsome, better than handsome, studies of Lowell. No rules will help, naturally, but can we seek guideposts? Suppose we try two: (1) When there is something imperfectly narrative, imperfectly dramatic, which obstinately *needs accounting for*, we allow ourselves, as readers, more liberty of interpreting than otherwise; (2) Where accident and coincidence seem implausible, we stick by the textual and psychological (even depth-psychological) probabilities. Both signs point to a connection of "Spartan" and "fox stain," though fifteen lines separate them. I have several times gone too far here, deliberately, in order to repudiate my (non-) findings. But I think we must allow, with some poets, for broad and complex areas of suggestion; and I would propose a third guidepost: (3) Whatever relates, however uncertainly, to the *ruling theme* of the poem deserves the reader's intimate attention. Thus, in the fifth stanza, the fact of its being a *dark* night may suggest in our tradition spiritual despair (St. John of the Cross), and the desolate "hull to hull" may look back to the "Nautilus," adventurous, submerged; or they may not. I have made no attempt to exhaust the poem. If we were a little longer civilized here, the poet would plainly be declared, in Japanese fashion, a National Cultural Asset, and exempted from coarse analyses of his subtle, strong, terrible poems.

1962

One Answer to a Question:

Changes

THIS SLIGHT EXPLORATION OF SOME OF MY OPINIONS ABOUT my work as a poet, you may wish to bear in mind, is the statement of a man nearing fifty, and I am less impressed than I used to be by the universal notion of a continuity of individual personality—which will bring me in a moment to the first and most interesting of the four questions proposed by Howard Nemerov. It is a queer assignment. I've complied with similar requests before, but never without fundamental misgivings. For one thing, one forgets, one even deliberately forgets in order to get on with new work, and so may seriously misrepresent the artist-that-was twenty years ago. For another, there are trade secrets. At the same time that one works partly to open fresh avenues for other writers (though one would not dream of admitting it), one has secrets, like any craftsman, and I figure that anyone who deserves to know them deserves to find them out for himself. So I do not plan to give anything away.

The question was this: "Do you see your work as having essentially changed in character or style since you began?"

I would reply: *of course*. I began work in verse-making as a burning, trivial disciple of the great Irish poet William Butler Yeats, and I hope I have moved off from there. One is obsessed at different times by different things and by different ways of putting them. Naturally there are catches in the question. What does "essentially" mean? What is "character"? What is "style"? Still the question, if semantically murky, is practically clear, and I respond to it with some personal history.

When I said just now "work in verse-making," I was leaving out some months of protoapprenticeship during which I was so inexperienced that I didn't imitate *anybody*. Then came Yeats, whom I didn't so much wish to resemble as to *be*, and for several fumbling years I wrote in what it is convenient to call "period style," the Anglo-American style of the 1930's, with no voice of my own, learning

323

chiefly from middle and later Yeats and from the brilliant young Englishman W. H. Auden. Yeats somehow saved me from the then-crushing influences of Ezra Pound and T. S. Eliot—luckily, as I now feel—but he could not teach me to sound like myself (whatever that was) or tell me what to write about. The first poem, perhaps, where those dramatic-to-me things happened was (is) called "Winter Land-scape." It is mounted in five five-line stanzas, unrhymed, all one sentence. (I admit there is a colon near the middle of the third stanza.)

Winter Landscape

The three men coming down the winter hill
In brown, with tall poles and a pack of hounds
At heel, through the arrangement of the trees
Past the five figures at the burning straw,
Returning cold and silent to their town,

Returning to the drifted snow, the rink
Lively with children, to the older men,
The long companions they can never reach,
The blue light, men with ladders, by the church
The sledge and shadow in the twilit street,

Are not aware that in the sandy time
To come, the evil waste of history
Outstretched, they will be seen upon the brow
Of that same hill: when all their company
Will have been irrecoverably lost,

These men, this particular three in brown
Witnessed by birds will keep the scene and say
By their configuration with the trees,
The small bridge, the red houses and the fire,
What place, what time, what morning occasion

Sent them into the wood, a pack of hounds
At heel and the tall poles upon their shoulders,
Thence to return as now we see them and
Ankle-deep in snow down the winter hill
Descend, while three birds watch and the fourth flies.

This does not sound, I would say, like either Yeats or Auden—or Rilke or Lorca or Corbière or any of my other passions of those remote days. It derives its individuality, if I am right, from a peculiar steadiness of sombre tone (of which I'll say more presently) and from its peculiar relation to its materials—drawn, of course, from Brueghel's famous painting. The poem is sometimes quoted and readers seem to take it for either a verbal *equivalent* to the picture or (like Auden's fine Brueghel poem, "Musée des Beaux Arts," written later) an *interpretation* of it. Both views I would call wrong, though the first is that adopted in a comparative essay on picture and poem recently published by two aestheticians at the University of Notre Dame.* After a competent study, buttressed by the relevant scholarship, of Brueghel's painting, they proceed to the poem—where, there being no relevant scholarship, they seem less at ease—and so to the relation between the two. Some of the points made are real, I believe. To quote the two with which they begin: they say the poem's "elaborative sequence urged on by the sweeping carry-over lines"— they mean run-on—"within the stanza or between stanzas—preserves the same order of presentation and the same grouping of elements as the Brueghel composition . . . Purposively restricting himself to a diction as sober, direct, and matter-of-fact as the painter's treatment of scene and objects, Berryman so composes with it that he achieves an insistent and animated pattern of strong poetic effect." And so on, to the end of the article, where the "disclosed affinities" of the two works are found testifying to the "secret friendship" of the arts. Nowhere is anything said as to what the poem is *about*, nor is any interest expressed in that little topic; the relation between the works is left obscure except for the investigation of affinities. An investigation of *differences* would have taken them further.

Very briefly, the poem's extreme sobriety would seem to represent a reaction, first, against Yeats's gorgeous and seductive rhetoric and, second, against the hysterical political atmosphere of the period. It dates from 1938–9 and was written in New York following two years' residence in England, during recurrent crises, with extended visits to France and Germany, especially one of the Nazi strongholds, Heidelberg. So far as I can make out, it is a war poem, of an unusual negative kind. The common title of the picture is *Hunters in the Snow* and of course the poet knows this. But he pretends not to, and calls their spears (twice) "poles," the resultant governing emotion being a certain stubborn incredulity—as the hunters are loosed while the peaceful nations plunge again into war. This is not the subject of Brueghel's painting at all, and the interpretation of *the event of the poem* proves that the picture has merely provided necessary material

* If anyone is *truly* curious, this can be found in the University of Texas *Studies in Literature and Language*, v. 3 (Autumn 1963).

from a tranquil world for what is necessary to be said—but which the poet refuses to say—about a violent world.

You may wonder whether I dislike aestheticians. I do.

Very different from the discovery made in "Winter Landscape," if the foregoing account seems acceptable—namely, that a poem's force may be pivoted on a missing or misrepresented element in an agreed-on or imposed design—was a discovery made in another short piece several years later. (It also is twenty-five lines long, unrhymed, but, I think, much more fluid.)

The Ball Poem

What is the boy now, who has lost his ball,
What, what is he to do? I saw it go
Merrily bouncing, down the street, and then
Merrily over—there it is in the water!
No use to say "O there are other balls":
An ultimate shaking grief fixes the boy
As he stands rigid, trembling, staring down
All his young days into the harbour where
His ball went. I would not intrude on him,
A dime, another ball, is worthless. Now
He senses first responsibility
In a world of possessions. People will take balls,
Balls will be lost always, little boy,
And no one buys a ball back. Money is external,
He is learning, well behind his desperate eyes,
The epistemology of loss, how to stand up
Knowing what every man must one day know
And most know many days, how to stand up.
And gradually light returns to the street,
A whistle blows, the ball is out of sight,
Soon part of me will explore the deep and dark
Floor of the harbour . . . I am everywhere,
I suffer and move, my mind and my heart move
With all that move me, under the water
Or whistling, I am not a little boy.

The discovery here was that a commitment of identity can be "reserved," so to speak, with an ambiguous pronoun. The poet himself is both left out and put in; the boy does and does not become him and we are confronted with a process which is at once a process of life and a process of art. A pronoun may seem a small matter, but she matters, he matters, it matters, they matter. Without this invention (if it is one—Rimbaud's "*Je est un autre*" may have pointed my way, I have no idea now) I could not have written either of the two long poems that constitute the bulk of my work so far. If I were making a grandiose claim, I might pretend to know more about the administration of pronouns than any other living poet writing in English or American. You will have noticed that I have said nothing about my agonies and joys, my wives and children, my liking for my country, my dislike of Communist theory and practice, etc., but have been technical. Art is technical, too.

So far I have been speaking of short poems and youth, when enthusiasms and hostilities, of an artistic kind, I mean, play a bigger role in inspiration than perhaps they do later. I do not know, because I see neither enthusiasm nor hostility behind "The Ball Poem." But I was nearly thirty then. I do know that much later, when I finally woke up to the fact that I was involved in a long poem, one of my first thoughts was: Narrative! let's have narrative, and at least one dominant personality, and no fragmentation! In short, let us have something spectacularly NOT *The Waste Land*, the best long poem of the age. So maybe hostility keeps on going.

What had happened was that I had made up the first stanza of a poem to be called *Homage to Mistress Bradstreet* and the first three lines of the second stanza, and there, for almost five years, I stuck. Here is the passage:

> The Governor your husband lived so long
> moved you not, restless, waiting for him? Still,
> you were a patient woman—
> I seem to see you pause here still:
> Sylvester, Quarles, in moments odd you pored
> before a fire at, bright eyes on the Lord,
> all the children still.
> "Simon . . .": Simon will listen while you read a Song.
>
> Outside the New World winters in grand dark
> white air lashing high thro' the virgin stands
> foxes down foxholes sigh . . .

The dramatic mode, hovering behind the two meditative lyrics I've quoted, has here surely come more into the open; and also here I had overcome at once two of the paralyzing obstacles that haunt the path of the very few modern poets in English who have attempted ambitious sizable poems: what form to use and what to write about. The eight-line stanza I invented here after a lifetime's study, especially of Yeats's, and in particular the one he adopted from Abraham Cowley for his elegy "In Memory of Major Robert Gregory." Mine breaks not at midpoint but after the short third line; a strange four-beat line leads to the balancing heroic couplet of lines five and six, after which seven is again short (three feet, like line three) and then the stanza widens into an alexandrine rhyming all the way back to one. I wanted something at once flexible and grave, intense and quiet, able to deal with matter both high and low.

As for the subject: the question most put to me about the poem is why I chose to write about this boring high-minded Puritan woman who may have been our first American poet but is not a good one. I agree, naturally, and say that I did not choose her—somehow she chose me—one point of connection, at any rate, being the almost insuperable difficulty of writing high verse at all in a land that cared and cares so little for it. I was concerned with her though, almost from the beginning, as a woman, not much as a poetess. For four-and-a-half years, then, I accumulated materials and sketched, fleshing out the target or vehicle, still under the impression that seven or eight stanzas would see it done. There are fifty-seven. My stupidity is traceable partly to an astuteness that made me as afraid as the next man of the ferocious commitment involved in a long poem and partly to the fact that although I had my form and subject, I did not have my theme yet. This emerged, and under the triple impetus of events I won't identify, I got the poem off the ground and nearly died following it. The theme is hard to put shortly, but I will try.

An American historian somewhere observes that all colonial settlements are intensely conservative, *except* in the initial break-off point (whether religious, political, legal, or whatever). Trying to do justice to both parts of this obvious truth—which I came upon only after the poem was finished—I concentrated upon the second and the poem laid itself out in a series of rebellions. I had her rebel first against the new environment and above all against her barrenness (which in fact lasted for years), then against her marriage (which in fact seems to have been brilliantly happy), and finally against her continuing life of illness, loss, and age. These are the three large sections of the poem; they are preceded and followed by an exordium and coda, of four stanzas each, spoken by the "I" of the twentieth-century poet, which modulates into her voice, who speaks most of the poem. Such is the plan. Each rebellion, of course, is succeeded by submission, although even in the moment of the poem's supreme triumph—the presentment, too long to quote now, of the birth of her first child—rebellion survives. I don't remember how conceptual all this was with me during the months of composition, but I think it was to a high degree. Turbulence may take you far toward a good short poem, but it is only the first quarter mile in a long one.

Not that the going is ever exactly tranquil. I recall three occasions of special heat, the first being when I realized that the middle of the poem was going to have to be in *dialogue*, a dialogue between the seventeenth-century woman and the twentieth-century poet—a sort of extended witch-seductress and demon-lover bit. The second was a tactical solution of a problem arising out of this: how to make them in some measure physically present to each other. I gave myself one line, when she says:

A fading world I dust, with fingers new.

Later on it appears that they kiss, once, and then she says—as women will—"Talk to me." So he does, in an only half-subdued aria-stanza:

It is Spring's New England. Pussy willows wedge
up in the wet. Milky crestings, fringed
yellow, in heaven, eyed
by the melting hand-in-hand, or mere
desirers, single, heavy-footed, rapt,
make surge poor human hearts. Venus is trapt—
the hefty pike shifts, sheer—
in Orion blazing. Warblings, odours, nudge to an edge—

Noting and overconsidering such matters, few critics have seen that it *is* a historical poem, and it was with interest that I found Robert Lowell pronouncing it lately, in *The New York Review*, "the most resourceful historical poem in our literature." The third pleasant moment I remember is when one night, hugging myself, I decided that her fierce dogmatic old father was going to die blaspheming, in delirium.

The Bradstreet poem was printed in 1953 (as a book here in America in 1956 and in London in 1959) and a year or so later, having again taken leave of my wits, or collected them, I began a second long poem. The first installment, called 77 *Dream Songs* (recently published in New York) concerns the turbulence of the

modern world, and memory, and wants. Its form comprises eighteen-
line sections, three six-line stanzas, each normally (for feet) 5-5-3-5-5-
3, variously rhymed and not but mostly rhymed with great strictness.
The subject is a character named Henry, who also has a Friend who
calls him "Mr. Bones." Here is the first section, or Song, where the
"I," perhaps of the poet, disappears into Henry's first and third persons (he talks to himself in the second person, too, about himself).

Huffy Henry hid the day,
unappeasable Henry sulked.
I see his point,—a trying to put things over
It was the thought that they thought
they could do it made Henry wicked & away.
But he should have come out and talked.

All the world like a woolen lover
once did seem on Henry's side.
Then came a departure.
Thereafter nothing fell out as it might or ought.
I don't see how Henry, pried
open for all the world to see, survived.

What he has now to say is a long
wonder the world can bear & be.
Once in a sycamore I was glad
all at the top, and I sang.
Hard on the land wears the strong sea
and empty grows every bed.

This is Number One of Book I (the first volume consists of the
first three books), and editors and critics for years have been characterizing them as poems, but I do not quite see them as that; I see them
as parts—admittedly more independent than parts usually are. Once
one has succeeded in any degree with a long poem (votes have been
cast in favour of, as well as against, *Homage to Mistress Bradstreet*),
dread and fascination fight it out to exclude, on the whole, short
poems thereafter, or so I have found it. I won't try to explain what I
mean by a long poem, but let us suppose (1) a high and prolonged
riskiness, (2) the construction of a world rather than the reliance
upon one already existent which is available to a small poem, (3)
problems of decorum most poets happily do not have to face. I cannot discuss "decorum" here either, but here is a case:

There sat down, once, a thing on Henry's heart
so heavy, if he had a hundred years
& more, & weeping, sleepless, in all them time
Henry could not make good.
Starts again always in Henry's ears
the little cough somewhere, an odour, a chime.

And there is another thing he has in mind
like a grave Sienese face a thousand years
would fail to blur the still profiled reproach of. Ghastly,
with open eyes, he attends, blind.
All the bells say: too late. This is not for tears;
thinking.

But never did Henry, as he thought he did,
end anyone and hacks her body up
and hide the pieces, where they may be found.
He knows: he went over everyone, & nobody's missing.
Often he reckons, in the dawn, them up.
Nobody is ever missing.

Whether the diction of that is consistent with blackface talk, hell-spinning puns, coarse jokes, whether the end of it is funny or frightening, or both, I put up to the listener. Neither of the American poets who as reviewers have quoted it admiringly has committed himself; so I won't.

1965

V

Thursday Out

I HAVE LEFT AN ORDER AT THE DESK FOR A CAR AT SIX, AND told the bearer to call me, with coffee, ten minutes earlier, but not trusting him I am up at a quarter of and thinking of washing. I am only thinking of washing because there issues no water, neither from the left tap nor the right, nor from either of the shower taps. After buzzing for the bearer I unbar the door to put my head out into the arcade and call him, without hope. He does not come. I dress, and pack. In a darkening mood I go out to the lobby to see about my car. There is no car, and nobody in the lobby. Shouts bring a bearded sweeper, who has no English and calls here and there about the offices, softly, in vain. For no reason I return to my room, where the bearer has turned up with tea, and we have an unsatisfactory interchange about taxis. There is no time for the tea and I forget about the water. The barber appears, eager to shave me. The sun is to rise at quarter past six.

I move rapidly out of my court, leaving the bearer gesticulating and the barber stoical, into the drive, which is jammed with cars without drivers. It is a fine day, already bright, and they were right at the desk last night about the sun. The only human beings in sight are a few pedestrians in the road, a man in a tonga, two passing in pedicabs. Again nobody is in the lobby and I can start only the alarmed sweeper, which does not please but does not surprise me, for this is almost the only hotel in India I have found for myself. It is true the lights in my room did not work when I arrived, though there was water, and the air conditioning was merely a blower, and breakfast was an evil farce shared with unusually large lizards and roaches, and the bearer could never be found, but I thought, For twenty-four hours what does it matter? Worried, with my traveling clock in my pocket (my watch many cities ago ceased running), I emerge into the road and get a pedicab, who turns at once in the direction opposite to all three of my earlier trips out to the Taj.

We have a kind of conversation about this, as he plunges north into the Old Quarter. I prevail upon him to seek advice, and we do so, of a distinguished-looking man, naked except a loincloth, standing calmly in his raised shop front toweling himself. His English is good and I am wrong: this is *also* the way. Soon we bear off right, come out into the deep-green, mildly rolling country, with little ruins that I know, and after twenty longish minutes we are here. Telling the boy to wait, I hurry along the enclosure and turn left toward the gigantic Gateway. The sun is full up, its light level on the great tomb, and my luck is better than it was yesterday, except for the moon.

I walk down the steps and follow as usual the broader promenade to the right of the watercourse with its narrow walks, watching the building. I skirt the platform midway the watercourse, and sit down on the bench I like best. This is in the far northwestern corner of the second court of the garden, or one court away, and off on the right, from the vast plaza up from which, on its colossal platform, the Taj rises. The view straight on is stagy and exhaustible; here is one reason photographs produce little sense of the monument. And a large scaffolding, as maniacal in appearance as other Indian scaffoldings, disfigures at present the southeast corner, which is least seen from where I sit. Many years in the world, besides, or partly in it, have taught me I see things better from the right; to be on the left ends by making me feel wall-eyed. I sit here for a while. The light brightens but does not deepen, and the building less continuously changes than it did yesterday or last night. I sit here.

The central dome, two thirds of a sphere, with its spire, withdraws, from this angle, is less flagrant and crushing among the lesser domes, and does not sit flatly on the immense central bay with its Saracenic arch, but is removed. Its relation to the towering minarets at the corners of the platform—so removed, so intimate—is clearer, too, from here than from elsewhere.

I am perfectly happy. Sways the great work and steadies, flash from the high corner nearest me its gems, in the wide washed monsoon light of the risen sun.

Presently I make my way into the western plaza, under the overpowering marble mass, four or five times my height, of this side of the platform. People are waking, looking out immobile over the broad river, talking. The environs of the Taj are a sort of hotel in this weather, lightless but well patrolled, quiet. The watercourse platform, marble, with its benches and steps, this plaza, and the Taj platform itself, seem to be the places, not the gardens; a group of twenty-five or thirty—men, of course—in keen, low conversation, smoking, thronged the northern steps last night when I wandered past at ten, late for India, waiting for the moon. Now as I come around to the front, to have the loose cloth slippers bound on my offending shoes, men are washing themselves busily in the six inches of scummed water. I mount by the inside stair to the platform, cross, and enter directly where the screen stands solid under the huge dome.

The light here is not strong, even now, though there is more of it than there was at noon. This is the most solemn place I have seen. The pattern thrown from the man-high screen on the tombs—hers dead center, his larger, close by it, left—lies light, not easy, like flowers, filtered through the high outer screens into and through this three-inch solid marble eight-sided massive screen encompassing the tombs. Each quiet shattering panel is six feet by ten in one piece, and dustless—no one has been able to tell me why. Acquaintance here begins with one's fingers, palm, upon the not believable, cool, not quite smooth, nervous, vigorous surviving inventions that create these lucid openings. From without, the building wants thought; in the chamber below, emotion; here, a gravity of sensual experience neither emotion nor thought. The tombs blaze, austere. Large, his larger, higher by a little, ascending through their terraced rectangles to the crowning casket shapes that would hold, each, one of the bodies, they bulk to me in brilliant gloom, their black and reddish floral inlays in the rigid gray-white marble alive as not before. Half a small cylinder, recumbent, super-crowns his. The only mysteries here are the force of the commissioned imagining—a Venetian brain; the decades' effort of faultless carving; the enigmatic light falling over the symbols of their deaths. She had thirteen children and one more of whom she died. She had a long wait for power, this Persian woman. He caused her husband to be murdered, but then, after she was brought to Delhi, he would not see her and made her a very poor allowance. She embroidered and painted on silk, selling things in the harem. She became famous. There is a scene when, hearing of her at last, he visits her apartments, to find her simply attired among her gorgeous attendants. She was extremely beautiful. Some dialogue reaches us. "Why this difference between the Sun of Women and her slaves?" "Those born to servitude must dress as it shall please those whom they serve; these are my servants, and I lighten the burden of bondage by every indulgence in my power, but I, who am your slave, O Emperor of the world, must dress according to your pleasure and not my own." Thereafter he lived agreeably and passionately under her thumb, saying he required nothing beyond a measure of wine and an amount of meat, while she ruled, celebrated alike for wisdom and benevolence. They say the Emperor stared out from his chamber across the river, in his last night's hours, upon the high pale form, long complete, of the Taj. In our world, it reminds me solely of the love Isotta degli Atti drew from Sigismondo, past their children, through the machinations, beyond the marriage, beyond the affairs. Cut flowers, real, lie on the grand base of her tomb, and upon its top, scarlet, white. I take one, white. Yesterday the State's watchman offered me one going out, I refused; last night, below, I picked up a little red one—where is it? I take one, white. It resembles a gardenia, smaller, but I know nothing of flowers. Jasmine—for eternal life—I remember dominates the fretwork of the true tombs below, and I have to go out.

There is no time to circle the platform once more, wondering, touching. I look up at the immense black marble inscription inlaid in the frame of the central bay, and descend. The boy who undoes my slippers has become a friend and wants no tip. Will I ever come back? It seems impossible that I shouldn't, the building has become so familiar and necessary. It must be impossible to take one's way without any regret off down the long garden, but I leave India today and my feeling is strong. We very hardly, Americans, relinquish things. I have not time even to go across to my bench, but I pause and turn. I was lucky to come at all, reluctantly, ill, without expectation, urged, my reservations out just allowing it; and yet this at the end, and the Ryoan-ji garden at the beginning, are the most remarkable things, single works, I have seen in Asia, and for the garden, so far as books, photographs, plans, study can prepare, which is not well, I was prepared. For the Taj nothing prepares. There is the matter of its size, enormous, though even at this short distance it begins not to seem so, balanced amid its quartet of tapering minarets (but these are 137 feet high) and between—here knowledge enters, affecting vision—the thin perpendicular watercourse before, the broad horizontal river behind. Murray's states that a side is 186 feet, and the central bay of each is 63 feet high, and in certain lights, as now, the whole prodigious bulk floats on its giant platform. Then, notwithstanding this, it is perfect as a jewel, like a jewel, the work of a jeweler: a matter again for fingers, in the bays, the pearl-smooth gleaming inlays of jacinth, chrysoprase, agate, some translucent blue stone, semiprecious stones unknown to me, in most chaste scrolls. Nor even apart from these is the Taj white, but thousand-hued, like the word invented by Paul for the wisdom of God, "*polypoikilos*," in marble veined and tinted, violet, gray, cream, tan, set off with black marble picking out the minarets, with huge flowing characters inlaid black alongside and above the front main bay.

In unshielded sun the tomb is glowing with its own removed life, as, after sunset last evening, when the overcast sky was almost lost, it held its light. Sumptuous it certainly has to be called; but such was not my ruling impression yesterday. Both the splendour and the grace stand at the service of something else, and this so strictly that my impression of severity, accompanying that of sumptuousness, overcame it. This is bound to be partly an effect—accidental for us—of art from which all images are of course excluded, whether of God or man; especially after the human and divine complexities of Buddhist and Hindu temples—it is a month only since I was at Bhuvaneshwar, two since I halted along the serried ten hundred life-sized figures gleaming in Sanjusangendo. But anyway, the clear essence of the Taj has, it seems to me now, to be named otherwise.

The Ryoan-ji garden—sand, fifteen stones—is a work devoted wholly to thought (tumbling Zen thought, it's true), and purely symbolic. But here is a performance devoted wholly to death, and not symbolic at all, embodying no protest of any kind, inspiring no sadness. I suppose—I know—that pain—well-nigh infinite calculation—hardly endurable fatigue—exasperation, agony—went into the making of the vivid thing. They are incidental, like the awe inevitable below in the crypt in darkness or the wonder at the miraculous echo above, where my merest mutter stirred forth a low far thunder long in the dome. Some other word—tranquil—will have to do for the essence of this work entirely beyond our Western quarrel with time, free from all longing. The echo and the awe were by-products. No one, I think, ever looked on the Taj, since the Emperor, with sorrow or passion. There is something limited or missing at the heart of this, accounting for the nature of its beauty; for, I suppose, this is the most beautiful of man's buildings. Can I account for it to myself by the anomalous inspiration? If it is true that the work was designed for Shah Jehan by a jeweler of Venice, who took as his model Humayun's superb tomb, then new, at Delhi, I can imagine what is missing; and there exists evidence, very early, Jesuit evidence, moreover, for the ascription. Geronimo Veroneo was the name of this transcendent genius, who, dying when the Taj was ten years underway, half done, in 1640, is buried here at Agra, three or four miles away in the Catholic cemetery northwest: his executor, a Jesuit, said to another Jesuit who came here that year that Veroneo designed it. Will a man whose executor is a Jesuit have lost his faith? I long since joined those who see Islam as a Christian heresy. But the work is Mohammedan in inspiration, Mohammedan in end, and neither faith is really here present. Few masterpieces so little vague, so definite, make a sense so curiously nonassertive; it has no theology, it offers neither hope nor consolation, and belongs—as against the *Mahābhā-rata*, Sainte-Chapelle, the *Commedia*—among the sublime uncommitted works, with the *Iliad* and *King Lear*. I expect I am wrong about all this, as I turn away again, anxious already about the world outside, my plane, but we get teased into thought. That young man's formulation, Keats's, of a few men's ability—negative capability—to be tranquil and effective, *between* faiths or doubts, is one of our deepest; and I wonder at the tumultuous energy of quiet mind in this astonishing Italian, creating in another culture its supreme achievement, when I turn for the last time on the steps of the Gateway to glance back at the great calm building above the cypresses, in the less bright sky. It looks as if it had just been finished, or were being finished now. It is secular: the content of the inscriptions is nothing, was nothing: it is mere love that everything here is at the service of, love for one actual woman—a love without eagerness of future.

I shut my eyes and bear the sight away.

My rickshaw boy is waiting and my troubles begin immediately. "Republic Hotel," I say urgently. "Republic. Where we came from," with gestures. "*Vite! Schnell! Molto rapido! Diritissimo!*" When at a loss in a language, as I am in Hindi—also in Japanese, Bengali, Oriyan, Gujarati, and Mahrashta, to mention other tongues that would have been helpful this tour—I fall back on languages in which I am also at a loss. In the right direction, but then there is only one, he sets off very slowly. His eye said nothing, nor did he shake his head (Indian for "yes," agreement, or comprehension) at the name of the hotel; he looked, indeed, as if he had not had an idea for three years and was not having one now. We drift toward Agra, where my plane connection leaves at eight-ten.

I encourage him freely to increase his pace, but it is where we are going that truly bothers me, particularly when he takes a turn I don't remember. The road is more uphill, too, than it was coming—a point neglected in my calculation—and he frequently gets down to wheel the pedicab. I would like to get down myself, but he won't hear of it. It is time for me to begin worrying about money; we are going so quietly, however, that the hotel gate is as far ahead as I can see. Is my clock right? Is this the right way? I should know it, or them, by now, but besides being dazed by the Taj, I am still full of German and Swiss medicines against a virus I picked up long ago in Calcutta which then laid me flat in Ahmedabad. Pedestrians are getting thicker. Making him stop beside three who look like students, I implore help in going to the Republic Hotel, suddenly. "Republic Hotel," one of them says to him. An expression of sharp surprise comes into the boy's face and he shakes his head with assent. What was in his mind I will never know. The student says something else; we are off like a rocket. "*Meherbanii!*" I call back. I never use Hindi except when it is unnecessary.

We are in at one minute past eight. I give him four chips, and he acts as though I had bought the cab and then returned it to him. This leaves me about one rupee over my bill, if I am right about it (and I have reckoned on a lemon soda that it took me three quarters of an hour to come by last night, and soda with both meals), and if I can get the bill.

I am wrong about everything. At the desk, which is now inhabited, my bill is ready. This has never happened to me in India before; campaigns are fought to a conclusion in desolate countries while a hotel bill is being prepared; the British taught these peoples paper work and they have learned the lesson. I have forgotten the service charge. One anna for matches does not signify, but the service charge brings the bill over forty rupees, or two more than I have. Knowing money is waiting for me in Delhi, and anxious not to go over the mark as I leave the country, I am bare as a bone. The tiny shopping I did yesterday was ruinous. I explain this to the manager, identifying myself as a traveller on official business and offering to post or wire him the odd rupees from New Delhi later this morning. He is sympathetic, but I can see the suggestion holds no attraction for him.

I feel stopped. If the government had made my reservation, as always before, there would be no difficulty. For forty cents I am going to miss my plane, my planes. Then I see my ten-dollar bill, tucked in the back of my wallet.

"Ha," I say, extracting and virtually brandishing it. "You can change this."

"The bank," he says. "We no longer have authority to change money." He glances up at the big clock. "The bank opens at ten."

With ten dollars in my hand, I argue, like Tantalus. I put forward my desperation: I would be happy to stay in Agra for days, forever, but with great difficulty, at last, the government has got me a reservation out for Karachi this afternoon, by BOAC, and if I miss it, there is no saying when I can have another; my family are waiting for me in Italy, and have been; dollars are money, this bill is excellent, here is my passport; good heavens! etc.

I am irresistible, because all my arguments are true and because the money is clearly real and because Indians dislike government as much as I do. "If I don't see your passport," he says at last, "I can do it. But not officially."

"I won't tell anyone," I promise intensely.

While he is making the calculation, I stand here flooded with gratitude. I love this abominable hotel and I love all India, and once again it looks as if I were really about to get out. But it is nine minutes past eight. "The airline bus!" I cry. "Oh, that doesn't leave until later," he says, looking up, "eight-thirty or eight-forty." Then he is counting out the good chips and I am solvent once more. "May I have a receipt?" I ask. "Oh no," he begins. "Well, that's all right," I say, understanding, voluble. "When my wallet was stolen from my room in the Grand Hotel in Calcutta—look at it, will you, it looks as if it had been under the Ganges for a month, it was put in a postbox, emptied of money, and the police returned it to me—it had three or four American dollars in it but not the ten, which I'd locked with my large rupee notes in a bag—well, I can just say they got it all—" I feel I would like to tell him the story of my life.

Pulling up short, I pay the bill, he sends a bearer off for change, and I shoot around to my court to be shaved. The barber is squatting patiently by my door, water has come on, this takes five minutes, when I ask him how much, he shrugs and smiles and I overpay him absurdly. Farewell to the bearer, and I give him eight annas, for nothing.

Back in the lobby I collect my change, wait. My bag comes. At last coffee is brought round and I am drinking it from the top of a showcase when the plane connection, a bus larger than a jeep, comes at eight-fifty-five.

What is so agreeable, withdrawn, timeless, as a ride to an airport? Some tourists have come in and are waiting in the little passenger cottage that occupies what used to be the stage of a small amphitheatre—this was an American air base during the war, like half the other places I have visited. The pocket-plane takes off, unsteadily, on time—as usual. The smiling, sullen hostess is wearing the usual blue sari, which hampers as she crosses and recrosses the shin-high barrier midway the plane, brushing her bottom into my shoulder every time. This is not seductive but Indian indifference. She wears lipstick, and no gum-gum. I did not see the fort, or anything else, but regret nothing but Veroneo's grave—which I determined long ago to visit if I ever went to Agra—but there was no time. I should have liked to stand with reverence beside the grave of this man who exerted his ultimate stretch of imagination in a monument, to be created in an idiom not his own culture's, to the love for a woman who had been another man's. We are in cloud. I see the hostess is curled up behind us (the other passenger and myself) with a film magazine. I doze.

1958

The Lovers

HE USED TO COME TO SEE US ONE SUMMER WHEN WE LIVED on the Island. As I reached the corner of the house wheeling my bicycle, which I was not permitted to ride on the lawn, dirty and hot in the late afternoon, he would be the first person in view if he was there, sitting stretched at full length but hardly at ease in a beach chair just at the edge of the tulip bed, balancing his drink on its wooden arm, with his head lifted staring out toward my mother and listening to my father, who sat invariably a few feet away in an angle formed by the house and garage, also facing the cannas bordering the lawn at the back. No matter how quietly I approached, my mother always‘ heard me and had turned from her care of the cannas by the time she came into sight as I advanced, her face pale above the blooms, her inexhaustible brown hair blowing, her garden glove dark against the orange sky, raising a hand to me. I never waved in reply without a twinge, an impulse of remorse for my absent day, the anxiety I knew she was feeling,—for this was the year when what she called my violent indolence first showed itself. It was the summer I was in love with Billie. Billie was an interesting blond girl who lived half a mile from us, the daughter of a notable playwright; but the relation, if it had lost none of its tenacity, was complicated because her mother had left him— they had been the centre of an artistic set in some Middle Western city, and she had then written a book about him—and was now married to an ace of the last war, a small shattered man, a European, who was kind to me and seemed nearly invisible in the rambling noisy suburban mansion filled night and day with hangers-on, suitors, unclassified cosmopolitan guests. The unsubstantiality, for me, of this ménage was enforced less by its confusion, or my shyness, than by my sense of wonder at its names; Mme Durand had living with her her mother, Mrs Austin, and in a reaction of feeling after her last divorce she had changed Billie's name—the playwright's—to the irrelevant name of another former husband, Neville; so that of the three women in this family still dominated by the memory (and the existence, productive erratically of extravagant gifts for Billie, nearby in New York) of the excommunicated celebrity, none bore his name, and their own names senselessly differed. "Billie," too, which I knew as I knew my biceps, flexed and felt endlessly in hope, would disappear for minutes into its incomprehensible original, Wilhelmina; and I loved her as against a set of uncertain troubled lights. Of Madame I remember little except her intolerable fatness, the nascent snobbism in Billie which I associated with her, and a luncheon described to me long afterward by my mother, one of Mme Durand's large hen parties, at which one of the guests, a tall fair woman who had been told by her psychiatrist that she could attain normality only by giving way immediately to her impulses, of whatever sort, amazed the assembly of fifteen women by suddenly reaching into the centre of the table, snatching up the odd-appearing main dish, sniffing it, and making loudly a remark so atrocious that I only after years, with the greatest difficulty, learned what it was. Repeated hesitantly, with recovered horror, in my mother's charming voice, it seemed at the moment of shock nakedly to score the tone of that society of the distant summer of the executive class, a society abrupt and sordid enough—the weekend parties in the Clubhouse, the sleeping, the desertions—not much to suffer under a symbol of such concise ferocity; only my father and my mother were distinct from it. But he, too, our visitor, and aside from the accident of my not liking him, appeared to stand somewhere else, apart from the Lennoxes and Clouds and Gores, the people who lived along the Lane and their friends, who would be drifting and drinking and flowering on the lawns when I returned in the afternoon. The sun was setting always behind them in my mind, because I rarely saw them at any other time. I left the house at eight-thirty every morning on my bicycle, raced to Mme Durand's, and waited restlessly on her drive below the grove of trees for Billie to come out, and off we went. We made this arrangement because I avoided entering her house. The sense of unreality which in itself it gave me was heightened by a feeling, which I began to have that summer, that I was not appearing in my true character. Although I could have given no account of that character, I was aware of the discontinuity between my life at school, absorbing if horrible, and my frenzied useless vacations; and I had an intermittent consciousness of guilt. My English master had given me a list of books to read during the summer, nineteenth-century novels, for the most part, and I remember I went faithfully to the public library every few days and brought volumes home, two or three at a time, returned them, and brought others; but it was my brother who read them; and the advantage, although years my junior, he then established over me he has never relinquished,—in our discussions of fiction he still assumes a tone, dating from that summer, of immeasurable experience and superior judgment.

What our visitor thought of the life we led, or of the life, rather, which at my level I shared and in the midst of which my parents had their different life, I doubt that it occurred to me to wonder, self-absorbed, going and coming. I saw him at most every few days, for an hour at five or six o'clock; save once, he never came in the evening, and he never arrived before my father, who drove out from the city, changed at once, and was facing the cannas, armed with that admirable brand of Scotch which I have scarcely tasted since those illegal days (our porter's charge for "bringing it in" was invariable and so heavy that with the indulgence of despair my father ordered liquors and wines more expensive and rare than seemed sensible later across a counter), ready for anyone, by five o'clock. My mother adjusted her time between the guests and the flowers, never appearing distant, although when she tossed, as now and then she hospitably did, a comment from across the lawn, it came to us with a diminished sound. The Clouds and Parkers would be there, perhaps Justin and Margaret, perhaps Macomber and Mrs. Tench, or the Dimmings. Or he would be there alone. I sat on the edge of the porch with a limeade, if I was not indoors following the dance bands, and listened to my father's familiar, ever-changing accounts of the life of his young manhood, his leaving college at his father's death, the Continent before the war, old Baltimore, old New York; of conditions on the Market—it was an unsettled but promising summer; of hunting, and the theatres of the past, restaurants and women. Our visitor listened also; I watched him, for I had already learned that these stories which interested me, no matter how frequently told, so intensely—so spacious and free the life in them seemed to me, so daring and rich their recital by my father—could be tedious to others; I watched him for a sign of disloyalty, and I never saw one. Yet I thought that somehow they did not deeply engage him. His mind in the immense head kept on working; when he looked at me I saw it, and I thought sometimes I could see pain, or longing—although it may be that my father's reminiscence interested him more than I imagined, for one afternoon, coming when my father had stayed in town for dinner, he seemed restless with my mother and left at once.

He said little, at any rate; of himself, nothing. We did not understand clearly what he "did," and he never, although my mother several times suggested it, brought anyone with him. This was why I disliked him, perhaps: he seemed singular,—independent, as no one else I knew was. And then he looked at me, he looked at all of us, most at my mother, when his chair was turned as my father's was, with uncomfortable intensity; he looked at me sometimes as if he did not believe I existed. Again, when I would be included in the talk and he turned to me with his slow, holding glance, I felt the obscure pressure of a real interest, and I avoided his eyes. To his rare questions about Billie, whom he met one afternoon when I brought her home, although they were put with the gravity which was habitual with him and with which I was unfamiliar in such questions, even was pleased by,—I replied as shortly, with as great nervousness, the same tortured grin, as to anyone else's questions. What he said to my father, however, often fixed my attention and remained with me for days. He spoke deliberately, with a kind of constraint which gave his words unnatural, memorable emphasis. One day, on my father's referring to an unexpected Congressional vote of the day before and asking his opinion, he said instantly, almost with impatience, that politics did not concern him. "What does concern you then?" asked my father, more nearly indifferent to politics himself than any other man in his set, but surprised to hear the blank disclaimer which he could never have made and would have contradicted had it been made of him. "Work!—a wife, and work!" our visitor said after a pause, during which Billie's face hovered so vividly before me, its round blond brows and low forehead conjured by the question, that his reply reached my ears to stun me; I did not understand the words in their starkness—"work" particularly fell into my mind like a word unknown, with its special weight from the idiom of workers in science and art—I did not understand them, but I recognized that their energy and sentiment were inimical to the beloved face which they had caused to vanish, as I felt them to be utterly strange to any answer which I might have made to the question, and I resented them, at the same time that their formality charmed me into the wish that I might have summoned, or might sometime summon, such a response myself to another question at another time.

Often thereafter this reply recurred to me, always mysterious, with incomprehensible reaches behind its bluntness, evoking dissonant emotions, and always with the power, which nothing else possessed, of banishing the face which haunted me; or if, after a time, not quite of causing it to disappear, of driving it to a certain distance,—at least of touching the springs of its ghostly force. No doubt I was in love with Billie; I said so a thousand times daily to her with my lips, with every motion, every impulse; I cried it to myself at night, lying uncovered on my bed sweating, lively with ecstasy; but the undiscriminating violence of my feelings would be better suggested by saying that she obsessed me. She was a torture, an enchantment. Her figure running, loose in its short light dress, her golden hair tossed in the morning light as she flew toward me down the turn of the drive, made me weak, like a repeated blow upon the muscle of my upper arm. My whole body, braced, eager and weak, at once shrank and yearned toward the moment of meeting, when we would cling kissing, hidden by the trees above and the wall below, for the first time that day together. Childish those embraces certainly were, in their crude clouded view of what union might be, in their awkwardness, restlessness, such that at any second either of us might break causelessly away; an adult, watching, might have found us absurd or pretentious, experiencing the emotion with which a professional man in the audience observes, smiling, the efforts of an actor who is impersonating a member of his profession, and how badly. Yet as we pressed together our lips and breasts helplessly, wantonly, we were in darkness—the darkness of touch and magnification of sound, the splitting of the eardrum at a murmur, the precipitation of the soul into a palm. The delicacy and the flow of darkness; the darkness broke—not when our bodies parted—long before, when the possibility, the far view of parting lighted my mind again with the abruptness and brilliance, blinding the eyes, of a switch pressed. In a second it will be over! I thought, agonized, and the irresolutions of pleasure and pain which are a child's first lesson in the world hung over me anew, so that I could not have told whether I was glad or sorry when at last we drew apart, her face smiling already and hot, my hands trembling, and I said, "Get on." She jumped on the crossbar then, her arms inside mine on the handles, her hands on mine in an old joke that she steered better than I, and leaned back swerving against my left shoulder—the unnerving moment of each day,—while her massed hair brushed my neck and cheek; I got the bicycle rest up; we started slowly in the gravel and picked up suddenly, coasting down the steep final turn of her drive into the road.

The days passed like a coasting, a hot wind. They were Billie agile in the glare of the beach, shouting above the Sound pounding the sand, Billie across the net bent forward, balancing from foot to foot, waiting for service, Billie bounding away toward the sideline, turned for a backhand, Billie's throat going back for a lob, her eyes gleaming as she grinned out at me from a tunnel in the fortification we were building, her voice, her weight against my shoulder and arm, her small breasts we examined on the porch in darkness, marvelling and tremulous, with the fearful anxiety of the traveller who lingers in a strange city and rushes to the next and lingers again, waiting for news—what news? what news?—from his half-forgotten, absorbing home. Late in the summer, the worst days, when nights held the heat still, the pavements never cooled, the float dried as we dived and burned us when we climbed back,—we were bold and wild. Of the famous innocence of first love, celebrated and remembered with desire by the poets whose childhood was solitary, we had never much, or if in the beginning we were so, I lose it now in memory; what I recall is a plunge down, deeper daily in forbidden complex experience, hesitations and curiosities and indulgences of the porch in darkness. But late in the summer we passed feverishly into regions so wicked and pleasant that we seemed to ourselves by August's end old in vice: by the time of the masquerade at the Clubhouse it seemed to us that we had no more to learn—not that we were exhausted, not that we did not suffer our privations, but the capacity of our selves was measured. Purity of feeling, selflessness of feeling, is the achievement of maturity; we begin in the slime, the naked beating self. Yet in a civilized view our diversions that summer left us unsoiled, and Billie went back pure, intact, to school, an image of tan youth, with candid eyes,—to be violated next year, perhaps, casually across the kitchen table of a fraternity house, tipsy in the vague light from a door half-opened into the passage, the dance music faint at this distance, by a boy who did not know her name, her magical name, against which no fatigue or incantation had power to preserve me except our visitor's grave words, repeated by me to the ceiling, like a rite, with envy and relief, as meaningless as for some stray from the street, crept into a church for a moment out of the sun, the Elevation of the Host.

It may be that he preserved me, or was able to provide my only aid, because he preserved himself—I did not know from what, but I had a sense, related to his solitude, that he did. Not from feeling, certainly: I had the testimony of his phrase and the weight of his eyes when I intercepted their glance flowing across the lawn while my father talked. Perhaps from the expressions that others used, the forms men's feelings regularly take; these he seemed to avoid as by nature; he never greeted my parents, never thanked them when he left; he made no effort that we could see,—was not, as we say, involved,—and when he walked into our living room on the night of the masquerade dressed merely in a white linen suit, I was not surprised, although with what emotion I could spare from my own excitement I exulted over his mistake. This was the first year I was allowed to go to the great September party which closed the season in the Lane; it was known as "the masquerade" but was simply a fancy-dress ball, very fancy, to which everyone looked forward for weeks; Billie was going, too, for the first time—all the day before she had talked of nothing else, intoxicating herself with it, her first grown-up dance. We would meet there. Now our guest was late, and my mother was keeping us. My father, dressed as a musketeer, from the figure of Athos in the illustrated volume of Dumas he had given to me at Christmas, posed amiably at the mantel and said nothing about our guest's lack of costume. I sat tense and silent. But they talked while we waited for my mother to come down, and it struck me, through my distraction, that our friend was in an extraordinary mood. It was impossible not to listen to him. I never at any other time heard him so little reserved. His voice, even, as he swung up and down the room, talking rather rapidly, not loudly, was rich with anticipation and what, to me who knew him, was almost recklessness, although to a stranger he would have appeared controlled enough. The burden of his talk I forget; he made images, he recalled, he dallied, he soared, and the unaccustomed tide of that wonderful voice—stilling quite, during the spell, my dislike—filled our rooms like the beating of wings, the leap of the heart in devotion and hope.

"Ah!" said my father. I turned, and there on the stairway, in gold, queenly and strange, stood my beautiful mother, taller and younger, smiling down at us. She stood for a long moment in the bright lamplight, triumphant, happy in our gaze, before she continued her descent. "Good evening!" she greeted us. "But you don't look the man for a party—" Her tone and startled air turned me again to our friend—another stranger—his face rigid, with such despair in the passionate eyes, such black depth as of a vision of Hell, that I could have struck him. It was as if the room darkened and whirled with bitterness. In another second his features had softened, his glare died out. What I had seen seemed phantasmal as he came a step forward and said in his normal serious voice that if his astonishment had surprised her he was sorry: it had been, really, a tribute, and should be forgiven: "You *are* magnificent"—turning to my father—"I congratulate you!"

The expectations of youth are its oblivion. I had forgotten my amazement, forgotten the incident five minutes later, when we mounted to the open floodlit doorway of the Clubhouse, where groups and couples in motley costumes, outrageous, exquisite, clownish, passed and repassed, shouting, laughing, the orchestra sighing from within a sweet lament. "Here are the brother and sister," someone said as we entered the light—Mrs. Lennox. My father bowed. At this moment, however, the pleasure which I never failed to take in this compliment—in that the metaphorical relationship seemed closer, for my mother and me, than our familiar one, and made me appear to myself older—was blocked as it rose. Across the ballroom by a table I caught sight of Billie, in a blue dress, waving a glass, not at me; she was gesturing, talking with three boys, or men, grouped before her. My breathing seemed oppressed. I started around the dance space. Halfway, she laughed—I could not hear her above the music—and, handing her glass to one of the men, danced away with another, a Spanish gentleman. Danced away with another—danced away with another—while I followed, disappointed and anxious. When at last I got her attention and cut in, she merely said "Hello" without surprise or warmth, we danced ten steps, another man cut. I leaned against the wall for a moment while the music rose and fell. Then as I followed, my heart throbbing and sick, my brain hot with betrayal, dominoes, slaves, gentlemen, warriors swarmed in my sight toward her,—divided her,—the room turned on the blue dress like a wheel. The tunes changed, the noise increased, my terror grew. She seemed not to see me, stared past or looked carelessly across as if I were a little boy with whom she played once, years ago. And she herself seemed to me strange. While night before last . . . I tried to call up and hold an image of the porch, but it slipped from me in my distress, the gathering unreality. What I wanted at last was to go outside and weep, but I dared not leave, hoping still for change, at any instant—turning in a glide step there, ten feet from me, radiant, blind—a sign, recognition, our love, made once more whole. I wandered back and forth, trying to control my face, confused, more and more tired, watching my mother whirling and shining like a shower of gold and gold-brown hair across the room, waiting, waiting. Several times I saw our friend against the wall near the doorway, and once he beckoned to me. I edged my way around the dancers, trying to catch a glimpse again of Billie, whom I had lost.

"Why are you not dancing?"

"You aren't dancing yourself. I haven't seen you once," I said, too sick and desperate for manners.

He looked out into the throng with a curious expression, as of an intensity of search which had ceased to be personal—the expression he has in most of his photographs of recent years, and the one I remember, since we never saw him again. "That's true," he said. "But you can hardly have my excellent reason."

"What's that?"

"I am in danger," he said, looking down at me seriously.

I was puzzled or angry. "You keep out of everything, don't you?"

"Keep out?" he was startled. "Here I am: I came! But the arrangements are not mine."

His answer, although I did not try to make it out, touched another bitterness in me. "Is that why you haven't got a costume on?"

He smiled. "I have. I wear it against danger."

But as he spoke I had seen Billie again, and muttering something quickly, I left him on my hopeless terrible quest, blown from corner to corner by the music of the dance. It is my fate, I thought: to follow her, to be near her if I can. As I went, the part of my mind which was not eyes tried to recall the sign I had had, the phrase, of which his last words had almost reminded me; but I could not, and in any event—while my eyes fixed her glowing face and my heart heard her name—I knew that it would be of no use to me now.

1945

All Their Colours Exiled

I'M NOT SURE SHE EVER TOLD ANYBODY ELSE. SO WHAT THE hell if I never was any writer, I believe I'll put the whole thing down. I thought it was odd and sad, and everybody tells me their troubles. I don't mean she made me any revelations exactly. This was a bright woman. She knew I didn't care *why* they separated. I gathered she "left" him—that is, kicked him out, as he more or less forced her to. In short, a usual case. Why people divorce each other is their own business, inscrutable. They seldom, in my experience, know why themselves—know what was most important, I mean, along the camps of the Everest of dissatisfactions nearly any human being feels with any other human being he knows inside out. Maybe nothing is most important. It's the mountain, and you must get too weary to climb on.

I never understood, though, that there were any arrangements for a divorce. They were both Catholics, what people seem to call now "cradle" Catholics; which made it rough. Of course, you can always get an annulment or leave the Church; or so I hear, as every year I know more Catholics; but I don't notice they seem to can as a rule, the original ones.

She got to telling me about it—I haven't seen him since even once, he moved to the Coast—in a bar on Third up in the Sixties, where at that time you could still get (this was nine thousand years ago) ale chilled, not iced. Now they ice it all and I have—excuse me, had—another Irish place, farther up on Lexington. I generally get hold of a loft in the Village when I'm in the city, but of course you can't drink there any more. Not that she drank.

He does. I knew him better, in fact I introduced them. She just happened to ring me up this time when she came down from Boston. But I knew her damned well, too, the way you know the wives of some friends. I put him out of his own living room one afternoon, needing some emotional information from her for a figure that was stalled, which I decided only one other friend's wife or her or my sister could give me and I couldn't get hold of them; models have always never had children. Besides, she studied with me when she was a kid. No promise. Colour; she couldn't make colour. I doubt if she sees it. Right of dead centre in one Gauguin there's a spread of green you could eat, and I found she'd never noticed it. Browns crowd it. What she had was genuine virtue, loyalty, self-effacing human passion; all that stuff, another matter. She quit long ago.

How she came to tell me, I think, is that she was just getting over it—I don't mean the thing itself, which I thought she'd never be over, but the funny immediate *hoping* that she told me about; it must have been a month or less; also, she knew I was fond of him. The reason I listened is, what can you do. And the reason I really listened is that it became clear right away that she wasn't going to come over me with any explanation. A dignified woman with a soft chin told me one day, twenty minutes after I met her, that *she* left her husband because—it's a little complicated: they both got in bed at night and drank, read and drank; pretty soon they passed out; but in the morning—this is what she couldn't stand—he'd finish his old highball before getting up; so she left him, keeping the children. A very full explanation. Never having married, I don't understand how people are *able* to separate. I can hardly bear to get rid of a model and I am a very casual type. But Phil and Treva were past all the quarrelling, Treva said, and friendly to each other, and they both still absolutely loved each other, though he didn't show it too much, when she said to him one evening, "You know, I'm leaving you." What could he do, blazing with guilt? He had no one on at the time though, she thought, and I believe she was right about this, though he wasn't too faithful, to tell you the truth. He was just a charming, affectionate, self-indulgent, gifted, and strong bastard who spent most of his time in despair. The night she told me about was some ten days after that: he hadn't left yet, and there was a question of their going to dinner at the house of some old friends who had been away on vacation. He'd accepted for both of them. She refused to go, and he wouldn't go alone. He was furious.

"I know," she told me, "it had to be sometime. He'd have gone on like that for months."

He went out, leaving her to make the phone call.

She said she felt drained and helpless, sitting in the wing chair, and the reproduction over their mantel looked drained, too—it was a golden Renoir, his choice—as blank as the flowers in a garden that frightened her once by moonlight, all their colours exiled. That's his now, she thought; this is my chair, that's my piano: nothing is ours any more. She shuddered and wanted to bolt, too. She felt as shocked and eager to be elsewhere, she said, as the tall fair girl had done, the only other girl in her first life-class, when the model stepped out from behind the screen and proved to have nothing on and the tall girl fled. But Treva had braced herself and stayed.

It must have been twilight deepening while she sat there.

The bar was a very quiet place and I worried about somebody hearing her. But she was muttering really, dry-eyed, trying to tell me how she'd felt—not quite for sympathy, but with a sort of minimum plea, as of "this too being a possible point of view." It was nerve-racking. I probably drank ten ales. I can't remember all she said up to the Indian story and the final conversation. She wasn't extremely coherent.

—He was even sober. But he shies like a horse. See how he always manages to get out of everything. Here I am, stuck with it again. *He* ought to have to call: they're as much his friends. More. They're all his friends. (Here she wept, she said; but by the way it didn't turn out to be true.) *He* really has always run everything, but he makes me seem to. What is wrong with him? How could we go to dinner there together and pretend? I might burst into tears. He might himself; he did yesterday. He is just crazy. He refuses to see what is. Everything I do exasperates him: he can't stand it—and he hates this, he can't stand the fact that he can't stand it—and neither can I. Oh, when he *admitted* it was necessary. When everything that happens has shown over and over again that nothing else is possible. When he brought it up himself *years* ago. And now he is trying to put it all on me. What's left of me.

"I'll tell you what I thought of," she said across the booth, with her big light-gray eyes withdrawn and level on my cigarette. "A thing my father told me." Meanwhile, I had got oppressed by a kind of dreadful stasis about her: I wished water had been flowing under that house in Waltham, or a dog stretching and barking. All their turmoil was mental. They had a baby once, a girl, years ago, but it died and they never had another; I don't know why. Just facing each other like that, complicated people, and they were never apart, it's impossible. On the other hand, maybe he *was* active enough, in painful ways, and so responsible. But then if she allowed it? Anyway, this was her father's story:

Waddy Wildcat, he said, was the handsomest Indian he ever saw; broad-shouldered, but tapering-delicate, even in jeans, like a masculine dancer. When he rode into town on the black stallion he owned, Treva's mother would go to the window sometimes—keeping behind the curtain—to look out admiringly at his tranquil, power-hard face. This being in the Southwest, where they moved for a while when Treva was a little girl. Waddy Wildcat was a Seminole, about twenty-three, but quiet. But one evening when he rode out home late and his wife came into the yard to meet him, she said something that he did not like, and he trampled her in the yard. There was truly no body left at all, and the horse's legs were wet with blood way up. Of course he was drunk. Waddy Wildcat was taken to Wewoka, and got bail until the court would sit; he had money. Then he came in town less, off and on for two months, until one night there was a brawl, when a young man named Edmund Tiger cut his head completely off, with a bowie knife, from behind. Now Edmund Tiger had no connection with Waddy Wildcat's wife, and also he was a stripling, maybe seventeen, whose neck Waddy Wildcat could have broken with one hand; so that the general opinion was, no matter how Edmund Tiger came to cut him from behind, Waddy Wildcat was disheartened and not defending himself. This was her father's story, she remembered in the dusk.

"He kicked me," she looked across at me and said clearly, "to death."

I was knocked out by the story, but I couldn't tell whether she realized the other reason she'd thought it, though she knew how Phil must be feeling; or the third, revenging reason. I didn't say anything. Are matters supposed to be cleared up on this earth? Besides, for all her sensitivity, she kept a certain black-and-white way of looking at things that comes from spending too much time in your own country.

Mourning women! I see now I began with my aunt. My uncle died. Their fidgets, their liquid tense eyes, their too much make-up, untears, inconsequence, bar crawls, their longing voices. I specialize in widows, but I'm strong in all kinds. I have great respect for them, too. Yet even a mourning woman's self-sufficiency has something frantic about it. To mourn, by the way, it is not necessary to have lost anything actual. Hope will do. Yes indeed, bucker. Hope will *do*.

They look . . . the same! They look much the same.

How they never tell you *exactly* what happened. And I'd like to know. But how can one break in on that self-reverent scattering recital?

Why do I go in for it? Well, I have sort of had it myself, so I feel sympathetic. And then too . . .

Aren't most people here—Americans—in mourning? For self-love? Are there any buckers left in the audience?

At last, that evening, she'd turned on a lamp, got a sweater, and gone to the telephone. There was some noise in the bar now, and I relaxed and sort of made up the real conversation behind her report of it. I've heard this other woman on the phone. In fact, I got to know her fairly well once when staying with Phil and Treva. Remarkable woman, very kind, inconspicuously on top of everything while keeping somehow wholly to herself, in spite of being very beautiful. She has a high warm eager voice and pronounces the question mark after "Hello" as if she were on her way somewhere and only picked up the phone in passing. Runs her servants like a Japanese print, nothing but what matters, when. A housewife, a ravishing housewife.

"Hello?"

"Hullo, Pam. Treva. I'm sorry to be so late in calling—"

"Hello! Now just how soon do you want to come out? We haven't seen you for ages. We're wild to see you. Are you ready? There's no hurry but do come straightaway if you can. David's been talking about you a blue streak. You ought to see him now: he's all protocol with Jack and me, and enormous," etc.

At last Treva would be able to say, "Pam, I'm sorry we can't come tonight. In fact, we can't come. Phil and I are separating."

"Atrocious connection it is, I can't hear a thing," she would hear Pamela say after a little moment.

"Phil and I are separating. We're separating, and so—"

"It can't be serious," the vivid voice hurriedly, "you probably just need a rest from each other. I know this last month—"

"No, Pam, really, we are. So for a bit I don't think I ought to see anybody—"

"Treva, you come anyway." Pamela very decided. "It will do you good. You can't keep shut up, feeling as you must be. We haven't seen you for *six weeks*. Let Jack come and pick you up right now, you say when."

"No," she said as if begging and in the wrong, "truly I mustn't. You're very sweet . . ." and somehow the conversation ended. She'd agreed to come to dinner with them as soon as possible—"You let us know now, soon. Promise? You rest now."

She leaned against the side of the booth as I suppose she had leaned back against the wall, feeling, she said, exhausted, shamed, relieved, and grateful.

"No questions," she said without emphasis. "I was not going to be asked questions after all. But I felt a very strange and intense resentment, too. I thought, Naturally! what do they care? First Pam pretended not to hear. Then it wasn't serious—as if she didn't *know* Phil and me. Then I was to come to dinner anyway. And yet she's devoted to both of us—I think—yes, Pam does love us both. I decided that it had just knocked her out, and she had only acted as kindly as she could." (I had my own opinion about this.) "Then I felt worse. I'd been wrong to torture myself over the scandal. Phil was right, that it didn't matter or there wouldn't be any. So we have many close friends—many even very close friends. Nobody was going to take it up. Nobody was going to help take it up. There was no way to distribute it. It is *ours*."

I won't bother telling you how I felt, as she let the word ring. And yet, imagine trying to get rid of the most grievous and interesting thing that has ever happened to you! That's American.

Her eyes were almost bright in her shadowed face. And wasn't she, anyway, at it again, with me? I paid the check as the bar shut, and dropped her off.

She was in absolutely first-class condition, last thing I heard; stunning-looking, big-deal hostess, boiling with admiration and dough. The whole palette, nearly. As for Phil, *Christ.*

?1954

The Imaginary Jew

THE SECOND SUMMER OF THE EUROPEAN WAR I SPENT IN New York. I lived in a room just below street-level on Lexington above Thirty-fourth, wrote a good deal, tried not to think about Europe, and listened to music on a small gramophone, the only thing of my own, except books, in the room. Haydn's London Symphony, his last, I heard probably fifty times in two months. One night when excited I dropped the pickup, creating a series of knocks at the beginning of the last movement where the oboe joins the strings which still, when I hear them, bring up for me my low dark long damp room and I feel the dew of heat and smell the rented upholstery. I was trying as they say to come back a little, uncertain and low after an exhausting year. Why I decided to do this in New York—the enemy in summer equally of soul and body, as I had known for years—I can't remember; perhaps I didn't, but was held on merely from week to week by the motive which presently appeared in the form of a young woman met the Christmas before and now the occupation of every evening not passed in solitary and restless gloom. My friends were away; I saw few other people. Now and then I went to the zoo in lower Central Park and watched with interest the extraordinary behaviour of a female badger. For a certain time she quickly paced the round of her cage. Then she would approach the sidewall from an angle in a determined, hardly perceptible, unhurried trot; suddenly, when an inch away, point her nose up it, follow her nose up over her back, turning a deft and easy somersault, from which she emerged on her feet moving swiftly and unconcernedly away, as if the action had been no affair of hers, indeed she had scarcely been present. There was another badger in the cage who never did this, and nothing else about her was remarkable; but this competent disinterested somersault she enacted once every five or ten minutes as long as I watched her,—quitting the wall, by the way, always at an angle in fixed relation to the angle at which she arrived at it. It is no longer possible to experience the pleasure I knew each time she lifted her nose and I understood again that she would not fail me, or feel the mystery of her absolute disclaimer,—she has been taken away or died.

The story I have to tell is no further a part of that special summer than a nightmare takes its character, for memory, from the phase of the moon one noticed on going to bed. It could have happened in another year and in another place. No doubt it did, has done, will do. Still, so weak is the talent of the mind for pure relation—immaculate apprehension of K alone—that everything helps us, as when we come to an unknown city: architecture, history, trade practices, folklore. Even more anxious our approach to a city—like my small story—which we have known and forgotten. Yet how little we can learn! Some of the history is the lonely summer. Part of the folklore, I suppose, is what I now unwillingly rehearse, the character which experience has given to my sense of the Jewish people.

Born in a part of the South where no Jews had come, or none had stayed, and educated thereafter in states where they are numerous, I somehow arrived at a metropolitan university without any clear idea of what in modern life a Jew was,—without even a clear consciousness of having seen one. I am unable now to explain this simplicity or blindness. I had not escaped, of course, a sense that humans somewhat different from ourselves, called "Jews," existed as in the middle distance and were best kept there, but this sense was of the vaguest. From what it was derived I do not know; I do not recall feeling the least curiosity about it, or about Jews; I had, simply, from the atmosphere of an advanced heterogeneous democratic society, ingathered a gently negative attitude toward Jews. This I took with me, untested, to college, where it received neither confirmation nor stimulus for two months. I rowed and danced and cut classes and was political; by mid-November I knew most of the five hundred men in my year. Then the man who rowed number three, in the eight of which I was bow, took me aside in the shower one afternoon and warned me not to be so chatty with Rosenblum.

I wondered why not. Rosenblum was stroke, a large handsome amiable fellow, for whose ability in the shell I felt great respect and no doubt envy. Because the fellows in the House wouldn't like it, my friend said. "What have they against him?" "It's only because he's Jewish," explained my friend, a second-generation Middle European.

I hooted at him, making the current noises of disbelief, and went back under the shower. It did not occur to me that he could be right. But next day when I was talking with Herz—the coxswain, whom I found intelligent and pleasant—I remembered the libel with some an-

noyance, and told Herz about it as a curiosity. Herz looked at me
oddly, lowering his head, and said after a pause, "Why, Al *is* Jewish,
didn't you know that?" I was amazed. I said it was absurd, he couldn't
be! "Why not?" said Herz, who must have been as astonished as I was.
"Don't you know I'm Jewish?"

I did not know, of course, and ignorance has seldom cost me such
humiliation. Herz did not guy me; he went off. But greater than my
shame at not knowing something known, apparently, without effort
to everyone else, were my emotions for what I then quickly discovered. Asking careful questions during the next week, I learned that
about a third of the men I spent time with in college were Jewish; that
they knew it, and the others knew it; that some of the others disliked
them for it, and they knew this also; that certain Houses existed *only*
for Jews, who were excluded from the rest; and that what in short I
took to be an idiotic state was deeply established, familiar, and acceptable to everyone. This discovery was the beginning of my instruction in social life proper—construing social life as that from which
political life issues like a somatic dream.

My attitude toward my friends did not alter on this revelation. I
merely discarded the notion that Jews were a proper object for any
special attitude; my old sense vanished. This was in 1933. Later, as
word of the German persecution filtered into this country, some sentimentality undoubtedly corrupted my no-attitude. I denied the presence of obvious defects in particular Jews, feeling that to admit them
would be to side with the sadists and murderers. Accident allotting me
close friends who were Jewish, their disadvantages enraged me. Gradually, and against my sense of impartial justice, I became the anomaly
which only a partial society can produce, and for which it has no name
known to the lexicons. In one area, but not exclusively, "nigger-lover"
is cast in a parallel way: but for a special sympathy and liking for Jews
—which became my fate, so that I trembled when I heard one abused
in talk—we have no term. In this condition I still was during the summer of which I speak. One further circumstance may be mentioned, as
a product, I believe, of this curious training. I am spectacularly unable
to identify Jews as Jews,—by name, cast of feature, accent, or environment,—and this has been true, not only of course before the college
incident, but during my whole life since. Even names to anyone else
patently Hebraic rarely suggest to me anything. And when once I
learn that So-and-so is Jewish, I am likely to forget it. Now Jewishness
may be a fact as striking and informative as someone's past heroism or
his Christianity or his understanding of the subtlest human relations,
and I feel sure that something operates to prevent my utilizing the plain

signs by which such characters—in a Jewish man or woman—may be identified, and prevent my retaining the identification once it is made.

So to the city my summer and a night in August. I used to stop on Fourteenth Street for iced coffee, walking from the Village home (or to my room rather) after leaving my friend, and one night when I came out I wandered across to the island of trees and grass and concrete walks raised in the center of Union Square. Here men—a few women, old—sit in the evenings of summer, looking at papers or staring off or talking, and knots of them stay on, arguing, very late; these the unemployed or unemployable, the sleepless, the malcontent. There are no formal orators, as at Columbus Circle in the nineteen thirties and at Hyde Park Corner. Each group is dominated by several articulate and strong-lunged persons who battle each other with prejudices and desires, swaying with intensity, and take on from time to time the interrupters: a forum at the bottom of the pot,—Jefferson's fear, Whitman's hope, the dream of the younger Lenin. It was now about one o'clock, almost hot, and many men were still out. I stared for a little at the equestrian statue, obscure in the night on top of its pedestal, thinking that the misty Rider would sweep again away all these men at his feet, whenever he liked,—what symbol for power yet in a mechanical age rivals the mounted man?—and moved to the nearest group; or I plunged to it.

The dictator to the group was old, with dark cracked skin, fixed eyes in an excited face, leaning forward madly on his bench toward the half dozen men in semicircle before him. "It's bread! It's bread!" he was saying. "It's bittersweet. All the bitter and all the sweetness. Of an overture. What else do you want? When you ask for steak and potatoes, do you want pastry with it? It's bread! It's bread! Help yourself! Help yourself!"

The listeners stood expressionless, except one who was smiling with contempt and interrupted now.

"Never a happy minute, never a happy minute!" the old man cried. "It's good to be dead! Some men should kill themselves."

"Don't you want to live?" said the smiling man.

"Of course I want to live. Everyone wants to live! If death comes suddenly it's better. It's better!"

With pain I turned away. The next group were talking diffusely and angrily about the Mayor, and I passed to a third, where a frantic olive-skinned young man with a fringe of silky beard was exclaiming:

"No restaurant in New York had the Last Supper! No. When people sit down to eat they should think of that!"

"Listen," said a white-shirted student on the rail, glancing around for approbation, "listen, if I open a restaurant and put The Last Supper up over the door, how much money do you think I'd lose? Ten thousand dollars?"

The fourth cluster was larger and appeared more coherent. A savage argument was in progress between a man of fifty with an oily red face, hatted, very determined in manner, and a muscular fellow half his age with heavy eyebrows, coatless, plainly Irish. Fifteen or twenty men were packed around them, and others on a bench near the rail against which the Irishman was lounging were attending also. I listened for a few minutes. The question was whether the President was trying to get us into the war,—or rather, whether this was legitimate, since the Irishman claimed that Roosevelt was a goddamned warmonger whom all the real people in the country hated, and the older man claimed that we should have gone into the f...ing war when France fell a year before, as everybody in the country knew except a few immigrant rats. Redface talked ten times as much as the Irishman, but he was not able to establish any advantage that I could see. He ranted, and then Irish either repeated shortly and fiercely what he had said last, or shifted his ground. The audience were silent—favouring whom I don't know, but evidently much interested. One or two men pushed out of the group, others arrived behind me, and I was eddied forward toward the disputants. The young Irishman broke suddenly into a tirade by the man with the hat:

"You're full of s. Roosevelt even tried to get us in with the Communists in the Spanish war. If he could have done it we'd have been burning churches down like the rest of the Reds."

"No, that's not right," I heard my own voice, and pushed forward, feeling blood in my face, beginning to tremble. "No, Roosevelt as a matter of fact helped Franco by non-intervention, at the same time that Italians and German planes were fighting against the government and arms couldn't get in from France."

"What's that? What are you, a Jew?" He turned to me contemptuously, and was back at the older man before I could speak. "The only reason we weren't over there four years ago is because you can only screw us so much. Then we quit. No New Deal bastard could make us go help the goddamned Communists.

"That ain't the question, it's if we want to fight *now* or *later*. Them Nazis ain't gonna sit!" shouted the redfaced man. "They got Egypt practically, and then it's India if it ain't England first. It ain't a question of the Communists, the Communists are on Hitler's side. I tellya we can wait and wait and chew and spit and the first thing you know they'll be in England, and then who's gonna help us when they start after us? Maybe Brazil? Get wise to the world! Spain don't matter now one way or the other, they ain't gonna help and they can't hurt. It's Germany and Italy and Japan, and if it ain't too late now it's gonna be. Get wise to yourself. We shoulda gone in—"

"What with?" said the Irishman with disdain. "Pop pop. Wooden machine guns?"

"We were as ready a year ago as we are now. Defense don't mean nothing, you gotta have to fight!"

"No, we're much better off now," I said, "than we were a year ago. When England went in, to keep its word to Poland, what good was it to Poland? The German Army—"

"Shut up, you Jew," said the Irishman.

"I'm not a Jew," I said to him. "What makes—"

"Listen, Pop," he said to the man in the hat, "it's O.K. to shoot your mouth off but what the hell have you got to do with it? You aren't gonna do any fighting."

"Listen," I said.

"You sit on your big ass and talk about who's gonna fight who. Nobody's gonna fight anybody. If we feel hot, we ought to clean up some of the sons of bitches here before we go sticking our nuts anywhere to help England. We ought to clean up the sons of bitches in Wall Street and Washington before we take any ocean trips. You want to know something? You know why Germany's winning everything in this war? Because there ain't no Jews back home. There ain't no more Jews, first shouting war like this one here"—nodding at me—"and then skinning off to the synagogue with the profits. Wake up, Pop! You must have been around in the last war, you ought to know better."

I was too nervous to be angry or resentful. But I began to have a sense of oppression in breathing. I took the Irishman by the arm.

"Listen, I told you I'm not a Jew."

"I don't give a damn what you are," he turned his half-dark eyes to me, wrenching his arm loose. "You talk like a Jew."

"What does that mean?" Some part of me wanted to laugh. "How does a Jew talk?"

"They talk like you, buddy."

"That's a fine argument! But if I'm not a Jew, my talk only—"

"You probably are a Jew. You look like a Jew."

"I *look* like a Jew? Listen," I swung around with despair to a man standing next to me, "do I look like a Jew? It doesn't matter whether I do or not—a Jew is as good as anybody and better than this son of a bitch—" I was not exactly excited, I was trying to adapt my language as my need for the crowd, and my sudden respect for its judgment, possessed me—"but in fact I'm not Jewish and I don't look Jewish. Do I?"

The man looked at me quickly and said, half to me and half to the Irishman, "Hell, I don't know. Sure he does."

A wave of disappointment and outrage swept me almost to tears, I felt like a man betrayed by his brother. The lamps seemed brighter and vaguer, the night large. Looking around I saw sitting on a bench near me a tall, heavy, serious-looking man of thirty, well dressed, whom I had noticed earlier, and appealed to him, "Tell me, do I look Jewish?"

But he only stared up and waved his head vaguely. I saw with horror that something was wrong with him.

"You look like a Jew. You talk like a Jew. You *are* a Jew," I heard the Irishman say.

I heard murmuring among the men, but I could see nothing very clearly. It seemed very hot. I faced the Irishman again helplessly, holding my voice from rising.

"I'm *not* a Jew," I told him. "I might be, but I'm not. You have no bloody reason to think so, and you can't make me a Jew by simply repeating like an idiot that I am."

"Don't deny it, son," said the redfaced man, "stand up to him."

"Goddamn it." Suddenly I was furious, whirling like a fool (was I afraid of the Irishman? had he conquered me?) on the redfaced man. "I'm *not* denying it! Or rather I am, but only because I'm not a Jew! I despise renegades, I hate Jews who turn on their people, if I were a Jew I would say so, I would be proud to be: what is the vicious opinion of a man like this to me if I were a Jew? But I'm not. Why the hell should I admit I am if I'm not?"

"Jesus, the Jew is excited," said the Irishman.

"I have a right to be excited, you son of a bitch. Suppose I call you a Jew. Yes, you're a Jew. Does that mean anything?"

"Not a damn thing." He spat over the rail past a man's head.

"Prove that you're not. I say you are."

"Now listen, you Jew. I'm a Catholic."

"So am I, or I was born one, I'm not one now. I was born a Catholic." I was a little calmer but goaded, obsessed with the need to straighten this out. I felt that everything for everyone there depended on my proving him wrong. If *once* this evil for which we have not even a name could be exposed to the rest of the men as empty—if I could *prove* I was not a Jew—it would fall to the ground, neither would anyone else be a Jew to be accused. Then it could be trampled on. Fascist America was at stake. I listened, intensely anxious for our fate.

"Yeah?" said the Irishman. "Say the Apostles' Creed."

Memory went swirling back, I could hear the little bell die as I hushed it and set it on the felt, Father Boniface looked at me tall from the top of the steps and smiled, greeting me in the darkness before dawn as I came to serve, the men pressed around me under the lamps, and I could remember nothing but *visibilum omnium . . . et invisibilium?*

"I don't remember it."

The Irishman laughed with his certainty.

The papers in my pocket, I thought them over hurriedly. In my wallet. What would they prove? Details of ritual, Church history: anyone could learn them. My piece of Irish blood. Shame, shame: shame for my ruthless people. I will not be his blood. I wish I were a Jew, I would change my blood, to be able to say *Yes* and defy him.

"I'm not a Jew." I felt a fool. "You only say so. You haven't any evidence in the world."

He leaned forward from the rail, close to me. "Are you cut?"

Shock, fear ran through me before I could make any meaning out of his words. Then they ran faster, and I felt confused.

From that point, nothing is clear for me. I stayed a long time—it seemed impossible to leave, showing him victor to them—thinking of possible allies and new plans of proof, but without hope. I was tired to the marrow. The arguments rushed on, and I spoke often now but seldom was heeded except by an old fat woman, very short and dirty, who listened intently to everyone. Heavier and heavier appeared to me to press upon us in the fading night our general guilt.

In the days following, as my resentment died, I saw that I had not been a victim altogether unjustly. My persecutors were right: I was a Jew. The imaginary Jew I was was as real as the imaginary Jew hunted down, on other nights and days, in a real Jew. Every murderer strikes the mirror, the lash of the torturer falls on the mirror and cuts the real image, and the real and the imaginary blood flow down together.

1945

Wash Far Away

Long after the professor had come to doubt whether lives held crucial points as often as the men conducting or undergoing them imagined, he still considered that one day in early spring had made a difference for him. The day began his deeper—deepest—acquaintance with "Lycidas," now for him the chief poem of the world, to which he owed, he thought, as much as anything else, his survival of his wife's death. The day had humbled him and tossed him confidence. One decision had come out of it—to give up research. He had gone back, of course, two or three times, but briefly, guiltily, without commitment and without result, abandoning it again each time more firmly; now he had not touched it for years. He knew that his appointment with tenure, four years later, must have been opposed on this ground, and barely managed through by his department chairman. The sense of stepping up on Alice's body came bitterly back—she had just died, and he had even at the time seen clearly what silenced the opposition. Not that he had cared for promotion, for anything, then. And that day seemed to him the last day of his youth, though he was already a year over thirty and had not for a long time thought of himself as young.

He sighed and smiled awry: he *had* been young. He closed his eyes.

This is not exactly what he remembered.

He stepped down into the brilliant light, blinked, sweating, and set out. My God, away. The small leaves of the maple on the corner shook smartly as he passed. Alice's fierce voice echoed. Sunlight plunged to the pavement and ran everywhere like water, vivid, palpable. I am a professor, he reflected, moving rapidly, or a sort of professor; there is a breeze, a wild sun. As he levelled his palm sailing along the even hedge, it tingled. He felt his toes in his shoes. The hedge danced faintly.

My life is in ruins, he thought. She begins the quarrels, but they are my fault. Here is this weather and we are desperate. Hugh and Penny never quarrelled. I'm no further on than when we started—*I* started.

He groped back seven years to the brimming fear that had choked him while he waited in the hallway before entering his very first class. He had handled it, empty, irrecoverable. But the students had been friendly. What passion that year called out! Hugh and he had been worked like Percherons, and they had stood it and done more than anyone wanted, half the night up with papers, all day with students, planning coups in class, coaxing, worrying, praising, ransacking like a bookshop the formless minds in front of them for something to be used for understanding, levering rich in alternatives, roaming the real world for analogies to cram into the boys' world for truth. He saw the faces strained, awed, full, at the hour's end. I must do it again.

He had been teaching for seven years and he felt quietly that he had been dead for the last five. The Dostals' garden, anemones, snapdragons, crimson, yellow, rose-pink; colors swimming, the air sweetened, he went by. He thought: I enjoy myself, I quarrel, but I am really dead.

What could change? Hugh, it seemed to him with the first resentment he had ever felt for his friend, kept steadily with him like a deadweight he could never live up to. He had once thought of himself as going-to-be-a-writer; but he had never actually written anything except his dissertation, some unfinished stories, three articles. Hugh *had* been a writer. They had been going to revolutionize scholarship, too. The professor acknowledged that he had no such wish now. He was just a teacher (word he didn't like—assistant professor was better); not a very good one, and stale.

Of the class that was meeting this afternoon, he really knew—what? Nelen was dark, from Philadelphia, lazy. Warner was articulate and disconcerting; the blond fashion plate who sat by the door, Stone, was not so dull as he looked; Landes, who was always carefully prepared, always grinned; Holson twitched and could not keep to the issue; Rush was a wit. The others were dimmer, except Smith, who took in every point made, a likable boy. He liked them all, and he was aware that they liked him (he wondered why), but he didn't know them. Yet he could still write out, he supposed, half the troubles and strengths of his students of that first year of teaching.

He was doomed to the past or an unalterable present. What could change his hopeless relation with Alice?—quarrel and reconciliation; quarrel and reconciliation. Another emotion mounted new to the history of his memory of Hugh: he felt that Hugh was lucky—if he had lived, he and Penny might have quarrelled. They had had two years only; that was lucky.

The bell rang slowly down from the campus.

He could determine to teach today as he hadn't for a long time, to swing the whole class to a fresh, active relation, an insight grave and light. Well, he did determine. What must it come to, under the inescapable routine? Since the first year, the boys repeated each other. He repeated himself. Teaching was worthy, and indispensable; but it was dull. No riskiness lived in it—not after the beginning. Perhaps when one came to organize one's own courses; but he doubted that. It was no use pretending: what had truly counted—the reciprocal learning—who older could set up again? He thought he was a man modest enough, but greater modesty than his was wanted to hope to learn from Landes or Stone.

Yet he was glad of his resolution. It seemed to bring forward for possible settlement some issue that he could hardly define but knew should be at stake. He glowed, unsmiling, and strode faster, confident.

The professor paused for traffic and experienced a disappointment. "Lycidas." He was teaching "Lycidas." He crawled across the street.

There was no poem he liked better. In his junior year he had written a defense of Dr Johnson's supercilious remarks about it, then had his position swept away by his experience of the poem when reading it next. But he knew the boys would find it formidable, egotistical, frozen, their hatred of Milton developed to a fine pitch in the schools. A burden fell on him—that unpleasant majesty, cold grandeur of Milton. And the poem was about Death and Poetry; what did they care for either? He could substitute some attractive poem of the period in their anthology. The boys not having been assigned any other, time would be wasted; he cast about all the same, dawdling, magnolias gleaming on the wall ahead. He would have to do "Lycidas."

If he shirked the greatest poem in English—he turned into the gate—what could his resolution be worth, or his teaching? Nothing, and his confidence returned in the sunlight. "A dreamy and passionate flux," he remembered Robert Bridges's phrase, though none from his own essay, and entering the high doorway of his building smiled at himself for the comparison, half pleased nevertheless with himself and remembering that at any rate Bridges hadn't known Milton borrowed his river-god Camus from Fletcher, not made him up. Except for one student and a committee meeting—no, called off—he would have the whole morning for preparation. Which Fletcher? He had forgotten (not John, anyway); and he found two students waiting to see him.

One rose and stood forward, diffidently holding a paper while he unlocked the door of his office. Sperry, dull and willing. Don't know the other, do I? "Good morning, come in."

The professor was no scholar, though he had wearied through several Elizabethan authors to find a degree; but he had once noticed Camus, he had a memory, and it vexed him to forget. Settled at his desk in the low bright room, he answered questions and helped the boy normalize a small bibliography, feeling attentive, virtuous, competent. Phineas, I expect, but where? ". . . and remember that the authors' names are *not* inverted in the footnotes; only for alphabetizing. Good luck with it."

Sperry closed the door. In a moment there would be a knock. The sun lay level across his blotter, photographing the dust on a dust jacket. Abruptly he saw it in a line-end, "old *Chamus* from his cell," guarded by a hundred nymphs or something—some short piece of Phineas'. "Come in!" he called, radiant.

This was a young man with a high forehead and a nervous smile who wanted advice about majoring in English, his adviser having given him less than satisfaction. He explained that the professor had had his brother several years before, so that he— Oh yes: what was his brother doing now? His brother was lost in Italy.

The professor's mind as well as his brow clouded.

He remembered Sutton: a broad brow like this boy's and large eyes, a yellow sweater, smoking. Once they had had an argument about *Volpone* in conference, and he had an impression later that Sutton was right. He remembered it all. Indeed—he thought with a vacant grind—do I do anything ever but remember? Does anything *happen?* Why yes . . . yes . . . students in yellow sweaters die. "Camus, reverend Sire, came footing slow." As the line sounded heavily in his ear, its movement was terrifying, as if Camus were Death. It would be good to say, "Sutton, you were quite right about *Volpone*, I hadn't considered it deeply enough." A ranging mind, original. "Sutton, Wade" on a course or casualty list, the name forever reversed. With the most serious effort he had required for some time, the professor wrenched himself to expectancy, muttering, "I'm sorry . . ."

Sutton's brother kept him nearly half an hour. After the first ten minutes, urgent for the afternoon, he itched to come at "Lycidas," but he couldn't bring himself to hurry the boy, and the record, the possibilities, dragged on. The portrait of Hugh, with its living depthless eyes and indefinable unease, watched them from the low shelf over the books at the back of the desk. The sunlight died, returned, died. He spun an ashtray, talking. At last the boy stood up, effusively grateful, knocking a book on the floor, effusively contrite, and undecided departed.

Instead of plunging into Milton, the professor went to his window with a fresh cigarette and looked down a little into the bright, sunless lawn. The rememberer. Teaching is memory. If it came to that, he could remember enough. How proudly he had begun at some point to say, "I haven't read that for ten years." Hugh's golden stories the summer in Canada. Tunes that summer. This was the superiority of aging one waited for: just to remember. True or false, evil or gay, never mind. The Nobel Prize for Memory. Recipient a suicide en route to Stockholm, having remembered all his sins at once, sitting in a deck chair sharpening a pencil.

Now the sun moved out from a cloud, and forsythia blazed by the walk. ". . . think to burst out into sudden . . ." Hugh lay on a couch in the August sun, his short beard glinting, saying, "It's just as well. I could never have got done what I wanted to." Later, when he had got very weak and was chiefly teeth and eyes, his wandering mind wanted pathetically to live, certain he would. But the professor clung still to the resignation, the judgment on the couch; he himself had done nothing he wanted, and he had come to believe that Hugh was right. He had come to believe this after his grief had dimmed. When he took over Hugh's classes, he had felt, perhaps, as a tree would, growing into a dry riverbed grieving still for water—good, but unexpected, trembling, and wholly inadequate. He stared at the forsythia beyond the flat green. "Came footing slow . . ." Came footing fast. But it was "*went* footing slow," and recalling this he exorcised suddenly the ominous in the line. He felt unaccountably relieved, normal; he enjoyed an instant the luminous scene, and turned back to his desk under the torn beloved print of the "Anatomy Lesson."

The professor was a systematic man. He opened his Milton and read the poem thoughtfully, twice, before he laid out side by side two other Miltons got from the library early in the week and began to work his way through the editors' notes. The professor was also honest. Though he'd not looked at the poem for months, he felt very little as he read except admiration for the poet's language and minute flirts of emotions he had probably experienced in previous readings, and he did not pretend to feel more. Consistently Lycidas was Hugh—even was Sutton—but without pressure. What were teachers if not shepherds? "Henceforth thou art the Genius of the shore," he whispered reverently to the brown portrait, thinking of his class, ". . . and shalt be good / To all that wander in that perilous flood." The second time through he was uncomfortable with the sterile complaint, "What boots it with uncessant care / To tend the homely slighted Shepherd's trade . . ." Both times he was gently moved by the exquisite melancholy of a semi-couplet at the end of the flower passage:

> For so to interpose a little ease,
> Let our frail thoughts dally with false surmise.

He wrote "exquisite melancholy" in the margin the second time.

The editors he read closely, he read long, and he was astonished when he learned that "flashy" meant insipid. What were the "songs"? Preaching . . . teaching. Insipid teaching, like his. Was all this preparation a mistake? His teaching during the first years had been very disorderly, quick, dialectical, free. He and Hugh had hated elaborate plans—sometimes, too, they hadn't a moment to prepare, but for reading the assignment—but they had learned and worked things out *with* the students, and that made the difference. Today he would be as free as he could. He wanted still to learn, he didn't feel superior to the students (Smith, Sutton) more now than then. But his experience was what it was. Who would know "flashy" unless he told them? He went eagerly on.

A student knocked, went off with a book.

As Milton's imitations and telescopings multiplied, he commenced to feel restless, distant, smaller. What one editor neglected, another observed, and he began to have a sense of the great mind like a whirring, sleepless refinery—its windows glittering far out across the landscape of night—through which poured and was transformed the whole elegiac poetry of Greece and Italy and England, receiving an impress new and absolute. *Mine!* it seemed to call, seizing one brightness, another, another, locking them in place, while their features took on the rigidity and beauty of masks. Through the echoing halls they posed at intervals, large, impassive, splendid; a special light moved on their helms, far up, and shadows fell deep between them. The professor collected himself and glanced at the time.

Naturally he wouldn't finish. It would take fortnights to weigh all the notes. And questions marked for further study would have to go—not that they were likely to come up. Making a late lunch, he ought to be able to do everything else. He stretched, luxurious, warm. When had he felt so thoroughly and profitably occupied? Throwing the window wider, he went rapidly, speculationless, through the notes to the end of the poem. This done, he closed the books except one, put them aside, pulled his ear, and stared at "Lycidas."

Now came the part he called "penetration." Although he knew very well what the subject of the poem was, he pretended he didn't, and pondered it, pencil in hand, to find out. Elegy by an ambitious, powerful, obscure man of twenty-eight for a successful junior of twenty-five, drowned. Academic status: Non-Fellow (grand poet) for Fellow (little poet). Probably commissioned or at least requested.

> Invocation, or *complaint*.
> Elegy proper: another invocation
>   (his own death)
>   their friendship
>   Nature's lament
>   Nymphs, where?
>   (Fame: Apollo)
>   the cause? Triton, Aeolus
>   University mourns: Camus
>   (Clergy: St. Peter)
>   flowers for hearse
>   where now? Nature godless
> Consolation, by metamorphosis (Christian, pagan)
> Ottava rima "Thus sang . . ." & so an end.

Four sections, with three personal digressions. And the opening was really another personal digression, this unpleasing insistence on his being compelled to write. No one *made* you, after all. The Milton passages came to less than a third of the poem—but where the power was. Reasonable enough; Milton may never have spoken to Edward King, except to ask for the salt. The professor studied the text and his notes, waving his pencil slowly by his ear. Cunning. He saw that. The testimony of Triton and Aeolus, and the speeches of Camus and Peter, actually made up a sort of trial—so that the poet's diverse materials would be given an air of unity. What on earth made Milton think of a trial? . . . *Oh.* His own inquisition of the nymphs above! They had deserted Lycidas when he needed them: who then *had* been with him, for evil? Let a court find out.

The professor leaned back in his chair with surprise. All this revealed only in the word "plea" and the sense of the passages. And one meaning of "felon." His vision of the refining plant recurred to him, but he grimaced impatiently at it. Better say Vatican. Only the "privy paw." A Puritan Vatican then, with catacombs.

Bending to the poem again, after a new cigarette and a dozen notes made compactly on a small yellow pad, he approached almost warily, as if toward an animal long familiar suddenly displaying resources unsuspected, even dangerous. But in the first moment he saw that his discovery made the fame passage more obviously than ever an excrescence, and with a touch of indignation he relaxed. It split the trial. Milton's mounting sense must have worked strongly indeed if he was willing to do this; and then that fantasy of arrogance wherein Phoebus singles him out by touching his ears! The professor, no poet, pulled his own ear.

He drew up a schedule for the discussion. How many hours, he wondered, would it take to teach "Lycidas" properly? I might give a course (first semester) English 193: "Lycidas" 1–84. He stretched again, smiling, crinkling his eyes toward the light stream.

And finally—it was very late—the "lesson." He wouldn't have admitted to anyone, of course, that this was what he called it, but call it this he did, had for years. He remembered a time when he hadn't used the "lesson," when in fact he had detested above all things a "message" (his derisive tone he heard still) of any sort. So had Hugh. His face shadowed, and he shifted his eyes to the portrait, which the sun reached. Have I betrayed you? Here in the sun? Feeling melodramatic, he set his mind uneasily to the "lesson."

Then all at once he felt hopeless. What could a one-hour class do to change what he had become? He had been a fool. One class, he raged, and the new man leaps from the old skin. With his schedule and his "penetration" and his "lesson." He stops catering to the boys' shiftlessness, he develops tongues of fire. A marriage like a tiger lies down and purrs. Dark in his office at one-thirty, he sat clamped in despair. And the despair threw him onward. No, he *had* been a fool, but he was a fool still, a worse one. You have to start. You have nothing to lose. Jump overboard now, you might as well try. At least you can become serious, and let the rhetoric take care of itself. If you fail, you fail anyway. He would finish his preparation and do everything he could do this afternoon, and see. Even the "lesson." Why not? It was only a joke with himself. Hating "teacher," he pretended to submit to "lesson"—merely the general moral truth, or some general moral truth (God knows, he wasn't dogmatic) arising out of whatever they were doing. Nothing pretentious, or original, but if you didn't make a form for it you might pass it by altogether. Hastily he wrote at the bottom of the schedule, cramping his hand, his "lesson" for today, and as he wrote an image sprang up of Milton rapt forward unconscious at a window table in the twilight, his drastic mind and dull eyes on the shade of King, his pen and the swirling threshold forces on himself: "Whatever we do and think we are doing, however objective or selfless our design, our souls each instant are enacting *our own* destinies." Moral enough! Did the boys even believe in souls?—they didn't give a hoot for immortality. But this was the point of teaching.

He arranged his notes and ideas with returning satisfaction. Hat, window. But after these hours he was tired, very tired, and the breeze and the blaze brightened him less than he would have liked as he hurried toward the club, deciding to have—how rare for him, how usual for others—a cocktail before lunch.

The bar was nearly empty, the martini firm and immediate.

Through lunch he resisted the silly recurring desire to say aloud what he heard again and again in his head, "Nor yet where Deva spreads her wizard stream," a line that gave him intense pleasure; for example, to his speechless neighbor at the round table, a dry short man, very hungry, evidently, in Classics. The verb seemed as brilliant as the epithet. King sailed from Chester-on-Dee. Deva, the Dee, like Wordsworth's Winander. Charles Diodati lived on the Dee; maybe he and Milton (Milton the diva of Christ's—beaten, disappointed genius) had sat on the bank the summer before and traded legends of the sacred stream . . . "youthful poets dream on summer eves by haunted stream." "What do you think of Edward King?" a soft voice. "I doubt he deserves a fellowship," a stern one from the incredibly youthful face, "and it came to him too soon." Behind the slight body, clenched grass. "Your luck, John, wait, will change." The late-afternoon airs, the dappled water. There was more in that line than the fatal sailing. He didn't even mention King in his letters to Diodati between the death and "Lycidas." However. Had he written to anyone of Hugh? None ever: how? Diodati had a year to live. Who did Milton write to then? God-given, God-withdrawn. The Dio stoops to the Dee; twice. And stoops no more.

He drank his coffee slowly. He hoped the boys had prepared well; he had told them to use the stacks. The dining room had emptied, a waiter hovered, still he lingered. He was remembering a lunch he and Hugh had had together once on a day as bright as this one—Friday, too—in a restaurant neither could afford. Italian bread. Something had gone very wrong for him, and Hugh was consoling and sympathizing with him in the merriest, gentlest way imaginable. They had told jokes, and were free together as two old friends can be in a strange, agreeable setting. He was leaving next day, he recalled; so that the occasion had urgency forward as well as back. But what was odd? He couldn't hear their voices. He could see the glints and sheen from the table, his own arms on the table, hand on a wineglass, he saw Hugh's face and the white wall, he saw the whole scene, but he heard nothing. It was completely silent. The professor struck his palm on his table and rose, his heart beating, and left.

The breeze had died away, leaving the campus placid, almost hot. Crossing, however, he looked forward eagerly like a defendant facing the last day of a suit that had so far gone well: anxious and confident, pacing out the final hour of his imputed, fantastic guilt. He went by his office for a book and notes, opened the window, touched the frame of the portrait, and arrived in his classroom just before the bell.

Where were the others? The high, dark-brown, sun-filled room, too large for a class of fourteen anyway, seemed all but deserted, and he looked around it annoyed while the bell rang. Who were missing? Only Cotton, it appeared, in the infirmary ("A good place for Cotton," said somebody), and Fremd. He smiled, throwing his Milton on the table, and felt better, although where was Fremd?

"Well, gentlemen," he went over to the windows—well known for roaming and for picking up chairs, he knew, but he had long ceased trying to refrain, "how do you like it? I assume you acquired an unholy aversion to it in school, as also to *Macbeth* and some other works not perfectly uninteresting. But what do you think of it this time, Mr. Rush?"

"Marvelous," the young man said mildly.

"Your diction is rich, but your tone is slack"—the professor smiled—"as applied to the most celebrated poem in our language. What precisely is marvelous about it?"

Rush grinned above his olive tie and thought. "There is a marvelous lack of emotion."

"Oh?" Crossing for the book, he read the opening lines aloud. "Unemotional? Did the rest of you feel the same way?"

No, they didn't.

"I meant emotion about his friend," Rush amended.

"Well, what about these?" Refusing to be hurried into his thesis, he read aloud some other lines:

> But, O the heavy change, now thou art gone,
> Now thou art gone and never must return!

Their languid gloom oppressed him. "Those are about King straight enough."

"Well . . . all those nymphs and flowers and wood gods . . ."

"Such properties needn't be inconsistent with strong emotion, as we'll see presently. But let's find out what Milton's subject is. What's the poem *about*, gentlemen? What lay essentially in his mind as he set about it? We have a poem in the form of a pastoral elegy, heavy in certain parts with passion. What about?"

"It's about his friend's death, isn't it?" Wright duly said.

"No!" Landes's high, confident voice broke out. "It's about Milton himself. In other words, it has a subject he felt very strongly about, and it's very emotional whenever it comes to him or things that interested him. King was just the occasion. If his cat had died instead, the poem might have been just as good."

"Hardly his cat," said the professor, "though Gray did well enough. But I agree with you that the poem is not on the whole passionate about King . . ." He talked easily and warmly, striding about the room with restless sudden turns, his ideas thronging. As he sat down lightly on the table edge, the sun streamed in afresh, glowing on the rim of Warner's glasses and white collar.

". . . In his crisis of discontent with hard long solitary study and protracted obscurity, *doubt* of the poetic priesthood he'd entered, *scorn* for the worthless pastors of the priesthood he had refused to enter," he caught Hale's eye back in the corner and realized with vexation that the tall, bland youth was engaged on some very different speculation of his own, "in this crisis all his passions and anxieties welled up at sight of a young man, dedicated as he was himself, though hardly in the same degree, *cut off*. Ah! To what end, then: self-denial, labor, patience, wisdom even? King's had simply vanished, and so might his."

"I don't see why he was worried about dying," said Nelen's good-natured, empty face.

A real young man's remark. "Two things. One I just indicated—a colleague five years younger suddenly being killed. The other is that there was some actual danger. The plague was fierce. People had died even in the little place where Milton was, Horton. And he planned to go to Italy the next year. As you sit here, a voyage from England to Italy seems safe enough, but travel was risky three hun-

377

dred years ago. If King had drowned going just to Ireland, why couldn't he, going farther?"

"But there are only four lines about his own death," Smith drawled, in the voice that made everything he said sound like a man dreaming.

A hand moved, Nelen's again. "Sir, who *is* King?"

Ugh. "Edward King," the professor explained with Oriental restraint, "was the *friend* of John Milton about whose death the poem we are discussing ostensibly is." Or rival.

"It seems to me the poem is about King," Stone said doubtfully, uncrossing his legs.

"Critics pretty much agree—Legouis and the rest—that Milton's feelings about himself are the real subject."

"Could they be wrong?"

Warner's simple, uninflected question somehow moved the professor very much. The trust, the measureless respect both for them and for *his* judgment of them, entered him so deeply that he couldn't answer for a moment but merely looked at the dark boy tilted back in his chair smoking. Perhaps it *was* after all an honour to be a critic, or even a teacher. But how deserve such confidence, this privilege?

"They certainly could. I've told you all year not to take anybody's word for anything if you feel competent to judge it yourself and can bring evidence forward. Sometimes, it's true, in matters of *feeling* there isn't much evidence. But here there is a good deal. Take the last line: 'To-morrow to fresh woods, and pastures new.' What do you make of that? Anybody."

Smith sat forward. "He doesn't want to be any more where his friend was with him, and all the things he sees will remind him of his loss."

Dumbfounded he looked down at the page. Smith's rapid intelligence working through the incantation of his voice had often affected the professor, but this time he felt as if an oracle had spoken. . . . Why not? "Yes, it seems possible. It's simpler . . . What I was going to say was that the line is usually taken as a reference to Milton's plans either for moving to London or traveling to Italy. Of course, there might be an allusion to this anyway. But your contemporary meaning is better—after all, his readers knew nothing and cared less about Milton's plans."

"Sir? Did people like this poem when it came out?" asked Holson, crawling about on his seat.

Did they? "No, they didn't, so far as we know. In fact, at least a century passed before any attention was paid to it at all, before any of his minor poems were recognized."

Curiously, from Rush, "Who recognized them?"

The professor, puzzling still over Smith's point, felt cornered. He cast back. "I think Warton was the first important critic on their side, but Pope and Gray knew them well. It was really the beginnings of Romantic taste that rescued them." Or so I say.

"Classics don't like them?" Landes wondered.

"Well, Milton is a classical poet, but he is also a Romantic. The word is difficult, as you probably know . . ."

He described its ambiguity, called Johnson's *Life of Milton* a model of respectful churlishness and vindictive merriment (he remembered his undergraduate phrases, after all), and glanced at the Pound-Eliot campaign against *Paradise Lost*, abbreviating, anxious to get on.

". . . But let me ask *you* some questions. Who are the 'rout'? In fact what does 'rout' mean? It's in line sixty-one."

"The Maenads," said Warner.

"No doubt. And who were they?"

Nobody knew, or nobody answered: he explained; and nobody knew that "rout" had any but its modern sense. Holson, indeed, thought the modern sense would be better. Briefly, and without expressing the asperity he felt, the professor laid down precepts of submission to a poem and fidelity to an author's sense. He was aware of some resistance in the class. He should have been fuller. What was "welter"? Nobody knew exactly. He read a few lines aloud, farsing. For five minutes he probed their familiarity with the meaning of details.

"You've got to look these things up, gentlemen. It's not only the matter of intellectual responsibility" (who would ever have taught them that? the major thing?), "it's a matter of enjoyment. We miss quite enough anyway, inevitably. How many of you know jessamine, crow-toe, woodbine—have visual images when you see the words or hear them?"

One hand hesitated.

He went off to the windows. "I don't myself," he said, looking out. Forsythia, daffodils, snapdragons. "Now it's true the passage has literary sources and a symbolic intention, but if the flowers are nothing more than words for us, we miss a good deal. Jammed in cities, we have to. The whole country experience is disappearing. Not only the country. Do you know the old rhyme about London bells? I can't

379

remember it all, most of it though, but each couplet rings the bells of some church, at first senselessly, and then a frightening continuity commences to emerge.

> Brickbats and targets
> Say the Bells of St. Marg'rets,
> Brickbats and tiles—it was *Bull's-eyes* and targets—
> Say the Bells of St. Giles, and so on.

It's violent and beautiful still, for a modern reader. It sometimes stands my hair on end. But how dim must the effect be, compared to its effect on its first hearers, accustomed all day to hear the ringing of the peals, high and low, now here, now there, from the hundreds of churches all over London, pealing like friends and warnings across the otherwise more or less silent city. No traffic or machinery, only the voice of the militant Church, the bells. The poem must have been a nightmare of reality. From this point of view, in fact, our prolific, active cities, with all their noise, have become in truth absolutely still—stiller than that," he gestured to a print of the Roman Forum high on the sidewall. "You lose out of literature some experience every year, and you need all the knowledge you can get." Hugh would have liked that. How quiet the room feels. Here comes Warner, here comes a chopper.

"What's the knowledge *for?*" said Warner in a loud voice bristling like his hair. "Poetry is supposed to be dreamy and vague, like Keats. Why pick it apart? I'd like to know how a super-jet works, that's useful knowledge, but I don't care how a poem works. This poem makes me feel half asleep. I like the feeling. I don't think a poem *does* work, I think it loafs, and teachers pretend to—no offense, sir—pretend to know all sorts of things about it that don't really exist."

The professor picked up his chair. A true feeling, though lazy enough; "dreamy and passionate flux"—and then all the claptrap.

"Tell me, Mr Warner, would you admit that there are conventions in 'Lycidas'?"

"Sure," the boy stretched. "They're not real shepherds, they're Milton and his friend. The nymphs are fanciful, and so on. But that's all obvious."

"We might be more definite than that, and fuller . . ." He elaborated a little, dangling his chair, on the artificial character of the properties. The poem seemed Watteau-*ish* as he talked—he did not like Watteau—and he felt abruptly that he was tired. Was he doing as well as he wanted to? What had happened to his excitement?

". . . So. Now: who is the 'blind Fury,' Mr Warner? Line seventy-five."

"What's-her-name. Atropos. The one who slices."

"Very accurate." (The yellow sweater smoked on, faceless.) "Except that she isn't a Fury."

"She's not? The fellow I read said she was."

"I doubt if he did. Atropos is a Fate. The poet in his rage against her *calls* her a Fury." He put the chair down.

Warner was decided, superior. "What's the difference?"

The professor suffered a flick of rage. The cold self-assurance in the voice cambered as from endless metallic contempt for these subjects, these feathers.

> They age, like ours, O soul of Sir John Cheke,
> Hated not learning worse than toad or asp.

"The difference is between understanding a world-poet, Mr Warner, and not. Or between cultivation, and Ignorance truculent." Warner sat straighter. (Fatuous, and then unjust?—as to Alice) "Of course I don't mean yours, but the difference is frankly as great as if one of your friends referred to your mother as an aging woman—say she is one—and another called her a witch, an evil witch." Frank, indeed. "The point is that the anger and horror of the line will be wholly felt only by a reader who already knows that Atropos is not properly a Fury but a Fate. As most readers, I suppose, do, or did." He didn't look at Warner, then made his voice general, "Let me give you an analogy. Some time ago, a century and a quarter, say, an audience assembled to hear a new piano concerto in Vienna. Piano, orchestra, conductor, a large aristocratic uncomfortable room, ladies, gentlemen. Now there is nothing very striking about the concerto's opening phrase but, as the piano began it, every nerve in the audience tightened." He stopped.

Silence, curiosity.

Doubtfully, at last, from Holson, "Did you say the *piano* began . . . ?"

"Yes. Why not?"

"The piano played the introduction? But the orchestra always does," the boy said nervously.

"That's the point. It's the orchestra, gentlemen, in a piano concerto, that begins and prepares for the entrance of the piano, which is the star of the occasion. That night, for the first time in history, a piano concerto began *not* in the orchestra but with the piano. It was Beethoven's Fourth. What sort of position is a listener to it in who simply does not know that concerti begin in the orchestra? He won't even hear the most important thing about the opening phrase. This is an affair, isn't it, of pure knowledge? No quantity of attention or insight will assist your ignorance, if you happen to be ignorant."

Hale wanted something! "Yes?" That admirable courtesy.

"Is there a good recording of that, sir?"

"What it comes to—just a minute—is that what the artist does is sometimes even more interesting in its negative aspect, that is, in the alternative or other possibility that it displaces, than in what it is itself. So in 'Lycidas.' The fact that Milton couldn't keep to his subject, or his nominal subject, shows that he had powerfully other matter on his mind. The digressions are in a way the poem's best testimony to his complete seriousness. But the reader observes them precisely in the sudden disappointment of expectation; that is, the poem ceases to be about King. Mr Hale, I think there is a recording by Schnabel, if not, there is one by somebody else, and a question more remote from the drowning of King I haven't heard for fifteen minutes." He looked at his watch, "Sixteen minutes."

Several boys laughed.

The professor had looked at his watch, however, to see what time it was, having lost during the Warner moment his usual sense of what piece of the fifty minutes had lapsed and what remained. More remained than he had feared, but it wasn't much.

"Sir," Smith spoke just before he hurried on, "what do you mean, that the poem ceases to be about King?"

Surprised, he explained: the two long, intense passages on Fame and the corruption of the clergy were obvious excrescences.

"But Milton qualifies their differences from the rest, doesn't he?"

"He does? Where?"

The slow-voiced, serious boy bent, scanning. Motes waltzed in a sunbeam across Hale.

"Here, eighty-six. He says *that strain* 'was of a higher mood' . . . from a god, that is. And 132, 'the dread voice is past.' At the end of each."

The professor studied the lines. He felt, uneasily, as if he had never seen them before.

"Maybe '*various* quills' at the very end is more of the same explanation," the boy went on.

"I don't quite see how these *explain* them. It would be easy to invent transitions at the ends after you had left your theme—or come to it, rather, nakedly, since Milton is his own theme."

"But they grow naturally out of the situation," Smith argued. "Each of King's masters gets a word in: Apollo, Cambridge, St. Peter. Orpheus perished horribly, like Lycidas; therefore, why break your neck to be a poet? Then the Church mourns, right after the university—promising son lost. What's out of order about that?"

"It's not so much that they're out of order, as that they're about Milton, not King," the professor repeated.

"Well, Milton felt them hard. It might be his own situation. It *is* King's though, isn't it? The only things I know about him are that he was a scholar and poet and was going to be a clergyman." The boy considered. The others were listening to him with interest. "It's King's life that got slit, and then Apollo consoles Milton by saying that his lost friend, after all, will be judged in Heaven, not here. So will Milton, but that doesn't keep it from being about King."

"But it's Milton Apollo singles out by touching his ear," exclaimed the professor, resisting a weak sense that the discussion was getting— how?—past him, dragging him.

"Only to defend him," Stone said unexpectedly. The blond, handsome boy lifted his book, "My editor said if your ear trembles, you're being talked about, that is, people would be saying Milton had his own fame in mind, so Apollo reproved them—for him. Fame is only Heaven's judgment, where King is."

"But the genuine rage is in the other passage," drawled Smith. "It seems to me King's death is awful to Milton, especially, because the Church needed good men."

"Why didn't Milton go in then?" Rush asked.

"How do I know?" Smith tilted his chair to see past Holson. "You don't have to do something yourself to want other people to do it well. Milton was a damned serious man. Maybe he thought poetry was more important."

"He quit it for politics for years. He probably was too aggressive to be a clergyman," Stone said from his corner.

The professor found his voice. The storm that had seemed to be gathering around him, from Smith, had somehow not descended. But was the boy right? What do I think? He wished the hour were over. Milton or King, he wondered wearily, what matter? He smiled at "aggressive" to raise his spirits; Stone it was who had remarked admiringly that Shakespeare's Cleopatra "had *id*."

Pacing the front of the classroom again, he told them his discovery of the morning, the Trial that linked Triton-Aeolus-Camus-Peter. "What brought into Milton's imagination, do you suppose, the notion of a trial?" he asked, sitting on the warm sill and lighting a cigarette. "Mr Nelen, any ideas?" Mr Nelen had no ideas, he revealed. "Mr Holson?"

While Holson was reflecting the professor made a short excursion. He climbed, dripping, under a blinding sun, up and up a sand dune, one of the vast dunes hanging over Lake Superior, panting. He was laughing and calling up. Once he looked back, fearful. Hugh helped him at the top, and as he stood up a wind caressed all his skin. The miles of blue lake gleamed. No other dune so white as this. The sky was full of the sun. He wanted to say. But he knew Hugh was saying, "It's wonderful," running back toward the edge. "Just step as far as you can with each foot," then disappeared over it. Now he had to? Yes. He shuddered, cold, came toward the edge, shrank. Feet moved by strong love on. Fought. He leaned erect off the world's edge, toppling, and stept! Through empty air straight down, terror of the first, the bounce and astonishment of the second. Pure joy the third, his eyes cleared. He rushed through the sunlight wild with delight in deep jumps, foot far to foot, touching the earth, down and down toward Hugh, bounding far below. Far off, another world.

"Himself," Holson said.

"I'm sorry?" said the professor, getting up.

"Did he want to show what a trial it had been for himself?"

"Hardly. The trial, I think, gentlemen, continues the dramatic method of Milton's own inquisition of the nymphs, earlier. It's a way of clamping his material together, producing an illusion of unity."

"Why the inquisition in the first place?" Stone's voice, after the pause, was thoughtful.

"Why not?" He smiled.

"Well," the young man in the corner went on deliberately, "but if the unity or the meaning isn't real, is just an illusion, how can the poem be good or true?"

The professor reached for his book, but a light came on in his brain. *Why!* He heard his voice sudden and tense: "Why the inquisition! What does a man think when a friend dies, what does he do? He *asks questions*—'not loud, but deep.' *Why? Where now? Why? Where?*" He saw the class again, and realized he was trembling. "But you can't just ask these questions over and over again in a poem, as you do in life. You have to have something to ask them about. What situation will let you ask the most questions? A trial. An inquiry, a trial. It doesn't matter what the questions pretend to be about. Where the nymphs were on Tuesday, which wind blew. What matters is that there *be* questions. Behind all the beauty we haven't had a chance to discuss, the versification, the imagery, behind the foliage, there is this urgency and reality."

His difficult, morning sense of the poem as a breathing, weird, great, incalculable animal was strong on him again. He returned to the table excited, constrained, for the book.

"That's like what I meant," Smith hastened his drawl. "He really asks the questions about King. They're his questions, but he kept himself out of the poem as much as he *could*."

His questions. Did he? The professor as he opened the book felt that all things were possible, and seeing the flower passage he imagined a rustling, as if his metaphor were true, and under the passage moved the animal, the massive insight of the grieving poet.

"Yet the flowers are to satisfy himself, not King. Of course, the whole elegy is in King's honour, but I mean their pathos is less than their beauty. The melancholy is all Milton's. Listen.

> Bid amaranthus all his beauty shed,
> And daffadillies fill their cups with tears,
> To strew the laureate hearse where *Lycid* lies.
> For so, to interpose a little ease,
> Let our frail thought . . ."

At this point, an extraordinary thing happened. The professor saw the word "false" coming. FALSE. He felt as if snatched up by the throat and wrung. "False" threw its iron backward through the poem. The room shook. Then the unutterable verse mastered his voice and took it off like a tempest:

> "dally with false surmise.
> Ay me!"

The cry rang hopeless through his mind—

> "whilst THEE the shores and sounding seas
> Wash far away, where'er thy bones are hurled;
> Whether beyond the stormy Hebrides,
> Where THOU perhaps under the whelming tide
> Visit'st the bottom of the monstrous world—"

A bell sounded, and the professor was able to dismiss the class a moment later—remembering that he had forgotten after all the "lesson." But whether he could have read a line more he wondered, as he closed the strange book and held it in both hands. The students made for the door. The sun shone steadily in at the windows. The class was over.

The professor sat a long time in his office, not thinking of anything and perhaps not unhappy, before he went home. Once he read over the transfiguration of Lycidas, and was troubled by the trembling of light on the page; his eyes had filled with tears. He heard the portrait's voice. At last he rose, closed the window, and took his hat. Shutting the door as he left, in the still-bright hall he looked at the name engraved on his card on the door. He felt older than he had in the morning, but he had moved into the exacting conviction that he was . . . something . . . not dead.

1957

Notes

MARLOWE'S DAMNATIONS. Published here for the first time. Judging by internal evidence, it was written in 1952.

THOMAS NASHE AND "THE UNFORTUNATE TRAVELLER." Written to introduce a new paperback edition of *The Unfortunate Traveller; or, The Life of Jack Wilton,* by Thomas Nashe. Edited by Louis F. Peck with an introduction by John Berryman, G. P. Putnam's Sons, 1960.

SHAKESPEARE AT THIRTY. Originally printed in *The Hudson Review,* vol. VI, Summer 1953, pages 175–203.

NOTES ON "MACBETH." Originally printed in somewhat different form in *The Arts of Reading,* co-edited by Ralph Ross, Allen Tate, and John Berryman, Thomas Y. Crowell, 1960.

SHAKESPEARE'S LAST WORD. Published here for the first time. The date of composition is not certain, probably 1962.

THE DEVELOPMENT OF ANNE FRANK. Published here for the first time. It was written in 1967.

CONRAD'S JOURNEY. Published here for the first time. It was written in 1962.

THE MIND OF ISAAC BABEL. Originally printed in somewhat different form in *The Arts of Reading,* co-edited by Ralph Ross, Allen Tate, and John Berryman, Thomas Y. Crowell, 1960.

"THE MONK" AND ITS AUTHOR. This introduction to the Grove Press edition of Matthew G. Lewis's *The Monk* originally appeared in 1952.

THE FREEDOM OF THE DON. Published here for the first time. The date of composition is not certain, probably 1960.

THE WORLD OF HENRY JAMES. Originally printed in *Sewanee Review*, vol. 53, no. 2, Spring 1945, pages 291–7.

STEPHEN CRANE'S "THE RED BADGE OF COURAGE." Originally printed in *The American Novel from James Fenimore Cooper to William Faulkner*, edited by Wallace Stegner, Basic Books, 1965.

STEPHEN CRANE'S "THE OPEN BOAT." Originally printed in somewhat different form in *The Arts of Reading*, co-edited by Ralph Ross, Allen Tate, and John Berryman, Thomas Y. Crowell. 1960.

THEODORE DREISER. First printed in *The New York Times Book Review*, March 4, 1951, page 7. Later reprinted in *Highlights of Modern Literature*, edited by Francis Brown, Houghton-Mifflin, 1954.

DREISER'S "THE TITAN." Originally printed as an Afterword to the New American Library paperback edition of Theodore Dreiser's novel, 1952.

F. SCOTT FITZGERALD. First printed in *The Kenyon Review*, vol. 8, Winter 1946, pages 103–12.

THE CASE OF RING LARDNER. First printed in *Commentary*, vol. 22, November 1956, pages 416–23.

HEMINGWAY'S "A CLEAN, WELL-LIGHTED PLACE." Originally printed in somewhat different form in *The Arts of Reading*, co-edited by Ralph Ross, Allen Tate, and John Berryman, Thomas Y. Crowell, 1960.

A NOTE ON "AUGIE." First printed in "Speaking of Books," *The New York Times Book Review*, December 6, 1953, page 2.

"SONG OF MYSELF": INTENTION AND SUBSTANCE. Published here for the first time. It was written in 1957.

HARDY AND HIS THRUSH. First printed under the title " 'The Darkling Thrush' by Thomas Hardy," in *Master Poems of the English Language*, edited by Oscar Williams, Trident Press, 1966, pages 788–90.

THE RITUAL OF W. B. YEATS. First printed in *The Columbia Review*, vol. 17, May–June 1936, pages 26–32.

THE POETRY OF EZRA POUND. Originally appeared in *Partisan Review*, vol. 16, April 1949, pages 377–94.

PRUFROCK'S DILEMMA. First printed in somewhat different form in *The Arts of Reading*, co-edited by Ralph Ross, Allen Tate, and John Berryman, Thomas Y. Crowell, 1960.

THE SORROWS OF CAPTAIN CARPENTER. First printed under the title " 'Captain Carpenter' by John Crowe Ransom," in *Master Poems of the English Language*, edited by Oscar Williams, Trident Press, 1966, pages 985–8.

DYLAN THOMAS: THE LOUD HILL OF WALES. First printed as review of *The World I Breathe* by Dylan Thomas, in *The Kenyon Review*, vol. 2, Autumn 1940, pages 481–5.

ROBERT LOWELL AND OTHERS. Originally printed in somewhat different form as an omnibus review under the title "Lowell, Thomas, & Co." in *Partisan Review*, vol. 14, January–February 1947, pages 73–85.

POETRY CHRONICLE: 1948. First printed in somewhat different form as an omnibus review of ten books of poems under the title "Waiting for the End, Boys," in *Partisan Review*, vol. 15, February 1948, pages 254–67.

FROM THE MIDDLE AND SENIOR GENERATIONS. Originally a review of books of verse by Theodore Roethke, Karl Shapiro, Cummings, and Williams in *The American Scholar*, vol. 28, Summer 1959, pages 384–90.

DESPONDENCY AND MADNESS: ON LOWELL'S "SKUNK HOUR." First printed in a symposium on Lowell's poem by Wilbur, Nims, Berryman, and Lowell in *New World Writing 21*, Lippincott, 1962. Later reprinted in *The Contemporary Poet as Artist and Critic*, edited by Anthony Ostroff, Little, Brown, 1964.

ONE ANSWER TO A QUESTION: CHANGES. First printed in *Shenandoah*, vol. 17, Autumn 1965, pages 67–76. Reprinted in *Poets on Poetry*, edited by Howard Nemerov, Basic Books, 1966.

THURSDAY OUT. First printed in *The Noble Savage*, edited by Saul Bellow, no. 3, Spring 1961, pages 186–94, but written in 1958.

THE LOVERS. First printed in *The Kenyon Review*, vol. 7, Winter 1945, pages 1–11. Reprinted in *Best American Short Stories*, edited by Martha Foley, 1946, and also in *New Directions 9*, edited by James Laughlin, 1946.

ALL THEIR COLOURS EXILED. Published here for the first time. The date of composition is not certain, but probably 1954.

THE IMAGINARY JEW. First printed in *The Kenyon Review*, vol. 7, no. 4, Autumn 1945, pages 529–39, and awarded first prize in the magazine's story contest. Reprinted as an appendix to Berryman's posthumous novel, *Recovery*, 1973.

WASH FAR AWAY. First printed in *American Review 22*, edited by Theodore Solotaroff, 1975, pp. 1–26. It existed in draft form in 1957 and may have been written somewhat earlier.